PUBLISHED ON THE FOUNDATION ESTABLISHED
IN MEMORY OF
CALVIN CHAPIN OF THE CLASS OF 1788, YALE COLLEGE

The Gentleman from New York: A Life of Roscoe Conkling

By Donald Barr Chidsey

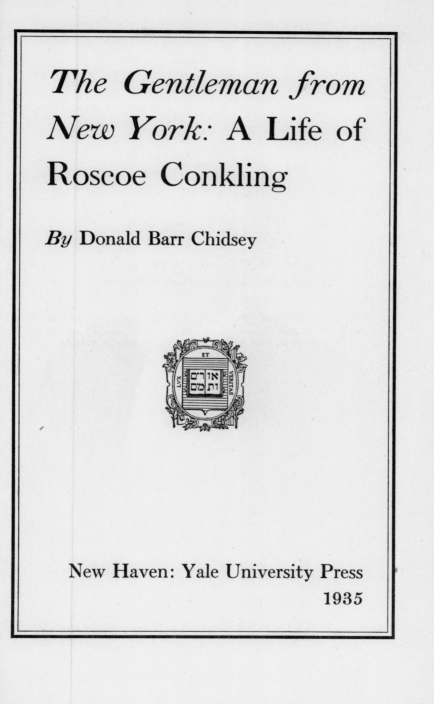

New Haven: Yale University Press

1935

To Billy

Contents

The cartoons in this volume have been reproduced from illustrations
in *Leslie's Weekly* and *Harper's Weekly*.

ROSCOE CONKLING

I. Such a Handsome Man

HE must not be introduced by way of his ancestors; or as a squawling, squirming babe forefingered by doting relatives; or even as a promising young man upon the threshold of his career.

No, he should stalk upon our stage in his maturity (it was early enough, at that!) and preferably to a blare of trumpets. This is the way he would have wished it.

The echoes of the trumpets die, and after a properly dramatic pause the Senator begins to speak. Think of him this way: speaking slowly, and with great distinctness, an erect and beautiful figure, his head back, his blue-gray eyes flashing, the left thumb hooked into a side trousers pocket, the right foot slightly advanced—standing, in fact, precisely as he stands today in bronze near the southeast corner of Madison Square. For he stepped naturally upon a pedestal, after his death. It suited him. Indeed, in the eyes of thousands he always had been there.

One of the handsomest men of his time, six feet three inches, straight, broad shouldered, he had wavy hair, which was dark yellow with glints of red, and a reddish, exquisitely curled beard. In the center of his broad forehead hung a Hyperion curl. Very arrogant he was, but very earnest.

If you had asked him his profession, and he had consented to reply, probably he would tell you that he was a statesman, sir. But the world called him, more accurately, a politician. A political boss, indeed; and one of the harshest, strictest, most narrow-minded of all political bosses.

Possibly like Pooh Bah he was *born* sneering. Some sniffed at him as a pouter pigeon, to learn that he was in fact more of an eagle. He was touchy, temperamental as the fabled prima donna, incalculably conceited. It is possible, but a mistake, to smile depreciatingly upon the figure he made. As Henry Adams put it, in the *Education:* "Great leaders like Sumner and Conkling could not be burlesqued . . . their egotism and factiousness were no laughing matter." The Senator's path was not broad perhaps, but it was long, and it led through a highly important period of our national history; and on either side of that path you can see headless trunks and trunkless heads, the mouths fixed in gory grins of astonishment, representing persons who were foolish enough to esteem the Senator a stuffed shirt and nothing more.

THE Civil War was an interesting fight; but much more significant was the period which followed it, the twenty years or so during which millionaires and political manipulators were creating the nation we know today. It is a figure of speech to say that a new country emerged from that conflict. The same country emerged—a bit battered, and simmering with more than a normal share of hard feelings, but essentially the same. The changes came soon afterward, and they were tremendous. Our whole concept of government was altered. The period doesn't lend itself to dramatics; it is not a subject calculated to make any painter of heroic canvases chortle with joy; the American people, perhaps a shade ashamed of it, ignore it, preferring the more orthodox glories of Gettysburg, and historians until recently tended to treat it with a wry face, hurriedly.

Yet in the final test tubes of history it may well be that the Fathers of the Constitution will be rated as of no greater importance than the members of the Joint Committee on Reconstruction, including Roscoe Conkling. Some day it may be thought that, far-reaching as was the effect of the struggle between Hamilton and Jefferson, it was of no greater influence upon the history of this country than the struggle between Thaddeus Stevens (young Conkling was called his right-hand man) and Andrew Johnson. Some day, too, the belief may become prevalent that no nation is any sounder than its own currency; and our whole system of currency changed during and just after the Civil War, with Conkling at all times battling—usually leading the battle—for hard money.

Rogers groups, fans pinned to the wall, bustles, thunderous references to the Boys in Blue—these bring a smile? But remember that in this period also were born more enduring phenomena of American life, such as the Standard Oil, the three-ring circus, the militant prohibition movement, the farm problem, inescapable and passionately rendered arguments about the Rights of Women, the cowboy, civil service reform, the holding company, organized baseball and also college football, inflation, the Veterans' Lobby, Protection with a capital "P," the Solid South, strikes and boycotts and lockouts, spiritualism as a paying proposition, the hobo. . . .

The millionaire, too. That is, the conventional conception of an American millionaire, the blusterous, boasting, vulgar, art-collecting personage of great wealth and no traditions. He had not existed here before the Civil War, and during that conflict his kind were not numerous and not notably vocal. But soon after the last shot he elbowed his way to the foreground, and for many years now he has been considered peculiar to this nation.

IT is impossible accurately to estimate Roscoe Conkling's influence upon the national history. He had a profound hatred of publicity, and preferred to do his work behind the scenes in caucuses, executive sessions, committee meetings, closed conferences. He refused to write his memoirs or even to authorize a biography, and he did not leave papers, manuscripts, or letters. He was, generally, too proud to try to explain, to publicly justify his acts. He walked alone. Hundreds of babies were named after him,[1] but he never stooped to kiss one of them; and though thousands of men believed for many years that he would be and should be President of the United States, he scorned to reach for that office. During the greater part of the two Grant administrations he was the most powerful politician in the country. He was only forty-three years old when he refused to accept the chief justice-ship of the United States Supreme Court. He might have been Secretary of State, Ambassador to the Court of St. James's. He preferred to remain in the Senate, where he was always sure of finding a fight.

With the exception of Thaddeus Stevens, he probably did more than any other one man to frame the reconstruction policy of the federal government. He was at least as prominent as John Sherman (who got all the glory) in the fight for a firm dollar. His very enemies admitted that he was chiefly responsible for the Electoral Commission compromise of 1876–77, which brought the nation through one of its greatest crises and averted a second civil war.

Even his meannesses were magnificent. And when finally he fell it was with a terrific crash, and he dragged the whole Republican party down with him—for it was Roscoe Conkling's personality, and not any real issue, which brought about the Stalwart–Half-Breed war, the assassination of President Garfield, the Republican split of 1884, the defeat of Blaine and election of Grover Cleveland.

A POLITICAL boss? That is so difficult to believe after a glance at Roscoe Conkling.

For a political boss in these United States is primarily an affable fellow, a handshaker, one of the boys, genuinely or affectedly democratic. And Roscoe Conkling (blare of trumpets, roll of drums!) was haughty, supercilious, aloof. It is impossible to think of him slapping a back. He disliked all physical contact. He hated men who put hands on his shoulders, or tried to hold his arm, while they were talking to him. Crowds he found agreeable enough if they were in front of him and a little below, respectfully listening; but he could not bear to be a *member* of any crowd, a pusher and joggler. It infuriated him if anybody sat close to him, or tried to read something over his shoulder. His nephew and only previous biographer, Alfred R. Conkling, records that the Senator, in a court room, invariably insisted upon having one end of a table entirely to himself, and was made irritable if another person even placed a foot on a rung of the Conkling chair.

A political boss is or affects to be homely, perhaps a trifle sloppy. Conkling was a Brummel, in the exact sense that while he did not originate fashions he sported them incomparably, and like the Beau he was clipped, well trimmed, a model of cleanliness, but not garish.[2] He usually wore a black cutaway, seldom a Prince Albert, which he considered somewhat informal for a man of his position. His ties, however, were bright—vivid red or blue butterfly bows.

Everything about him must be neat, clean, exactly in place. He always folded a newspaper just so, before he started to read. He creased his money precisely in the middle, first lengthwise, then sidewise, before putting it into his pocket. He did not like to borrow or to lend books. He hated tobacco smoke, cigar ashes, men who spat.

A machine politician, somehow he rose without obsequiousness and reigned without amiability. He had no sense of humor. Reformers, whom he despised, considered him dangerous, sinister; yet the man was almost absurdly honest in financial matters. If he had not gone to Congress so early in his life, he could have built up a great fortune, for his talents as a lawyer were amazing; yet when he retired to private life he was not merely poor but in debt.

This honesty is worth emphasizing. Roscoe Conkling was the power behind the throne throughout the two Grant administrations, admittedly the most lush period of graft in the history of American politics; but when scandals were exploding around him like firecrackers, he was not remotely touched, was not even singed. It was a time when the public readily forgave the grafter who grafted successfully—forgave him and even honored him as a "smart man." And to some it seemed impossible that the Conkling skirts were spotless through it all: to some it seemed that this man must be *super*-smart. But they were wrong. He was only honest.

You wouldn't have liked him, personally. Few did. He had a genius for embroilment, and fought in a white-hot fury, lashing out at anything and everything that said "no." Nor did his rage ever cool. He "used to get angry with men simply because they voted against him," records Hoar, and Stewart wrote that "The great fault of his life was his inability to forgive an enemy, or even to pass him without a kick." More downright was the comment of Andrew D. White: "Conkling seemed to consider all men who differed with him as enemies of the human race."

Eventually he antagonized most of the few friends he did have—and this was quite satisfactory to him, for he did not desire friends, only worshipers.

II. The Bright Young Lawyer

ANANIAS Conkling and John Conkling, from Nottingham, England, landed at Salem, Massachusetts, in 1638. Probably they were brothers. At least, Ira Conkling says they were; though Thomas Prosch, another member of the family who had dabbled in genealogy, goes no further than the assertion that there is "abundant reason for supposing they were brothers." Nobody seems to know which was the elder.

They were glass workers, not very successful. Later they became farmers. They drifted through Orange County and Rockland County, New York, and got into Long Island, Ananias settling at East Hampton about the year 1653, while John settled at Huntington. There are Conklings in that vicinity today, though most of them have dropped the final "g."

Our Senator was the sixth in direct descent from Ananias. His father got away from the soil, achieved an education, moved to Albany and later to Utica, was sent to Congress at the age of thirty-one, and served the last twenty-seven years of his life as the United States district court judge for northern New York State. He was a distinguished ornament of the bar, author of sundry learned books, a friend of most of the important Whigs of his time. So far as can be learned, he was the first member of the family to be a college graduate (it was Union College, at Schenectady) and the first to get into politics. He was married to Eliza Cockburn, "the Belle of the Mohawk Valley," an exceptionally beautiful woman, wealthy as wealth went in those days. They had four sons and three daughters. Roscoe was the youngest son, and he was born at Albany on October 30, 1829.

THEY named him after William Roscoe, the English historian, poet, barrister. Roscoe, who was tall, pompous, without humor, a writer of commendable if uninspired verse, still was alive at the time. Judge Conkling, "a better lawyer, though less brilliant man" than his celebrated son,[1] had long been a profound admirer of Roscoe.[2]

At ten, Judge Conkling's youngest son was kicked by a horse, and his jaw was broken. This didn't mar his beauty, nor did it cause him to lose his taste for horses: he was always an enthusiastic horseman.

Boxing was another sport he loved. He was big, strong, fast, immeasurably self-confident. And he seemed really to enjoy fighting for its own sake.

He was thirteen when they sent him to the Mount Washington Collegiate Institute in New York City, where he studied for not more than a year under the guardianship of his eldest brother, Frederick, who was thirty then and a wholesale drygoods salesman.

Then Auburn Academy for three years, and this completed his formal education, aside from his law studies. So he was not, like his father, a "college man." The reason is not clear, since the father was a firm believer in college education and the family was well-to-do. Perhaps Roscoe was too impatient; a good guess might be that he refused to take orders even at that tender age, and even from school teachers or parents.

Politically his learning extended over a longer period. In New York, with brother Frederick, he had read *The Art of Speaking*, at that time a celebrated textbook; and one of his instructors at the Mount Washington Collegiate Institute, a Dr. Harvey, had recently come from England, where he listened to speeches by Daniel O'Connell, Sir Robert Peel, and other giants.

Oratory today is a minor asset for a politician. *Then* it was a necessity. Roscoe Conkling always was an impressive speaker. Tireless, too—which was important in a time when crowds expected two- and three-hour speeches. It was not unusual for him to deliver a *four*-hour speech; and nobody ever quit the hall. Indeed, a few of the greatest Conkling addresses were delivered in sections, occupying two or three different afternoons, and had to be heard in their entirety, like a Eugene O'Neill drama, to be properly appreciated.

In his father's home, too, there were visitors an ambitious youngster was fortunate to meet—associates and friends of his father—men like Enos Throop, Martin Van Buren, John Quincy Adams, Thurlow Weed.

From the beginning he had that indispensable adjunct, Pull.

WHEN he had completed the three years at Auburn Academy he started to study law under excellent auspices. Joshua A. Spencer and Francis Kernan were admittedly two of the greatest of upstate attorneys at that time, who sometimes charged, and got, as much as fifty dollars a case.

It is not probable that the youth "went into" politics. It is more likely that he was always there, that he took the condition for granted. Joshua Spencer is said to have induced him to make his first speech at the age of seventeen, but there is no record of this. The following year he spoke publicly for charity, spoke in behalf of the Irish famine victims.

He called himself a "Seward Whig" or "Woolly-Head Whig"—that is, a free-soiler. He felt very strongly about slavery.

He was only about twenty when he was admitted to the bar. His first case was tried before his own father, in Utica. He won it.

On April 22 of that year, 1850, Governor Hamilton Fish appointed him district attorney of Oneida County. It was six months before his twenty-first birthday, but nobody seemed to care.

He held the office for one year. Then he hung out his own shingle as a practicing attorney. For five years he was in partnership with former Mayor Thomas R. Walker of Utica, and later, for a few years, he had other partners; but most of his life he went it alone, refusing to hunt with the pack.

"P'ter O'Dactyl"[3] remembered meeting him in that first year of his law career. It was in Rome, N. Y., and the youth asked the way to the courthouse: "He had two law books under his arm, was apparently about twenty years of age, and looked like a tall, blonde young lady; had on a tall silk hat, a frock coat with a velvet collar; his cheek was as fresh as a rose, and he had long red ringlets clustered about his neck."

In the campaign of 1852 he was tolerably active and made many local speeches. He was very high tariff, declaring that the English were backing Pierce as a free trader.

America cannot, and, for one, I trust in God she will never, sink so low in wretchedness that she can compete unaided in cheapness of products with the pauper labor of England . . . a system exists in England, a system of double-distilled slavery, a system of grinding oppression, a political and social system, which enables the rich man to wring from the poor man the products of his labor at prices at which an American mechanic would starve . . . human beings in England live like beasts, and the tariff of wages is so adjusted as just to prevent starvation, without leaving to the laborer one farthing for any of the necessities peculiar to human life.

American slavery was "one of the blackest and bloodiest pictures in the book of modern times." Yet

American slavery compared to English slavery, compared in the magnitude of its horrors with the oppression of the laborers of Great Britain, compared with the condition of things which must exist here before Americans can compete with Englishmen in cheapness of manufactured production—American slavery, when brought into contrast with these, is as much to be preferred as the Christian religion is preferable to the dark idolatry of chance.

He traveled as far as Schenectady, where he met General Scott, his party's candidate.

There was a local Whig bolt that year, and Joshua Spencer, Roscoe's good friend and mentor, was nominated for Congress as an independent; but the young man remained regular. Scott, incidentally, lost the election; and so did Spencer.

ELOQUENCE never was forgotten. He was reading Chatham, Fox, Pitt, Goodrich, Erskine, Mansfield, Grattan, Burke. His taste in literature, too, tended toward the resounding. He liked Shakespeare, Milton, Macaulay, Byron, Scott. He could quote whole pages of the Bible, and was very fond of doing so.

Even as a youth he could thunder magnificently, and from the beginning he had been an expert at the business of making jurors weep. This, for example, at the age of twenty-four:

Dark and dreary as is the day, it is far too bright for such a deed. "Hang be the heavens with black," and let the courthouse and all Herkimer County be hung in mourning on the day when twelve of her sons will take from their fellow-man his life or his liberty on such testimony as this. . . . The day is too bright and too beautiful for such a deed. Nature and man should shudder! Heaven and earth should give note of horror; the skies should be weeping; the winds should be sighing; the bells should be tolling; the courthouse should be hung in mourning; the jury-box should be covered with crape—on the day when a father, a husband and a citizen of Herkimer County is sent to a prison or a gallows upon such testimony as this.

He had another talent, too, which was useful. He was an adept at bullying witnesses. The audience loved it, and in the audience must be included the twelve men who sat in the jury box.

Not that he depended upon words alone. Then, as later, his cases were exceptionally well prepared. He was a hard worker. Days, weeks sometimes, would be spent in the preparation of an important speech; everything would be checked, tabulated, properly arranged; and there would be innumerable dress rehearsals in the privacy of his room. Yet he was also a good extemporaneous speaker.

He got good cases, too. And his fees were high. He was extraordinary, and he was willing to have others realize this. He argued with the supreme confidence of a man who has never doubted himself; and confidence like that is always effective. Very early, he was opposing his former instructors at law. In 1853, for example, he defended Sylvester Hadcock in Herkimer County Oyer and Terminer before Judge W. F. Allen, and Spencer was his opponent. Hadcock, who was accused of forgery, had a large family. Young Conkling, after a blistering assault upon the integrity of the

State's star witness, dwelt upon the picture of that empty
chair at the Hadcock table so effectively that most of the
jurors were weeping before he was finished. Incidentally, but
only incidentally, he established that the prisoner was illiter-
ate. The jury found for acquittal.

There was no apparent limit to his ambition. At twenty-
five he aspired to be the State Attorney-General, and he
attended the Whig State Convention in October, 1853, in
search of nomination: election was almost a certainty for the
Whig nominees that year, for the Democrats were split.

Perhaps this was a trifle too audacious. His opponent was
a New York City man, Ogden Hoffman, sixty years old, a
former Congressman, a former United States judge too, and
a well-known orator. Hoffman won on the third ballot; and
our brilliant young lawyer continued in private practice. He
had been attending Whig State conventions since his sixteenth year. He was a vice-president of the convention of
1854, in Syracuse.

The very next month he handled a case which brought him
considerable publicity. It was, in fact, precisely the sort of
case he handled best. *Martha Parker by Guardian* v. *The
Reverend F. A. Spencer* of Westmoreland, tried in Rome before Mr. Justice Bacon—it lasted three days and caused a
tremendous sensation.

The real complainant was a young and pretty choir singer
at the Hampton Presbyterian Church, in Westmoreland,
and the defendant was the pastor of that church. The charge
was slander. Judge Conkling's son had been engaged by the
prosecution.

The pastor having asserted that the choir singer was no
better than she should have been, the defense put on the witness stand a young man who said he'd had relations with the
girl. The case hung upon this fellow's testimony. Conkling
tore it to pieces.

Gentlemen, have you daughters? I have sisters, and I would rather follow their hearse, than that one of them should receive an injury so irreparable as that which has been inflicted by the defendant upon this orphan girl. I would rather the clods should fall upon their coffins than that one of them should be robbed of that priceless reputation, without which a woman is a casket without a jewel, a ship without a rudder, a helpless, hopeless wreck on Fortune's lonely shore.

There was, be sure of it, a booming reference to the biblical admonition against casting the first stone.

What should I say of the act if committed by one absorbed in human matters, and pretending no higher standard of action than the honor and morals of the world? I might say it was cruel as the grave, I might say it was unpardonable, malignant, mean; but tell me, gentlemen, tell me what I shall say of it when perpetrated by one who professes to devote his life and his thoughts to learning and teaching that great rule of charity, of mercy and of love, whose seat is the bosom of the Almighty, and whose voice is the harmony of the world? How shall I describe the enormity of such a violation of the laws not only of man but of the King of Kings by one who, when he thus bids defiance to reason and to right, must have heard, ought to have heard, the pleadings on Calvary, the warnings on the Mount of Olives, and the thunders of Mount Sinai still ringing in his ears?

The summation lasted two hours, and the verdict was a record one, $2,500. Conkling had convinced the jurors.

He had convinced the spectators; and such eloquence can be dangerous. Men were muttering, and their fists were clenched. Drunk with Conklinian phrases, they gathered in little groups, whispering, scowling; and soon they started for the hotel where the star witness was roomed. Friends hurried that frightened young man to the roof, and from there he was lowered by a rope to the back yard, eventually making his escape to another town. The mob, after stamping in vain through his hotel room, burned him in effigy. They also hanged him in effigy.

He had convinced somebody else, too. The slandered songbird was married less than a year later.

Oh, he was very successful! He defended a lawyer in a slander suit brought by a woman, and got him off with a verdict of six cents. He acted for Sanford Snell, a cheese buyer, who brought suit for slander against his uncle, the venerable Suffrenus Snell. Popular sympathy was all with the older man, an honest farmer, and no less a lawyer than Francis Spencer had charge of the defense; but Conkling won a verdict of $1,000.

He was charging $50 a case now, regularly, and sometimes $75, occasionally even $100. Attorneys were advising their clients to pay him a retainer, if only in order to keep the other side from engaging him. Samuel Earl, an old Herkimer County lawyer, remembers: "I once brought action against a young man for breach of promise of marriage, and Conkling was retained to defend. Such was his reputation that when my client heard he was retained, she fainted."[4]

At all times, and in everything, he worked furiously, pauselessly.[5] Yet he was no pedant. He seldom tried a case on appeal. "He had not then, nor did he ever have, a very great fondness for the drier or more curious learning of the law. He was neither a bookworm, boring into antiquated volumes, nor an intellectual ferret, exploring what may be termed the underground passages of jurisprudence."[6] It is impossible, for example, to think of him doing what his father did—writing a work on the law of admiralty, and an elaborate treatise (a standard work to this day) on the jurisdiction and practice of the courts of the United States.

He changed associates frequently, for all partnership was obnoxious to this fastidious man. In 1855 he formed a law firm with Montgomery H. Throop, nephew of Enos Throop, and recently a schoolmate at Auburn Academy. It lasted six or seven years, a long time for Conkling.

On June 25 of that year he contracted a more durable if no more satisfactory partnership when he was married to Julia Seymour, daughter of Henry Seymour and a sister of Horatio Seymour, governor of the state and one of the nation's most distinguished Democrats. The Seymours were a good family to marry into—wealthy, cultured, influential.

THE Whig party in New York at that time, and the Republican party for some time subsequent, was controlled by three men, who of course were known as the Big Three.

William H. Seward, blue-eyed, sandy-haired, was not a good speaker, but he had a simple, convincing manner, informal, earnest. Henry Adams remembered him well, and loved him—remembered "a slouching, slender figure; a head like a wise macaw; a beaked nose; shaggy eyebrows; unorderly hair and clothes; hoarse voice; offhand manner; free talks, and perpetual cigar."[7] He was brilliant, erratic. He had been chief executive of New York State, and everybody called him "Governor" even after he had been elected to the Senate, even after he had been appointed to the cabinet. There seemed not the slightest doubt that he would be his party's next nominee for the Presidency. He lived in Auburn, and was a close friend of Judge Conkling.

Thurlow Weed of Albany was large, dark, shrewd, silent. He avoided the open platform, public places. Henry Adams again:

His mind was naturally strong and beautifully balanced; his temper never seemed ruffled; his manners were carefully perfect in the style of benevolent simplicity, the tradition of Benjamin Franklin. . . . Manipulation was an instinct with Mr. Weed; an object to be pursued for its own sake, as one plays cards; but he appeared to play with men as though they were only cards; he seemed incapable of feeling himself one of them. He took them and played them at their face value . . .

Adams, who really didn't know Weed well, liked and admired him. Horace Greeley, who knew the man very well indeed, didn't. Greeley, the third member of the Big Three, in his *Recollections* characterized Weed as "of coarser mould and fiber than Seward . . . resolute, and not over-scrupulous—keen-sighted, though not far-seeing." His mouth was rarely open, and he smoked cigars constantly.

Now Horace Greeley neither smoked nor drank. Also he was a vegetarian. He stood 5 feet 10½ inches, but seemed shorter, perhaps because of the enormous head, perfectly round, almost completely bald, with a bulging forehead and a preposterous (even for those days) goatee. He was so pale, and his hair was so thin and silky, that at first you would almost take him for an albino; but you learned that his eyes were not pink but a mild, washed-out blue. He wore glasses which he was constantly mislaying, he carried a fat umbrella, his voice was high and thin and easily rose to a screech when he was excited, he was always in a hurry, his absent-mindedness was proverbial, he (literally) couldn't read his own handwriting. It goes without saying that this "sublime old child"[8] was a genius. He had read the Bible through before he was six years old; was lecturing women against the use of corsets when he was thirteen; and while still in his early twenties was editing two highly successful New York newspapers and planning to start a third, was admittedly, even then, one of the greatest of American journalists and one of the most promising of the Whigs, and was lending $50 to a cheerless young poet by the name of Poe.[9]

They were a curious trio. Seward and Weed were close friends; the swarthy man from Albany was either Seward's guiding angel or the devil who brought about that statesman's ruination—depending upon how you feel about it. Greeley, in time, fought with both of them, for Greeley was a born nonconformist. Seward accepted high positions naturally: he seemed to be made for them. Weed, who might have annexed any number of titles if he'd been interested, preferred to remain in the background pulling strings. So *they* were happy enough. But Greeley, not satisfied with being the greatest journalist the country had known, was plagued by a desire to hold office—almost any office. He tried to be governor, then lieutenant governor, then senator. In time he tried to be President; but the people simply refused to take him seriously. For this he blamed the machine operators, and particularly Weed.

THERE was no secret about the fact that Seward might have had the Presidential nomination of the new Republican party in 1856, but Thurlow Weed advised against it. The party had not yet grown big enough, Weed thought, and '56 would not be a Republican year. There was no profit in running unless you were going to win. Seward, Weed decided, should wait until 1860, when unquestionably he would be nominated and probably he would be elected.

So Fremont received the nomination. Young Conkling worked hard for him in New York State, which Fremont carried. But Weed had been correct about at least the first part of his prediction: it was not a Republican year, yet, and Buchanan became President.

The Conkling rise, meanwhile, continued. On April 27, 1857, two days after the death of Francis Spencer, he was elected secretary of the Oneida County Bar Association; and not many months after that, rather unexpectedly, he was made mayor of Utica. His nephew says he didn't want the job. It paid $250 a year and probably interfered with his much more lucrative law practice. Besides, his eye was on Washington.

Congress was none too safe a place for Republicans then. Southern members, wildly excited about slavery, passionately hating all members of what they considered an out-and-out abolitionist party, were, many of them, resorting to cheap bullying tactics. Challenges were not rare, threats more common still, and occasionally there was a real meeting on the field. Northerners didn't believe in that sort of thing; but dueling still was an accepted practice in the South. Charles Sumner of Massachusetts, the most vocal of all abolitionists in the Senate, had scorned repeated challenges. Preston Brooks, representative from North Carolina, only a few years previous had deliberately attacked Sumner in the Senate chamber when that body was not sitting, approaching him from behind while Sumner was bending over his desk, and beating him unmercifully with a heavy cane. Sumner suffered for years—in fact, never fully recovered. Brooks resigned from Congress, to be unanimously reëlected by his district: the South made a hero of him.

Likely enough all this only whetted the Conkling appetite. He was a crack pistol shot, an expert boxer. "Boys, we must nominate muscle as well as brains for Congress," Ben Allen, fifth ward leader in Utica, told his friends. "Let's send Conkling. I guess they won't hurt him!"[10]

Conkling was more than willing. The county convention met at Rome, September 21, and he won the nomination on the first ballot, 62–23, defeating Charles H. Doolittle. They cheered for him; and graciously, and at considerable length, he addressed them. There was plenty of thunder in the speech, and lightning, but some oil, too; for he still was young, and all was not well within the ranks.

The nomination you have bestowed upon me is the offspring of a contest full of endeavor and heated animation. . . . Harsh words have been spoken and published and things said in too great excess, by Republicans, one of another. For my own part I have written not a word which has been printed in the canvass, but if any hasty expression has crossed the lips of any friend of mine, or fallen from my own, in which injustice has been done to any true Republican, I here recall it. Let things of this sort be forgiven on every hand and let the waters of forgetfulness conceal them from future view.

No, all was not well, all was not harmonious. Something

Conklingesque was needed; and six days after the convention the Republican candidate wrote to the Democratic candidate, P. Sheldon Root, challenging him to a series of debates in various parts of the district. Root was much too shrewd to snap at this bait. "I am aware the custom you refer to prevails generally at the South and to some extent in the Western States," he replied gently. "That mode of conducting a political canvass, however, has never been adopted in this county or State, and I am disinclined to assume the responsibility of introducing it at the present time." Root did not make any public speeches in that campaign, but the energetic young Republican spoke at least once in all thirty-six towns and wards of the district.

A series of public debates would have been wonderful. Failing that, the next best thing was to get Seward to speak for him. Seward was the most popular man in the State, and a friend of Judge Conkling.

So Seward was induced to address a meeting at Rome, October 29, and so was Henry Stanton, an eminent Barnburner. Seward was perhaps too good natured on this occasion. Opposition to the young candidate was running strong, even inside the party, O. B. Matteson, a publisher, being particularly bitter; and Senator Seward, who never could bear to hurt anybody's feelings, desired to say a good word too for his friend Mr. Matteson. Stanton tells it:

Wrapped in a blue broadcloth cloak, with elegant trimmings, Conkling surveyed the large audience with anxious eye. I spoke first, eulogizing Seward and Conkling. The Senator commenced his address with a hearty encomium upon Matteson, by way of preface to the matter in hand. He then spoke generally in support of the Republican cause, and eloquently commended his young friend Conkling to the voters of Oneida. I have been told that this eulogium of Mr. Matteson was retained in the published report of Mr. Seward's speech under the special direction of Mr. Seward, and against the earnest protest of Mr. Conkling's friends. The next morning I went to Utica, and was

amused to see that nearly the only notice taken of the Rome
meeting, by the general press, was a full report of Mr. Seward's
eulogium of Mr. Matteson. This, of course, would go the grand
rounds of the newspapers of the state. I met Mr. Conkling. My
acquaintance with the English language is not sufficiently intimate to enable me to describe how angry he was.

However, he was elected. He was twenty-nine years old,
and his parents were very proud of him.

III. War Was Coming

TRADITION (but apparently nothing else whatever) has it that Roscoe Conkling dramatically
justified his selection as muscle man for the Republicans on the second day of the Thirty-sixth
Congress. Thaddeus Stevens, the tale goes, was ranting
against the South and Southerners; and Stevens, though a
cripple and a very old man, was not one to pull his punches.
There was a rumble of threat from the Democratic side, and
some fire eaters, fists clenched, advanced toward the speaker.

At this point there strode forward the husky Roscoe, who
placed himself directly in front of the gentleman from Pennsylvania. The Conkling arms were folded, the Conkling
brows were low; and the chivalry of the South, faced with
the prospect of clearing this mountain in order to reach the
cripple, decided against hostilities and returned sheepishly
to their seats.

It makes a pretty story, and possibly it's true.[1]

The first two months of that session were spent in trying
to select a speaker. The Republicans had a plurality but not
a majority, there being 109 of them, together with 101
Democrats and 27 members of the American ("Know-Noth-
ing") party. Candidates were John Sherman and Galusha A.
Grow; and at the end of eight weeks, when both lines re-

mained unbroken, the House elected ex-Governor William Pennington of New Jersey, a man who had never before even been in Congress.[2]

The new congressman from Oneida, when finally a speaker had been picked, was named a member of the District of Columbia committee. He did very little talking in that first session.

But he was talked about. There were rumors that he had passed a note to Barksdale of Mississippi—rumors both of them denied. Indeed, Congressman Conkling was kept busy denying just such rumors. There is not a vestige of evidence that he ever did formally receive or accept any challenge to a meeting on the field of honor, either for himself or for a friend; but his quick temper, his tremendous dignity, his infinite capacity for hatred, were noted promptly; and it was known too that he was a crack pistol shot. He appealed to the popular imagination as a man who *ought* to be a duelist.

But, in fact, the new congressman appears to have been quiet enough, and well behaved. He was a close friend of Thad Stevens from the beginning,[3] but he was not at this time the radical he became after the war. Indeed, he seems to have been rated as a conservative. He voted against the proposed Thirteenth Amendment, a desperate, last-minute effort to prevent war, an amendment that would have made slavery a perpetual institution, sacred, untouchable even by subsequent amendments, in all the South and in all the territories. His well-prepared and well-received speech in opposition to what he believed to be an unconstitutional assumption of power on the part of the Supreme Court was made into a pamphlet which was widely circulated during the campaign of 1860; but though the language of that speech is strong, it is not bellicose; when the speaker's allotted hour had expired, it was on the motion of a Democrat that he was permitted to finish.[4] He voted in favor of the Crittenden resolution.[5] Even his enemies never considered him an unconditional abolitionist. If he did no more than his share to prevent the war, neither did he do more than his share to help start it. His record here is conservative, unremarkable, generally "good."

Nevertheless, he looked as though he *ought* to have been a fire eater. And because he was friendly with the ferocious Stevens, and also because of his later record as a relentless radical, "the great American quarreler," he has gone down on the popular pages as a South hater. The accusation, always indirect, hurried, mumbled, is an unjust one.

NOT only did he fail to indulge himself in any personal, physical combat during those tense days just before the guns began booming, but according to his nephew he did much to prevent one. This story, too, is unsupported. John B. Haskin, a Douglas Democrat from Kansas, whose seat was directly in front of Conkling's, was orating violently, and representatives from below the Mason-Dixon line again were muttering threats and stirring impatiently in their places. Congressman Haskin reached into a trousers pocket for a handkerchief with which to mop his anti-Southern brow; and as he drew it forth a pistol fell to the floor. It is difficult to guess what would have happened if that pistol had been seen by certain other representatives. But it wasn't. The gentleman from Oneida reached out with a long leg and quietly kicked the thing under Haskin's seat. Later, just as quietly, he picked it up and returned it to Haskin.

BUT the war was coming, anyway. That seemed certain.

Another thing that seemed certain was that Seward would be the Republican candidate in 1860. Thurlow Weed and all of Weed's friends were convinced of it. So was Seward himself. Probably Roscoe Conkling was, too: it would mean a lot to him, politically, if his friend from Auburn were put into the White House.

National conventions in those days were lighted by gas, and there were no amplifiers, or women on the floor, but otherwise they were almost exactly the same as national conventions today—not a whit more fair, or sensible, or predictable.

Still, it seemed to Seward's friends in New York and elsewhere that here was one convention the result of which could safely be foretold. An upset they considered almost impossible. Had not Thurlow Weed told his friend not to be a candidate in '56, definitely and confidently predicting his nomination and probable election in '60? And was not Thurlow Weed in personal charge of the New York delegation? That long, dark, silent man, puffing his long, dark cigars, was esteemed an infallible prophet, incalculably sagacious. He made his full share of mistakes, and perhaps a few more, like all others who are hailed as master-minds in American politics; but the people hadn't learned this, yet.

So the New York delegates went jubilantly to Chicago. Roscoe Conkling was not one of them: he remained in Washington. And Seward stayed at home, in Auburn, where his neighbors worshiped him. Stanton, who was there, describes the scene:

On the day the convention was to ballot for a candidate, Cayuga County poured itself into Auburn. The streets were full, and Mr. Seward's house and grounds overflowed with his admirers. Flags were ready to be raised and a loaded cannon was placed at the gate whose pillars bore up two guardian lions. Arrangements had been perfected for the receipt of the intelligence. At Mr. Seward's right hand, just within the porch, stood his trusty henchman, Christopher Morgan. The rider of a galloping steed dashed through the crowd with a telegram and handed it to Seward, who passed it to Morgan. For Seward, it read, 173½; for Lincoln, 102. Morgan read it to the multitude, who cheered vehemently.

Yet they must have been puzzled, even as they cheered. For Lincoln was a second-rate Illinois lawyer, almost unknown outside of his own state.

Then came the tidings of the second ballot: For Seward, 184½ for Lincoln, 181. "I shall be nominated on the next ballot," said Seward, and the throng in the house applauded, and those on the lawn and in the street echoed the cheers. The next messenger lashed his horse into a run. The telegram read, "Lincoln nominated. T. W." Seward turned as pale as ashes. The sad tidings crept through the vast concourse. The flags were furled, the cannon was rolled away, and Cayuga County went home with a clouded brow.

In Chicago, Thurlow Weed had burst into tears.[6]

ROSCOE CONKLING was unanimously renominated by his party, and he worked hard for the Lincoln-Hamlin national ticket. He told a ratification meeting at Utica on June 5 that "You may well cheer his [Seward's] name. . . . He filled the whole country with his renown. . . . If the question at Chicago had been, Who shall be President? instead of, Who shall be the candidate? beyond all doubt the choice would have fallen upon New York's illustrious statesman."[7] And this was probably the truth.

Conkling was reëlected easily, running exactly even with the ticket.

So Lincoln prepared to go to the White House, and the country prepared to go to war.

THE Weed boss-ship was wobbling. Business conditions in the city, in the whole State, were bad. " 'Do you think the South will secede?' became as common a salutation as 'Good-morning'; and, although a few New Yorkers, perhaps, gave the indifferent reply of Henry Ward Beecher—'I don't believe they will; and I don't care if they do'—the gloom and uncertainty which hung over business circles made all anxious to hear from the leaders of their party."[8] For New York sold a lot of merchandise to the South, and nobody likes to lose a good customer.

In addition, the people suddenly were deciding that Thurlow Weed didn't know what he was talking about. This was unfair; for practically every important political leader in the State, and many of them elsewhere in the country, had believed with Weed that Seward's nomination was inevitable; but it was a natural reaction.

Finally, and perhaps most important of all, Horace Greeley, with all the power of the *New York Tribune*, then easily the most influential newspaper in the country, picked this moment to rebel against the leadership of the man in Albany. Weed was a Unionist, and conservative; Greeley was declaring that if the Southern states wished to secede they had a perfect right to do so. There were also, of course, numerous personal reasons for the rift.

Seward's term in the Senate had been about to expire. There is no doubt that he would have been reëlected if Lincoln had not appointed him Secretary of State. As it was, the Weed-Greeley fight centered around the naming of his successor.

Weed's candidate was William M. Evarts, forty-three years old then, who had not held any public office, a great lawyer, a great wit—and later a great enemy of Roscoe Conkling. Greeley's candidate was Greeley. The leaders at Albany, Greeley was complaining, were glad to have him do a lot of work but they never were willing to give him a job he really desired. And now he was determined to be senator, Weed or no Weed.

Weed was sixty-three. For more than thirty-five years he had been a prominent Whig and Republican leader, and most of this time his dictatorship had been undisputed. He had plenty of fight left in him.

A couple of newspapermen. It was an historic battle. Greeley himself did not go to Albany in February, when the legislature was to pick a senator, but he was ably represented by his assistant, Charles A. Dana, later editor of the *Sun*.

Both sides appealed to the President-elect for support, but Lincoln wisely kept out of it.

For two weeks the preliminary, unofficial balloting continued, and nobody got a majority. On the night of February 4 the caucus assembled. Weed sat with Evarts and Governor Morgan in the executive chamber, Dana was in the rooms of Lieutenant Governor Campbell at Congress Hall. Speaker Littlejohn, a Weed man, scurried back and forth between the caucus room and the executive chamber.

The first ballot gave Evarts 42, Greeley 40, Ira Harris 20, with 13 scattering. On the second Evarts dropped to 39, Greeley rose to 42. Then four more ballots, showing little change. But on the seventh Greeley went up to 47, while Harris dropped to 19, Evarts remaining at 39.

The boss was "pale as ashes" when this was reported to him. "Unmindful of the fact that he had a cigar in his mouth, Weed lighted another and put it in, then rose in great excitement and said to Littlejohn, 'Tell the Evarts men to go right over to Harris—to *Harris*—to HARRIS!' " And, Stanton continues, "They wheeled into line like Napoleon's Old Guard, and Harris was nominated."

Alexander believed that "had Weed delayed a moment longer, Greeley must have been a United States Senator."[9]

So the master-mind myth was restored to a fond public which probably had missed it.

Nevertheless, the Weed boss-ship was wobbling.

ONE by one the Southern states were declaring themselves out of the Union. Congress assembled, and the proposed Thirteenth Amendment was rejected; whereupon such Southern senators and representatives as had remained walked out. They were not going to wait for the gawky lawyer from Illinois. Long before that person had roped his battered trunks and penned on their labels "A. Lincoln, White House, Washington, D. C.," the South was on its own.

The gawky lawyer, somewhat pathetically, was one of the few men who retained any hope for peace. Certainly Roscoe Conkling didn't. "From the outset of this session, I have had little hope that anything could be done here or in the other end of the Capitol to arrest the revolution now prevailing in some portions of the country," he told the House on January 30. And in the same speech:

In this connection there is one remark I want to make about war—war, whether it be waged in resistance of laws or for any other purpose. In this material age, war is a very humdrum thing. The battles known to the crusaders, and sung by the troubadours, have all been fought. War is no longer a question of personal valor or individual prowess; but a mere question of money—a question who can throw the most projectiles, who can indulge in the most iron and lead. It is no longer regulated by the laws of honor and chivalry, but entirely by the laws of trade.

In spite of which warning, Sumter was fired upon and war was declared.

IV. A Matter of Millions

IT was, like all big wars, an amateur affair. Men who never had handled so much as a shotgun abruptly found themselves colonels of regiments; and before the business was completed—it took much longer than anybody here or in Europe had expected—they were likely to be, if still alive, generals.

The title, easy enough for any able-bodied politician to achieve then, subsequently became a valuable political asset. Why Roscoe Conkling did not grab a generalship while he had the chance is not clear. Nobody ever accused him of being a coward, a weakling; he was married and the father of a daughter, but though not rich he was not obliged, like Grover Cleveland, to consider money matters and an invalid mother; and it would seem, offhand, that the trappings of war—the orthodox stimulants, band music, epaulets, shining swords, the cheering of crowds—would appeal to his nature.

A deeper dip into the man's character, however, might produce an explanation. He was a fighter, yes, but fighting was to him always a personal matter. It is impossible to imagine him keeping in step, literally or figuratively, or wearing just such-and-such a uniform with every button in its proper place, or bearing in mind a thousand and one conventional regulations and restrictions; discipline was something for his followers, not for himself. He spouted glamorous periods at public meetings, at rallies, but off the platform he was singularly clear-headed about it all. Had he not told his fellow congressmen that fighting in the field was, after all, only a small part of successful warfare? And there were plenty of good soldiers.

We cannot be sure: but it is a careful guess that Roscoe Conkling really believed that he could do more for his nation behind the lines, in civilian clothes.

His record was good. He supported the administration in everything. He worked hard. Valiantly, though without success, he opposed inflation of the currency and fought for a hard-money plan for financing the conflict. He did not object, as he certainly would have done in peace time, when the executive branch of the Government took over powers never granted to it by the Constitution.

IT is silly to speak of business or professional men "making great financial sacrifices" to serve their country in a non-military capacity. That is, they deserve no special praise for this. If they desired money more than the thrill of politics, they would stick to their desks. There is no law which forces any person to hold a public office.

So it is not argued here that Conkling deserves any special commendation for overlooking his own financial interests and working so hard in Washington while clients at home were clamoring for his services. His nephew says that in later life Roscoe Conkling frequently expressed himself as wishing that he had not gone into Congress quite so early, that he had lingered in Utica at least long enough to build up a moderate fortune.

However, he did find time between sessions to try a few cases. It was in August of the year the war started, for example, that he acted as counsel for the defense in the Budge murder mystery.

The Reverend Henry Budge was a Port Leyden, N. Y., clergyman, who sometimes worked out as a farmhand on week days to increase his pitifully small income. He and his wife were not on the best of terms; she was in poor health, and she disapproved of the farm work as unbecoming; they slept in different rooms. On the morning of Sunday, December 11, 1858, their daughter Priscilla, taking a pot of tea to her mother for breakfast, found her dead in bed, her throat cut from ear to ear. The bed, 4 feet 4 inches wide and the usual length, stood in one corner of the small bedroom, its head against one wall, its right side against another. The dead woman's face was peaceful, the head turned slightly to the right. The bed-clothes were pulled up smoothly over the upper part of the body, and the arms were outside. The left arm was bent, so that the hand rested on the breast. The right arm was extended at the side, and under it, between the elbow and the wrist, but nearer the wrist, was a blood-covered razor which was half open.

The coroner called it suicide, and the body was buried. But it happened that the Reverend Mr. Budge had bitter enemies inside his own church. A minority party, annoyed because the call had been issued to him instead of to another pastor, battled furiously with the other members of the congregation. Precisely what it was all about is not clear now, and not at all important; but the fact is that the fight was being carried on with a degree of rancor rarely attained except when churchmen fall to fighting among themselves. And so, very soon, there were whispers that the Reverend Mr. Budge had killed his wife.

The whispers broke into print, and the pastor brought a suit for libel. The answer to this was the exhuming of the body, four months after the death, and an autopsy performed by a Dr. Swinburne, who found that Mrs. Budge had been suffocated or strangled before the cutting of her throat. The pastor was arrested on a charge of murder.

From this distance, it is difficult to appreciate the excitement the case created, not only locally but all over the state. You were either pro-Budge or anti-Budge, and to many persons the war itself was not a matter of such great interest. The local ramifications, perhaps partly political, were indescribably complex. Feeling ran so high that a change of venue was obtained, from Lewis County to Oneida County; and Roscoe Conkling was engaged by the defense.

His preparation is characteristic of the man both in his legal and his political careers.

Apparently he was defeated before he started. Almost two years had passed since the death of Mrs. Budge, and to exhume the body again, for another autopsy, obviously would be foolish. For a layman to dispute the word of a reputable physician in such a matter as this was unheard of. Conkling broke all sorts of precedents when he engaged Dr. Alonzo Clark of New York City.

He went into everything, the whole history of the case, the whole history of medicine too. He had the sort of mind that could soak up knowledge like a sponge. "He learned in a few days what it took me thirty years to find out," Dr. Clark later told a friend.[1] He even procured a human cadaver and caused medical men to dissect it in front of him, in order that he might know precisely what he was talking about. And when the case was called, at Rome, he was ready.

He scoffed at the strangulation theory. Dr. Swinburne could not prove it: an examination of a body four months after death could not possibly show marks of any sort on the throat, embalming methods being what they were then. Besides, the lawyer for the defense quoted from high medical authorities to show that a person being strangled or smothered would instinctively resist, yet where were signs of resistance upon the face or in the muscles of this corpse?

The prosecution, shifting its attack, contended that Mrs. Budge would not have had the strength to cut herself so deeply. Conkling proved, again by means of medical authorities, that any person capable of lifting twenty-five pounds could easily make such a cut. Dr. Swinburne had testified that the trapezius muscle had been cut; but Conkling proved that the razor had not come within half an inch of it—a small point, perhaps, but it tended to weaken the jury's respect for the star witness.

But, said the prosecution, a woman in such a bed could not possibly have cut her own throat with her right hand—would not have had *room* in which to do so! This was refuted in a manner understandable to the twelve good men and true, by use of a table, a toothbrush, and a set of measurements, plus the testimony of those who had examined the body before it was moved.

Finally there was Dr. Swinburne's testimony as to the condition of the lungs. They were congested, the doctor had said. Conkling, cross examining, ripped this testimony to pieces, quoting yards of medical authorities, giving dozens of figures, tripping up the witness on small technical inaccuracies in his statements, using breathlessly long words with perfect ease, and establishing at last that the presence of blood and serum in the pleural cavities behind the lungs was nothing more than the result of post mortem drainage through the tissues.

Nor at any time did counsel for the defense lose a chance to perform one of his favorite court room tricks. He bullied witnesses unmercifully; he confused the jurors, and made them laugh, and made them weep; Henry A. Foster, the spe-

cial prosecutor, must have been ashamed to look at himself
in a mirror after Conkling (thereby acquiring another political enemy) had called him, among other things, a "bull
dog snuffing for blood around a slaughter house"; the Conkling newspaper, raised in contempt, was lowered in feigned
amazement, the Conkling eyes were opened very wide, and
"Are you going to sum up *this* case?" greeted Foster when
he rose to address the jury for the last time. The defense's
own summation, of course, was a masterpiece. People talked
about it for years afterward.

The jury said "Not guilty."

THE war was on, though it could not properly be described
as being in full swing. The President had called Congress
into special session in July, and Roscoe Conkling had become chairman of the now suddenly important District of
Columbia committee. The call for volunteers was issued. The
new Ninety-seventh New York regiment called itself the
Conkling Rifles—and the Congressman, in the spring, made
the boys a stirring speech before they started for the front.
There had been some fighting, not encouraging from a
Northern point of view. For instance, there had been a skir-
mish at Ball's Bluff.

Ball's Bluff, scarcely a footnote in military histories today, at the time caused almost as much gloom in the North
as the first battle of Bull Run. There is no need to rehearse
its details here; but it was as obvious then as it is today, even
to a lay mind, that somebody had made a ghastly mistake.
And on the first day of the regular session, December 2,
1861, Roscoe Conkling offered a resolution, which was
unanimously adopted, requesting the Secretary of War, "if
not incompatible with the public service, to report to the
House whether any, and if any, what, measures have been
taken to ascertain who is responsible."

The secretary replied that General McClellan, in charge
of the army, "is of the opinion that an inquiry on the subject

of the resolution would at this time be injurious to the public service." This enraged Conkling, who got the floor on a question of privilege.

To a question of whether a particular thing has been done, the Adjutant General reports that, in the opinion of the General-in-Chief, it would be injurious to do some other thing. This, however inadvertent it may have been, raises a very high question of privilege. We sit here as the representatives of the people; we sit here as their only representatives. In our organism this is the only place to which the people can come, or in which their voices can be heard, and among the most undeniable and sacred of their prerogatives is the right to inquire into their own affairs.

His resolution "relates to a lost field; to a disastrous and humiliating battle; to a blunder so gross that all men can see it,—a blunder which cost us confessedly nine hundred and thirty men,[2] the very pride and flower of the States from which they came." He described the battle. And when the last echoes of his slowly enunciated but impassioned words had snuggled to rest in the remotest corners of the chamber, there could be no doubt that the congressional blood was stirred and that thereafter West Point need not expect to save the Union unqueried.

There was much debate. Richardson of Illinois and Crittenden of Kentucky contended that the generals should be permitted to fight their own battles. Owen Lovejoy of Illinois solemnly declared that Bull Run and Ball's Bluff were arranged by God to punish the North for not abolishing slavery. Wyckliffe of Kentucky said that slavery was all right, and expressed a desire to "throw the Abolitionists overboard." Mallory of the same state believed slavery could be maintained, but declared that if it came to a question of saving either slavery or the Union, the people of Kentucky would save the Union. There were loud cheers then. Dunn of Indiana, while agreeing with this sentiment, said he was un-

willing "to accept Mr. Lovejoy as prophet, priest, or king,"
believing that "the gentleman from Illinois was not authorized to interpret God's providence in the affairs of men."
Thad Stevens characteristically brought the debate back to
where it belonged, supporting the Conkling resolution. "Has
it come to this," he asked, "that Congress is a mere automa-
ton, to register the decrees of another power, and that we
have nothing to do but find men and money?"

The resolution was passed 79–54, but the second reply of
the Secretary of War was no more enlightening than the
first.

Nevertheless, the agitation had some effect. The Senate,
though refusing to pass a similar resolution, did pass one offered in the ensuing debate by Grimes of Iowa, calling for a
permanent Joint Committee on the Conduct of the War,
consisting of three Senators and four Representatives. The
House concurring, this committee was formed, and it was

for four years one of the most important agencies in the country. It assumed, and was sustained by Congress in assuming, a
great range of prerogative. It became a stern and zealous cen-
sor of both the army and the Government; it called soldiers and
statesmen before it, and questioned them like refractory school-
boys. It claimed to speak for the loyal people of the United
States, and this claim generally met with the sympathy and
support of a majority of the people's representatives in Congress assembled. It was often hasty and unjust in its judg-
ments, but always earnest, patriotic, and honest; it was assailed
with furious denunciation and defended with headlong and in-
discriminating eulogy; and on the whole it must be said to have
merited more praise than blame.[3]

IT has become customary to speak of Roscoe Conkling as a
protégé of Thaddeus Stevens. This was not the case. Conkling was nobody's protégé, nobody's pupil. It is true that the
gall-bitter Thad and the gentleman from Oneida partnered

it to a considerable extent during the latter stages of the
battle between Andrew Johnson and Congress, just before
Grant moved into the White House; and it is also true that
the men appear to have been friends off the floor, though
perhaps not intimate. But in the early years of the war the
parliamentary differences between them were many, the
clashes not a few. Indeed, it is difficult to conceive of two
such men working together for any length of time. Both
were masters of sarcasm—good, harsh sarcasm with a sting
that hurt. Thad Stevens was the more supple, the less ponderous, and at this time the more effective. He was, of course,
a much older man; and he was majority leader of the House,
a resistless disciplinarian, a fiend in a fight.

The figure is familiar and easily remembered, because like
Conkling the man was an island of ill-nature in a monotonous expanse of professional amiability; like Conkling he
didn't ask that anybody like him, or even admire him, but he
demanded that his associates fear and obey him—and they
did.

He was thin, almost six feet tall, and had been a great
horseman and swimmer, in spite of his club foot. But now, in
his 70's, a dying man who somehow refused to die, he seemed
rather shorter than he was. He was a bachelor, a radical of
radicals, had no particular religion, loved poker, and wore a
black wig. Harsh, unforgiving, perfectly willing to hit below
the belt in any fight, nevertheless he was honest; he had a
wealth of sound, common sense; and he worked hard and got
results. Highfalutin' ideals were not for Thad Stevens. Other
men might fondle them if they wished: so long as they voted
his way, Thad didn't question their reasons.

Like Conkling, too, often he was deliberately insulting.
He would finish a speech with a wave toward the congressman who was to follow him: "My friend, the gentleman from
——, will now make a few feeble remarks." And those remarks *would* seem feeble, after Thad Stevens'! Nobody

started for the cloakrooms when the whip from Pennsylvania began to talk. He was often wrong, but never half-hearted; he was called many hard names, but nobody accused him of being a bore.

Simon Cameron was Secretary of War at the beginning of Lincoln's first administration. Stevens once told Lincoln what he thought of this fellow Pennsylvanian. "But," Lincoln cried, "you don't really think Si Cameron would *steal* anything, do you?" No, Thad didn't think Si would steal a red-hot stove. Lincoln couldn't resist the temptation to repeat this, and of course Cameron heard of it. The President apologized to Thad, told him Cameron was demanding a retraction. "Yes, I'll take it back," said Thad. "I was wrong when I said Si Cameron wouldn't steal a red-hot stove. I retract it. I think now that he would."

THESE two had sundry scrapes in the 1861–62 session. When Roscoe Conkling presented in the House a resolution calling for federal coöperation with whichever states might desire to institute plans for gradual compensated abolition—as requested by the President, and in fact framed in the President's own words[4]—Thad Stevens, always the extremest sort of abolitionist, couldn't see why so much excitement was caused. The resolution, he thought, meant nothing one way or the other, and would come to nothing, whatever its fate on the floor. "I think it is the most diluted milk-and-water gruel proposition that was ever given to the American nation," said Thad. It was passed, 89–31.[5]

Earlier, Stevens, as chairman of the Ways and Means Committee, had brought in a bill levying a direct real estate tax of $30,000,000, and Conkling had the temerity to fight this. To be sure, Conkling's district was a rural one, and his objection that the tax would bear too heavily upon farm property would be popular at home: "I protest against taxing farms until everything else is taxed!" Still, men didn't usually oppose the fury from Lancaster. In this case, Thad was obliged to compromise, and $10,000,000 was cut from the levy.

But their greatest fight was over the legal tender acts.

THE United States was rich in possibilities, but otherwise not notably opulent. Congress' chief job, with a war started, was to raise a lot of money right away. Compared with that, nothing else mattered.

Stevens' real estate tax was trivial. There were to be many other taxes too, particularly a heavy tax on manufactures, which was to be offset by a boost of tariff rates. But these were not enough. So Thad Stevens and his Ways and Means Committee reported the first legal tender bill.

The argument for inflation was simple, then. Admitted that the nation needed money: admitted that the Federal Government had the power to print, or engrave, pieces of paper which were money: then why shouldn't the Government print or engrave a lot more of those pieces of paper? Surely an act of Congress, duly signed by the President, would create anything, even a few hundred millions of dollars? It might be objected that people would refuse to consider such notes as real money, since they were not backed by hard, cold gold.[6] It might be pointed out that unbacked paper currency had been tried, and found wanting indeed, by Turkey, Austria, France during the Revolution, England during the Napoleonic wars, the Continental Congress while the War of Independence was in progress; and that already the Confederate states were beginning to experience the evils of confusion resulting from such money. It might even be argued, and perhaps a few irreverent persons did argue, that a good way to get more money into circulation would be to repeal the laws against counterfeiting.

Thad Stevens was no fool, and he realized that the legal tender acts, which purposed to create $450,000,000 worth of pieces of paper, undoubtedly would lead to nasty complications. He had been convinced that *something* must be done, and that promptly; and legal tender seemed to him the best device.[7]

It didn't seem so to Roscoe Conkling.

"The Treasury will control and decide the war, not the war the Treasury," he declared, opening the fight against the first of three legal tender bills. "Armies and navies may perish, and a public credit well preserved can replace them; but if the public credit perishes, the army and navy can only increase the disaster and deepen the dishonor. . . . It [the bill] will proclaim throughout the country a saturnalia of fraud; a carnival for rogues. . . . Every debtor of a fiduciary character, who has received from others money, hard money worth a hundred cents on the dollar, will forever release himself from liability by buying up for that knavish purpose, at its depreciated value, the spurious currency which we shall have put afloat. Everybody will do it," he added, "except those who are more honest than the American Congress advises them to be."[8]

Like others of the opposition, he called the legal tender scheme not merely dangerous and dishonest, but unnecessary even as an emergency measure. In addition, he believed it to be unconstitutional. It should not be resorted to, at least, until everything else had been tried. Why not impose heavy taxes first, increasing the public credit even before they were collected, and then issue bonds against this increased credit? He offered two alternative plans. Whether these would have proved better than the legal tender acts is something for economists to discuss among themselves, arriving at no conclusion. It is difficult to see how they could have proved worse.

Sell $500,000,000 of 6% bonds payable in 20 years, at rates not lower than the equivalent of par 7% stocks. "The banks [of Boston, New York and Philadelphia] would issue unlimited amounts of what would become trash, and buy good hard-money bonds of the nation," cried Thad Stevens. "Was there ever such a temptation to swindle?" Well then, as another admittedly emergency measure, providing at least a breathing spell, why not authorize the Secretary of the Treasury to issue $200,000,000 of United States notes, carrying no interest, redeemable in coin in one year? Stevens snorted: "Does he not know that such notes must be dishonored, and the plighted faith of the government be broken? If we are to use suspended notes to pay our expenses, why not use our own?"[9]

Conkling fought to the last ditch, but Thad Stevens cracked his whip and the Congressmen fell into line. Cried Lovejoy of Illinois, at the very last minute: "There is no precipice, no chasm, no yawning bottomless gulf before this nation, so terrible, so appalling, so ruinous, as the bill before the House," and the gentleman from Oneida sprang to his feet to declare that he concurred "in every word" of this.

The bill was passed 93–59.[10]

ROSCOE CONKLING was fulfilling his destiny. Men were becoming aware of him in Washington—disliking him perhaps, but admiring and fearing him. The fellow had tilted with Thad Stevens and still was on his feet, still was talking. And how he could talk! Very slowly always, his anger cold, rich, musical, his invective a trifle elephantine but crushing, he pronounced his vowels with the greatest care, and used few gestures. At first he would walk back and forth nervously while he talked, but he conquered this habit early in his career; thereafter he stood very straight, his head thrown back, one foot forward; and he never bellowed or shouted or stamped, never pounded with his fist, never bent, figuratively or literally. During his set speeches, his greatest, he would refer occasionally to notes on the backs of envelopes, reminder notes resembling newspaper headlines; but usually this was no more than a trick to give the impression of extemporaneous speaking when in fact the speech had been perfectly memorized.[11]

Ben Perley Poore looked down upon him from the gallery

and found the sight a good one, commenting on the dark frock coat, the light-colored waistcoat, the trousers "with gaiters buttoned over his shoes," the large and prominent nose, the bluish-gray eyes, heavy dark eyebrows, sidewhiskers closely curled. But others were not so favorably impressed. "Vain as a peacock, and a czar in arrogance," Breen found him; and Welles, that humorless, bad-tempered Pepys of the period, thought the man "vigorous and vain," and again "an egotistical coxcomb . . . who would, at any time, sacrifice the right to benefit his party."

Three Oneida Republicans called upon him with some suggestions regarding patronage, for young, recently elected members of the lower house usually are good listeners when such delegations approach. But not Judge Conkling's son! "Gentlemen, when I need your assistance in making the appointments in our district, I shall let you know."[12]

Surely this is no way for a Congressman to talk to his constituents, especially if they be persons who, as in this case, had been prominent in the campaign just past. One cannot fancy James Gillespie Blaine, for instance, talking that way to persons from his home state of Maine. That young man was making his first appearance in the halls of Congress, and he was promptly compared with Roscoe Conkling—no, not compared, perhaps, nor yet contrasted, so much as *linked* with Conkling as a name, though the differences were both essential and superficial—very much as the names of Thackeray and Dickens always have been linked.

Blaine was polite, Blaine was charming. He was thirty-two years old, tall, robust, erect, with a white skin and delicately pink cheeks, prematurely grayish hair, and big, brown, sympathetic eyes. An excellent talker, too, and naturally good tempered, he didn't have an enemy in the House, yet. Thad Stevens found the *mot juste* for him in '64, when after grinding under heel one of Blaine's pet bills, he referred with a grudging grin to "the magnetic manner of my friend from Maine." Yes, "magnetic!" The public took it up and never forgot it.

But Roscoe Conkling had no time, then, to worry about Blaine of Maine. There was work to be done at home. There was everything to indicate that in New York State at least, and probably all over the North, this year of '62 was going to be a Democratic one. The war was going very badly for the Union forces, and nowhere was it so unpopular as in New York. Conkling, as a Republican, represented the war; he was whole-heartedly with the administration, and in his stock of vituperative adjectives he could find none hot enough, sharp enough, properly to express his opinion of Copperheads.

It happened that the leading Copperhead in the state at the time was his own brother-in-law, Horatio Seymour, whom the Democrats had nominated again for Governor. Seymour did not believe that the Federal Government had any right to prevent a state from seceding from the Union, and he honestly thought that the war was a ghastly mistake. The issue was made even clearer when the Republicans nominated Wadsworth, a military hero.

On September 26, the Republicans of Oneida County, assembled in convention, unanimously renominated their Representative in Congress. But the Democrats nominated Francis Kernan, who in any year would have proved a strong opponent.

It was in the offices of Kernan and Spencer that Roscoe Conkling had studied law. Francis Kernan was forty-six, Roscoe Conkling thirty-two. The Congressman had a brilliant record, and he was easily the better orator. But it was going to be a Democratic year.

The Seymour-Wadsworth contest was one of the bitterest in the history of the state, and Conkling stumped vigorously in opposition to his brother-in-law. But it was a Democratic year, no doubt of it. Seymour got in by more than 10,000

majority, while Roscoe Conkling lost his district by a scant
98 votes, and became a lame duck.

V. Work at Home

HE continued to be warlike, but unmilitary. On
March 20 he addressed a meeting of the National
Loyal League at Cooper Institute in New York
City, supporting the President. On April 12, the
anniversary of the firing upon Fort Sumter, he addressed
another meeting of the same organization—a mass meeting,
in Union Square. On May 26, at Mechanics' Hall, Utica, for
the benefit of local members of this league he scorched Val-
landigham and his supporters, the hated Copperheads, calling them a "whole swarm of sharks and pestilent beings" and
"hypocrites." In July and August he acted for the Government against Charles E. Hopson, arrested as a deserter, and
had the satisfaction of again defeating in the court room the
man who recently had defeated him for Congress, Francis
Kernan. In September he handled two more such cases for
the Government, both successfully. He was one of a committee of eight which framed six resolutions enthusiastically endorsing Lincoln and the war, which resolutions were adopted
by a mass convention of Oneida County Unionists at Rome,
February 26, 1864.

The Lincoln support was not forgotten by that President,
who knew how to pay political debts. On August 26, 1864,
Lincoln wrote to Roscoe Conkling's friend, Ward Hunt, that
"I am for the regular nominee in all cases, and . . . no one
could be more satisfactory to me as the nominee in that district than Mr. Conkling." The President added, cautiously:
"I do not mean to say that there are not others as good as
he in the district, but I think I know him to be at least good
enough."[1]

For New York was an important state always, doubly important now as a hotbed of the anti-war faction opposed to another four years of Lincoln. The President was nervous, worried—troubled even about the nomination. "A more anxious candidate I have never known," recorded Colonel McClure, who conferred with him at this time. Lincoln wished to have a Southerner, and a Democrat, for his running-mate, and was not eager to repeat the name "Republican," preferring, as did so many others then, including Conkling, "Unionist."

The custom of nominating for the Vice-Presidency a man in almost every personal and political respect the opposite of the Presidential nominee, was coming to be a fixed one. It might be supposed that after unfortunate (for them) experiences with Tyler and Fillmore, the men who manipulated national conventions would have refused to gamble again in the matter of the secondary nomination, and would have proceeded on the assumption that even a President might die. But they didn't; they still don't. And Lincoln persuaded Colonel McClure and a few others to work for the nomination of Andrew Johnson of Tennessee as the Emancipator's running-mate.

Andrew Johnson was born to poverty, and a self-educated man; he was a staunch believer in the Union; but there the resemblance to Lincoln ceases. Johnson was an egotist, a rough and tumble fighter, without tact, stubborn, straightforward, utterly humorless. But he was a Southerner, born in North Carolina, a resident of Tennessee, and he was a Democrat; so he should go excellently well on the ticket with a Northern Republican who was modest, humble, diplomatic, peaceable, and possessed of a sense of humor his nation never will forget. They would both be "Unionists" together—not Republicans, not Democrats, but Unionists.

For it would be a hard fight, this election of 1864. The war, by far the most expensive the world ever had known, was costing $4,000,000 a day; and things were going very badly for the Union forces, in spite of, or perhaps because of, a continuous shifting of commanders-in-chief. Who, Democrats were asking, cares for the South anyway? Who wants it? Let it secede, if secession would make it happy, and let this costly slaughter cease. It might not be so bad, Democrats conceded, if there were a victory now and then to cheer Northern taxpayers. And they themselves were preparing to nominate the most popular commander-in-chief of them all, the fiery George McClellan, a diminutive egotist from East Orange, N. J.

Of course Abe Lincoln was troubled in mind.

Roscoe Conkling was troubled too. In the company of the faithful Ward Hunt, he called upon Chauncey Depew, a precocious young man from New York City who engaged in railroading for a livelihood but loved politics, and who recently had been elected secretary of state of New York. He "delivered an intense attack upon machine methods and machine politics, and said they would end in the elimination of all independent thought, and ultimate infinite damage to the state and nation." In view of Conkling's later record as head of the State machine, this pronouncement of a man seeking a second election to Congress was rather amusing, as Depew remembered when he came to record it in his memoirs. The machine, Conkling continued, had defeated him at the last election, but it could defeat him again only by running Erastus Clark against him. Now, would Mr. Depew consent to appoint Erastus Clark his deputy secretary of state, thereby removing this obstacle? Mr. Depew, always good natured, said that he would do so. Whereupon Conkling made a speech.

It was his habit, when emotionally stirred, to break into an oration. Frequently he startled men, and sometimes delighted them, with these declamations, delivered without any warning.

On this occasion he "rose as if addressing an audience, and

as he stood there in the little parlor of Congress Hall in Albany he was certainly a majestic figure. He said: 'Sir, a thing that is quickly done is doubly done. Hereafter, as long as you and I both live, there will never be a deposit in any bank, personally, politically, or financially to my credit which will not be subject to your draft.' "[2]

COMMODORE VANDERBILT's bright young protégé was to be of great service to Roscoe Conkling at least once more in this campaign. The New York legislature had passed a law, approved by the Governor, designed to take the vote of New York soldiers in the field. This law made it the duty of the Secretary of State to provide ballots and see that they reached the soldiers. There was no machinery by which this work could be done. Chauncey Depew applied in vain to the express companies, who protested that they were not properly equipped, and finally he persuaded John Butterfield of Utica, a retired expressman, to organize a company for this specific purpose. Then it became necessary to learn where the New York troops were stationed, and Depew went to Washington.

He was there for several months, and accomplished nothing. The Secretary of War, Edwin M. Stanton, was an executive genius, but he also was one of the most ill-natured men in all history, who seemed to take a genuine satisfaction in saying "no." It was generally supposed at the time, and has been generally supposed since, that Lincoln appointed him for this very reason, knowing his own tender-heartedness.[3] Depew himself thought this. "If the boy condemned to be shot, or his mother or father, could reach the President in time, he was never executed." But Stanton could withstand oceans of tears, and did. He was extraordinarily efficient. Everybody hated him.

Depew, who found him "brief and disagreeable and . . . very brusque," finally tried hammering the desk. "If the ballots are to be distributed in time, I must have information at once!" But Stanton "very angrily refused" and said: "New York troops are in every army, all over the enemy's territory. To state their location would be to give invaluable information to the enemy. How do I know if that information would be so safeguarded as not to get out?"

Depew, sighing, quit the office, and was walking down a long corridor, "which was full of hurrying soldiers returning from the field or departing for it," when he encountered Congressman Washburne of Illinois, a close personal friend of the President; and to Washburne lugubriously he told his tale. "To protect myself," he explained, "I must report to the people of New York that the provision for the soldiers' voting cannot be carried out because the administration refuses to give information where the New York soldiers are located."

"Why," said Washburne, "that would beat Mr. Lincoln. You don't know him. While he is a great statesman, he is also the keenest of politicians alive. If it could be done in no other way, the President would take a carpetbag and go around and collect those votes himself. You remain here until you hear from me. I'll go at once and see the President."

About an hour later Chauncey Depew found himself chatting with a Secretary of War who suddenly had become "most cordial and charming." And he left Washington on the midnight train, with the information he'd come to get.

It should be remembered that at this time New York State had more than three hundred thousand soldiers in the field, most of them voters, and a majority of them Republicans.

A convention at Rome nominated Conkling for Congress, September 22, 1864. Unexpectedly coy, he asked if he might decline, and was informed that he mightn't; so he accepted.

It was a few days after this that he received a letter asking him to attend a proposed anti-Lincoln conference for the purpose of calling an independent national convention at

Cincinnati. The matter, still a secret, was no mean one. The men who had either signed or approved this letter—they included such celebrities as Salmon P. Chase, Horace Greeley, Mayor Opdyke, David Dudley Field, Daniel S. Dickinson and Lucius Robinson—really believed that Lincoln could not win. The supposedly sagacious Thurlow Weed (who, however, had nothing to do with the letter) had told Lincoln that his reëlection was "an impossibility."[4]

But Conkling, though he was an "out" at the time, and thus presumably more susceptible to such temptation, refused to have anything to do with the matter. "I do not approve of the call, or of the movement, and cannot sign it," he wrote. "For that reason it would not be proper or agreeable that I should be present at the conference you speak of."[5]

The proposed convention never assembled. And the Conkling fidelity was rewarded when military men suddenly turned the course of the campaign with some dramatic victories, notably Sherman's capture of Atlanta, which stimulated Northern enthusiasm and made it clear that the end of the slaughter at last was near.

So Lincoln won, though he carried New York State by a scant 6,749, thanks largely to the soldiers' vote.

Roscoe Conkling also won.

New York is a big state. As it had produced the most Copperheads during the Civil War, so it produced the most Unionists. No other state numbered among its citizens so many patriots or so many thieves.

The end of the war found the Congressman from Oneida busy prosecuting bounty frauds, and making a host of new enemies. Desperately needing volunteers, the Government had offered a substantial enlistment bounty, and of course the system was abused. Men enlisted, accepted the bounty, deserted, enlisted elsewhere under different names, got another bounty, deserted, enlisted elsewhere. . . . The business was organized; and necessarily it had the coöperation of many bounty brokers and military officers.

Roscoe Conkling had tilted many times with Major Haddock, the deputy provost marshal for the western New York district. He was convinced that Haddock was crooked. Besides, Haddock had summarily removed the Congressman's friend, Captain Peter B. Crandall, assistant deputy provost marshal in charge of the Oneida congressional district, and Conkling, for all his fury, hadn't been able to get Crandall re-instated.[6] So it must have been with considerable satisfaction that he accepted a commission as special judge advocate to prosecute Major Haddock before a military court, the major at last having been accused of corruption.

The trial, the whole business, created a great deal of excitement. It is an exceptionally complicated matter; and here it should be sufficient to record that Conkling surpassed himself in his summation, winning additional admirers, and additional enemies as well.

. . . the Rebellion, now ended, seems to have been appointed to illustrate, in manifold ways, the shame not less than the glory of humanity. A vessel tossed and groaning in a gale, a crew heroically manful, and a myriad of sharks following the ship— such is a faithful emblem of our condition during the mighty convulsion which has just subsided. The nation was in the last peril of existence. The continent quaked under the tramp of an uncounted host, eager, from general to private, to suffer all, and dare all, for the salvation of the Government of their fathers. But with them came knaves, titled and even shoulder-strapped, a darkening cloud of vampires, gorging themselves upon the heart's blood of their country. Shoddy contractors, bounty gamblers and base adventurers found their way even into the army . . .

So people were declaring that he was indecently eager to prosecute this case? Good! He was proud of such condemnation.

Give me a certificate of my zeal, that I may leave it as a legacy to my children; and bid them say of me: "He did his utmost to gibbet at the crossroads of public justice all those who, when war had drenched the land with blood and covered it with mourning, parted the garment of their country among them, and cast lots upon the vesture of the Government, even while they held positions of emolument and trust."[7]

Haddock, found guilty, was cashiered and was sentenced to pay a fine of $10,000 or serve five years in jail. He paid the fine.

THE war had been ended, and everybody was glad of that. Congressman Conkling, in Utica, welcomed the troops home.

At the country's call . . . you left fireside and home for the camp, the trench, and the hospital. Then it was that you went out to defend on far distant battle-fields the life and glory of your country . . . You have conquered in fights which will be historic forever. You have belonged to the most glorious army which ever assembled on earth . . .[8]

But old General Scott had predicted, back in '61, that when the war was ended it would require the whole force of the nation to restrain the fury of the noncombatants. The general had been correct. For another conflict was brewing, a political one, not less bitter than the Civil War itself, not less shameful either, and not a whit less interesting.

The whole matter was greatly confused when, scarcely a month after the surrender at Appomattox, a bombastical young actor shot and killed President Lincoln.

VI. The Biggest Problem

IT has been asserted by some writers that Lincoln had a plan of reconstruction carefully drawn, and that Congress, under his guidance, would have avoided hideous mistakes in its treatment of the South. There isn't any proof of this. Lincoln was too shrewd a politician to plan very far in advance. Business men can do that, sometimes with success, but the preposterous assertion that the national government should be run like a gigantic business, "along business lines," at that time had not even been heard in the land; adoration of the Man on Horseback had not yet given way before adoration of the Man at the Big Desk; and it was generally taken for granted that politics must be conducted in a political manner.

Lincoln did have the beginnings of a plan for readmission of the seceded states; but nobody can say, nobody is even on safe ground guessing, what would have come of this plan. The President had been given extraordinary powers during the war, and Congress, properly jealous, was prepared to snatch those powers back. Lincoln would have had a terrible fight on his hands, had he survived Booth's bullet. Andrew Johnson, the man Lincoln himself had selected for the Vice-Presidency, inherited a bomb already lit and sizzling.

Johnson's place in our history, even his approximate place, has not yet been fixed. For many years he was cursed as a stubborn drunkard, a ranting, egotistical fool who had been thrust into the White House by accident or perhaps by murderous design (for thousands believed or came to believe that he was behind the plot to kill Abraham Lincoln) and who had made a tragic mess of his work there. More recent biographers and historians, and notably Beale, Stryker, and Bowers, have praised the man so loudly that he seems actually to have had something godlike about him.

And it is conceivable that under different circumstances,

and in less turbulent times, Andrew Johnson might have become a national hero. His virtues were rugged, unvarnished, the sort Americans like. He had been born to poverty. He was a tailor. He never had spent a day in school; and it was his wife, small, frail, a Scottish woman, who taught him to read and write. But nobody had been obliged to teach him how to fight. Tennessee politics were very rough indeed; but he fitted naturally into the turmoil. A familiar anecdote has him, in his early career, mounting a platform in a neighborhood where his opinions were unpopular, drawing a loaded pistol and cocking it and placing it on the speaker's stand in front of him, and then announcing that he had been given to understand that if he repeated his views on this platform he would be shot and killed before he was finished. Well, he intended to repeat those views, so perhaps it would be as well to have the shooting first and get it over with? A long pause. Nobody stirred. Finally the man on the platform uncocked the pistol, put it back into his pocket, and launched into the bitterest speech of the campaign. Nobody shot him.

The story is very likely true. But what is more important is that Andrew Johnson really was that sort of man.

He was of medium height, but broad shouldered and erect, so that he seemed somewhat taller. His complexion was swarthy, and this, with his high cheekbones and sparkling, penetrating eyes, his dark, thick hair, his dignity, and his lack of any sense of humor, frequently suggested the noble Indian. He had a good voice, but rarely spoke except when he was angry—and then he roared. He was laconic, stubborn, suspicious. He worked seventeen or eighteen hours a day, and had absolutely no outside recreations or amusements. He never smiled. He was very methodical about everything, the first President to keep complete files of his business memoranda and correspondence; he was a neat dresser. Aristocrats he hated. His greatest love was for the Constitution of the United States, several copies of which he always kept somewhere on his person or near at hand: he had a disconcerting habit of presenting these to visitors or chance acquaintances.

Men called him a drunkard; and it is true that he had been scarcely able to stand when he made his inauguration speech as Vice-President. But this episode was partly explained by his illness at the time. Certainly Lincoln himself was untroubled by it: "I know Andy—he's all right—he's no drunkard." Persons who knew him well, saw him constantly while he was President, and in some cases had no special cause to love him, have testified that in fact he drank very little.[1] Even this evidence is not necessary. No heavy drinker could have done so much work.

His home life seems to have been in the most admired American Presidential tradition. His wife was an invalid, thoughtful, dignified, consumptive, who stayed in her room, in a little rocking chair with her needlework and her books, seldom appearing downstairs. She was able to quiet him with a "Now, Andrew!" when he was in one of his rages. The social duties were performed by his daughters, Mrs. Stover, mother of three small children, and Mrs. David Patterson, mother of two more such: the President was passionately fond of children. Mrs. Patterson was attached not only to her family but also to her dairy. She made, with her own hands, all the butter consumed at the White House. "You mustn't expect too much of us," she sometimes told startled ambassadors. "We're just plain Tennessee folks." Yet there were many exemplary if not gay receptions and dinners at the Executive Mansion during the Johnson régime.

THE great question was, what to do about the Confederate states. Nothing like this ever had been known before.

Perhaps the most remarkable thing was the absence of rancor in the North and at Washington. Only a fool would contend that the reconstruction job was perfectly performed, and that a saintly dictator, equipped with the power of peering into the future, would have been unable to rearrange things in a manner more satisfactory to the contemporary population and to posterity. The fact remains, however, that at the close of hostilities, the people of the North generally, and most of their representatives in Congress, had no thought of treating the secession states as conquered territory. Nobody dreamed of the carpetbag era, then. And subsequent force acts were inspired not by an angry desire to humble the South and break up its economic life, but rather by well meant stupidity and, sometimes, sheer partisan blindness. The truth is, Washington didn't hold enough men capable of performing the most difficult task of statesmanship—the making of a just peace.

The Civil War had been the greatest of all wars. It had involved the largest number of men, had featured the bloodiest battles, had covered the greatest area, had cost more money, consumed more supplies, taken more lives, than any other single conflict. And the result had been decisive, the defeat of the Confederacy complete and final, the Government of the North and its military position stronger at the finish than at any other time. Yet nobody was executed, formally or otherwise; nobody was exiled, or thrown into prison for any mentionable time; except for Robert E. Lee and Jefferson Davis, nobody was permanently disenfranchised; not a penny of reparations was paid or demanded; not an acre of land was confiscated. This was, truly, unprecedented clemency! Some wild talk there was of hanging at least a few of the principal leaders of the Confederacy, and many persons believed to the end of their lives that it had been a mistake to permit Jefferson Davis to go free. But the fact remains—there isn't the slightest doubt of it—that an overwhelming majority of residents in the North and West were concerned only with forgetting about the whole affair (except for sentimental purposes) and getting back to work.

However, the men at Washington couldn't do this, even if they had been so inclined. They were faced with the fact that eleven states were out of the Union, and with the problem of how, and how soon, and under what auspices, those states should be readmitted.

There were various ways of accepting this situation.

Abraham Lincoln apparently had thought of the seceding states as erring children, who should be gently rebuked perhaps but permitted to reënter the home promptly and to resume their places at the family table.

Andrew Johnson had been angry with the leaders of the Confederacy, abhorring them as traitors; but against Southerners as a whole he had no animosity. Wasn't he one himself? He had been a poor white in Tennessee, where class feeling was exceptionally strong, and he hated the rich planters and their kind—the men who, in his opinion, were responsible for all the bloodshed—with a hatred bitter as gall. He would gladly have hanged them, and said so. He would have been delighted to see the Federal Government seize their property. But he believed that the Southern states themselves, secession being unconstitutional, never had been out of the Union in the first place, and that they should be permitted to resume their duties and privileges as soon as they could organize, or he could organize for them, acceptable state governments—that is, governments acceptable to him, personally.

Charles Sumner, the greatest leader in the Senate at this time, held what was known as the "States suicide theory." A soaring idealist, he believed that all Negroes should be placed immediately upon an equal basis with all white persons, and that until this was done the Confederate states should not be readmitted. By seceding, he contended, those states had forfeited all the rights guaranteed to them by the Constitution, and so were neither in the Union nor out of it, having approximately the status of territories, and being subject to the will of Congress rather than that of the executive.

But the true leader of the Republican party after Lincoln's death, and possibly even before that event, was Thaddeus Stevens of Pennsylvania, and that salty, hard-boiled statesman pointed out that there had been a war which the North had won and that therefore the Southern states could be treated as conquered provinces. And *should* be, too. They should be readmitted whenever the North was damned good and ready to readmit them; and the North should see to it that their appearance was altered before that event. "The whole fabric of Southern society *must* be changed," Stevens cried, "and it never can be done if this opportunity is lost."[2] He too believed that Congress and Congress alone should direct the reorganization of the Confederate states and set forth the conditions for readmittance.

WHAT the South itself thought about it all, no man can say. The South was dazed, dizzy, blinking in bewilderment as the dust settled and the last echoes of artillery chased themselves to rest. Defeat was everywhere admitted—it was undeniable —and probably most Southerners, like most Northerners, were chiefly concerned with getting back to business and trying to make things as much as possible as they had been before the whole fight started.

The South had become a land of mystery, a vast, indefinite expanse of darkness out of which drifted from time to time the most amazing stories. It is and was then a mistake to think of the South as one place, over all of which conditions were uniform. Some portions suffered much more than others. Some resumed their peace-time functions readily, some with great difficulty. The Negro population, around which most of the discussion centered, was by no means evenly distributed. And just as there was a vast difference between the planter aristocracy and the poor whites, and between city residents on the one side and the hill people of Tennessee, Virginia, and the Carolinas on the other, so also there was an immeasurable gulf between the former house slave, who usually was intelligent and reliable, and the plantation slave, who was a black mass of ignorance. The plantation slaves were greatly in the majority, and they caused the worst fears in the hearts of white people. Would they go back to work? And if so, on what terms? And if not, what *would* they do?

Nobody knew just what was the condition of the South, not even Southerners themselves. So sightseers with note-books began to pour into and through that strange land —editors and politicians, authors, military observers, mer-chants, journalists, philanthopic workers; official or semi-official or not official at all; wise men, "smart" men, earnest but stupid busybodies. For the most part they went with pre-conceived opinions, and saw what they had expected to see, and heard what they had expected to hear, returning with their opinions conveniently confirmed. No two of them agreed.

Perhaps the best answer to the question, What will the South accept? was given by one of these observers near the end of the long book he published after his return.

"The South," he wrote grimly, "will take—now as at any time since the surrender—whatever it can get."[3]

ANARCHY? Well, for a time there was something of the sort. But amazingly little, in view of the circumstances. The innate amiability of the American Negro, and the fact that the South was wholly agricultural, centers of population being few, small, and far between, probably account for the ab-sence of large-scale disorders. The Negro was free, but what of it? He had been freed, not simply by the Emancipation Proclamation, a mere war-time measure, but by the adoption of the Thirteenth Amendment to the Constitution of the United States. There were many who thought that this amendment had been adopted illegally; if you believed, with Andrew Johnson, that secession being unconstitutional in the first place, the Southern states never had been *out* of the Union, then obviously you must believe that the Thirteenth Amendment had not been properly ratified, since the South-ern states had not been given a chance to vote upon it. Nevertheless, ignoring this, it was generally admitted by intelligent persons in South and North alike that the Negro was, should be, *must* be free.

So the Negro was a free man; but he was not technically a citizen of the United States, nor was there any law or machinery to make him such. Yet, perplexingly, he was not an alien either. He had no status at all. He could not sue or be sued in the courts, local, state or national. He could not marry. He could not own property. Of course he could not vote: at this time none but the wildest fanatics even thought of making him a voter.[4] He could not sign a contract (or make his mark) and be held by it. Who was he? What to do about him?

The Negro himself was as confused as anybody else. In many cases he had come to think of this "freedom" he'd heard so much about as a material thing, an article which would be delivered to him, handed to him. In almost all cases he believed that it meant at least freedom from work. It never had occurred to him that all this fuss was being made merely for the purpose of giving him the choice of which ankle to wear his ball-and-chain on. What was the use of freedom, he asked, if a nigger had to work *anyway?*

It would be pleasant to believe romanticists who tell of slaves clinging to the ol' plantation, remaining faithful to the ol' massa, in spite of everything. No doubt a few of them did. But the truth is that most of them took to pedestrianism. They wandered. And when they were asked where they were going, they replied honestly and good-naturedly that they didn't know—that they were "enjoying their freedom." And when they became hungry, they stopped and asked for food; if they weren't given food, often they took it. Why not? Weren't they free now?

Their former masters did what they could to keep the slaves at home, to set them to work again in the fields. It wasn't much, at first. There were other influences. The Federal army, scattered pretty much all over the South, fed

them, sometimes clothed and sheltered them, and kept them
out of mischief. They hovered in great black swarms around
all army encampments, and followed the soldiers everywhere,
doglike, till they became a great nuisance. And the Freedmen's Bureau, a temporary Federal organization set up during the war to care for former slaves in conquered Southern
territory, and designed to continue in existence for one year
after hostilities had ceased—the Freedmen's Bureau did
what it could. And so did the Union League, and numberless
other well-meaning Northern organizations.

Still, there were hordes of footloose and carefree Negroes
tramping all the roads, singing, laughing, expecting to be
fed, "enjoying their freedom." And the fields were idle, while
Englishmen were offering fabulous prices for cotton.[5]

LINCOLN's plan—framed as a war-time measure, an executive, emergency measure for operation in the seceded states
as they should be conquered by the military—was to have the
Southern states form their own governments under military
supervision but without military interference, after 10 per
cent of the legal voters (but none who had borne arms
against the Union) had expressed in the form of a petition
to the President their willingness to do so. These governments, he believed, should be recognized promptly by the national Government, and their senators and representatives
received in Congress. This plan already had been started in
some of the Southern states, and notably in Tennessee, where
it seemed to be working well. But then, Tennessee was not
like the states of the deep South. It is doubtful whether a
majority of the adult whites in Tennessee had been in favor
of secession in the first place: certainly the hill people and
the poorer classes generally had been opposed. Tennessee
had been under Northern military government almost from
the beginning of the war. It was a border state, and probably
as loyal as Kentucky, which had refused to secede. So Tennessee was a poor example.

Possibly Lincoln would have stuck to this plan. We do not know, and cannot know. If he had, certainly, he would have been obliged to modify it. But Andrew Johnson wished to put it into effect without any modifications. He himself, he, the executive branch of the national Government, would be the one to say which Southern states should be readmitted to the Union, and when, and under what conditions, if any. Congress, he believed, had nothing to do with it. Wasn't he, the President, by authority of the Constitution commander-in-chief of the army and navy of the United States? Reconstruction was an executive function.

Congress didn't feel that way about it. Too long had Congress been a secondary branch of the government, an obedient body which produced an appropriation when called upon to do so, and offered suggestions for the conduct of the war, and obligingly passed the legislation requested of it, but which did not assume any real direction of affairs.

The war ended in March. Lincoln was killed in April. By law, unless a special session was called by the President, the new Congress would not meet until December 4. Andrew Johnson, refusing to call a special session, had lots of time to himself.

But his enemies weren't idle, either. When Congress finally did assemble, and even before that time, the radical trenches had been dug, the radical bayonets sharpened, scores of congressmen were preparing before scores of cheval glasses, and all was in readiness for the greatest political battle in the nation's history.

VII. Stronger Than Ever

THE radicals, wailed the *New York World*, "did not wait till the opening of Congress today, to give that plan [Johnson's reconstruction plan] the honor of a decent burial under the clerk's table, but put the party bow-string around it, and pitched it at midnight out of the window of a partisan caucus."

The *World*, being Democratic, felt very strongly about it. Nevertheless, this is the unexaggerated truth of the matter.

The Republicans had large majorities in both houses, almost two-thirds majorities, and a few days before the opening of the session, at a party caucus, the saturnine Stevens proposed a resolution, which was accepted, calling for a committee of six senators and nine representatives

who shall inquire into the condition of the States which formed the so-called Confederate States of America, and report whether they, or any of them, are entitled to be represented in either House of Congress, with leave to report at any time, by bill or otherwise; and until such report shall have been made, and finally acted on by Congress, no member shall be received into either House from any of the so-called Confederate States; and all papers relating to the representation of said States shall be referred to the said Committee without debate.

Observe the final clause. The "said Committee" was to be put in complete and unchallengeable charge of all reconstruction matters.

Assuredly it was impolite thus to tell the world how they, the Republican members of Congress, intended to do this thing, before they even listened to the President's formal announcement of how *he* intended to do it—how he had already started to do it. (It was especially unfortunate in view of the fact that the new President's message was admittedly a masterpiece of literature and statesmanship. It should have been! It was written by one of our greatest historians.)[1]

It was impolite, but it was understandable. For the Lincoln 10 per cent plan already was in operation in all the Southern states, which had organized their own governments and elected their senators and representatives. And who were these senators and representatives? Why, they were the same ones who had been in Congress before secession, or else they were younger men holding the same opinions, ex-officers of the disbanded Confederate army, just as arrogant, just as intolerant as ever.

There was nothing strange about the Republican reluctance to permit these men to return to Congress on the assumption that the states they represented were back in the Union already, or else that they never had been out of the Union. After all, there *had* been a war. And while forgiveness is admitted by all Christian gentlemen, and by many others as well, to be a most commendable virtue, still it would be asking too much of anybody except angels to take those Confederate fire eaters back on the same basis as before the fight, at the command of a Democrat. And there were no angels in Congress that session.

So Congress, even before the opening gavel-tap, showed its teeth—told the President what it thought of his reconstruction plan, and told the Southerners they could linger in the ante-rooms until the insiders were prepared to summon them.

Stewart (Rep., Nev.) in the Senate debate on the Stevens resolution made an interesting point. The resolution declared that no senator or representative from any "of the eleven states which have been declared to be in insurrection" should be seated in Congress until that body had agreed to readmit that state into the Union. Stewart asserted that no *state* ever had been "declared to be in insurrection," and quoted from Lincoln's proclamation of August 16, 1861: "I hereby declare that *the inhabitants of certain states and parts of states* . . . are declared in a state of insurrection against the United States."[2]

This passed almost unheeded, Stewart himself doing nothing about it, and the resolution was adopted—but with one significant change.

As originally proposed by Stevens, it was a *joint* resolution, not a *concurrent* resolution, as the Senate subsequently made it. The difference is a signature, the President's.

Yet a concurrent resolution carried precisely the same authority. Stevens knew this. The matter was strictly a Congressional one; and why did Stevens, always jealous of Congressional power, wish to drag in the President?

There could be but one answer. Stevens knew a fight was coming, and he saw no reason for shilly-shallying. If Andrew Johnson signed the resolution he placed himself on record as admitting that the legislative and not the executive branch was charged with the responsibility of reconstruction. If he refused to sign it (and he *would* refuse: Stevens, who had conferred with him at the White House a few days earlier, was sure of this) he would antagonize many members of both houses who otherwise would be willing to go along with him. An open fight—that was what the Pennsylvanian wished. But the conservatives of the Senate were not so bellicose; and though the resolution went into their chamber a joint, it emerged therefrom a concurrent, and the President was unembarrassed.

However, there were other methods of provoking a fight, and Stevens knew every one of them.

THERE were no angels in the Thirty-ninth Congress. But there were persons more amusing, more immediately important.

There was a fellow from Ohio named Rutherford Birchard Hayes, an undistinguished general with the customary sidewhiskers. He was quiet, untidy, affable, and was reputed to be a tolerably good lawyer; but nobody paid much attention to him, and he wasn't on any important committee. He wrote to his masterful wife, back in Columbus, that when Thad Stevens rose to speak "everyone expects something worth hearing," and added some similarly chatty comments on other fellow congressmen, among them: "Roscoe Conkling, of New York State, delivers measured sentences in a grave, deliberate way that is good."[3]

There was James Abram Garfield, a much more spectacular Ohio general, well liked, an excellent party worker, conscientious, an omnivorous reader. He was brainy, but a weather vane. He meant well; there was no malice in his soul; but since childhood he'd had great difficulty making up his mind about anything, and no difficulty at all in changing it. A tall and handsome man, erect, his well-shaped head thrown back, his gray eyes bright and friendly, he had prominent cheekbones, a thick, muscular neck, and (though he didn't look it) chronic indigestion. He enjoyed being popular. For all his reading, there was nothing of the stooped scholar in his appearance or his manner. Quite the contrary. He was a great handshaker and backslapper, who really liked people.

There was tall, cold, humorless John Sherman, very ambitious, but not at all popular. He wasn't a general, but his brother was—a good one, too.

There was General John ("Black Jack") Logan, a somewhat ferocious-looking personage, a hard-hitting politician from Illinois, adored by the ex-service men.

There was James Gillespie Blaine, that brilliant, that magnetic young fellow from Maine, who already was pushing ahead, somewhat to the annoyance of older statesmen. Yet Blaine was Blaine, from the very beginning. His private secretary once told Stanwood of overhearing one Southern member saying to another: "Now there's Blaine—but damn him, I do love him—"

There was Ben Butler of Massachusetts, another general, fat, bald, with a squint; he was an amazing vulgarian, noisy and vituperative, not to be squashed by anything.

There was Schuyler Colfax, neat, nimble, shiny, on his face a constant smile which might easily be called a smirk. They had made him Speaker at the same caucus which adopted Stevens' reconstruction resolution. He stood high in the councils of the Methodist Episcopal Church. He was a clever man who would have gone far, very far, if he hadn't happened to get caught in the sticky claws of the worst congressional scandal in the history of the nation. But at this time, when the Thirty-ninth Congress first assembled, he was a very important and highly respected person.

And there was Roscoe Conkling, that pavonine giant from upstate New York.

He had come back stronger than ever. At thirty-six, he was virtually a veteran in the House, and very much a Republican, one of the inner circle, a man to be treated with respect, even with awe. He didn't swagger—that would have been beneath his dignity—but he was at all times conscious of his own importance, and he made others conscious of it as well. He was, as before, pompous, and dangerous, and indescribably eloquent.

Schuyler Colfax appointed him to the Committee of Ways and Means, which, now that the war was over, was the most important standing committee of the House.

And in addition, Schuyler Colfax appointed him a member of the Joint Committee of Fifteen on Reconstruction.

The Committee of Fifteen has been accused of the basest sort of partisanship, the most heinous offenses against justice. Thad Stevens has been called its master mind, the other fourteen members merely his puppets.

Well, members of the committee made mistakes, but they were not devils intent upon doing wickedness just for the fun of it. Nor were they Thad Stevens' trained dogs, though that sardonic fellow was easily the most conspicuous among them and probably the most able.

There were radicals and conservatives then, but the words did not mean what they mean today. A radical was a person who believed that Congress should take charge of reconstruction, and that the seceded states should not be readmitted to the Union until they had conformed with certain requirements fixed by the victors. A conservative was a statesman who wasn't a radical. Or, a radical was an anti-Johnson man, a conservative more or less pro-Johnson.

But the distinction, when the Committee of Fifteen was organized, was not so clear as some historians have made it seem. The committee *became* radical. At first, it was inclined to be conservative. The chairman, Senator Fessenden, was decidedly a conservative. Roscoe Conkling was rated as one too, in the beginning.

This committee came to be Congress' army in its long, ungentlemanly war with the President.

Andrew Johnson had the advantage of a good start. Generally, at the time Congress assembled, the people were with him; the Democrats always were with him; he had the support of the Republican conservatives; and many of his enemies were afraid to attack him, or reluctant to do so while he seemed to be enjoying a moderate popularity. His 10 per cent plan already was in operation in the former Confederate states.

It was only natural that those states should elect to Congress the men who had led them into secession—the men who were the true leaders of the Southern people, the instinctive leaders, almost the only ones. It was natural—but it was highly indiscreet. It made previously complacent Northerners suspicious; it frightened conservatives; and it gave the more radical radicals an argument against executive reconstruction.

The radicals soon were given an even better weapon. The

Southern states, no doubt thinking more about local conditions than about the effect of such moves upon public opinion throughout the rest of the nation, began to pass the celebrated series of "Black Codes." This, too, was natural but indiscreet.

Something, it was explained impatiently, must be done about those droves of darkies drifting here and there across the countryside, potential and occasionally actual troublemakers. Something must be accomplished to define their status, put them to work, take from them the opportunity to do mischief—and raise the cotton.

Northerners agreed that something must be done, but they wished to do it themselves. And Southerners believed that only Southerners knew "how to handle" Negroes, and believed also, and with more justification, that there was no time to wait for Congress to make up its mind. So the Black Codes began to appear.

Mississippi's was the first, and the strictest. Under it, all Negroes below the age of eighteen were made the wards of the state; and all Negroes of eighteen and older who could not show that they were self-supporting and had established homes—which of course included practically every one of them—were rated as vagrants, and were to be farmed out by the state pretty much as the state desired. No Negro was permitted to own firearms. Negroes were authorized to marry, but intermarriage with whites was made punishable by life imprisonment. The law, ostensibly meant to benefit Negroes as well as whites, gave the former slave a legal status: he could make contracts, could plead or implead in any state or local court, and could own, buy, sell, and lease property—though only in incorporated towns, never in the country.

Other states followed, and in most cases their laws were much the same. In South Carolina Negroes were obliged to get licenses from district judges in order to be anything but farmers or farm laborers. Georgia fixed a death penalty for arson, rape, burglary by night, and horse-stealing, applicable only to Negroes. Texas had strict labor laws, and Negroes with no apparent means of support were made apprentices. In Virginia, vagrants could be farmed out for three months, their wages to go toward their upkeep; and if one escaped, a month could be added to his sentence. The use of the ball and chain was authorized in Virginia, provided permission was obtained from a magistrate. North Carolina, though its Negro laws were somewhat more liberal than most, imposed a death penalty upon Negroes convicted of assault with attempt to rape. Florida's Black Code likewise was comparatively liberal, and though the vagrancy law was strict, this included whites as well as Negroes. Only Arkansas and Tennessee, at least on paper, had no race discrimination. All of the states passed laws defining "persons of color," the definitions ranging from persons with $\frac{1}{4}$ to persons with $\frac{1}{16}$ Negro blood.[4]

Not cynicism on the part of Northern statesmen, but plain common sense, suggested that under the provisions of the various Black Codes, Negroes could be treated precisely as they had been treated before the war. They still would be slaves, except in name. Inevitably they would be declared vagrants—most of them in fact *were* vagrants—and the states could farm them out as apprentices or as official prisoners, and by means of a succession of petty regulations keep them in that status indefinitely.

To be sure, under the provisions of these same laws, Negroes could be made gradually into good, self-respecting citizens, and their lot greatly bettered. But that depended upon the men who administered the laws, and those men were the old slave owners, whom Northerners, with very good reason, did not trust.

Yes, there were excellent arguments for the Black Codes, as well as excellent arguments against them. But the side which was against them happened to be the side which had won the war.

THE committee broke up into subcommittees, to each of which was assigned the responsibility of investigating conditions in two or three of the former Confederate states. It was not considered necessary to go to those states. Instead, witnesses were summoned to Washington.[5]

Roscoe Conkling was on the subcommittee delegated to look into the affairs of Virginia, North Carolina, and South Carolina.

But there was plenty of time for this. It was too big a matter to be rushed. And meanwhile, the army was governing the South, and doing an extremely good job of it.

What concerned the committee members more immediately was the matter of representation. It is easy to sneer at their interest in this as a partisan one, inspired by a determination to keep control of the national Government. And it is true that many or most of them believed (as some persons do to this day) that the Republican party is the only party fit to rule the nation. But it must be remembered that what this committee was to do would probably change the whole structure of Congressional representation, and that another opportunity to change it as they wished was not likely ever to be vouchsafed to them again. They wished the North represented equally with the South. It had not been, before the war. It isn't today. But that is not the fault of the Committee of Fifteen.

The original framers of the Constitution had compromised in the matter of representation. Three-fifths of the slaves were to be counted with the white men, and Congressmen apportioned on the basis of the total. But what now—now that there were no slaves?

Again Roscoe Conkling was a member of the subcommittee. And on January 22, 1866, when the time had come for the committee to present its first report, Thad Stevens selected the young man from Oneida to speak for the majority. His opponent, speaking for the minority members, was something less than worthy. The debate was to be a set-up;

and Conkling should have been ashamed to match silvery inflections with so poor a talker and so violent a Negro hater as the Democrat, Rogers of New Jersey.

The majority's resolution provided simply that

representatives and direct taxes shall be apportioned among the several states which may be included within this Union, according to their respective numbers, counting the whole number of persons in each state, excluding Indians not taxed; provided that whenever the elective franchise shall be denied or abridged in any state on account of race or color, all persons of such race or color shall be excluded from the basis of representation.

In other words, if the South enfranchised the Negro, then he would be counted. But not until then.

Rogers spoke, and he was passionate, over eager.

Then an icy (at first) Roscoe Conkling, beautifully self-possessed, and equipped with extensive tables calculated to answer the contention of New Englanders that their states would be harmed by the reapportionment. For Blaine of Maine (Conkling didn't like that man!) the previous month had complained that the New England states would have too few Congressmen under the proposed plan, partly because of their stricter suffrage requirements, which were mostly of an educational nature, and partly because so many New England men and so few New England women were moving to Western states.

"If a black man counts at all now, he counts five-fifths of a man, not three-fifths," Roscoe Conkling declared.

"Think of them! Four millions, each a Caspar Hauser, long shut up in darkness; and suddenly led out into the full flash of noon, and each, we are told, too blind to walk, politically."

He produced the tables, elaborate, carefully drawn. He showed that in 1860, when the last census had been taken, the Southern states had elected eighty-five members of the House of Representatives; whereas if three-fifths of the slaves had not been counted there would have been only 65, and if *all* of the slaves had been counted there would have been 94.

But there were no slaves now, and was the South to be permitted to increase this injustice?

Shall the death of slavery add two-fifths to the entire power which slavery had when slavery was living? Shall one white man have as much share in the government as three other white men merely because he lives where blacks outnumber whites two to one? Shall this inequality exist, and exist only in favor of those who without cause drenched the land with blood and covered it with mourning? Shall such be the reward of those who did the foulest and guiltiest act which crimsons the annals of recorded time? No, sir! Not if I can help it.

His tables showed that under the proposed reapportionment New York would gain four congressmen, Massachusetts two, Connecticut and Maine one each, California three. No New England state would lose, he said. Pennsylvania would lose two, and Illinois and Ohio one each.

Thad Stevens had wished to have the whole debate finished that afternoon, and Rogers' speech and Conkling's the only ones. But this was not to be. For one thing, Blaine of Maine interrupted the gentleman from New York, producing his own figures, his own tables. Conkling, of course, was furious.

Hurlburd moved for unanimous consent to extend Conkling's speaking time, but Conkling himself did not ask for this, and Stevens objected on the ground that Rogers' time had not been extended. Stevens was sufficiently sure of his measure to be fair about it.[6]

The following day Blaine brought up his figures again, and this time Roscoe Conkling, speaking extemporaneously, was less dignified. These two men had disliked one another from the very beginning, and the whole House was waiting for an explosion. It didn't come this day, though a few promissory firecrackers were set off.

Mr. Conkling: I desire to answer not so much the argument as the witticism of my friend from Maine.

Mr. Blaine: Oh, no; no wit, either perpetrated or intended.

Mr. Conkling: Well, Mr. Speaker, we consider it very witty over here; but then we are so far off.

Mr. Blaine: Glad the gentleman thinks my wit will carry a long distance.

Mr. Conkling: It is said that New England is the focus of fanaticism—

Mr. Blaine: I thought the gentleman only rose for an explanation?

Mr. Conkling: I am going to make a very brief explanation. New England is the place where the man said the sun riz and sot in his back yard, and it is alleged that such regard is had to it here that we cannot do anything here that militates against New England, and that various persons here—myself among the number—are opposed to the suffrage basis merely because it takes away some part of the power of fanatical New England. Now, I desire to relieve the proposition before the House of any imputation that it comes here or is supported in the interest of New England, and in preference to the other proposition, because the other proposition hits New England. I deny that it hits New England and I deny that this proposition benefits New England; in other words, I support this proposition on account of its own merits and not for local or electioneering purposes.

Mr. Blaine: I am very much obliged to the gentleman for the patronizing care with which he looks after the interests of fanatical New England.[7]

The resolution which Thad Stevens had wished disposed of in a single afternoon was debated for a full week, after which it was reported back to committee, where the words "and direct taxes" were taken out—for New England seems to have been less alarmed about the lack of additional congressmen than about the possibility of getting higher tax bills from the Federal Government—and in this form it passed the House on January 31. In the Senate, however, Charles Sumner and some others thought it not radical enough, and after a long and desultory debate it was killed, March 9.

VIII. He Didn't Like Blaine

CONGRESS, groaning, surveyed the nation's financial muddle as a savage might survey and poke at a modern adding machine.

At the outbreak of the Civil War the man didn't live who could remember when the United States had been embarrassed by any real national debt. There had been almost no need for internal revenue taxes; the customs duties, occasionally supplemented by a sale of public lands, provided sufficient income. Sometimes there were small, short-term loans, but more often there was a surplus. Only twice, and then but briefly, in 1798 and in 1814, had Congress found it necessary to exercise its constitutional right to levy a direct tax upon the states.

But wars are expensive, as statesmen should learn; and on August 1, 1865, a few months after the last shot had been fired, the national debt amounted to $2,756,431,471, which represented all manner of obligations—five-twenty bonds at 6 per cent, ten-forty bonds at 5 per cent, currency bonds at 7.3 per cent, one-year and two-year notes, compound interest notes, legal tender notes, fractional currency.[1]

There was, at least in the North, a false flush of prosperity; but taxes were terrific. David A. Wells, the Government's financial expert, estimated that Washington was collecting from 8 to 15 per cent on every finished product manufactured in the nation, in addition to the income tax which was then 5 per cent up to $10,000, and 10 per cent above $10,000.[2] And all sorts of obligations were about to fall due.

Obviously, something must be done.

It is very easy to recall that the tariff duties had been raised only as a war-time measure, to offset the high internal taxes of all sorts but particularly the manufactures and sales taxes; and that after the war the internal taxes were generally removed, whereas the tariff duties were not lowered until 1872 and then only for three years, at the end of which time they were raised again to the war-time level. It is very easy to rage that this constituted a breach of faith.

It was somewhat more difficult for the men charged with the task of putting the Government back on its financial feet. No doubt there were hidden influences at work; and it is true that the word "protection" was coming to be uttered by many Eastern statesmen with large-eyed awe, with reverence. But the immediate demand, from all sides, was for a reduction or elimination of truly troublesome personal taxes; and to cut those taxes, and cut the tariff rates at the same time, probably would have been impossible—certainly it would have been impractical.

The war was over; but financially the nation still faced a crisis which called for emergency measures. Apparently a great majority of the people preferred to be taxed indirectly, by means of a tariff on imports. This method had been tried and found not wanting; collection machinery existed; and the public clamor against all other methods proposed or actually in operation was very loud indeed.

Also, import duties were payable in gold. But internal taxes, naturally, were payable in greenbacks.

For those greenbacks had come home to roost, giving Roscoe Conkling and a few others an excellent opportunity for crying "I told you so!" The Government might assert that, officially, a greenback dollar was worth exactly one dollar in gold; but here the Government sang a solo. At one time, during the darkest period of the war (in July of 1864), $2.85 in fiat money was needed to buy one honest gold dollar. Victory brought the value of the greenback a little higher than this, but it remained "soft" money, and Congress might have passed laws until Doomsday without making it anything else.

The chief objection to a high tariff schedule would have come from the agricultural South. But the South was silent, then.

Most congressmen are automatically in favor of lower taxes. But Roscoe Conkling, at this trying time, really worked for them; he interested himself in financial matters, he who had very little money of his own and never tried hard to make more; he fought long and valiantly for economy in government, for more equitable taxes, for hard money. He had opposed the legal tender bill. He had opposed placing too heavy a tax (as he believed) upon farm property, and had suggested a plan for saving vast sums in the collection of the direct state tax by requisitioning the governors of the states instead of creating an expensive and awkward federal machinery.[3] Generally he was a high tariff man, but he was not a fanatical protectionist. He had once even proposed cutting Congressional salaries and mileage; once, too, with no greater success, he proposed elimination of the franking privilege. When, near the end of the lame duck session of '66–'67, members of Congress blithely raised their own salaries from $3,000 to $5,000, and made this retroactive, thereby awarding themselves large bonuses, the gentleman from Oneida once again voted with the minority. He voted, however, for contraction of the legal tender, and later for resumption of specie payments; he voted for reduction of the burdensome internal taxes; he voted against a bill for extension of the income tax; as much as any man, perhaps more than any other one man, he was responsible for blocking inflation moves which followed the panic of 1873.

NOT only financial legislation suffered from the fight between Congress and the President. "It was like a pair of shears from which the rivet was gone," Senator Hoar thought. Andrew Johnson still believed that he alone was constitutionally charged with the task of restoring (he didn't think of it as reconstructing) the Southern states; and nothing could budge him from this attitude. He was suspicious of Congress, angry, scorning compromise. Yet compromise is the very essence of successful politics. Politicians thunder well about "uncompromising stands," but if they were to take such stands very often we would have no legislation at all, or else vicious legislation. In the fight with Andrew Johnson, the members of Congress, like the President himself, stood pat. And the result was a crush of bad laws, a paradise for extremists, altogether unfortunate for North and South alike.

It is easy, today, to find fault with the radicals of the Republican party. They put through their plan, eventually, and it proved to be a poor one. It always had been full of inconsistencies, and certainly some features of it were unconstitutional.

But inconsistencies would have been found in any plan. And even today, even theoretically, on paper, it is impossible to devise a plan which would not have included some extra-constitutional features. Most battles can be fought over again, with maps and suchlike, and generals can be proved to have been wrong here or there or in some other place; but reconstruction was not like that. There was absolutely no precedent for it.

Andrew Johnson, who wouldn't budge, sometimes seems rather a martyr, sometimes a fool. Unquestionably he was sadly wronged. He was called a drunkard, which was false.

He was called faithless to the Republican party, which was unfair, since he never had pretended to be a Republican and had originally accepted the Vice-Presidential nomination of the Union party (not the Republican party) at the urging of Abraham Lincoln. He was called egotistical, and he was; but who were congressmen and senators to call anybody that? It was asserted that he was ambitious, but as much might be said of most of his enemies. It was asserted that he was preparing to take advantage of his executive position to build up a personal machine and force his own renomination. Who, in his place, wouldn't do the same? It is true that he did perform some low political tricks, but he performed them from the noblest of motives, and only when forced to do so by Congress.

Congress had been accustomed to weakness from Buchanan, and from Lincoln vast amiability and tact and an humbleness which was gratifying. But Andrew Johnson was angry, impatient. He was of greater service to the radical party than Thaddeus Stevens himself. Man after man who had been inclined to be conservative when Congress assembled, was driven by Johnson's acts and his manner into the radical camp—able and powerful men like Blaine, Conkling, Morton.

Fessenden, chairman of the Committee of Fifteen, leader of the conservatives in the Senate, was potentially Johnson's best friend in Congress; but even Fessenden was driven away from the President by the veto of the Civil Rights Bill.

There were, in fact, very few real fanatics of the Stevens-Sumner stamp, at first. Roscoe Conkling himself was not naturally a radical, in the usual meaning of the word; inherently he was conservative. Nor was he ever under the spell of the terrible Thad Stevens: an examination of the journal of the Committee of Fifteen will show that he voted against Stevens almost as often as he voted with him, and his outspoken opposition to the proposed judicial murder of Lamden P. Milligan made the Pennsylvanian furious. But Conkling believed passionately in the right of the legislative branch to dictate the terms under which the seceded states should be readmitted.

It became almost a formula. Johnson refused to recognize the congressional attitude, and Congress refused to recognize Johnson's plan. The Southern states had governments which at least functioned locally. Johnson believed they should function nationally as well, believed that until they were duly represented at Washington the current Congress had no right to legislate for them. But the radical strategy was to refuse even to recognize these as proper local governments. They should be torn down completely, and new governments set up in their place.

So Congress passed bills, and the President vetoed them, carefully and lengthily pointing out his reasons for doing so, and Congress then proceeded to pass them over the veto.

Harper's Weekly (April 14, 1866) solemnly observed that "he (Johnson) makes a profound mistake if he regards the situation as a struggle between himself and Mr. Thaddeus Stevens." But this is just what Johnson did. Thad Stevens and a few others, he supposed, and publicly declared, were usurping his own powers, were plotting to overthrow the true constitutional form of government. He was quite as bigoted, quite as stubborn, in his attitude toward the majority members of the Committee of Fifteen as those gentlemen were in their attitude toward him. And between the two, the public suffered unspeakably.

It was generally agreed that Tennessee should be the first state readmitted. It had been the least disloyal, by whatever definition. Testimony taken by the Committee of Fifteen showed that about 40,000 citizens, mostly in eastern Tennessee, had voted against secession in the first place.[4] The state had ratified the Thirteenth Amendment, and was eager to be readmitted.

The subcommittee of the Committee of Fifteen recommended readmission. But another subcommittee was appointed to examine the testimony, and this one, headed by Roscoe Conkling, brought in a report to the main committee recommending readmission only on the condition that all persons who had taken any part in the Confederate cause be disenfranchised for at least five years.

The maneuver has been interpreted as an intentional slap at Andrew Johnson, who was understandably eager to see his own state back in the fold. It is much more likely that it was prompted by a reluctance on the part of congressional leaders to establish a precedent before they had fully worked out their own plan for reconstruction.

At any rate, no action was taken on the Conkling report. It was not necessary to take action, from the radical point of view, since Johnson was expected on the very day the report was made (February 19, 1866) to veto the Freedmen's Bureau continuation bill and thereby make for himself many more enemies in the legislative branch. This Johnson obligingly did. So the Conkling report died, and Tennessee stayed out.

The Freedmen's Bureau had been established during the war as a Government agency designed to aid the Negroes in conquered territory, and it was to exist for one year after the end of the war. As that year was drawing to a close, it seemed to most members of Congress that the bureau should be continued indefinitely. Johnson didn't think so. He thought, with other Southerners, that the bureau was unconstitutional, a Federal interference with the right of the states themselves to decide what to do about their own Negroes. So he vetoed the continuation bill, which was promptly passed over his veto.

Johnson likewise vetoed the Civil Rights bill, designed to make the Negro a citizen, though not a voter—to give him that official place in the population which he had lacked since the final ratification of the Thirteenth Amendment. And the Civil Rights bill was passed over the veto.

Johnson did not, as he might well have done, make whole-sale removals from office, filling the vacancies with his own supporters. But it was feared that he was preparing to do this in order to break the radicals' two-thirds Congressional majority in the coming elections. So the tenure of office act was passed, vetoed, and duly passed over the veto, on March 2. It was probably unconstitutional.[5] It forbade the President to remove any official appointed with the advice and consent of the Senate (which of course included members of his own cabinet) without first getting the consent of the Senate; and it was based upon the theory that since the constitution gave the Senate power to confirm appointments it also inherently gave that body power to confirm removals.

At the same time Congress specifically forbade the President to give any orders to the military except through the General of the Armies; or to order the General of the Armies out of Washington without the consent of the Senate.

For the radicals were getting control of Grant, whose prestige was invaluable to them. They feared, or pretended to fear, that Johnson was planning to use his position as commander-in-chief to set up a dictatorship. Today it seems preposterous. But the *fear* was genuine, at least in many cases. And it appeared to be substantiated by the rumor, which probably was authentic, that Johnson meant to appoint Grant a member of the commission to go to Mexico City and help arrange for the removal of the annoying Maximilian. Certainly one prominent military man was needed on that commission, if only as a frightener. Grant was the logical selection. But the radicals wished to keep Grant in Washington.

There was the usual veto, the usual passage-over-the-veto, and Sherman went to Mexico City while Grant stayed where he was.

And so the fight proceeded, waxing hotter all the time. It couldn't be called ludicrous only because it happened to be tragic; but one example of what a tangle it resulted in might be worth citing.

J. H. Reeves's term as postmaster of Newburgh, N. Y., had expired, and he was renominated. The Senate of the United States, not at all interested in Newburgh, N. Y., but very much interested in the business of baiting Andy Johnson, refused to confirm the renomination. The President appointed Reeves twice more, and twice more the Senate of the United States rejected this appointee. The President appointed Benjamin H. Mace. The Senate rejected this. The President appointed a Mr. Lomas. Rejected. Then Reeves once again. Rejected. Then William A. Boyce. Rejected. Finally Lomas again; and this time, possibly because the Senate was wearying of the sport, the nomination was confirmed.[6]

MEANWHILE, on a smaller stage, there was another, more personal fight. The Conkling-Blaine explosion everybody in Washington had been expecting at last occurred.

James G. Blaine was the most affable of men. Often sarcastic but quick to apologize. A grand fighter while the fight actually was in progress, but prepared to shake hands the moment hostilities had ceased. A forgiver. A friend-maker. He really liked his fellow men.

But he didn't like Roscoe Conkling. Somehow, Conkling irritated him. The scrape during the debate on Conkling's representation tables has been mentioned. Later Conkling, politely enough, for him, called Blaine's attention to a possible mistake in his speech on a bill limiting the power of the President (Congress was fond of passing such bills at this time) to appoint to West Point. On that occasion Blaine was furious, and his reply was bitter.

Conkling didn't like Blaine, either. He treated the man with great aloofness. The story of the disputed quotation was familiar to everybody in national politics at the time.

Blaine and Conkling were fellow guests at a formal dinner, and somebody jokingly referred to Conkling's home town with:

> *No pent-up Utica contracts our powers,*
> *But the whole boundless continent is ours.*

Oh yes, smiled Conkling, Addison's lines. Oh no, said Blaine, the quotation was from Sewell's "Epilogue to Cato." The gentleman from Oneida, properly proud of his amazing memory for poetry (he could quote whole pages of rhyme or blank verse) haughtily replied that the gentleman from Maine was mistaken. *Addison* wrote those lines. No, Blaine persisted, it was *Sewell*.

So they bet a bottle of champagne on it, and Blaine won. Conkling always was a poor loser. They say that he refused to attend the party Blaine gave when the bottle was opened.

But all this was mere background for the fight itself, which started on Tuesday, April 24, 1866, and lasted for the rest of Roscoe Conkling's life.

IX. The Turkey-Gobbler Strut

GENERAL SCHENCK, chairman of the committee on military affairs and a celebrated authority on draw poker, had introduced his army reorganization bill.

One section provided for a permanent Bureau of the Provost Marshal General, until that time generally thought of only as a war-time organization. The soldier who held the post of Provost Marshal General was to have the rank of brigadier general. The incumbent, General Fry, was not specifically mentioned, but it was understood that he would be given the permanent post.

Now Conkling didn't like General Fry. He had had only one personal meeting with the general, and that one brief;

but they had battled at long distance when Conkling, in Utica, was acting as a special judge advocate prosecuting bounty grafters, and Fry, in Washington, was trying to give his subordinates all the possible benefit of every conceivable doubt.

Conkling rose:

I move to strike out section 20 of that bill. My objection to this section is that it creates an unnecessary office for an undeserving public servant . . . I have never heard any serious attempt to justify by argument the permanent continuance of an officer whose administration during the war had in it so little to commend, so much to condemn. . . . The Provost Marshal's Bureau was a temporary expedient resorted to in an extreme emergency to bring volunteers hastily to the field. Its mission is ended, and it should be buried out of sight . . .

Blaine, a member of the military affairs committee, was in the diplomatic gallery, chatting with a friend. But he stopped at the first sound of that familiar voice. He listened for a few moments; then excused himself, and galloped downstairs, helm lowered, lance at rest.

. . . they turned the business of recruiting and drafting into one carnival of corrupt disorder, into a paradise of coxcombs and thieves. . . . We were victimized by constant uncertainty and deception . . . the whole machinery of Government was subject to miscreants and robbers. . . . The most palpable wrongs were refused redress. Men immeasurably the superiors of General Fry represented and protested, but they were spurned with magnificent disdain. Never was the "insolence of office" more offensively portrayed. . . .

Blaine was waiting, white with rage, to get the floor.

If there was no design at headquarters to do wrong, there was a capacity to muddle, to befog, to misunderstand facts, and to misread and misstate figures and simple results, which is nearly inconceivable. . . .

He produced a letter from General Grant, which seemed to favor elimination of the Bureau of the Provost Marshal General.

There never has been in human history a greater mockery and a greater burlesque upon honest administration than the conduct of this bureau, taking the whole country together.

A trifle exaggerated perhaps, but the effect was good.

But here was Blaine, contending that Fry was "a most efficient officer, a high-toned gentleman whose character is without spot or blemish" (though in fact he scarcely knew the general);[1] and producing another, earlier letter from Grant, which seemed to show that Grant thought the Bureau of the Provost Marshal General an excellent thing indeed.[2]

Boutwell of Massachusetts reminded the speaker that the adjutant general was carrying on the army's recruiting work now, in peace time, and was doing it well. Blaine replied sharply, impatiently. Boutwell could keep out of this, please! This was not his fight.

Mr. Speaker, I do not suppose that the House of Representatives cares anything more than the Committee on Military Affairs about the great recruiting frauds of New York, or the quarrels of the gentleman from New York with General Fry, in which quarrels it is generally understood the gentleman came out second best at the War Department . . .

Now Conkling was on his feet. *Second best!*

. . . I must say that I do not think it is any very creditable proceeding for the gentleman from New York here in this place to traduce General Fry as a military officer when he has no opportunity to be heard. I do not consider such a proceeding the highest specimen of chivalry that could be exhibited.

Conkling got the floor.

Mr. Speaker, if General Fry is reduced to depending for vindication upon the gentleman from Maine, he is to be commiserated certainly. If I have fallen to the necessity of taking lessons from that gentleman in the rules of propriety, or of right and wrong, God help me. . . . I am ready to avow what I have here declared elsewhere . . . I have stated facts for which I am willing to be held responsible at all times and places.

So much for the assertion that there was anything unchivalrous about speaking frankly of an army officer while enjoying Congressional immunity! Also the statement about quarrels was false—

Mr. Blaine: What does the gentleman mean to say was false?
Mr. Conkling: I mean that the statement made by the gentleman from Maine is false.
Mr. Blaine: What statement?
Mr. Conkling: Does not the gentleman understand what I mean?
Mr. Blaine: I call the gentleman to order. I demand he shall state what was false in what I stated. I have the parliamentary right.

The speaker asked Blaine to make a point of order. Blaine said he had already done so. The speaker asked what it was —and overruled it.

Mr. Blaine: One single word more—
Mr. Conkling: I do not yield!

But eventually Blaine, an expert in parliamentary law, got his point of order on the ground that the use of the word "false" was unparliamentary.

Conkling wasn't finished:

I could not remain silent when I knew that in my own district and elsewhere men who stood up honestly and attempted to resist "bounty jumpers" and thieves were stricken down and trodden underfoot by General Fry. I affirm that the only way to acquit him of venality is to convict him of the most incredible incompetency. I am responsible for that, sir, everywhere.

There was a further squabble about who had the floor. Conkling won.

I have stated but a very small part of what I know from my own investigation of the matter. And I want it distinctly understood that in my judgment no officer of this government holding a similar position has done so much harm and so little good as the officer of whom I am speaking. If that is offensive to anybody, so be it. To the particular individual to whom it may give most offense, I will answer not here but elsewhere, when it becomes necessary.

This made an impressive, if somewhat familiar, ending. He yielded the last four minutes of his allotted time to Spalding of Ohio, who spoke against the proposed retention of the bureau.

But when Spalding was finished, Blaine was up again.

Sir, even were I in full health (and I ought to be in my bed to-day) I could not consent to go into this cheap sort of stuff about answering "here and elsewhere" and about "personal responsibility" and all that sort of thing. . . . When we had gentlemen from the eleven seceded states, they used to talk about answering "here and elsewhere"; and it was understood that they meant a duel. . . . Whenever a man says that he is ready to answer "here or elsewhere" he means that he is willing to receive a note outside of the District of Columbia. Well, now, that is very cheap, and certainly beneath my notice. . . . When I have to resort to the use of the epithet "false" upon this floor, and this cheap swagger about being responsible "here and elsewhere," I shall have very little faith in the cause which I stand up to maintain.

Conkling sizzled in silence, for a time. (*Cheap! Beneath my notice!*) But his motion to strike out Section 20 still was before the House. Thad Stevens, who like everybody else present had been enjoying the fireworks, proposed a substitute motion which would direct the Secretary of War to end the Bureau of the Provost Marshal General within six months. The gentleman from Oneida, graciously consenting to this, withdrew his own motion. General Schenck defended Section 20, but Stevens' motion was passed.

But this didn't mean that the fight was finished.

GENERAL FRY wrote a longish letter to Blaine. He later explained that he intended this merely as an expression of thanks to Blaine for Blaine's defense on the floor, and as a personal explanation of his own case—the sort of thing military men like to write whenever they get into trouble. But it doesn't read at all like that. Fry had consulted a few friends first, and then "a rough draft was shown to Mr. Blaine, by whose advice some of the expressions were sharpened." No doubt.

Fry said he didn't know that Blaine intended to have this letter read before the House, but simply gave it to Blaine to use "as he thought best."

House rules provided that if a person reads a letter as part of a speech from the floor, he is personally responsible for statements in that letter; but if he gets the clerk to read it, then the House itself is responsible. A fine point, but sometimes an important one.

Late in the morning of Monday, April 30, six days after the army reorganization bill debate, Blaine rose to request that the clerk read General Fry's letter. The speaker reminded him that this would require a suspension of rules, which called for unanimous consent. Did anyone object? Everybody looked at Roscoe Conkling.

"I infer that this has some reference to me," that personage said slowly. "I shall make no objection, provided I may have an opportunity to reply to whatever the letter may call for hereafter."

This was agreed to; and Blaine made his formal motion for suspension of rules. But then the speaker remembered that the House already was considering a bill under suspension of rules, so the letter was not read until that afternoon, when it created a sensation.

General Fry declared that Conkling "made a case for himself" in the summer of '63 by wiring the War Department that the deputy Provost Marshal General in the western New York district needed legal assistance. Also that in April, 1865, "without notifying me," Assistant Secretary of War Charles A. Dana appointed Conkling a special judge advocate; that Conkling was paid $3,000 for this work, and perhaps got more from the district—"I am now unable to say." Also that Conkling

was as zealous in preventing prosecutions at Utica as he was in making them at Elmira; and the main difficulty between Mr. Conkling and myself arose altogether from my unwillingness to gratify him in certain matters in which he had a personal interest. It is true, also, that he was foiled in his efforts to obtain undue concessions from my bureau, and to discredit me in the eyes of my superiors.

The one brief meeting of the two men was mentioned: it was in Dana's office in Washington, and the letter said Conkling was "worsted." The letter denied that the convicted Major Haddock had been a "crony" of the writer. It made a dignified and convincing defense of the bureau as operated in war time, and finished on a manly note: "That there were frauds in my branch of the service I admit, but that they prevailed to a greater degree than in others, or that earnest and zealous efforts were not made by me to pursue, correct, and punish them, no man dare have the hardihood to assert."

This rings clear; but the beginning of the letter was weak, indiscreet. It made rash half-statements, for which it offered no support; it advanced improper insinuations against a Congressman of unspotted reputation, a fighting man as touchy about his personal honor as any storied knight. This alone was definite:

He [Conkling] can, therefore, only escape the charge of deliberate and malignant falsehood as a member of Congress by confessing an unpardonable breach of duty as judge advocate. He held both offices and took pay for both at the same time; he has certainly been false to honor in one, and perhaps, as the sequel may show, in both.

For Conkling, though not a member of Congress at the time the bounty graft investigation was started, was technically a member of that body before the investigation was finished—and he received his fee November 9, 1865, according to Fry.

The letter was indiscreet. One wonders whether it was this part of it which Blaine had "sharpened." If so, that was a foolish move, and not like the sagacious gentleman from Maine. Certainly he should have known that his fellow members would not forgive a general, a mere outsider, who spoke ill of a representative.

There was an ominous hush when the clerk had finished reading the letter. The dignity of the House had been hurt. On paper, James G. Blaine was not accountable for this affront. In fact, he was.

Blaine wouldn't ask that the clerk read through all the documents which were attached to this friendly, personal letter of thanks, but only that they be printed in the record, since—

"I ask that everything be read," boomed Roscoe Conkling. "I enjoy it very much."

So the accompanying documents—letters, credentials, copies of telegrams, etc.—all, all were read. Which gave Roscoe Conkling more time to consider what action to take. And presently he was demanding an investigation into Fry's charges. He had expected, he said, to be attacked by "thieves, marauders, and miscreants who have battened upon the necessities and needs of their country," and was perfectly prepared to "maintain my allegations of wrong in the Provost Marshal's Bureau at all times and places. I will not," he added, "say 'elsewhere,' for fear of unsettling the nerves of some who may hear me."

A Democrat, Ross of Illinois, asked him to answer the charge that he had held two government jobs at the same time. Conkling evaded this by scorching "that distinguished mathematician and warrior, Provost Marshal General Fry," and averring that it would be extraordinary if certain gentlemen of Congress, whom he would not name, "had subjected themselves to the criticism of the gentleman from Illinois, or of anybody whatever, always excepting, of course, Provost Marshal General Fry." He denied that he had concealed anything. He pointed out that there had been no direct charge against him, only insinuations. He read aloud from the *Globe*. He did about everything else a congressman can do who hasn't got the right answer ready but wishes to appear unafraid; and he did it well.

(There is an old political adage that it is best not to handle a red-hot poker on the front porch. Take the thing down cellar, if it *must* be handled.)

So he read from the *Globe*. . . . Blaine interrupted to declare that the gentleman from New York had interpolated the word "personal" before the word "quarrels."

"I hope," coldly said Conkling, who really had interpolated that word, "that the active member from Maine will preserve himself as free from agitation as possible."

Blaine got the floor and grimly read from the law forbidding any person holding office under the Government which paid $2,250 or more yearly (a congressman's salary at that time was $3,000) to receive compensation for "discharging the duties of any other [Government] office."

"And he cannot deny that he discharged the duties of judge advocate under the special commission which I have read, and he was paid for the discharge of those duties!"

Ah, but he *did* deny that! He had not, he said, been a member of Congress and a judge advocate at the same time. No. He never had received his commission as a judge advo-

cate. What had been read into the record was only a preliminary authorization, a mere announcement of Mr. Dana's
intention. Therefore the payment of November 9, 1865, was
nothing but a "counsel's fee," which was permissible. (Forced
at last to bring the hot poker out on the front porch, he was
juggling it with skill and apparent casualness.)

Mr. Blaine: Mr. Speaker—
Speaker: Does the gentleman from New York yield to the
gentleman from Maine?
Mr. Conkling: No, sir. I do not wish to have anything to do
with the member from Maine, not even so much as to yield him
the floor.
Mr. Blaine: All right.

But soon afterward Blaine did get the floor again:

Everybody knows that those preliminary authorizations are the
things on which half the business arising out of the war has been
done. Men have fought at the head of battalions and divisions
and army corps without having received their formal commissions. The gentleman was just as much bound to respect the
law under that appointment as though it had been a formal
commission with the signature of the Secretary of War.

But the technicality had been pointed out to the House,
and a House committee, under such circumstances, surely
would find a member not guilty as charged. "Counsel's fees"
were semi-sacred to many congressmen. (The poker was
cooling.)
    Said Conkling:

If the gentleman from Maine had the least idea how profoundly indifferent I am to his opinion upon the subject which
he has been discussing, or upon any other subject personal to
me, I think he would hardly take the trouble to rise here and express his opinion . . . an interruption which I pronounced the
other day ungentlemanly and impertinent, and having nothing
whatever to do with the question.

thing practical. In fact, the abstract theories had gone to the place where such things usually do go. The seceded states were being considered, officially, not as victims of their own acts of suicide, not as conquered provinces, and yet certainly not as full members of the Union either. The tendency seemed to be to treat them as unruly territories; yet nobody doubted that they would be readmitted sooner or later. And in some respects they were treated as full-fledged states. For example (it was one of the crowning inconsistencies of the congressional policy), the seceded states, though denied representation in Congress, were asked to ratify and did ratify the Thirteenth Amendment, by means of legislatures recognized by the President but not by Congress. Similarly, when the Fourteenth Amendment was proposed, almost nobody believed that it would be legal to have this ratified only by three-quarters of the states which had *not* seceded. The ex-Confederate states—or, as they were termed in Federal legislation, "the Confederate states so-called"—virtually were told that they would not be readmitted into the Union until they had ratified the Fourteenth Amendment, and yet the amendment was submitted to them as members of the Union!

Anyway, the big thing was to frame some sort of plan, make some sort of sense out of the whole mess. For business was bad.

The committee suffered from no lack of outside suggestions. There was, for example, the plan Stewart proposed from the floor of the Senate. It was turned over to the committee, where eventually it died. It would have readmitted all seceded states promptly to full Federal rights, provided they repudiated the Confederate war debt, acknowledged the Union war debt, yielded all claims for liberated slaves, and granted Negroes not only civil rights but also a vote. The Northern states, on the other hand, would be "respectfully requested" so to amend their constitutions as to enfranchise Negroes, but this would not be mandatory. A general amnesty would be proclaimed.

The Stewart plan certainly was too liberal for the radicals of Congress. Moreover, by the wording of it, though it would have granted suffrage to the Negroes, it held out a deliberate invitation to the Southern states to apply what has since come to be known as the "grandfather clause."

This plan never came to a vote in the committee, and how Roscoe Conkling felt about it is not a matter of record. He was a personal friend of the erratic, picturesque senator from Nevada.

Then there was the plan proposed by Robert Dale Owen, son of the celebrated British liberal. He suggested unofficially to Stevens, Fessenden, Conkling, and others a constitutional amendment which would give all Negroes full civil rights immediately and the franchise on and after July 4, 1876, the nation's one hundredth birthday anniversary. Confederate war debts were to be repudiated, the Union war debt acknowledged. All seceded states should be readmitted to full Federal rights when they had ratified this amendment, provided, of course, that the amendment was ratified by three-quarters of all the states, and became a part of the Constitution. There was one more provision, by way of compromise. No person who had been an officer of the army or navy, or who had held Federal office prior to the Civil War and had subsequently fought in that war on the Confederate side, should be permitted to hold Federal office until after July 4, 1876.

This plan, *as such*, never was voted upon by the committee, though it was much discussed. Owen later declared that Fessenden had been strong for it, and that Conkling and even Thad Stevens had told him that they favored it. Fessenden was ill and not present when the thing was tabled, but the Conkling and Stevens votes on the various amendments proposed and discussed, as recorded in the committee's *Journal*, do not indicate that either of these gentlemen was very enthusiastic. Probably Owen was over-optimistic.[2]

EVENTUALLY from this welter the Fourteenth Amendment emerged. It was an unwieldy thing, an omnibus compromise, consisting of five sections all of which were mauled a bit by Congress before the amendment was permitted to freeze into its final form, though only the third section underwent any really important change.

The committee report which followed submission of this instrument was long and explicit, finishing:

The conclusion of your Committee, therefore is, that the so-called Confederate States are not, at present, entitled to representation in the Congress of the United States; that, before allowing such representation, adequate security for future peace and safety should be required; that this can only be found in such changes of the original law as shall determine the civil rights of all citizens in all parts of the republic, shall place representation on an equitable basis, shall fix a stigma upon treason, and protect the loyal people against future claims for the expenses incurred in support of rebellion and for manumitted slaves, together with an express grant of power in Congress to enforce those provisions. To this end they offer a joint resolution for amending the Constitution of the United States, and the two several bills designed to carry the same into effect, before referred to.

Before closing this report, your committee beg leave to state that the specific recommendations submitted by them are the result of mutual concession, after a long and careful comparison of conflicting opinions. Upon a question of such magnitude, infinitely important as it is to the future of the republic, it was not to be expected that all should think alike. Sensible of the imperfections of the scheme, your Committee submit it to Congress as the best they could agree upon, in the hope that its imperfections may be cured, and its deficiencies supplied, by legislative wisdom; and, that when finally adopted, it may tend to restore peace and harmony to the whole country, and to place our republican institutions on a more stable foundation.[3]

A note of apology is there, unmistakably. For no one

thought very highly of the Fourteenth Amendment. To say, as has been the fashion, that Thad Stevens had the Committee of Fifteen under his thumb at all times, and that its work was a mere expression of his will, is to ignore patent facts. Stevens didn't like the amendment any more than did the conservatives. The strongest radical clause was the third, which was considerably softened (from Stevens' point of view) before the thing solidified.

But something had to be done.

The amendment was not greatly different from that proposed by young Owen, after all. The first section, which made "all persons born or naturalized in the United States, and subject to the jurisdiction thereof" citizens of the nation and of the state in which they lived, forbade states to make or enforce "any law which shall abridge the privileges or immunities of citizens of the United States; nor shall any State deprive any person of life, liberty, or property, without due process of law, nor deny to any person within its jurisdiction the equal protection of the laws."

This, if it did nothing else, gave the Negro a status. It made him a citizen. There were many arguments against it at the time, the most frequent being that it merely did what had already been done by the Civil Rights Bill. But a law might be altered or repealed. Besides, there was considerable doubt as to the constitutionality of the Civil Rights Bill.

It was argued also that the first section was unnecessary, since all of it, with the exception of the final clause, already was in the Constitution. But the Fifth Amendment is binding only upon the Federal Government, not upon the states. (All the early amendments were designed to limit the power of the Federal Government.)

This first section proved to be the only part of the amendment which has had any lasting effect upon our form of government.[4]

The second section concerned representation and was a compromise between the original Conkling and Blaine ideas, providing for representation according to the "whole number of persons in each State, excluding Indians not taxed," but adding that "when the right to vote at any election . . . is denied to any of the male inhabitants of such State, being twenty-one years of age and citizens of the United States, or in any way abridged except for participation in rebellion or other crime, the basis of representation therein shall be reduced in the proportion which the number of such male citizens shall bear to the whole number of male citizens twenty-one years of age in such State." Thus New England was satisfied, and the Southern states were given their choice of enfranchising the Negro or taking grave cuts in representation. However, the Fifteenth Amendment, following a few years later, made all this of little importance; and Congress never did cut the representation of any state because that state did not enfranchise the Negro.

The third section provided that no person "who, having previously taken an oath as a member of Congress, or as an officer of the United States, or as a member of any State Legislature, to support the Constitution of the United States, shall have engaged in insurrection or rebellion against the same, or given aid or comfort to the enemies thereof," should be permitted to hold any Federal or state office, civil or military. But it also provided that this disability could be removed by a two-thirds vote of each house of Congress; and, in fact, when passions had cooled a bit, it was removed for practically everyone.[5]

The fourth section declared the Federal debt sacred and the Confederate debt null and void, and denied any claim for loss or emancipation of any slave. Professor Kendrick thinks this "entirely unnecessary," as perhaps it was, and adds that "since it was designed to catch votes, especially those of the soldiers, it deserved to be classified as mere political buncombe,"[6] which is hardly fair.

It seems unlikely, now, that the South ever would have demanded remuneration for slaves freed, or made any effort to have the Confederate obligations taken over by the Federal Government. But remember, it had seemed unlikely to Unionists in 1860 that the Southern states would secede, would form an army and a navy, would fire upon Fort Sumter. Washington, while the Committee of Fifteen was in session, was filled with wild reports of the Southern attitude, and members of that committee were filled with memories of arrogant Southerners who had stalked the halls of Congress before the war. The fear might have been built on a poor foundation, but it was a very real fear. It is doubtful whether an amendment could have been passed which did not contain some clause providing for nullification of the Confederate debt and of claims for emancipated slaves. Also, the knowledge that this provision actually was a part of the Federal Constitution would do much toward stabilizing business and bolstering the national credit.

The fifth section was a simple enabling act.

It was not until June 13, 1866, that Congress handed the Fourteenth Amendment to the states for ratification or rejection, and even then the body was reluctant to adjourn. But there was home work to be done. To put through not only the amendment but also the rest of the congressional program of reconstruction, it would be necessary to keep that veto-smashing majority. For the election of 1866—nobody doubted it—was to be one of the most important in the history of the nation.

XI. Keynoting in Utica

IT was not a Presidential election, though this is difficult to remember. The issues were national, the candidates too—Andrew Johnson being one, Congress the other. Also there were national conventions. The first, at Philadelphia, was pro-Johnson. Democrats and Republicans alike attended, and the tone was moderate. Thurlow Weed was there, and Seward, but neither of these gentlemen was the power he had been a few years earlier. Another New York personage, Henry L. Raymond, editor of the *Times*, wrote the platform—and as a result sank to the bottom of the political sea with a swiftness which astounded even his enemies. A great effort was made to show that North and South alike were behind the Johnson policies. Delegates from Massachusetts and South Carolina walked into the hall arm in arm. So it was called, by its friends, the "arm in arm convention." Others, Conkling among them, had harsher names for it. Thomas Nast drew a picture for *Harper's Weekly* showing the interlocked delegates entering the hall, meanwhile mouthing with rolled-up eyes such ecstatic phrases as "Oh, blessed hour!" and "Charity covereth all!"—and followed by a dog and cat which were arm in arm too, and then a cat and a rat, likewise arm in arm.

There was much talk of organizing a separate political party, but nothing was done. Instead, the convention adopted resolutions commending the President's attitude toward reconstruction; a delegation waited upon Johnson and read these to him; and Johnson responded with a speech of thanks. The third party talk died in discouraged whispers.

Countering this, soon afterward, there was a radical convention in the same city. It attracted less attention. The *New York Herald*, pro-Johnson that month, called it "the Nigger Worshipers' Powwow."

Then a national convention of Union army and navy

veterans at Cleveland, designed to show that these persons were behind the President. It was followed by a much larger soldiers-and-sailors' convention at Pittsburgh, designed to show just the opposite, and termed by the *New York World* of September 26 "a feast of buncombe and a flow of bile."

Miles of newspaper copy and many hours of platform talk preceded, accompanied and followed each of these conventions; but this was about all they did produce, except hard feeling.

Roscoe Conkling attended none of them. He had a fight on his own hands, in New York.

THE New York State convention of the Union Party in September of 1865, deploring the death of Lincoln, had recognized Lincoln's successor as "a statesman of ability, experience, and high-toned patriotism and the most unsullied integrity," and had pledged him "cordial and effective support."

Ah, platforms! One year later a Republican state convention met at Weiting Hall, Syracuse, which was decorated with caricatures including a Nast enlargement of Johnson: it was conspicuous on the left of the speakers' platform, and, like the speeches at that convention, it did not flatter the President.

The convention was harmonious enough, probably because the pro-Johnsonites, including Weed, had deserted to the Democratic camp. The radicals had their way at Syracuse. They renominated Governor Reuben Fenton, a silent, somewhat sinister person who had beaten Horatio Seymour in the '64 election, running ahead of Lincoln on the Union ticket. This Fenton was a well-to-do business man, tall, erect, impressive in appearance, with wavy grayish hair and a sloping forehead; he was suave and gracious in manner, not a good orator, but inestimably ambitious, and shrewd, a great organizer. He was prepared to take Weed's place as Dictator. But then, so was Roscoe Conkling.

The Democrats nominated Hoffman, a Tammanyite. Weed had wished General Dix to receive this nomination, but Weed adrift among Democrats was not a brilliant figure, and Tammany tricked him easily. Hoffman was affable, highly popular, possibly crooked. Sundry charges against him as mayor of New York City—charges the *World* contemptuously dismissed as "bugabooing"—comprised almost the only non-national issue of the campaign.[1]

THE Irish question was important too, for the first time. The Irish, thick in New York City, were normally Democratic; but the Fenian movement was strong among them, and the Fenians recently had been making or planning to make various invasions of Canada—rather silly excursions, which failed noisily, but which were diplomatic dynamite. Andrew Johnson had maintained an attitude of strict neutrality, for which he should have been but wasn't commended. The radicals did not lose this opportunity. They fished for and caught many Irish votes with the promise (never kept) to work for neutrality laws which would permit American Fenians to plot the conquest of Canada with less danger at home.[2]

And Andrew Johnson's alleged drunkenness wasn't forgotten. Indeed, it was discussed more often than anything else in that campaign. The President, soon after the first Philadelphia convention, had started for Chicago, where he was to lay the cornerstone of a memorial to Stephen A. Douglas on September 5—but he went by way of most of the rest of the country. "Swinging around the circle," he called it. James Russell Lowell called it "an advertising tour of a policy in want of a party"; and Republican stump speakers generally referred to it as a disgraceful orgy.

For Andrew Johnson lost his temper again. In the East he behaved tolerably well, though there seemed to be a feeling that it was undignified for a President to go stumping in his own behalf (which was, of course, what it amounted to); but in Western cities he lost control of himself and shrieked back at hecklers. Of course the Republicans said he was Under the Influence all the time. Even so staid a publication as the *Atlantic Monthly* termed him "a spiteful, inflated and unprincipled egotist." And the stump speakers, Roscoe Conkling among them, said a lot more than that.

Conkling was his party's star performer in New York State that year. The Republicans were somewhat short of good speakers. Fenton was not one. Chauncey Depew was entertaining, but not thunderous, not of the sort that was needed then. Horace Greeley, though always effective, was erratic, unpredictable, and many persons refused to take him seriously. The two senators, Morgan and Harris, were indifferent speakers. So the heavy work went to Conkling, who was ready for it.

The Oneida county convention of September 8 renominated him unanimously, and in acknowledgment he gave them what they expected:

"The great and glorious party you represent, having stood by the country in its darkest hours, and borne it in triumph through the most trying of human struggles, has still a mission unperformed."

(Breathless pause. Conkling did this sort of thing extremely well.)

"The President of the United States, as he goes on his deceitful errand with an imperial condescension, a supercilious patronage, which seems to ape Louis Napoleon, repeats from place to place, 'I shall place the Constitution in the hands of the people.' "

(The reference to Louis Napoleon was shrewd. That potentate was extraordinarily unpopular in the United States at the time.)

This angry man, dizzy with the elevation to which assassination has raised him, frenzied with power and ambition, does not seem to know that not he, but the men who made the Constitution placed it in the people's hands. They placed Andrew Johnson in the people's hands also; and when those hands shall drop their votes into the ballot-box, Andrew Johnson and his policy of arrogance and usurpation will be snapped like a willow wand . . .[3]

But this was mere practice. The true opening gun, generally considered the keynote speech of the campaign, was fired at a meeting in Utica a few days later.

"You believe your country is at stake now. So do I; and therefore we assemble under the institutions which our fathers made, and which give us, as the remedy for wrongs in government, the silent, potent vote, and enjoin upon us the duty to use it wisely."

Reconstruction? Who was better qualified to speak about it than one who was a member of the Committee of Fifteen?

"We examined hundreds of witnesses, pushing the sittings into the night. We called witnesses of every shade of opinion, refusing none that anybody wanted to hear. Rebel and loyalist, civilian and soldier, officer and private, were all sought after, and members of the Committee, of opposite politics, were present to examine and cross-examine."

The result?

Here it is. It fills eight hundred fourteen pages of type too fine for an old man to read. Besides this, there are two hundred and sixty pages of documentary evidence. How many, think you, have read it, of these gentlemen who have suddenly started up to take charge of the business of Reconstruction? How many of them have taken the trouble to read a page of it, or to study the question at all in its various bearings, before undertaking to pronounce upon one of the greatest and most difficult problems in history? But then, after all, what are volumes of testimony, what are months of labor, compared to going to Philadelphia and seeing a man from Massachusetts and a man from South Carolina walk into a convention arm in arm? Who wants to fool away his time in investigating, after he has been to Philadelphia and heard Lee and Stonewall Jackson cheered, in reply to serenades where Dixie was played?

The "unseemly clamor of Southern rebels for immediate representation" had five objects: to enable "those who plunged the Southern states into secession to resume their old sway in the Government"; to obtain remuneration for emancipated slaves; to make the Federal Government pay for damage done by the war, most of which, of course, was in the South; to compel the Federal Government to pay the Confederate war debt; or else to repudiate the Union war debt.

He announced that "when the last of the Rebellion was beaten down, the insurgents would have accepted anything, but . . . under the patronage of the President everything is reversed."

He referred feelingly to the recent riots at Memphis and New Orleans, race riots from which the Negroes emphatically had come out second best, and intimated (but wilder orators were saying this outright)[4] that Andrew Johnson was at least in part responsible for them.

He defended the proposed Fourteenth Amendment, and notably that section which referred to representation.

Do you want to give up your interests once more to this alliance, with two-fifths added to the old slave power? Do you want to bind your country hand and foot, and lay it again on the altar at which it has been once offered up? What would become of it? What would become of the pension roll of soldiers and their widows and orphans? What would become of the public debt and the public credit? What would greenbacks, and five-twenties, and seven-thirties be worth?

Why, it stands to reason! Just suppose that "the rebels who did the sleight-of-hand at Philadelphia" were permitted to take control of the government at Washington—what would they do?

Will they say to the North, You have beaten us in battle; you have desolated our land with fire and sword; you have stripped us; you have annihilated four thousand million dollars by destroying slavery; you have compelled us to repudiate our debt; you have prevented our paying our creditors or soldiers; we are poor, we are naked, but we are going now to keep voting taxes on ourselves to pay the debt you made in destroying us? Will they say this? Is it rational to expect it?

So:

Are you ready, after staggering through four years of agony, to fool away and give away for nothing all you have struggled for the moment you have it in your grasp? The Committee of Fifteen thought not. They thought the graves should grow green, that the cripples should have time to limp back to their homes, that the inky cloak should begin to disappear before the authors of our woes come back into the presence of their surviving victims; and that when they do come, it should be on terms of equality with the rest of us, and with nothing more.[5]

YES, decidedly he was the star performer. He spoke in fourteen cities and towns of the state, always to huge audiences. Yet he was none too certain of his own district. His nomination had been unanimous, but that meant very little. Conkling always did like unanimous nominations. He always worked for an outer show of party harmony.

His friend Ellis Roberts, editor of the powerful *Utica Herald,* worked for him faithfully and well. But the *New York Tribune* was strangely silent. The *Tribune* was the recognized Republican mouthpiece of the state; its support was expected and gladly received by every regular Republican candidate. But it didn't support Conkling that year. Why? Was it because Horace Greeley, unwearied in search of a high title, eyeing fondly that senatorship which would be there for the filling when Ira Harris' term expired in a few months, was jealous of the increasing power of this young silver-tongue from Oneida? Many thought so. Even so cautious an observer as Andrew White thought so. Dr. White approved Roscoe Conkling:

I had never spoken with him; had hardly seen him; but I had watched his course closely, and one thing especially wrought powerfully with me in his favor. The men who had opposed him were of the same sort with those who had opposed me, and as I was proud of their opposition, I felt that he had a right to be so. The whole force of Tammany henchmen and canal contractors throughout the State honored us both with their enmity.

Well, what of Greeley? He was an old-timer anyway; while Roscoe Conkling had all the arrogance of youth.

The support of New York City papers was highly important then, for those papers were powerful upstate, and their editorials were copied by smaller journals. But if the *Tribune* was silent, the *Times* was kind. Congressman Conkling had not been so harsh in his treatment of Henry L. Raymond as had most of his fellow radicals; and possibly the editor was grateful.

WEED and Seward were not the only men who had stumbled into a strange camp that year. Indeed, party lines were almost unfindable. The Republicans didn't call themselves Republicans but Unionists—which greatly annoyed the Democrats, who didn't wish to see one party taking to itself all the credit for holding the nation together. The Democrats called Republicans Republicans. But a sizable portion of the population—not simply the uninterested citizens, but the political workers themselves—was uncertain where to go. They were not independent so much as merely lost.

Conkling's personal opponent in 1866, Palmer V. Kellogg, had been one of his earliest and heartiest supporters; but he had also been a member of that delegation to Washington which had been informed by the young man that when he needed help in making recommendations for appointments he'd ask for it; so now Kellogg wasted no love on the statesman. He was nominated by a group of men who called themselves Independent Republicans, and endorsed by the Democratic organization of the district. He went after the labor vote. He packed a hall—it was only a few days before the election—with friends, labor leaders, and their followers. A resolution endorsing the Kellogg candidacy was announced.

It never came to a vote. For Conkling himself had at least one friend in that hall, who admitted him, alone, at the crucial moment. Majestically he strode down the center aisle; he mounted the platform like an emperor mounting a throne; he threw back his head, tossing the Hyperion curl, and cleared his throat. . . . And after a time the turmoil subsided.

"Fellow laboring men! For I, too, am a laboring man, and claim the right to address you thus. It matters not, it seems to me, whether the sweat which toil and labor produces exudes upon the outside or the inside of a man's forehead. It is the sweat of honest toil just the same."

Of course they listened. And having listened, they cheered. He left alone, as he had come; but the rafters were ringing then.

It was a clean sweep for the radicals, in the nation, the state, and Oneida. The two-thirds majority in both houses of Congress was unbroken, and Andrew Johnson could look forward to two more years of wasted vetoes. Fenton was made Governor again, defeating Horatio Seymour by 13,000; and the state elected a Republican legislature and sent 20 Republicans and only 11 Democrats and independents to Congress. Conkling ran 39 votes ahead of his ticket.

He was back, then, and stronger than ever. But long ago his gaze had been fixed on a higher place. The new legislature at Albany would consist of 26 Republican senators to 6 Democrats, and 84 Republican assemblymen to 44 Democrats. And this legislature soon would elect a new United States senator. Roscoe Conkling was thirty-six years old.

XII. He Fitted Admirably

NOW there was such a thing as a professional politician. He had existed previously in this country, but his numbers had been negligible and the public hadn't taken the trouble to despise him.

It is a curious thing, this American propensity to look down upon the professional politician. Other nations appear more inclined to honor this class of men, at least such as are successful. But here, except when we wish to ask them a favor, we sneer at them. A rich man who goes into politics as a hobby—*that's* another thing! But it seems there is something reprehensible about making a living out of politics, and even the professional strives to create the impression that he is an amateur, stressing whatever alternative business or profession he may practice. "Officeholder!"—we say it with a snort. And our lips curl as we speak of "practical politicians," though it seems unlikely that we would care to be governed by impractical ones.

The permanent congressman had existed previous to the Civil War, but he was assumed to be a gentleman; politics had been an honorable estate; the public service was thought to be proper, decent, even laudable, as in England. But the public servants here, as they increased enormously following the war, lost caste. And another class appeared—the class of persons who seemed truly to believe that they were doing the nation a favor by consenting to hold public office for a short while, that they were helping to "raise the tone" of American politics.

Take John Hay. He had been abroad for a year and a half, and returned to Washington in February, 1867, to note in his diary: "I drove to Willard's, and saw the same dead beats hanging around the office, the same listless loafers moving gloomily up and down, pensively expectorating." He had, then as ever afterward, the most profound contempt for any "hoary old place-hunter" like General Dix. For he was a clever and accomplished young man who had been abroad for a year and a half—at the expense of the Government. His pull with Lincoln, a neighbor, had taken him to the White House as a lad in his early twenties; and from this secretaryship, after Lincoln's death, he went to Paris as military chargé d'affaires, a colonel in the regular army though still under thirty. But how he hated politicians! And how glad he was when Seward, with whom he had further pull, got him a second sinecure, in Vienna this time, which permitted him to meet many more royal personages and to travel all over Europe—again at the expense of the Government.[1]

Take Robert B. Roosevelt, born wealthy, member of half a dozen fashionable clubs, but notable chiefly as the uncle of McKinley's successor. From a platform he fumed about "that old fossil or father of corruption, Thurlow Weed, to whom our State and country are more indebted for the deterioration of the public service than to any other man in the land." Yet Thurlow Weed, starting penniless, had built up, honestly, a reasonable fortune as a newspaper proprietor, and in addition had found time to work many long, long hours, year after year, as a manager of that party to which Mr. Roosevelt belonged. What, really, did Mr. Roosevelt know about Mr. Weed, a man who had had to fight for everything he got? What *could* he know about him? How, with such immaculate, carefully wrapped and padded ideals, could he comprehend that manipulative genius?

Oh, there were crooked politicians too! There were men like Tweed of Tammany, who had moved recently from Henry Street to Fifth Avenue, who clanked with diamonds, whose country estate boasted stables of the finest mahogany, and whose daughter, when she was married to Ambrose Maginnis of New Orleans, received wedding gifts valued at $700,000, "completely eclipsing," as the *New York Herald* of June 2, 1871, patriotically pointed out, "the jewelry presents to the British Princess Louise, on the occasion of her union with the heir of the great Scottish Duke of Argyle."

Roscoe Conkling was not of this sort. He was, as Senator Vest said of him, "too proud to be corrupt." But he was at no time too proud to consider himself a professional politician. He saw in this nothing of which to be ashamed. Indeed, for all his personal hauteur, instinctively he allied himself with the men who did the real work, and he played the game as he found it, honestly, vigorously, but without any touch of the holier-than-thou. A born conservative, he despised reformers. He snapped at a reporter:

Yes, there are about three hundred persons here [in New York] who believe themselves to occupy the solar walk and milky way, and even there they lift their skirts very carefully for fear even the heavens might stain them. Some of these people would vote against a man because he had been nominated. The mere fact of nomination and selection reduces him in their estimation. They would have people fill the offices by nothing less than divine selection . . . they are after the unattainable in human government.[2]

No, he saw nothing shameful in being a practical politician. He was devoting most of his time to politics now, and central New Yorkers rarely were given an opportunity to hear that musical voice raised in a court room. In June, 1867, he successfully defended Filkins, leader of the mob which had burned the Loomis buildings and killed George Loomis at Sangerfield, in southeastern Oneida. And in September of that year, with Francis Kernan, he defended two physicians, proprietors of a drink cure asylum, accused of arson; separate trials were granted, and one doctor was acquitted in five minutes, after which the indictment against the other was quashed. But this was his last criminal case. Criminal law, somehow, was not dignified, not in keeping with the calling of statesman. And besides, he was busy with other things.

THERE was not the slightest doubt, now, that young Conkling was reaching for the United States senatorship which would become vacant when the term of Ira Harris expired March 4, 1867. More, he wished to grab the Republican leadership of the state. It would have been ambitious enough in any man: it was notably so in one who was unwilling to be pleasant, to smile the bland smile of the hypocrite. For the boss-ship of New York State is one of the most important executive jobs in the country. Like the governorship, it implies Presidential possibilities. Aaron Burr had missed the chief magistracy by one vote; DeWitt Clinton had wriggled within inches of the White House; Martin Van Buren actually got into that mansion. Yet even without this possibility, and even in itself, the suzerainty of New York State is a position of inestimable power.

Roscoe Conkling apparently never aspired to the governorship.[3] He preferred the brighter glare of the Washington spotlight, the higher ceilings of the national capitol, which echoed more awesomely his utterances. But control of the Republican party in the state was something else again.

Weed and Greeley, powerful still, but old men, were taking on an appearance of worn-out schemers. Fenton was the Congressman's chief rival—Reuben Fenton, who sat in the executive mansion at Albany, planning and planning, pulling strings, putting oil here and there in the machinery he had constructed—smooth, solemn Fenton, still young, very dangerous.

BACK in Washington, after that sweeping election of '66, which left the radicals in full control, Conkling voted for continuation of the Freedmen's Bureau bill, for the civil rights bill, for the tenure of office act—all these over the

Presidential veto, which now meant less than ever before. He introduced, on February 6, what became the supplementary reconstruction bill of March 2, fought successfully Bingham's attempt to soften it, and helped to pass it over Johnson's veto. Yet he quarreled again with Thad Stevens, complaining that Stevens wouldn't permit a meeting of the Committee of Fifteen, now that the second session of the Thirty-ninth Congress was so much more radical than the first. There were only two meetings of the committee that session.[4]

In everything, he outshone Senator Harris, whose term was about to expire, and who would be a candidate for re-election. Harris too was a member of the Committee of Fifteen, but he was undramatic, without color. In one way only was he remarkable, and this was in his zeal for jobs. Abe Lincoln had said of him: "I never think of going to sleep now without first looking under my bed to see if Judge Harris is not there wanting something for somebody."[5] Harris had been a Weed stopgap, utilized only to check the threatened Evarts flood. Dourly, Welles wrote in his diary that he was "sly and manoeuvering and had defeated himself," whereas Conkling "is vain, has ability with touches of spread-eagle eloquence, and a good deal of impetuous ardor. He may improve," Welles, a New Englander, added, "and he may not."

Long before the end of the session, in March, both Harris and Conkling found time to return to Albany and fight it out.

THERE were many aspirants—Harris; Conkling; Greeley, who however had no organization in the field, and who received no votes after the first ballot; Charles J. Folger, president and leader of the State Senate, a fine looking man, an impressive orator; Supreme Court Justice Noah Davis, of Erie County, who had the valuable support of the speaker of the house; George William Curtis, soft-spoken editor of *Harper's Weekly;* Ransom Balcom of Binghamton, another Supreme Court justice; Lyman Tremaine, who soon switched his votes to Conkling; Calvin T. Hurlburd of St. Lawrence County; Thomas G. Alvord, leader of Onondaga County.

The caucus assembled at 7 p.m. January 10, Folger presiding and the galleries crowded. The floor was crowded too: only one member was absent, Senator Parsons, and he voted by proxy.

Conkling was stopping at the Delavan House. "Great sums of money are among the influences here," he wrote to his wife. "I have resolutely put my foot upon the ground that no friend of mine, even without my knowledge, shall pay a cent, upon any pretext nor in any strait, come what will. . . . The gamblers say that I can have $200,000 here from New York in a moment if I choose, and that the members are fools to elect me without it; think of it!" Yet he was optimistic. "The whole thing has been amusing and instructive," he wrote, not too convincingly. "No political result personal to me can disturb or excite me, and so I have been as well able as the idlest spectator to enjoy the oddities and lessons of the thing."[6]

The western counties were demanding that they be represented. Burrows of Erie, placing Noah Davis' name in nomination, emphasized that never in its history had the state elected a United States senator from west of Cayuga Bridge. Reuben Fenton, jockeying for the senatorship which would become vacant in two years when Morgan's term expired, greatly wished an Easterner to get Harris' job. For Governor Fenton himself came from Chautauqua, the farthest west of all the counties. But by the time the balloting started, fearful that Conkling would win, he switched his support from Harris to Davis, the Oneida man's strongest opponent. "The fact of the matter is," commented the *World* of January 12, "the real contest was not Conkling and Davis, but

Fenton and anti-Fenton." The Fenton forces tried to rope in Curtis, in support of Davis, but he "declined absolutely" to make any deal.[7]

His good friend Ellis Robert, editor of the *Utica Morning Herald*, placed Roscoe Conkling's name in nomination. Andrew D. White, in the seconding speech, cried that what New York needed was not merely judicial ability but "a voice"—Morgan and Harris had been silent—New York had not had a good speaker in the Senate since Seward. The point was a shrewd one, and was received with great enthusiasm.

Fifty-five votes were necessary. On the first formal ballot Conkling had 33, Harris 32, Davis 30. On the second Conkling had 39, Davis took the lead with 41, while Harris fell to 24. Conkling got 45 votes to Davis' 44, then 53 votes to Davis' 50. And the fifth ballot showed: Conkling 50, Davis 49, Folger 1.

A few minutes later the disheveled, laughing Professor White dashed up to a tall man who stood leaning against a mantelpiece in Parlor 67 at the Delavan House. "God bless you, Senator Conkling!" They carried him downstairs and many times around the lobby. He made a speech, in which he twice referred to the "Union party" as the successor of the "Republican party." Lyman Tremaine made a speech, asserting that the election showed that "henceforth the young, vigorous, live men must rule." Professor White made a speech. They all made speeches.

REUBEN FENTON probably didn't like it much, but he said nothing. At least, the way remained open for his own election two years hence, and this had been his chief concern.

The *World* remarked:

He [Conkling] has a fair intellect, a bumptious kind of self-importance, and a restless desire to make a figure, which will perpetually spur him to make a display of his talents such as they are. That his radicalism is a little deeper seated than that of Mr. Harris, is of no consequence, since he does not carry guns enough to be a party leader.

But the *World* in those days was a sour, disagreeable paper. And surely it had no more cause to regret this prophecy than had George William Curtis of *Harper's Weekly* for writing (January 26): "Young, fearless, devoted, able: of the profoundest convictions: of much experience acquired in critical and stormy times: with all his brilliant powers disciplined and available, the country no less than the state will find him a man equal to the hour." Curtis, as it turned out, found him the most undesirable figure in American public life. But that was later.

SENATOR CONKLING, now. And whatever he might not have been, assuredly he was picturesque. Even in Washington, where picturesque senators always have been common enough, he was a personage to be pointed out, whispered about. Just as a little while before it had been impossible to believe that such a man was not a duelist, so now it was incredible that he was no Don Juan. A hundred reports linked his name with almost as many women. If capital gossip were to be believed, never since Casanova had there been such a heart-breaker. The rumors were shored up, moreover, by the fact that Senator and Mrs. Conkling (it was an open secret) did not get along well together. The nature of the quarrel, if there was a definite quarrel, is not a matter of record. Mrs. Conkling, quiet, lovely, retiring, preferred to remain most of the year in the Utica house the Senator had purchased recently, while the Senator himself spent much of his time in Washington.

The new house fitted the new dignity. It was, and still is, a square, gray stone, three-story affair, cold, aloof, fronted by a teardrop-shaped driveway and spacious if rather severe grounds, an uninviting but impressive sort of place in Rut-

ger Street, staring sternly down John Street. There Mrs.
Conkling devoted herself to her flowers and her charities. A
friend remembered her as "always composed, gentle and
firm." This friend recalled a dinner in honor of Grant, just
before his inauguration in '69, at the home of Senator Morgan:

> Mrs. Conkling, looking splendidly in a blue brocade with
> pearls, was taken in by Senator Sumner. After dinner I had a
> few words with Senator Sumner. I said, "I have been so fortu-
> nate as to sit next to Mr. Conkling, and we have talked poetry."
> Said he: "I have been so lucky as to sit next to Mrs. Conkling,
> and we have talked sense. Do you know that she is one of the
> few women who can talk sense?" Mrs. Conkling was very much
> admired in Washington, but her heart seemed never to be in that
> life. She told me later how much better she loved her life at
> Utica.[8]

Whisperers had it that the Senator was bitterly disappointed because his wife presented him with only one daughter, Bessie, and no son at all. Further whisperers averred
that in fact the Senator did have a son. There is a man in
New York State today, whom old-timers point out, who
bears a striking resemblance to the late Senator Conkling,
and whose son shows an even greater likeness. Also, there is a
lady, a schoolteacher in one of the southern counties, who
sometimes is designated as the product of another Conkling
liaison.

Probably the truth or falsity of these rumors could not be
established, even if a biographer cared to try. This is not
important. What *is* important is that the Senator was the
subject of such rumors, which were numerous, widespread,
and generally believed. And his reputation as a rake, albeit a
highly circumspect rake, harmonized with his appearance as
a beau, his always immaculate turnout, his dazzling personal
beauty. He was too dignified to snicker or sneer, too proper
to mention names or to drop double-edged remarks; yet he

was also, in the popular estimation, too good looking to be pure.

It is perhaps significant that his name should be used most frequently in connection with that of Kate Chase Sprague. For here was a woman indeed!

Poking about among the relics of the past, the historian is tantalized by a whimsical ambition—the ambition to be an absolute czar of recorded history, a sort of glorified city editor, unhampered by limitations of time, whose district would be the world, and whose reporters, perfectly obedient and perfectly efficient, would be those keen-eyed young college professors so expert in digging out unsunned or forgotten data. It does no harm to dream. . . . And if ever this were to come to pass, one of the first assignments might be: investigate the effect of women upon politics. Investigate that endless cavalcade of bright stories about female powers-behind-the-throne. Report upon the psychological reasons why otherwise hardheaded writers ludicrously tumble for tales which endow Pompadours with abilities and powers at least supernatural and possibly superdivine.

Now this assignment would mean a lifetime of work for the alert young professor to whom it was given; and it would be many years, and he would have achieved many gray hairs, before his researches brought him logically to the task of re-estimating the influence of women upon politics in the United States of America. Probably he would start with Mrs. Bingham and her sister hostesses of eighteenth-century Philadelphia, smile his way swiftly through Abigail Adams, Dolly Madison, Peggy Eaton, and some lesser females, and wind up with whatever women the public's imagination had by that time selected to follow Alice Longworth and Mrs. Franklin D. Roosevelt into the mythology. But surely, somewhere in the middle he would pause over the figure of Kate Chase Sprague.

She was the daughter of Chief Justice Salmon Chase, one of those distinguished personages who might have become,

wished to become, and almost did become President. From
childhood she had been his hostess (he was three times a
widower, and had been a senator, a governor and a member
of the cabinet) and also his chief lieutenant. Garfield thought
her "a woman of good sense and pretty good culture—has a
good form but not a pretty face, its beauty being marred by
a nose slightly inclined to pug";[9] but innumerable contempo-
raries, male and female alike, besides the surviving portraits,
make out Garfield an unchivalrous boor, or else a liar, or perhaps totally blind; for certainly the woman was lovely to look
at. She was slightly plump, and had tiny hands and feet. The
nose Garfield called a pug might better be described as saucy,
and it was set in an oval face containing also a low wide forehead, deep brown eyes topped by thick and drooping lashes,
and a small mouth. Her hair was a rich golden brown. She
could talk about anything at all and make it seem sweet music
—yet she could scheme like a cigar-chewing convention rig-
ger. Her husband, Senator Sprague (their marriage, November 12, 1863, in Washington, had been a national event which
for the hour almost outshone the war) was fabulously rich,
and came from Rhode Island, and drank. It was generally
believed that she had married him to help her father, her
hero, in his political career. When it became known that she
was pregnant the whole nation held its breath, snatching
every tiny detail which slipped from the showplace at Cannonsett, R. I., or from the mansion at Sixth and E Streets.

Even to be invited to one of Kate Chase Sprague's functions was a heart-thumping honor; to have the attention of
the hostess for more than a few minutes was to be established
in Washington society; while to be credited with being her
lover—in spite of the general knowledge that almost from
the beginning her marriage had been an unhappy one—was
a distinction reserved for one man.

Again, there is no proof. The conversation of ancients is
spiced with astounding stories (one such, an oft repeated
one too, has Senator Sprague escorting Senator Conkling off

the grounds of Cannonsett at the point of a double-barreled shotgun), but published accounts are wary and scarce. The human thing to do is assume that these two dabbled in adultery. The safest and perhaps the most sensible conclusion, however, is that they were very dear friends.

So he fitted admirably into the Senate, into that austerer chamber where speeches were not limited and the members frowned upon jostling, babbling vulgarity. There his accents found a perfect home. The Senate galleries and floor alike knew him, heeded him, held him in the reverence he believed to be his due. David Barry, then a page boy, more recently (till he took to writing for magazines) sergeant-at-arms of the Senate, remembers the figure: "When he summoned a page . . . he would slap his hands above his head as Roman emperors, according to ancient paintings, used to do, and would confide a message to the boy on a matter of the most ordinary routine as if he were conferring knighthood upon him." His turndown collars, and blue and red butterfly bows, his ice cream trousers, his moonlight-on-the-water waistcoats, were talked about everywhere, like his Hyperion curl and his reddish Venetian beard. He was the hero of the capital's favorite scandal. His oratory was breath taking. He was an excellent poker player—which ability was then, as it is today, a genuinely valuable social asset in Washington. He was reputed to carry a pistol always, and to write his personal letters in mauve ink. He was Senator Conkling, sir.

XIII. Andy Fights It Out

> EXECUTIVE MANSION,
> Washington, August 5, 1867.

Sir:

Public considerations of a high character constrain me to say that your resignation as Secretary of War will be accepted.

> Very respectfully,
> ANDREW JOHNSON.

To Hon. EDWIN M. STANTON,
Secretary of War.

Which inspired this answer:

> WAR DEPARTMENT,
> Washington, August 5, 1867.

Sir:

Your note of this day has been received, stating that public considerations of a high character constrain you to say that my resignation as Secretary of War will be accepted.

In reply I have the honor to say that public considerations of a high character, which alone have induced me to continue at the head of this Department, constrain me not to resign the office of Secretary of War before the next meeting of Congress.

> Very respectfully yours,
> EDWIN M. STANTON.

To the PRESIDENT.

So a long, disgusting squabble edged closer to its climax. Stanton, Abe Lincoln's no-man, a hold-over in the Johnson cabinet, was heart and soul with the anti-administration forces. Johnson would have done well to demand his resignation earlier, but the radicals, anticipating such a move, had passed the tenure of office act which forbade a President to remove a member of his own cabinet without the consent of the Senate. Johnson believed this act to be unconstitutional, and was eager to have a test case.

The wonder is that Johnson, suspicious by nature, always impatient of opposition, should have delayed as long as he did. "It is impossible to get along with such a man in such a position, and I can stand it no longer," he declared.[1] He had actually written the message five days before, and redated it before sending it, according to Colonel Moore, his private secretary.[2] And when Stanton refused to resign, he wrote suspending him. He was tempted to write "you are hereby suspended *and removed*," Colonel Moore says, but thought better of it. The tenure of office act only gave him permission to suspend a cabinet officer until the next session of Congress, when the Senate should consider the situation; and with a circle of watchful enemies so very close about him, it would be as well not to break a law, even a law in the constitutionality of which he didn't believe. He had a sharp temper, Andrew Johnson, and it was the chief hope of the radicals who bayed around him that he would lose it in this affair, as he had done before, giving them priceless ammunition.

So, for a time, the matter rested.

"IN a political warfare, the defensive side will eventually lose," DeWitt Clinton once told a friend; and added, "the meekness of Quakerism will do in religion but not in politics."

Senator Conkling had lost none of his aggressiveness in treating reconstruction matters, but he seems to have believed that the time had come for being more lenient with the Southern states, though ever vigilant, cautious. ". . . it seems to me that any State complying with the prerequisites of recognition, ought not to be compelled to abide the event in some other State," he wrote to Greeley that fall. "On the contrary the pioneer in good behavior should be commended in that character—as was Tennessee."[3] He was a member of the Senate judiciary committee, which had charge of reconstruction affairs for that body once the Committee of Fifteen was dissolved, and he participated in virtually all reconstruction legislation; but he was gentler than he had been. He supported Zack Chandler's unsuccessful resolution to count the Louisiana electoral vote in 1868. In company with such conservatives as Fessenden, Trumbull, Edmunds, Morgan, Morrill and Frelinghuysen, he voted for exclusion of Alabama from Stevens' reconstruction bill of June 9, 1868. He fought hard for admittance of Virginia without radical restrictions. He voted for the readmittance of Arkansas, North Carolina, South Carolina, Louisiana, Florida. He was strangely quiet, but generally conservative, in the debate about Georgia. He was a member of the Senate committee which helped to frame the Fifteenth Amendment, and took a conspicuous part in the long, involved and highly technical arguments which preceded the passage of that measure in the upper house: he thought it hopelessly inadequate because of its omissions, declaring it could be evaded by the passage of state laws fixing "disingenuousness of birth" as a disqualification for voting—more, such laws might be made especially severe by placing the *onus probandi* upon the would-be voter, requiring him to prove his "genuousness" of birth.[4]

In financial matters he always had been a "hard," and his move to another legislative chamber caused no change in this attitude. He helped to pass the contraction bill of April 12, 1866, which gave the Secretary of the Treasury permission to retire ten millions of greenbacks in six months and four millions a month thereafter; and when forty-four millions had been wiped out, and Congress proposed to suspend contraction, he was one of the four senators who voted against this.[5] Parenthetically, he was a member of the committee which framed the resumption bill of '74. He was at all times a bitter opponent of the so-called "Ohio idea," or "rag baby," that provided for payment of principal of the five-twenty bonds in greenbacks because the medium of principal payments of that issue, unlike the later four-twenty issue, was not stipulated, though the act expressly provided for coin payment of *interest*. And surely he guffawed as loudly as any when Andrew Johnson, in his annual message of December 9, 1868, naïvely proposed that since holders of Government war bonds already had made so much on their investments, "it would seem but just and equitable that the six per cent interest now paid by the Government should be applied to the reduction of the principal in semi-annual installments, which in sixteen years and eight months would liquidate the entire national debt."[6] Yet he was no servant of the millionaires. His bill to prohibit secret sales of Treasury gold, pushed in February, 1869, was bitterly opposed by Jay Cooke, the most influential financier of his time, the Robert Morris of the Civil War, whose words were as the tableted commandments down from Sinai to many senators. That bill failed of passage, but it had been accorded much solid business support, and Boutwell, when he became Secretary of the Treasury, in deference to public opinion began his administration by openly announcing his program as to purchases and sales.[7]

All this was in Washington. At home, there was even less of the meekness of Quakerism about him. At the '67 Republican state convention in Syracuse in September, he arrived early to find Reuben ("Spinach") Fenton, that sleepless schemer, maneuvering to make Lyman Tremaine permanent chairman. Conkling, through friends, put it to Fenton squarely: Make Conkling permanent chairman—or else fight. Fenton didn't fancy a fight, yet, and he hesitated for only a moment. Senator Conkling, presiding at the convention, promised amid cheers to "take no man's dust," and threw out a dark warning about possible impeachment proceedings at Washington. A few months later that warning was remembered.

On January 21 Roscoe Conkling was addressing his colleagues from the floor when a messenger deposited a paper on the desk of the Senate's President. Zack Chandler, that earlier Mark Hanna from Michigan, strolled over to the desk, glanced at the paper, gasped, hurried to Sumner.

There was a stir, and Senator Conkling paused, frowning. He didn't like any lack of attention on the part of his audience. This must be a matter of the greatest immediate importance indeed, he decided, to justify such behavior in the course of a Conkling speech.

And it was. It was a notification that President Johnson, goaded beyond his endurance, at last had definitely dismissed Edwin M. Stanton as Secretary of War. Johnson, in August, had suspended Stanton, but under the tenure of office act this suspension was in force only until the Senate acted upon it; and that body, when Congress assembled in December, had refused to endorse the President's act. But now Johnson, Senate or no Senate, bluntly was telling Stanton that he was fired. It was a declaration of war.

Sumner, delighted, wrote a one-word message to Stanton: "Stick." And in the excitement that followed, as the whisper went about, even a Conkling speech was forgotten. Senators, buzzing, tumbled toward the desk. So Andy was going to fight it out at last?[8]

Johnson's behavior now seems rash. Only the most popular President can hope to defy the Senate of the United States, even for a short time; and Andrew Johnson was perhaps the most *un*popular President in our history. But he was not an utter fool. He had arranged, or thought he had arranged, to have Ulysses S. Grant accept an appointment as Stanton's successor.

It would have spiked the radical guns. Grant's prestige and popularity were unbounded. Even the South respected and trusted him, and in the North he was worshiped as the savior of the Union. His was the most mauled and yanked-about name in the country. He disliked politics and politicians, but he was not strong enough, or clever enough, to keep them at their distance, as his colleague Sherman managed to do. "Washington is as corrupt as Hell. . . . I will avoid it as a pest house," General Sherman had written to his wife soon after the close of the war; and now, with an unprecedented brawl a-brewing, he wrote to her: "The whole matter is resolved into a war between parties and neither cares or seems to care a damn for the service of the country." So Sherman kept out of it; but Grant, who felt the same way, wasn't so fortunate. Grant was incalculably important to both factions. The radicals had been disinclined to trust him,[9] but they realized that he probably would be the next President, and they acted accordingly. Andrew Johnson appeared to think that he and Grant were in perfect accord, and that Grant had agreed to take over the war portfolio when Stanton was removed, regardless of what the Senate might say or do about its right under the tenure of office act. In that event, possibly the Senate would have been balked; for even the Senate would hesitate to turn out of office so popular a figure as Ulysses S. Grant.

But Grant insisted that though he had acted as Secretary of War during the period of Stanton's suspension, at the behest of the President, he never had agreed to flout the tenure of office act and give Johnson an opportunity to test its constitutionality. He and Johnson quarreled bitterly and very noisily about this, and Johnson to the end of his days thought Grant a liar and a betrayer of his word.

If Johnson wasn't right (we'll never know) at least he was honestly mistaken, and Grant's refusal to take the portfolio left the President in a dangerous predicament. Sherman refused to have anything to do with the matter, and so did General Schriver, and Potts, chief clerk at the war office, and probably others as well. Until at last General Lorenzo Thomas was induced to take the job.

Lorenzo Thomas (who should not be confused with Major General George H. Thomas, the war hero) was an office warrior, more accustomed to the pen than the sword, unused to the sound of bursting shrapnel but perfectly at home on dress parade. Likely enough he was delighted thus unexpectedly to be hoisted to the technical top of his profession, to be given an opportunity to boss fellow generals of equal or higher rank. He scurried over to the war office.

But Stanton had obeyed Sumner's one-word message. He was sticking. He knew he had the Senate behind him, and the Senate meant business. One member of that body, General Logan, Republican boss of Illinois, had mustered a force of one hundred men, some of whom were to occupy the basement of the War Department night and day, at Stanton's command. A siege? All right, then: it was a siege! Anyway, General Lorenzo Thomas was not admitted.

All Washington was in a turmoil. General Thomas, quivering with indignation, went to a masked ball in Mariners' Hall that night, and there boldly announced to anybody who cared to listen that unless he were admitted to the War Department the following day he would kick the door in. He drank sundry toasts to this resolution, and repeated it many times. It seems, though, that his own costume did not conceal effectively his familiar form and face; since a Senate official, at eleven o'clock that night, had no difficulty serving him with a Senate resolution declaring his appointment illegal.

Well, the President said he was Secretary of War, and the Senate said he wasn't; but he agreed with the President. If they didn't let him in, he'd kick the door in!

They say the ball was a notable success, and General Thomas might have slept late the following morning had not some rude persons awakened him with the information that he was under arrest by order of the Secretary of War, Edwin M. Stanton. They didn't give him time for breakfast, or even to drink a pick up. Wildly he appealed by message to Andrew Johnson, to Attorney-General Stanbery. He was taken to a police court, while he raged, threatening a damage suit of $150,000 against Stanton for false arrest. Bail was provided; and General Thomas stamped away to his new office.

This time he was admitted. Fuming, he confronted Stanton. "Next time you arrest me, don't do it before I get something to eat!" Stanton laughed nervously, and suggested a drink. General Schriver, in charge of the inspection bureau, was summoned into consultation, and he went to his desk and found a little whiskey—which he was careful to explain he kept there only as a medicine. They finished that. Stanton had determined, on senatorial advice, not to stir from the protection of his office, from his cordon of faithful desk generals and volunteer bodyguards, until the whole matter was decided; but he sent a messenger to his home for a full bottle of whiskey, and when this arrived he and Lorenzo Thomas (who was feeling a little less angry now) had a real drink. Stanton put his arm around Thomas' neck, and ran his fingers through Thomas' hair. All this was brought out later, and solemnly recorded, in a congressional investigation.

And the House of Representatives impeached President Johnson. And Thaddeus Stevens, smiling a thin, cruel smile, hobbled down to the other end of the capitol, where in a high-pitched voice he notified the Senate of this fact.

THE country as a whole appeared to have expended its not very reasonable hatred of Andrew Johnson in the '66 campaign. *It* had passed the climax. "Besides," as Clemenceau wrote to *Le Temps*, "the American people became accustomed to all sorts of excitement during the war and have become rather indifferent." A President of the United States was being haled before the bar of the Senate of the United States on impeachment articles found by the House of Representatives; but as General Sherman wrote to his brother, the senator, "the people generally manifest little interest in the game going on."

Not so the politicians, who fairly seethed. *Their* hatred of Johnson was greater than ever, and the passions they had stirred in that memorable campaign recently completed were hottest in their own bosoms. Many of them attended a regularly scheduled White House reception on the night of the twenty-third, "to see how Andy would take it." They found him taking it very well. Indeed, he seemed the only tranquil person in Washington, where hysteria was the rule then. His mail each day was packed with frenzied threats, and with prayers, and absurd advice. Numerous mediums, taking advantage of the after-war fad for spiritualism, and eagerly in search of publicity, called or wrote to offer their services, as did also astrologers and divers other soothsayers. But the President maintained his dignity throughout. When a bank employee, much embarrassed, informed him that a congressional investigating committee was demanding his private accounts, the President only laughed. "Let them have them, if they want them. I have nothing to be ashamed of."[10]

Oh, he could be calm! But not clever. He had made one mistake when he banked so heavily upon Grant's willingness to accept the war portfolio. Even after that, he might have extricated himself; for the radicals had blundered in arresting General Thomas and haling him before a magistrate. Johnson had proved slow witted there, or perhaps ill advised. Bail should not have been provided. Instead, a writ of habeas corpus should have been taken out, thus insuring a formal hearing before the Supreme Court of the United States—a test of the constitutionality of the tenure of office act—the very thing Johnson desired. But he lost that opportunity. And the radicals were not likely to make a second misstep.

Constitutional lawyers find the record of these impeachment proceedings fascinating stuff; but the average American can see in it very little that is not dull and almost nothing that is not shameful.

There were thirteen articles of impeachment, but the only real accusation was that he had violated the tenure of office act—an act he, with many another public servant, honestly believed to be unconstitutional.[11] Surely this was not high treason. Besides, even from a sheerly dog-eat-dog stand-point, there was very little the radicals could hope to gain by putting Johnson out. Very little, that is, except the mean satisfaction of hurting a man they disliked. He had only a little over a year to serve in the White House—less than a year, by the time the Senate started to try him; the radicals commanded a clear two-thirds majority in each house, and easily could and did pass laws over his veto, besides having much control of certain executive departments; and there wasn't the slightest cause for anybody, even Johnson him-self, to believe that he could be reëlected on any ticket, or could even be of any notable influence in selecting his suc-cessor.

Moreover, the man who would step into the White House for the few remaining months, if Johnson were ousted, was Ben Wade, President of the Senate. And nobody was over-proud of Ben Wade.[12]

As for Roscoe Conkling, at least he was no worse than most, not as bad as many. For all his campaign bluster, he was quiet now. He wasn't mentioned as a possible member of Wade's in-the-air cabinet. He took no active part in the proceedings, and made no speech, though he attended every session. He voted for conviction, but he did not, like twenty-nine other Senators, file an individual opinion.

Johnson was acquitted by one vote.

Colonel Crook, hurrying down from the balcony to rush the news to his boss at the White House, saw Thad Stevens emerging from the Senate chamber supported by friends (for he was dying, still). Thad was black with rage, and screaming: "The country is going to the devil!" Likely enough he believed that, too. Yet the country survived.

XIV. Strong, Silent, and Mysterious

THERE was a wholesome interlude that summer, when the Senator with eight friends made a trip west. They stopped at Harrisburg to see Si Cameron, Pennsylvania's Republican boss, and it was there that they heard of the death of Thad Stevens, who had kept his mulatto housekeeper with him to the end (men said she was his mistress, and he never denied it) and had refused to be buried in a previously selected cemetery when he learned that Negro corpses were not accepted there.

Then to Galena, where General Grant gave them a reception; to Dubuque, and St. Louis, where the Senator walked many times in admiration around the statue of Thomas H. Benton; and up Pilot's Knob, where a bottle of wine was opened and the health of Grant drunk. General Palmer joined them in St. Louis. They went to Kansas City, to Lawrence, where Roscoe Conkling was serenaded and where he graciously responded with a speech; to Fort Wallace, and Fort Harker, Kansas, where they met Phil Sheridan and walked around the fort. An escort of cavalry, supplied by Sheridan, traveled with them to Denver. Senator Conkling, scorning the carriages, rode in saddle the whole distance; and they camped nights in the open. They went to Georgetown and Boulder. They climbed Grey's Peak. There was thunder and snow that day, and some of the men quit, but the Senator pushed on to the summit. Always he had illimitable confidence in his own strength—the confidence of a man who never had known a day's illness and never had met the fellow man he couldn't whip. A stage coach took them to Cheyenne, and they traveled by rail to Bitter Creek, Wyoming, which was as far as the railroad went. They returned by way of Omaha, having been gone about six weeks.

The trip is interesting because it was the first time Roscoe Conkling had ventured far from his native state. The fellow

who is dreaming of the Presidency, as all men said Conkling
was doing, seldom misses an opportunity to show himself in
other sections of the country, especially if he be as handsome
a man and as good a talker as Conkling. Yet on this one trip
the Senator was not "on display." He avoided reporters, as
usual.

Rumors of the Conkling eloquence had penetrated other
states, and in a day when oratory, political or otherwise, was
esteemed a marvelous treat, invitations were showered upon
him. He refused them. Colleagues in Washington, faced with
campaigns for reëlection, implored him to take the stump
for them. He never obliged. Nor did he attend national conventions, or send open letters to newspapers, or embark upon
congressional junkets.

If he thought of himself as a Presidential possibility (he
had no real intimates, and his letters were so guarded, so
formal, that it is impossible to be sure about this), then certainly he was behaving in a very strange manner.

His political ideas were old fashioned; and it may be that
he subscribed to the belief that the office should seek the man,
particularly if that office be the Presidency. People in those
days thought there was something undignified about a truly
great statesman, or a man aspiring to truly high office, making appearances everywhere, shaking too many hands, spouting too many speeches.

At the same time, an ambitious fellow could see to it that
he was in plain sight in the event a job *did* come looking for
him. But the Senator was proud, and very stiff.

There was another reason for his reluctance to accept invitations to speak outside of his own state. He was admittedly
one of the greatest political orators this country ever has
produced (graybeards alive today, who have heard both,
will tell you that Bryan was a stuttering schoolboy compared
with Roscoe Conkling), but he was not glib. He was no spellbinder born, eager to mount any platform, pound any stand,

at the slightest excuse. He didn't meet people easily. In extemporary debate there was nothing extraordinary about him; and each of his truly great speeches was the product of weeks, even months, of painstaking preparation.

For if genius really is an infinite capacity for work, then Roscoe Conkling was a genius. First, he got together all pertinent facts, a great mass of material. Then he wrote or dictated the speech itself, dipping deep into his memory for scarlet quotations. Then he rewrote it many, many times, changing this, changing that, going over it again and again. Then, his long legs swinging, he would take walks through the countryside, out of sight of his fellow men, reciting the speech at the top of his lungs, sometimes perhaps pausing to declaim thunderously to a tree or bush, or else hurling more or less immortal invective at some startled cow. Finally there were the indoor rehearsals, themselves long, covering many nights. Hours, men whispered, were spent in front of mirrors. Chauncey Depew was acquainted with the target, or listening-post, one Lawrence, an employee of the Republican state committee, who was "a man of a good deal of receptive intelligence and worshiped the senator." Lawrence heard some of the speeches, the greatest ones, many times before Conkling delivered them. He was not expected to comment, and certainly he would not venture to dispute the construction or delivery of any sentence. Often he was up all night, listening, listening. But he never tired of this, never failed to be enthusiastic.

Yet when finally the speech was made, on the platform, it sounded as though Roscoe Conkling, inspired, was spouting it *ex tempore*.

There is evidence that Roscoe Conkling almost *thought* in terms of oratory. His informal speech was stately enough; but occasionally, in the company of intimates, he would discard even this, abruptly raising his voice, breaking into a pompous but wonderfully impressive diatribe complete with gestures. Nor did he seem to be aware of anything unusual about this, for he was merely expressing his thoughts in the manner in which he thought them. These unexpected, apparently impromptu speeches, which never failed to flabbergast the persons who heard them, came only when the Senator was especially angry about something. His rage, probably the strongest emotion in his make-up, sought a natural (for him) outlet.

THERE could be no question, now, that Grant would be the Republican Presidential nominee in 1868, and would be elected. The radicals, still powerful, were strong for him since his refusal to help Andrew Johnson out of the tenure of office trouble. But then, everybody was for him—even the Democrats, who for a time really hoped to persuade him to stand as their candidate. Grant himself, confused, frightened, flattered, didn't seem to know what to do. He did not know whether he was a Republican or a Democrat. The only time he'd ever taken the trouble to vote, in 1856, he had voted for Buchanan, a Democrat. But such things are easily forgotten.

If Grant didn't know much about politics, neither did the politicians know much about Grant—though they knew the most important thing about him, which was that he'd win, whatever he ran for, on whatever ticket, and whatever platform.

He was called a strong, silent man, and of the silence there can be no question. He was extraordinarily shy. General Badeau, once a member of his staff, and perhaps as close to him as any man, wrote in his understanding biography that Grant

had indeed a genuine liking for society; not only because wherever he went he was the chief and the idol, though this might make any one fond of the world; but he was social by nature. He not only had a pleasure in the company of his intimates, not only enjoyed the conversation of important men; but he liked to look at pretty girls and to listen to the talk of clever women. For a long time, however, he was not ready in replying . . .[1]

It is amazing how little was known about this man whose name was on everybody's lips. No one doubted that he would be the next President, yet no one had an inkling of the nature of his political philosophy, if any—of his opinions on the questions of the day. When asked things, he did not reply. He did not have to reply. He was Grant; and the politicians had to take him whether they liked it or not.

Henry Adams, who lived in the same Washington boarding house with General Badeau, sometimes caught that interesting gentleman at the dinner table when he (Badeau, of course) was not too drunk yet not too sober either, and so learned many things about Grant. The old-time West Point men described Grant as "vicious, narrow, dull, and vindictive," but Badeau really liked him.

He held that no one except himself and [General] Rawlins understood the General. To him, Grant appeared as an intermittent energy, immensely powerful when awake, but passive and plastic in repose. He said that neither he nor the rest of the staff knew why Grant succeeded; they believed in him because of his success. For stretches of time, his mind seemed torpid. Rawlins and the others would systematically talk their ideas into it, for weeks, not directly, but by discussion among themselves, in his presence. In the end, he would announce the idea as his own, without seeming conscious of the discussion; and would give the orders to carry it out with all the energy that belonged to his nature. They could never measure his character or be sure when he would act. They could never follow a mental process of his thought. They were not sure that he did think.

The rest of the country, too, was to know that feeling of doubt. But meanwhile, Grant was Grant. The New York state convention at Syracuse, February 5, picking delegates for the national convention, unanimously endorsed him—the first official state endorsement. The convention endorsed Reuben Fenton as a running-mate for the general. Why Fenton should have wished to be Vice-President, is not clear. At the national convention he ran third.

THE Republicans in New York were none too jubilant. They would have lost control of the legislature the previous year had it not been for the most unblushing sort of gerrymandering; and confidence was not high. So the acquisition of Grant as the head of the national ticket was very welcome indeed.

At the regular state convention, July 8, there was a scramble for the gubernatorial nomination. Fenton, committed to a try for the Senate the following spring, no longer was an aspirant. Horace Greeley emphatically was. The name of Roscoe Conkling's older brother, Frederick A. Conkling, was mentioned—but no more than mentioned. The Senator's own choice was his close friend John T. Griswold of Troy, who nosed out Greeley, thereby giving Greeley just a little more cause to dislike the Oneida giant.

The Democrats nominated John T. Hoffman, a Tammany creature. Tammany was riding high then, under Boss Tweed, at the apogee of his glory; and "Elegant" Oakey Hall, the mayor, a poet and social climber, an earlier Jimmy Walker; and "Slippery Dick" Connolly, that astounding bookkeeper; and Peter ("Brains") Sweeny, the outfit's Mephistopheles.

THERE was enthusiasm, but no astonishment, when the Republicans in national convention nominated General Grant. Much more interest centered around the Democratic national convention, which was opened in Tammany Hall, in East Fourteenth Street, on July 4. It was ninety in the shade that day. There were several aspirants for the dubious honor of being beaten by Grant, and one of the most conspicuous was Chief Justice Chase. Billy Hudson, a cub reporter assigned to cover the Chase headquarters in the Clarendon Hotel at Fourth Avenue and Seventeenth Street, found Chase's daughter, Conkling's Kate Chase Sprague, in "active and visible charge." Equipped with "brains of almost masculine fiber," she was entirely capable of running her father's campaign. He was beaten, partly because of a last-minute juggling of votes for which the Chase adherents held Samuel J. Tilden responsible,[2] and Senator Conkling's brother-in-law, Horatio Seymour, was nominated, much to his own consternation. Seymour, Colonel McClure believed, "had no more idea of being nominated for President than he had of becoming Czar of Russia." He accepted the nomination with no very good grace. But in view of his own indifference or dismay, the popularity of Grant, a hasty speaking running-mate, and a platform which embraced the "Ohio idea" (though Seymour himself was a hard-money man) and which declared "unconstitutional, revolutionary and void" the "so-called" reconstruction acts, but offered no concrete substitute—in view of these considerations, he made a fair run, winning New York, New Jersey, and Oregon, and getting a good vote in California, Connecticut, and Indiana. Excepting Louisiana and Georgia, where there were sensational Vigilante scandals, all the Southern states permitted to vote in that election went Republican.

His brother-in-law stumped the state vigorously against Seymour, and for Grant and Griswold. But New York went Democratic, thanks largely to some extra dirty work on the part of Tammany. The Senator, white with rage, called the election a "barbarous burlesque," and helped to instigate a congressional investigation which discovered some interesting facts (but ones which did nothing to change the result) about the proportion of voters to population in Tammany districts and the Tammany policy of naturalizing as many as one thousand immigrants a day immediately before an election.[3]

THERE was another disappointment the following January, when Reuben Fenton at last got that senatorship. Conkling opposed him, backing Morgan for reëlection. Greeley opposed him, blaming him for failure to support the Greeley gubernatorial campaign in '68, and backing Marshall O. Roberts. Noah Davis opposed him, contending that he had agreed to permit *him* to have the senatorship. Also there was a sniff of scandal in the air, mutters which involved Fenton and $10,000 and the always sinister name of Jay Gould— all duly denied, but not convincingly disproved.

Nevertheless, Fenton won, 52–40. For Fenton had the machine, and he had methods. When his man, Speaker Younglove, deliberately held up announcement of committee appointments in the lower house, legislators could easily comprehend what this meant. Either they voted "right," or else they didn't get the jobs they'd been expecting to get. It was the first time this unlovely trick was used at Albany, though it was not the last.[4]

THE directors of the Michigan and Southern, when they held their annual meeting in 1853, were obliged to borrow chairs from an adjoining office because the sheriff had taken all their furniture,[5] and as late as 1865, when Commodore Vanderbilt sold his steamship interests and began buying rails, many of his associates thought the old fellow was getting feeble minded. But by May 10, 1869, when the Central Pacific and Union Pacific met at Promontory Point, five miles west of Ogden, Utah, and gold and silver spikes were driven, the nation was railroad mad. It was a romantical fever. The railroad engineer was a semi-fabulous hero, and the railroad financier was esteemed a public benefactor whose behavior it was treason to call into question. The great companies could ask state and Federal governments for almost anything they wished—cash subsidies, credit, lavish gifts of public lands—and receive these things instantly, without regulation. They almost got them without asking. For a time they didn't even find it necessary to bribe.

Conkling was no railroad Senator. When Oakes Ames came whispering to him of a wonderful holding company called the Crédit Mobilier of America, which would take all the Union Pacific's profits, and which certain leading senators and congressmen were to be permitted to buy into very cheap indeed—in fact, with no cash outlay at all—he turned Oakes Ames down. When the grim old *World* was under the temporary "angelship" of Tom Scott, the czar of the Pennsylvania, a railroad robber baron who never pulled a punch, there was no let-up in its hostility to Roscoe Conkling.[6] When a bill was proposed in the Senate, in January, 1869, which would have guaranteed interest of some $2,900,000 on bonds of the Central Branch, Union Pacific Railroad Company, and in addition would have appropriated to that line an extra 2,000,000 acres of choice public lands, Conkling denounced it in a long speech and had the satisfaction of seeing it defeated by one vote. And on several occasions he wrung big sums from railroads in court, the most remarkable one being the Smith case in the summer of '69.

Norman T. Smith was a New York Central engineer, and was operating a special train from Syracuse to Albany. There were directors on that train, and divers high railroad officials, all in a hurry to get to a banquet at Albany. They were drinking champagne, after the manner of railroad directors in those days, and playing poker. The engineer had been told that the track would be cleared the whole distance, and had been instructed to go fast. He obeyed. At Oriskany, four miles from Utica, he swung around a curve and crashed into the rear of a gravel train. He was killed; and his family brought suit for damages.

Senator Conkling's old friendly-enemy, Francis Kernan, defending the case, tried hard to convince the jurors that corporations were not the cruel, heartless things they were reputed to be. But he had no chance against the Conkling eloquence. The Senator's summation lasted two hours, and long before its conclusion there was not a dry eye in the jury box. He made much of the fact that the rich and care-free directors had been drinking expensive wine and playing cards, while the sturdy, faithful engineer, hanging upon his throttle, was dashed to death at command of these rich, sneering men. Some of the very directors themselves, not undecorated, were in the court room. The Senator pointed to them. "In eternity," solemnly said the Senator, "the pebbles upon the grave of poor Smith will shine as brightly as do the diamonds upon the bosoms of these men." The jury found for $18,000 damages, the biggest award on record at that time. And when the railroad attorneys proposed to appeal, Commodore Vanderbilt snapped: "Pay it! If Conkling tries this case again he may get fifty thousand!"[7]

ANDREW JOHNSON, still angry at Grant, refused to ride with his successor to the inaugural ceremony. Instead, he stayed in the White House, clearing up his personal papers. And when finally he quit that building, by a side door, he remarked sardonically that at last he was doing something of which everybody would approve. There were only a few White House employees to wave him off. And in the distance they could hear the bands playing.

The ceremony itself passed off well enough, in fair weather, but a blizzard came soon afterward, and the inaugural ball that night was a hideous failure. It was held in the north wing of the Treasury Department. There was much confusion about admittance tickets, hats and coats were lost, carriage calls were badly mixed, and in the end hundreds of persons, many of them separated from their partners, were obliged to walk home through mud and snow and slush. Mrs. Grant wore white satin trimmed with point and pearls and diamonds, and almost everybody got at least a glimpse of the utterly silent little man who was now President of the United States.

XV. The New Boss: Conkling

CURIOSITY about Grant was quickly satisfied, at least in small matters. Never before had life at the White House been so exultantly publicized. Everybody very soon learned of the President's fondness for rolling breadballs during the service of dessert; of Mrs. Mullen, the small, bright-eyed German housekeeper; of the Presidential passion for cribbage, billiards, rice pudding, four-in-hands; of the many brooms sent from all parts of the country, the implication being a desire to have swept clean a Johnson-polluted government; of the enlargement of the stables, and the nine horses, the landeau, barouche, top buggy, phaeton, road wagon; of the black, indescribably strong cigars (Billy Hudson smoked one during an interview at Long Branch, and wasn't able to get any sleep that night); of the fact that his wife called the President "Uyles," while he called her "Mrs. G."[1]

Yes, these things were well and promptly known. Yet the General himself remained a mystery.

He seems to have started his administration with a sincere belief that a President should be above party considerations. He seems really to have supposed that politics could be run without politicians. This quaint notion was driven out of him swiftly, but not before the politicians themselves had received a shock.

It started with the first official act, announcement of the cabinet. The appointments, Grant's very own, were, to put it mildly, indiscreet. Henry Adams might have thought that they "had the singular effect of making the hearer ashamed, not so much of Grant, as of himself"; but the men who had helped to elect Grant didn't feel that way about it—they were furious. Generals and millionaires were especially favored. The President had an emphatic weakness for each of these classes—for millionaires because he stood always in great awe of wealth and the power of wealth, and for generals because he knew so many of them and because, whatever he was *not*, assuredly he was loyal to his friends.

In the Senate there was a considerable squawk about ratification. The new President, doubtless through ignorance, had flouted many a law. Conkling himself pointed out nine separate statutes which prohibited the appointment of A. T. Stewart, the New York merchant, as Secretary of the Treasury. This appointment, the most obnoxious, was withdrawn. So were others. The secretaries to which the Senate finally consented were not at all the ones General Grant himself had first selected. Nor did the cabinet ever stay firm. In the eight years Grant was President no less than twenty-three men held the seven portfolios.

There were fewer objections to the generals who were given private secretaryships and important diplomatic posts. But the politicians weren't pleased—and they were puzzled.

It was difficult to learn what the President was thinking, if anything. A congressman (or senator) would appear before him, talk to him by the hour, and he would listen unstirring while one cigar after another was converted into ashes. At last he would grunt. This was, for him, loquacity. And the senator (or congressman) would quit the White House all smiles, believing that the President had consented to everything—only to be dumbfounded later on learning that the grunt hadn't meant "yes" at all. To hurry back and talk for another hour or two (the general was an excellent listener), frequently enough only produced another grunt which might mean one thing or might mean another. Grant wished to be honest, straightforward, nonpartisan; but it was impossible for him to explain himself to those smooth-speaking fellows from Capitol Hill. Sometimes he seemed almost too shy to look them in the face. Not even the grunts were effortless.

Yet "because he did not speak was no reason to suppose he did not think or feel," Badeau tells us. "It seemed to him immodest to uncloak himself to the world. . . . He could not, if he would, expose his opinions and sentiments to every one he met. . . . He had secrets of business from one friend, of politics from another, of feeling from many; and no one knew all. I found out traits in his character in the last months of his life that I had not suspected before, and I doubt not that he had emotions and beliefs which he died without revealing to his wife and children. Yet no man ever loved wife or children more profoundly than he."

It would seem, at a glance, that such a man would have nothing in common with Roscoe Conkling. Grant was bashful, humble, torpid; Conkling was imperious, instinctively a great actor. Grant, always the military man, expected to be obeyed instantly and without question. Conkling never was prepared to obey anyone, but appeared to suppose himself born a czar, whose word it were treason to dispute.

Yet there were similarities, bridges for sympathetic feeling. Conkling, after all, was a true fighter who hated compromise, and no mere blustering bag of conceit; and Grant could appreciate a fighter. Conkling was trustworthy; there was nothing treacherous about him. He wasn't a crank, a leader of causes. Rather he was an efficient public servant, a molder if not an originator of measures, a person who got things done (or else had them killed) without shilly-shallying. And this too Grant could understand and admire.

Many other men bowed to Grant, but Conkling wouldn't bow. Conkling *couldn't* bow, if he would. He was not built that way. And possibly Grant preferred such a man.

Reuben Fenton could bow, and he did, asking the President for patronage. Grant seems to have been impatient with him, distrustful; but Fenton, smooth and suave, convinced the President that he, Fenton, was the true and natural Republican leader of New York State, and should be consulted about all appointments there.

The courtesy of the Senate was a recent thing. Originally, most of the Federal patronage was dispensed directly by the President himself. George Washington knew personally most of the men he appointed to office. Later, members of the cabinet took upon themselves the duty of making suggestions; and later still, for some reason not apparent, this pleasant work was delegated generally to members of the House of Representatives. However, when Grant took office in 1869 the patronage was coming to be a senatorial prerogative.

And the patronage, too, was coming to be very important to state leaders. Always there had been applicants, to be sure; but now, with Southerners virtually barred from public office, the armies demobilized, the public service vastly expanded, and the civil service act no more than a fond dream in the hearts of reformers—*now* the real rush for jobs began. The rush was toward the White House, but by way of individual Senators.

The man who controlled Federal patronage in New York, controlled New York. Fenton knew this, and so did Conkling.

Fenton worked hard for the ratification of Stewart as Secretary of the Treasury. He did many other things for the general. But when Tom Murphy's name was given to the Senate as nominee for collector of the port of New York, Fenton balked. We don't know his reasons. Possibly they included the fact that Tom Murphy, a common ward heeler, was unfitted for the post.

Conkling had not suggested the appointment, nor had he been consulted about it, and at first he was reluctant to fight in behalf of a man like Murphy. His friend Senator Stewart persuaded him to do so, arguing that if the Murphy appointment wasn't ratified the President probably would appoint somebody even worse. It was, Stewart cried, the great Conkling opportunity. Fenton was losing ground at the White House; patronage was being withheld, or granted to him grudgingly, for his obsequiousness disgusted the President. What better time for a death blow? a showdown?

It must not be supposed that Roscoe Conkling, proud and incorruptible though he was, was any knight in shining armor. There was nothing chivalrous about him. He respected no Queensberry rules, but fought with any and all weapons, butting, kicking, scratching, biting, and when it seemed advisable not hesitating to hit below the belt. In Reuben Fenton he had a skilled and unscrupulous enemy, and he saw no reason for withholding the misericord when such a one had been unhorsed.

He moved, on July 11, 1870, for immediate consideration of the appointment.

Fenton spoke for three hours, Conkling for one. Both were bitter, angry. But Conkling was by far the better talker. Besides, he had the last word.

Every sentence was replete with logic, sarcasm, reason, and invective. Sometimes the senators would rise to their feet, so great was the effect upon them. Toward the conclusion of his speech Conkling walked down the aisle to a point opposite the seat of Fenton. "It is true," he said, "that Thomas Murphy is a mechanic, a hatter by trade; that he worked at his trade in Albany supporting an aged father and mother and crippled brother, and that while thus engaged another visited Albany and played a very different rôle"—At this point he drew from his pocket a court record, and extending it toward Fenton, he continued,—"the particulars of which I will not relate except at the special request of my colleague." Fenton's head dropped upon the desk as if struck down with a club. The scene in the Senate was tragic.[2]

Undoubtedly a dirty trick, but effective. Fenton, earlier, had been sent to Albany with $12,000, and had arrived to say that he'd lost the money. He had been arrested, examined, discharged. But the whole matter smelled bad, and Fenton would not have enjoyed seeing Conkling lift the lid on the Senate floor.[3]

The Murphy appointment was confirmed 48–3.

ALL this was dramatic enough, but it did not make Roscoe Conkling the Republican boss of New York State. Fenton had builded well. There were those who esteemed him the greatest organizer since Martin Van Buren. His lieutenants were everywhere, his personal popularity not inconsiderable, and his prestige among the politicians of his home state, for all the Murphy setback, remained great.

The senior Senator had squashed Reuben Fenton's Presidential aspirations, but Reuben Fenton's home machine was of tougher material. Dramatics were not sufficient; behind-the-footlights behavior was not likely to impress men at a state convention—professionals, fellows who probably didn't care a hoot, most of them, whether Fenton had stolen that $12,000 or not—men who might enjoy hearing Senator Conkling make a speech, but who could be budged more calculably by such substantial things as jobs and votes.

The state convention that year was in Saratoga. Fenton was there early; but so was Conkling, and with him Tom Murphy.

Election of temporary and permanent chairmen, in state as in national conventions, is a highly important matter when a question of leadership is involved. The positions themselves do not carry great power, but the election is a show of strength carefully watched by those who are trying to decide which vehicle will prove to be the bandwagon.

Fenton wished to have his friend Charles H. Van Wyck made temporary chairman, and himself president, or permanent chairman. Conkling proposed, in the course of the preliminary dickering, that George William Curtis be made temporary chairman. (*Here* was a strange enough bedfellow!) Fenton, confident of his own strength, knowing Van Wyck's popularity and supposing that Conkling would not dare to fly in the face of that popularity, absolutely refused to compromise. Fenton went to sleep.

But Conkling stayed up almost all that night, in the company of Tom Murphy going from hotel room to hotel room, awakening delegates, talking to them—talking plainly. They had Grant behind them, and Grant meant all the Federal patronage. There was no need to mince words. Next morning George William Curtis was elected temporary chairman, 220–150.[4]

Then the cunning Conkling moved that the committee on organization report Van Wyck for permanent chairman—a position of greater honor, a position Van Wyck's friends probably would rather see him have. And this was done, the credit going to Conkling.

Senator Conkling himself took the chairmanship of the committee on resolutions.

The fight for the gubernatorial nomination was a sensational but bewildering business. Grant, it was known, wished his friend General Woodford to get the nomination, and therefore it was supposed that Conkling would back Woodford. Fenton, planning accordingly, supported Marshall O. Roberts. Conkling countered that by supporting (of all persons!) Horace Greeley. Roberts and Greeley were good friends, and Greeley considered himself something of a patron of Roberts; but Greeley longed still for high office. General Woodford offered to withdraw if Greeley desired it. DeWitt C. Littlejohn, dangerous as a dark horse, sidestepped. All of which left Fenton sure of only one thing, which was that whoever was nominated it must not be done through Roscoe Conkling. But who *was* Conkling's candidate? Now the man was passing word along the line to vote for Curtis!

But on the second ballot he switched to Greeley. There was much confusion. Conkling's own workers didn't know what

the Senator was doing—and it is just possible that he didn't
know either. He moved for adjournment. Fenton had every
reason to suppose that this was an act of desperation, that
Conkling sought breathing time, a retreat to the repair
shop. So Fenton blocked the motion.

Conkling spread the word to vote for Woodford, and
Woodford was nominated on the third ballot.

Afterward, hard feeling hung over the convention hall
like dust over a recently quitted battlefield. Fenton and his
friends had been completely routed, fooled, tricked at every
turn. Indeed, almost everybody had been tricked, even Senator Conkling's own friends. Greeley was angry, naturally,
and so was Curtis, who had finished a poor third; but these
fellows were foreordained enemies of Conkling in any event,
and he had lost nothing by hurting them, as he would have
gained nothing by helping them. The hardheaded delegates,
the in-betweens, the practical men, knew now which was the
bandwagon—and therein lay the senior senator's victory.
For whether he had proved himself a marvelously lucky man
or a genius at manipulation, or both, there could now be no
doubt that he was master of the Republican party in New
York State.

Parenthetically, General Woodford was not elected, for
the Democrats scored a victory that year in New York. But
this in no way affected the Conkling leadership. Conkling
had got Woodford the nomination, and Woodford was
Grant's friend. The Republicans were in power in Washington, and likely to remain in power there for a long time.
And nothing less than a landslide could give Democrats control of a shamelessly gerrymandered legislature.

CONKLING had a genius for embroilment. Godkin once called
him "the great American quarreler." His enemies constantly
increased in number, and he never forgave or asked forgiveness, either at home or in Washington. Fenton and Fenton's
friends were pursued, sought out, slaughtered. Greeley's Re-

publican city committee was branded pro-Tammany, and
Greeley men got no more mercy than the Fenton men. But
Greeley was better able to fight back. He had a pen, and a
very big paper; and he struck Conkling in Conkling's sorest
spot. He hit at "the pose of that majestic figure, the sweep
of that bolt-hurling arm, the cold and awful gleam of that
senatorial eye." For Conkling was "the Pet of the Petticoats
. . . the darling of the ladies gallery" who "could look
hyacinthine in just thirty seconds after the appearance of a
woman." And: "No one can approach him, if anybody can
approach him, without being conscious that there is something great about Conkling. Conkling himself is conscious of
it. He walks in a nimbus of it. If Moses' name had been
Conkling when he descended from the Mount, and the Jews
had asked him what he saw there, he would promptly have
replied, 'Conkling!' "[5]

Conkling might have raged in the secrecy of his bedcham-
bers, but his pummeling of the editor, always rather messy,
but thorough, never ceased for an instant. The Greeley men
protested that they had merely inherited the policy of "playing ball" with Tammany, and hadn't invented it. They
wailed that the city organization could be kept together in
no other fashion. And some of the Conkling lieutenants began to waver. On September 27, 1871, at the state convention, a friend of the Senator, Hamilton Ward, proposed a
compromise. The Fenton faction, and likewise the Greeley
faction, fell quickly into line, and there was much applause.
Ward was about to put the motion formally, with every reason to believe that it would be carried, when from nowhere a
great voice boomed: "Not yet the question, Mr. President!"
The convention froze to silence. The Senator wished to
speak.

The speech had not been prepared. It lacked the usual
Conklinian epigrams and beautifully rounded periods; nowhere is it graceful to read, and in many places it is not
even grammatical. Yet its effect was amazing, and some of

the Senator's friends afterward proclaimed it his greatest effort. Certainly it served its purpose. The motion to compromise was shouted down, the Greeley delegates quit the hall amid hisses and boos, and grimly the Senator made it clear that there was only one Republican boss in New York and that he was not and never would be, either directly or indirectly, an associate of Tammany Hall.[6]

Greeley, to be sure, went on saying nasty things about Roscoe Conkling in the convenient *Tribune;* but Greeley never again was a major power in New York Republican circles.

Conkling fought, too, with Ellis H. Roberts, editor of the *Utica Morning Herald* and a considerable power among the Welsh, who were strong in Oneida. Roberts always had been a staunch friend, had helped Conkling get into Congress, had placed his name in nomination for the Senatorship. Roberts had himself gone to Congress to represent Oneida, after Conkling had moved up to the Senate. And James G. Blaine, now Speaker of the House, had appointed him with disconcerting promptitude a member of the Committee of Ways and Means. Men serve for many years in the House before appointment to that most important committee, but Roberts was put there instantly. Be sure of it, the wily Blaine was aware that there was a Conkling-Roberts quarrel brewing, and he prodded the Conkling jealousy in this manner. The rift appeared to public view in 1874, when Scott Lord, a Democrat but a close friend of Conkling, ran against and defeated Roberts for reëlection. Conkling had declared for Roberts, but none too warmly, and Roberts charged that Conkling henchmen had worked against him. Thereafter the *Utica Herald* joined the *New York Tribune* in its assault upon the giant, and Roberts, in Conkling's conversation, became "little Roberts."[7]

HE was the Boss now. No longer was he considered the leader of the younger element, the shining knight who was to rescue the party from the mustiness of Weedism. The rescue, a *fait accompli*, seemed to some not so desirable after all. The change was in the attitude toward Conkling, not in himself. He always had been a conservative, even when he first had gone to Washington, a glittering young Viking of great promise—even when he had spluttered to Chauncey Depew that the progressive elements within the party were being held back by the controllers of a vast and crushing machine of reaction—even when, more recently, his election to the Senate was being hailed as a triumph of the younger, brighter political workers.

He always had been a conservative, despising liberalism and all reform. Yet it is true that until this time he had somehow seemed a young man. And after all, he was only forty-one in 1870 when the convention at Saratoga settled all doubt as to the leadership of the party in New York State. Yet Tom Platt, who met him for the first time at this convention, and who was thrilled by the "beauty of his apollo-like appearance" and "his noble figure, flashing eye and majestic voice," noted also that the hair at the Conkling temples was "beginning to get gray."

Well, perhaps this was fitting and proper. For he was the promising young man no longer. He was the Boss now.

XVI. Imperialism, Scandal, Munitions

THE Conkling-Blaine feud slumbered fitfully. These two were in separate houses, and their warfare, for a considerable time, was at long range.

Blaine was easily the most powerful individual in the lower house, the first of the boss speakers, possibly the greatest. Men compared him to Henry Clay. Perhaps he was not so great a statesman, but he was much more effective from a partisan point of view. Clay sometimes had entered debates, but always on such occasions he stepped down from the speaker's stand. Blaine stayed there, crushing his opponents officially and not merely through rhetoric. It was said of him that he could always find a good excuse for a bad decision.

Always amiable, Blaine kept on good terms with most of his associates. But elsewhere in Washington there was hard feeling aplenty. Seward and Sumner wouldn't speak to one another. De Catacazy, the Russian Ambassador, was *persona non grata* at the White House. Salmon P. Chase was jealous of almost everybody, but particularly of Grant. Sumner wouldn't speak to Secretary of State Fish; and Grant and Sumner, as Senator Hoar has it, "each looked with a blood-shotten eye at the conduct of the other." Andrew Johnson had gone back to Tennessee, trailing his animosities, but he was to return for a short time in 1875, as a senator, to renew some old enmities. "Conkling, Carpenter and Edmunds hate Sumner," Senator Morton wrote to his wife, "but they hate me more."[1] Schurz and Conkling battled, too. Conkling was very happy in Washington.

He defended the President in almost everything—and the President sadly needed defending. Indeed, General Grant appears to have been one of Conkling's few real friends. Both were reticent, shy, though Conkling hid his reticence behind a wall of bold words, while Grant drew back into silence like a turtle into its shell. They understood one another, trusted one another. Conkling even consented to try some of the Grant cigars—though he never smoked them, for he hated tobacco smoke: he chewed them, unlighted.

Logan and Morton and Conkling: they were the leading apologists, the chiefs of the "court party." They were called not the Big Three of the Grant Administration, but, in a burst of originality, the Three Musketeers.

Senator John ("Black Jack") Logan was operator of the Republican machine in Illinois. Ferocious in appearance and sometimes in manner too, the possessor of the longest and fiercest pair of mustaches in either house, he was an authentic war hero and the veterans worshiped him.

Oliver Morton was a paralytic, was carried in a chair, and spoke from that chair on the Senate floor. He was a huge man with black eyes, a black beard, thick black hair. He was clever, sarcastic, a contemptuous fellow, from Indiana.

There were others, too, who usually supported Grant in the Senate. They constituted something of a clique. There was Zachariah Chandler of Michigan, quiet, caustic, tall, equipped with a goatee and a decided talent for getting campaign contributions—a heavy drinker, he lived in H Street, and was rich, and gave talked-about entertainments—he was the party's best pre-Hanna business manager, at all times unencumbered by scruples. And George Franklin Edmunds, called "Moses" because he looked like that—shiny bald head, wavy white beard, long nose, a parsonic manner—he came from Vermont, sat in the first row, and habitually objected to everything, so that he got something of a reputation as a liberal. And Revels of Mississippi, a Negro sent by the carpetbaggers, schoolteachery in manner, modest, dignified, well educated. And Blanch K. Bruce, from the same state, the second (and last) Negro to achieve a Senate seat: he was tall and good looking, with wavy black hair parted in the middle, and a natty little mustache: he was not well educated, and kept quiet most of the time: he greatly admired the New York firebrand, and his firstborn (the event occurred soon after Bruce took his seat) was christened Roscoe Conkling Bruce. And Simon Cameron, the Republican leader of Pennsylvania, an old-time boss, the man Thad Stevens had believed *would* steal a red-hot stove after all.

A MINOR assignment the Czar of Recorded History might give out would be: Learn why President Grant, though retaining his iconic immobility while scandals exploded like bombshells around his head, became so wrought up about that silly matter of the annexation of Santo Domingo.

Santo Domingo was a West Indian republic nobody ever had heard much about, or cared much about, until the early part of 1872, when it created a most extraordinary stir in the United States Senate.

The nation at that time had been bothered but seldom by talk about the White Man's Burden. It was not and did not pretend to be an empire. There was Alaska, of course. Seward, mussy and lovable, had sat up with Baron Stoeckl on the night of March 29, 1867, smoking cigars and discussing Alaska. The Baron was Russia's Ambassador, and Russia, having no use for Alaska, and needing money, was willing to sell that country for $7,200,000, which was cheap enough even for a frozen waste not known to harbor gold. Besides, the Secretary of State and the Ambassador were good friends. And Washington at the time felt friendly toward Russia, which had refused to threaten recognition of the South during the war, as England and France had done. So Seward, at midnight, got Sumner out of bed—Sumner was chairman of the Senate Foreign Relations Committee—and the three of them worked until four o'clock in the morning framing a treaty which subsequently was ratified with little delay.[2]

Denmark, noting this, and also needing cash, soon afterward offered St. Thomas and St. John, in the West Indies, for $7,500,000. It seemed a lot for two islands comprising only seventy-five square miles between them and inhabited chiefly by mosquitoes and black men who made rum. Moreover, Denmark's luck was not good. While the proposed treaty was before the Senate Foreign Relations Committee, there was an expensive earthquake and hurricane at St. Thomas. The treaty was rejected.

There were sundry little islands here and there in the Pacific, upon which American naval officers had signed semi-official or entirely unofficial treaties with cannibal kings. Nothing definite had been done about the Hawaiian group, then called the Sandwich Islands, though they were filling rapidly with Yankee missionaries and Yankee traders, and it was generally supposed that sooner or later they would be annexed.

Now the Island of Hispaniola was divided into two republics, both black. In Haiti the inhabitants spoke French, in Santo Domingo they spoke Spanish; and they were usually at war. It was Santo Domingo which decided that annexation to the United States would be desirable. At least, President Baez, who feared that otherwise he wouldn't keep his life, much less his job, had been suggesting it for some time, though nobody paid much attention to him. Andrew Johnson, in his last message to Congress, had recommended annexation; but nothing had been done. It was Grant who stirred up all the excitement—Grant, who ordinarily only asked that things be kept quiet.

Soon after his inauguration he sent his private secretary, General Babcock, to Hispaniola, ostensibly to study the Bay of Samana, in Santo Domingo, as a possible American naval station. Babcock returned with one treaty for leasing the bay, and another for taking over the whole republic. Grant instantly became enamored of this second treaty.

Here he was almost alone. The average senator didn't see how the United States could possibly be benefited by the acquisition of half an island filled with truculent Negroes. Hadn't we had enough trouble with our own Negro population, at home? The Senate was cool, and Sumner shook his head, disgusted. There was no ratification. But Grant, in his annual message of December, 1870, pleaded for appointment of an investigating commission. Well, this could do no harm, and it might make the President happy. So a commission was appointed. It investigated, and reported against annexation.

Still Grant was not quieted. The phlegmatic general became very active. He had failed even to mention the framing of the treaty to his own Secretary of State, Hamilton Fish, and Fish, indignant, wished to resign—but Grant persuaded

him to remain. Grant called in Roscoe Conkling and Oliver
Morton and other faithfuls, and pleaded with them to bring
the matter up again in the Senate. They were obliging,
though not at all enthusiastic. Grant went to the capitol in
person, and buttonholed senators like any eager lobbyist,
and tried to talk them into voting for ratification of the
treaty. His interest was downright embarrassing, and certainly strange.[3] Even Badeau, intimate with the general
though he was, admitted that he couldn't understand why
Grant was so worked up about the matter, and hazarded the
guess that it was sheer stubbornness. And if Conkling knew
the secret, he never made it public.

It became a factional matter, a test of strength. Sumner
passed from disgust to alarm. Let Grant have his island, the
court party leaders were urging Sumner; but he was finding
great issues involved, sacred principles endangered. The
ratification resolution, he declared, "commits Congress to a
dance of blood." He was very eloquent, yet at the same time
a shade ridiculous. His frenzied idealism, which had seemed
glorious to some before the war, now seemed only rather
silly. He never had had a following, an organization. He
never had been a manipulator. He was a pompous, overedu-
cated man, and he'd outlived his time.

Conkling, answering the "dance of blood" speech, coldly
suggested that the foreign relations committee "ought to be
reorganized." There was much talk of forcing out either
Carl Schurz or Sumner himself, and filling the vacancy with
Conkling.

The treaty wasn't ratified. The whole business caused a
wave of feeling against the court party in the Senate, and
Sumner came in for huge, soft blobs of sympathy when, the
day after the rejection of the treaty, his dear friend Motley,
the historian, was removed as Ambassador to the Court of
St. James's. It looked like petty spite on the part of Grant,
though it wasn't.[4] Motley, like Sumner, was a highly intellectual gentleman from Massachusetts, and an insufferable

snob. Americans in London found it as easy to meet the Queen herself as the American Ambassador. The bluff Grant constantly was hearing complaints about this. Also, Motley dealt directly with his equal in Washington, Sumner, and in much of his official correspondence ignored the President and the Secretary of State.

Nevertheless, the removal of so distinguished a man as Motley, coming as it did immediately after Sumner had squelched the Santo Domingo treaty, was a bad thing for the Presidential prestige. Nor was public feeling soothed by the appointment of Motley's successor—a typical Grant appointment, another general. For it had become a fixed custom to give the St. James post to some wealthy admirer of escutcheons from New England, some personage more English than the English themselves. And Schenck was very American indeed. The home people were somewhat shocked; though the English themselves were delighted with Schenck, the more so when they learned that he was the author of a book on draw poker, which was all so quaint and exciting. Much of this delight faded, however, when General Schenck permitted the use of his name on an Emma Mine prospectus. Englishmen lost thousands of pounds in the Emma Mine, and Schenck went home hurriedly. This did not help General Grant.

THE Black Friday business, too—*that* had a bad smell.

Jay Gould, a mild-mannered, soft-spoken, apologetic little fellow who raised orchids and azaleas, but who during office hours was one of the crookedest, most treacherous, most cold-blooded operators ever known even in Wall Street, in 1869 essayed to corner gold—and very nearly succeeded. On Friday, October 4, the thing was climaxed. Millions were lost (though not by Gould!) and firm after firm went to the wall. Bankruptcies, suicides, broken homes, were the wake; the whole industrial structure of the nation was jolted in a few mad hours of trading precipitated by one man as a result of

many months of careful planning. The scheme had required
assurance that the Government, the largest holder of gold in
the country, would not release any of its store. The Government *did* release gold, and the panic was halted, but by that
time Jay Gould had got out from underneath—and by that
time, too, the damage had been done.

Gould and his associate, boisterous Jim Fisk, had sought
to convince Grant that the Government should not release
gold, come what might. Their methods had been devious, and
spread over a considerable period of time. They had pinned
most of their hope, however, upon A. H. Corbin, brother-in-
law of President Grant, who was to use pressure on the President, and who, incidentally, was to receive a million or so of
the profits.[5] When the President visited Corbin in New York,
Jay Gould and Jim Fisk entertained him, wined and dined
him, took him to a show, accompanied him on one of Fisk's
steamers to Boston, talking all the while about the wisdom of
keeping the Government gold intact.

This came out later, unofficially at first, then officially in a
congressional investigation which resulted in little else but
resounding phrases. It looked bad for Grant, whose childish
admiration for rich men and their appurtenances was well
known to everybody, and whose wife's relatives seemed to be
without number though never without good jobs. Not that
Grant was believed to be dishonest. But it does not comfort
the average citizen to think that his President has been a
dupe. As Henry Adams put it: "With the conventional air
of assumed confidence, everyone publicly assured everyone
else that the President himself was the savior of the situation, and in private assured each other that if the President
had not been caught this time, he was sure to be trapped the
next, for the ways of Wall Street were dark and double." A
man could be a fool twice. Indeed, a man usually was.

No doubt about it, Sumner had outlived his day in the Senate. Somebody more acceptable to the court party must be

placed upon the Foreign Relations Committee. A proposal
was made in caucus to substitute Roscoe Conkling for Patterson, but Sumner objected, and this was dropped. Sumner
was causing all sorts of trouble. He wouldn't deal with Grant
or with Secretary of State Fish. His egotism was appalling.
He thought that he himself should be Secretary of State—
thought he should have been under Lincoln, replacing Seward—thought he would have been under Ben Wade, had
Johnson been put out of office—and was furious when Grant
didn't give him the portfolio. He never hesitated to say that
he was the man best fitted for the position. And indeed, he
acted anyway as though he were the whole State Department.

Before the war Charles Sumner had been a great Abolition leader, and Preston Brooks with his cane had made a
martyr of him. Since the war, things had changed. But not
Sumner. "It sometimes seemed as if Sumner thought the Rebellion itself was put down by speeches in the Senate, and
that the war was an unfortunate and most annoying, though
trifling disturbance, as if a fire-engine had passed by."[6] He
affected ultra-English clothes, brilliant plaids, vivid con-
trasting colors, invariably white spats. So startling was his
appearance that when Jesse Grant, the general's son, first
saw him at the Grant home in I Street he wondered what
medicine show he was in.[7] Yet Sumner had fulfilled Abe Lincoln's idea of what a bishop should look like and talk like,
and his manner was such that being in his presence *was* like
being in a cathedral.

Now he was going wild, seemingly convinced that he could
do no wrong. He was always eager to have persons know how
extremely learned he was, and once he boasted to Welles that
he had read everything "on what constitutes a Republic,
from Plato to the last [latest] French pamphlet." Yet with
it all he was jabbering that England owed the United States
two billions of dollars, for hadn't the Civil War cost about
four billions? and hadn't England by reason of her sympa-

thetic treatment of Southern blockade runners caused it to last twice as long as it should have lasted? He was proposing that in payment England should cede Canada and other American possessions to the United States. It was perhaps as well that Charles Sumner was not appointed Secretary of State.[8]

Still, he was firmly placed. Seniority was not so important in the Senate then as now, but it was important enough, and Sumner had been chairman of the Foreign Relations Committee for many, many years. He believed that the position was his by right, and announced this so frequently and with such eloquence (for the man could talk!) that others came to believe it too. Such a person is not easily dislodged. It required the French arms debate, the last straw, to do that.

THROUGHOUT the Franco-Prussian War popular sympathy in the United States had been with Germany. Germans had been pouring into this country for some years. They became citizens, and good citizens too. Large numbers of them had fought for the Union. The German vote was an important consideration in many a Northern state, though notably in New York and Wisconsin. There were no French newcomers to offset this influence. Also, Americans had viewed the career of Louis Napoleon with mistrust. They saw nothing wrong with Bismarck; but Louis Napoleon seemed always to be threatening war, to be trying to emulate his well remembered but not wept-about uncle. The Maximilian business in Mexico, too, had been largely Louis Napoleon's doing; and Americans didn't like that.[9]

So it was that Sumner created all the excitement he probably had expected when on February 12, 1872, he made charges against the administration of violation of the neutrality laws by shipping arms or permitting the shipment of arms to France, and the following day offered a resolution calling for an investigation. The debate flared, got too hot even for this oratorical giant, and he summoned Carl Schurz.

Morton, Conkling, Logan, and the others promptly rallied around the President, and there were two weeks of indescribably bitter debate. Corbett, Frelinghuysen, Carpenter, Nye, and Trumbull all got into it, besides the Three Musketeers and Sumner and his friends; but Conkling and Schurz were the headline attractions.

"If we regarded the defeat of the renomination of General Grant as the sole object and end of political work at this moment," severely stated the *New York Tribune* of February 12, "we would be perfectly satisfied with the performance of his thick-and-thin partisans in the Senate and in the press."

The Senate was a caldron, and oratory hissed and seethed therein, and boiled and bubbled, while steam rose to the ceiling.

Sumner might be expected to make a damned fool of himself, members of the Grant apology squad thought, but Schurz was something new—and more dangerous. They trained their heaviest guns upon him. Did he plan, then, Morton demanded to know, to arrange for "a smelling committee to be set upon the President . . . just as you would put a detective upon a suspected criminal"? And did this tall, skinny, frowning, bespectacled *Herr Doktor* of a Schurz really believe, Roscoe Conkling asked, that he could speak for the great German population of this great country? Conkling himself did not pretend any right to speak for them, though he did "venture to say that the Germans of the State of New York and of the other States cannot be hoodwinked, or nose-led, or handed over, by any man, whoever he may be." What charges, after all, had these fellows brought? What was there to them? "There is not one substantial averment which has not been pulverized!" An investigation, eh? Very well!

Let us have investigation on all sides. Let there be no dark place, no nook, no corner anywhere. The American honor has been assailed; the American name has been hawked at; grave and offensive charges have been spread before the world. Let us know the truth, no matter at what cost of convenience. Let the witnesses be brought, if to bring them it be necessary to traverse continents, visit islands, vex seas. Let us know the very right and justice of this matter. Let us have laid bare the motives which have brought it about. Let justice be done, though officials higher or lower fall.

This was on February 19. Schurz replied the next day, and his speech was heartily applauded, in spite of all manner of interruptions by Morton and Conkling, who laughed and rattled newspapers until the chair was obliged to reprimand them. Schurz himself considered it his greatest parliamentary triumph.[10] Conkling, the following day, hotly accused him of swagger, showy threats, an attempt to bulldoze the Senate by posing as the spokesman for all German-Americans. Schurz was cold, his voice harsh, far carrying: "If I did and said anything yesterday that looked like strutting, then I most sincerely beg the Senate's pardon; for I certainly did not want to encroach upon the exclusive privilege of my honorable and distinguished associate from New York."[11] Those who dared, laughed. And at the other end of the building, when he heard about it, Speaker Blaine must have chuckled in his beard.

Conkling never spoke to Schurz again.

But there was no investigation. And the party whip was cracked sharply, an unmistakable warning; and a caucus decided that Sumner no longer should be chairman of the Foreign Relations Committee, this post being given to (of all persons!) Si Cameron.

XVII. Poor Horace Greeley!

IN those days people took need-for-a-third-party talk seriously. To some, in 1872, Grant and the regular Republicans appeared unstoppable. The Democrats had no strong candidate and could expect little if any help from the South, where most of the readmitted states still were under carpetbag governments. Yet there were many earnest little groups, so there were many national conventions.

As early as February there were two, both in Columbus, Ohio. One was the first national convention of the Prohibition party: delegates from nine states nominated James Black of Pennsylvania and John Russell of Michigan. The other was the convention of the Labor Reform party, a hastily organized group of men who favored paying everything with greenbacks, and who nominated David Davis of Illinois and Joel Parker of New Jersey. Davis and Parker postponed their decision as to acceptance, desiring to wait and see whether any other conventions would nominate or endorse them. When nothing of the sort happened, they declined—in June. Some of the Greenbackers got together again after that and nominated Charles O'Conor of New York instead, not taking the trouble to nominate a Vice-presidential candidate. O'Conor didn't accept, but the convention adjourned anyway. It didn't make much difference.

The women, too, held a convention, organizing as the Equal Rights party, contending that the Fifteenth Amendment had given them suffrage, and nominating the editor-banker-wife, Victoria Woodhull. It was the time of Charlotte Wilbour, Jocelyn Gage, Grace Greenwood, Isabelle Beecher Hooker, Rachel Moore Townsend, Elizabeth Cady Stanton, Josephine Griffing, Susan B. Anthony, Phoebe Couzens, Pauline Davis, Reverend Olympia Brown. . . . There had been a burst of woman's suffrage activity the previous winter, and Victoria Woodhull herself had shocked or amused the members of a congressional committee (not to mention everybody else in the country) by appearing before them in a "business suit"—a skimpy skirt of dark blue cloth, a jacket with coat tails, and a severely plain, steeple-crowned hat pulled down over her short hair.[1]

All this caused no consternation among those close to the throne. However, there was some fear that the liberal Republicans, if they banded with the Democrats and other discontented elements, and got a strong candidate, might yet be dangerous. Such a candidate, say, as Charles Francis Adams.

In April, Roscoe Conkling informally asked Charles Francis Adams if he would care to accept the Republican nomination for Vice-President. The austere New Englander, presumably with a snort, refused.[2]

When a call went out for a national convention of the Liberal Republican party at Cincinnati, May 1, it was understood that tariff reform was chiefly to be sought. Tariff reform and jobs. It was a conclave of cranks and high-minded idealists, ambitious youngsters and broken, cast-out veterans. "This is moving day," Carl Schurz announced, opening the proceedings. Joseph Pulitzer, an emotional young newspaperman from St. Louis, was secretary. Other newspapermen there were too—Henry Watterson, Whitelaw Reid (who couldn't convince the rest that his boss, Horace Greeley, had a chance to get the nomination), Murat Halstead, Horace White, Samuel Bowles.

Reuben Fenton was there. Where else could he go?

The platform started bravely enough:

The administration now in power has rendered itself guilty of wanton disregard of the laws of the land, and of usurping powers not granted by the Constitution. . . . The President . . . has openly used the powers and opportunities of his high office for the promotion of personal ends. He has kept notoriously corrupt and unworthy men in places of power and respon-

sibility. . . . He has used the public service of the government
as a machinery of corruption and personal influence. . . . He
has rewarded with influential and lucrative offices men who had
acquired his favor by valuable presents. . . . He has shown
himself deplorably unequal to the task imposed upon him . . .
and culpably careless of the responsibilities of his high office.

There were scorching sentences for "the partisans of the administration, assuming to be the Republican party and controlling its organization," who

stood in the way of necessary investigation and indispensable
reforms . . . kept alive the passions and resentments of the late
civil war, to use them for their own advantage . . . resorted to
arbitrary measures in direct conflict with the organic law, instead of appealing to the better instincts and latent patriotism
of the Southern people . . . degraded themselves and the name
of their party . . . by a base sycophancy to the dispenser of
executive power and patronage . . . sought to silence the voice
of just criticism, and stifle the moral sense of the people, and to
subjugate public opinion by tyrannical party discipline. . . .

But thereafter the platform waxed funambulistic. A guf-
faw rose from the ranks of old-line politicians when they
read the tariff plank, which asserted neither this nor that,
but steered a serpentine course, in and out, backward and
around, finally succeeding in saying nothing, except, apologetically, that the tariff was after all a local issue!

Even louder, much louder, was the laugh which rose when
the balloting had been completed. Charles Francis Adams
led until the seventh—though Adams himself had gone to
Europe—and on the seventh ballot Horace Greeley was
nominated.

A motion to make the nomination unanimous was howled
down.

HORACE GREELEY was a clever editor, no doubt of it, and
a brilliant man; but he was eccentric, erratic, unpredictable;

thousands even thought him mad. To look at him, merely to think of him, was to laugh. His baby-smiling face, his bald head, his always-misplaced eyeglasses, his bulging umbrella, the way his trouser legs kept coming out of the tops of his gaiters—these were things which needed no caricature but simply reproduction in exact detail. The work of the cartoonists was done for them in advance. So, too, was the work of the journalists and pamphleteers. For Greeley in the course of a scintillating career had said almost everything, and could be called upon to contradict himself, by means of past utterances and writings, upon almost any given subject.[3]

He was the worst possible candidate. Obviously the endorsement of the Democrats was needed; but would Democrats endorse a former Whig, a Black Republican? Southern support was necessary; and would Southerners vote for an Abolitionist? The candidate should have been personally impressive, to offset the strong-silent-man glamour which enveloped Grant. The candidate should have been at the very least noncommittal on the matter of the tariff, yet Horace Greeley boasted that he was "ferociously protectionist."

Nobody could understand it. Not even those who had done it.

THE Democrats, meeting at Baltimore, did endorse the Greeley candidacy, and even adopted the Liberal Republican platform. But they were not enthusiastic. And a group of indignant old-line Democrats called still another national convention at Louisville in September, adopted their own platform, exuberantly blasting "class legislation which enriches a few at the expense of the many under the plea of protection," and nominated Charles O'Conor.

". . . we proclaim to the world that principle is to be preferred to power," their platform stated. ". . . having been betrayed at Baltimore into a false creed and a false leadership by the convention, we repudiate both. . . ."

AT Philadelphia the clockwork was perfect. General Grant was renominated by acclaim, on the first ballot, with rafter-shaking shouts of approval. Colfax had said that he wouldn't run again for the Vice-Presidency. He changed his mind at the last minute—but it was too late then, and Henry Wilson was nominated. Everybody was happy, and nobody doubted that a record vote would be cast. Roscoe Conkling was not present.

The platform, an unread agglomeration of evasions, spoke well of the Republican party:

During eleven years of supremacy it has accepted with grand courage the solemn duties of the time. It suppressed a gigantic rebellion, emancipated four millions of slaves, decreed the equal citizenship of all, and established universal suffrage. Exhibiting unparalleled magnanimity, it criminally punished no man for political offences, and warmly welcomed all who proved loyalty by obeying the laws and dealing justly with their neighbors. . . .

Yes, the Republicans were well pleased with themselves.

ROSCOE CONKLING, rejoicing, proclaimed that the desertion of the liberals had cleansed the Republican party. On the night of July 23, at Cooper Institute, New York City, he made what was perhaps his greatest campaign speech.

The doors were opened soon after seven o'clock, and within ten minutes every seat was filled and men were jostling for places to stand in the aisles. Five thousand got inside. Also "a few ladies graced the assemblage with their presence," which was gratifying if unimportant.

This meeting, after the fashion of the time, had many vice-presidents and many secretaries, all honorary, most of them proudly seated on the platform behind a flag-draped bust of George Washington. There were 234 vice-presidents and 51 secretaries. Of course it was necessary to read the entire list, and the clerks waited for applause after each

name. It was in the middle of this, when everybody was getting thoroughly bored, that the Senator entered, all 6 feet
3 inches of him, head back, eyes straight ahead, features
fixed in an expression of gravity.[4]

He created the sensation he had expected. He had a talent
for entrances.

He did not immediately start to speak. It was well to keep
the audience in a state of suspense for some time first. But
the wait, they realized when finally the oration was begun,
had been worth it. Decidedly this was a one-man show.

Grant had been attacked! And the Senator had a real affection for Grant. Stains upon the Grant escutcheon were to
be treated like stains upon his own. Not many months earlier,
the Senator had written to his friend John A. Griswold: "He
has made a better President than you and I, when we voted
for him, had any right to expect; and he is a better President every day than he was the day before."[5] And every day
since then, too, there seems to have been an increase in the
Conkling admiration for the general. Furthermore, the Cincinnati attack had been made.

Grant had fought the war and won the war, and when
peace came:

How stood he then? The nation leaned and reposed upon him,
and blessed him. Both hemispheres gazed upon him as the
prodigy and wonder of the age. . . . Yet this man, honest,
brave, and modest, and proved by his transcendent deeds to be
endowed with genius, common sense, and moral qualities adequate to our greatest affairs; this man who saved the country,
who snatched our nationality and our cause from despair, and
bore them on his shield through the flame of battle, in which,
but for him, they would have perished; this man under whose
administration our country has flourished as no one dared pre-
dict; this man, to whom a nation's gratitude and benediction are
due, is made the mark for ribald jibes and odious groundless
slanders. Why is all this? Simply because he stands in the way
of the greed and ambition of politicians and schemers.

Gifts? They said that the President accepted a diamond brooch here, there a team of carriage horses, from persons who expected favors? Well, why shouldn't he? Didn't Wellington? Marlborough? Nelson? Cromwell? Fairfax? The salary of the President, the Senator reminded, was only slightly more than that of the General of the Armies, to which post Grant undoubtedly would be returned if he retired or was defeated. Moreover, the Presidential salary didn't go as far, for the General of the Armies had none of the crushing expenses of the chief executive. Grant, said the Senator, had not really desired to remain President. He had thought not to run for a second term. "But when the shower of mud and the beating of gongs and the foul-mouthed uproar burst upon him, all felt that we were safe. Grant does not scare well."

(The Senator stood for some time, head back, eyes flashing, until the clapping and shouting had subsided.)

A war of mud and missiles has been waged for months. The President, his family, and nearly all associated with him, have been bespattered, and truth and decency have been driven far away. Every thief and cormorant and drone who has been put out—every baffled mouser for place and plunder—every man with a grievance or a grudge—all who have something to make by a change, seem to wag an unbridled tongue or to drive a foul pen. . . . When a man turns Turk he spits upon the Cross, and when wide-throated Ultra-Republicans clandestinely trade with the enemy, and then turn open traitors to their party, they become the meanest and fiercest opponents, just as a Yankee slave overseer from New England was always more brutal than those born in the South. When men whose vanity was hurt, and others gnawed by ambition and cupidity, went out to ruin the party which they could not rule, madness drove them on. They have no polar star, except hatred of Grant and his supporters.

When all was said and done, this was a simple matter for decision. "The issue is narrowed to a single inquiry: Which is personally the safest, fittest man for the Presidency?"

Grant they knew. The Senator had told them about Grant. And Greeley? "Eccentricity and fickleness are Mr. Greeley's traits . . . peevish . . . eccentric . . . grotesque and harmless . . . a man of oddities, flattered by many, and most of all by himself."

Oh, it was a simple matter! Did the people wish a "safe, tried and stable government; peace with all nations and prosperity at home, with business thriving and debt and taxes melting away," or did they prefer "a hybrid conglomeration made up of the crotchets, distempers, and personal aims of restless and disappointed men"? He left it to them. He sat down.

Weak and dizzy from hours of rapt attention, nevertheless the five thousand succeeded in finding somewhere the strength to applaud almost forever. It was one of Roscoe Conkling's greatest triumphs.

FENCES at home seemed constantly in need of repair, which irritated the Senator. It *should* have been easy, once he became Boss. He *should* have been permitted to conduct greater affairs, at Washington, ruling New York State from a distance, untroubled by petty, local fights. But this was not to be. Always the machine screeched for oil—and Senator Conkling fed it vinegar. Incredibly it kept going anyway; but it continued to screech; and scores of monkey wrenches were hurled into it the instant the Senator turned his back.

Not that he lacked able lieutenants. He must be supreme, himself, but he was more than willing to permit obedient fellows to act as assistant engineers while he was in Washington. There was, for example, Chester A. Arthur, a Phi Beta Kappa from Union College, a lawyer and teacher, large, amiable, dandified, with impressive, beautifully kept burnsides; he spoke always in a low, pleasant voice; he eschewed publicity, and enjoyed nocturnal conferences during which decanters were frequently but unboisterously emptied; he liked life, and everybody liked him.

There was Alonzo B. Cornell, a big fellow, silent, cold, with cold dull eyes, a massive head, bulging brows. He was a son of the university founder, and had been phenomenally successful as a business man. He never said anything, so they called him "the Sphinx." There was something brutal about his appearance, something ponderous, terrifying: he suggested that steamroller which starts to crush us in nightmares when legs are made of lead.

And there was Tom Platt. Whiskerless at this time, nervous, alert, with hard shifty eyes, Tom Platt was a secretive, suspiciously affable fellow, skinny, delicate, acquisitive—"a cold-blooded, mousey, fidgety little man who walks cautiously cat-wise across his own bedroom floor."[6] He had been a druggist and liquor merchant at Owego, and now he was an express company executive and eager to shine as a politician. Nobody took him very seriously, yet; but he had a genius for obeying orders, no scruples at all, and a boundless admiration for Senator Conkling.

Henry Clews, the banker, also had a great admiration for Senator Conkling, though Clews could not be called a lieutenant: he was an amateur in politics, a dabbler, very proud of his little accomplishments and delighted to think of himself as an insider. Clews attended the state convention at Utica, August 21, and was met at the station by Roscoe Conkling's secretary, who asked him, in the name of the Senator himself, to be a guest at the big square house in Rutger Street. Pleased, Clews accepted. At dinner that night there were other guests—Chet Arthur, Cornell, William Orten, General Sharpe. Tom Platt was not present. He had not yet succeeded in slipping sideways, soundlessly, into this group.

The talk was about the nomination for governor. The Senator seemed to have no special choice. Opdyke was generally agreed upon, until Clews pointed out that Opdyke had been mayor of New York City during the notorious draft riots, and also that Opdyke had been mixed up in a shoddy army contract. These things would count against him, Clews said. The others, Conkling among them, appeared to agree. Cornell volunteered to break the news to Opdyke.

After that, the consensus appeared to be for William Robertson of Westchester County. Indeed, it was generally understood the following day, when Cornell had broken the news to Opdyke and Opdyke had slambanged back to the city in a rage, that Robertson was to be the organization's choice.

Clews, however, sprung a surprise. Without any warning, he put the name of General Dix in nomination. Dix was a friend of Weed, but despised Horace Greeley. He was inclined to liberalism, had presided over the arm-in-arm convention of '66, and was an uncertain party man. Moreover, he had said that he didn't wish the nomination. But Clews's motion was received with enthusiasm, and Dix was nominated. Clews went to Long Branch, where he persuaded President Grant to write a letter to Dix urging acceptance. Dix said he'd have to consult his wife, who was to return from Europe in a few days. Finally he accepted.

"The credit was awarded to Conkling, without any hesitation or inquiry," recorded Clews, "and he was either too proud or too indifferent to public opinion to explain." But "Senator Conkling had no idea of the deep-seated enmity that lodged in the breast of Robertson."

Clews devotes two whole chapters of his autobiography to the story of this nomination, insisting that it was all his own work and that Conkling had nothing to do with it. He alone, he crows, instigated the Robertson-Conkling feud, which was to have such stupendous consequences. One wonders. Conkling and Robertson probably would have been enemies anyway, sooner or later; though there seems to be no doubt that the Senator had not much cared who became governor in 1872, being much more concerned with who became President; and similarly there seems to be no doubt that Robertson always believed he had been stabbed in the back by the organization that year, and always held Senator Conkling personally responsible for this. Robertson wasn't the sort of man who would forget, either.

The Democrats nominated Francis Kernan.

No doubt the Senator would have preferred to rest upon his great Cooper Institute speech. He liked to think that when he consented to talk at all he said everything there was to say, and that thereafter, until the affairs of the nation called for another Conkling speech, the echoes of the last one should be sufficient nourishment for a worshiping public. Still, this was a Presidential year.

The Grants visited the Conklings in Utica, a little before the state convention, and the Senator gave them a reception. Four thousand persons shook the hand of the President, while Conkling, for once second man in his own home, loomed nearby, stern and impassive.

There was a soldiers and sailors state convention in Utica, August 20, and after one of the sessions the men marched behind a band to the house in Rutger Street, where they serenaded the Senator. Responding, he told them about Grant.

Crowned with the unfading glories already earned in paths of peril, you might repose upon your laurels, and leave others to bear the brunt of the remaining fight. But no; volunteers and heroes once cannot be laggards afterward. . . . Now you see plots to destroy the fruits of your valor and your toil, and again you appear in the field. . . . The worst elements of the Rebellion, which failed in war, now creep and prowl in the stealthy path of politics, but they lift a fallen crest in vain. . . . Not content with arguing who shall be President, the ringleaders of a sordid coalition seek to blacken the character and belittle the achievements of a great soldier and a stainless patriot. You and I know the sin of this attempt, and we mean that the result in November shall be not only a triumph, but a grand vindication of Ulysses S. Grant. Rest assured that your labor is not in vain. The skies grow brighter every day. The clouds are breaking everywhere. Calumny after calumny aimed at Grant explodes, and wounds the inventors. Grant's fame is one of the treasures of the nation, and his name and his deeds will be held in grateful memory when his vilifiers have vanished utterly. But I am not going to make a speech. . . .[7]

At the Republican state convention itself he played no conspicuous part, did not even seem greatly interested. But afterward, in September and October, he consented to make campaign speeches at Watertown, Rochester, Buffalo, Olean, Brooklyn, Bath, Saratoga, Albany, Utica, Norwich, Johnstown. . . . He told people about Grant.

Dix defeated Kernan by 40,000. Grant got 286 of the 352 electoral votes, though the popular vote was only 3,597,070 to 2,834,079.

Poor Horace Greeley, whose wife (she was insane) had died only a few days before the election, resumed the editorship of the *Tribune*. But all zest had gone from that job. No longer was he the tosser of journalistic bombs, the nation's brightest and most entertaining figure, who could dare tell any man to go to hell. Suddenly sick, suddenly nerveless, broken, he slipped into a daze, mumbling, gibbering; and then into a coma; and a few weeks after the election he followed his wife to her fresh grave. And the nation, which had been making cruel fun of him, screaming with unholy delight, now abruptly felt ashamed of itself, felt sorry for the poor fellow. Thousands wept, or at least swallowed biggish throat-lumps. President Grant himself attended the funeral.

XVIII. The Worst President

GRANT had poor luck with his inaugurations. March 4, 1873, was the coldest day on record in Washington. The mercury showed four above zero, and there was a nasty, wet wind. The parade was an agony of stumbling, with men dropping out of line all the time. The very bandsmen couldn't play: they couldn't catch a full breath.

The general, and his wife, had a real fondness for the trappings of society. Much work had gone into the inaugural ball. A temporary wooden building was erected in Judiciary Square, with five sub-buildings for the caterers. The main room was 300 by 150 feet, and 25 feet high. The floor rested on a foundation independent of the walls, because of the danger of vibration caused by dancing. White muslin was everywhere, and everywhere too were canary cages filled with yellow birds expected to sing joyously in the glare of thousands of gas jets. An enormous American eagle hung from the center of the ceiling, gripping a United States shield, and from this to the surrounding walls were stretched one-hundred-foot red-white-and-blue streamers, each terminating in the shield of one of the states.

But nobody had thought to make provision against the cold. There was no heat of any kind. "Mrs. Fish wore a rich pearl-colored gown, with flounces of point lace, an ermine cape and diamonds; Mrs. Boutwell, light blue silk; Mrs. Cresswell . . ." But who cared, when it was too cold to dance, or to talk, or to do anything at all? ". . . pearl-colored satin with cherry trimmings, with a bandeau of gold and diamonds in her hair; Mrs. Delano, a pompadour dress of blue and pink; Mrs. Cooke, wife of the District Governor, emerald satin and . . ." But all the wine and the ices were frozen solid. The affair was rumored to have cost $60,000; thousands of tickets, at $20 apiece, had been sold; but by midnight there wasn't a living thing in the place—except such canaries as were not already frozen, and even those had refused to sing a note.[1]

PERHAPS all this was significant. For it ushered in four years of scandal, four years of the most corrupt, most contemptible administration the nation ever had suffered.

Grant was not responsible for the temperature on March 4, 1873, but he was responsible, in however negative a degree, for many more terrible things which followed. People protested that at least he was honest, and was merely too trusting, too slow witted. But ignorance and ineptitude, pitiable elsewhere, are sins in a President of the United States. Grant was the worst President we ever had.

He didn't seem to care. He kept his mouth shut, and smoked his cigars, and drove his four-in-hands, and loafed in Long Branch from June to October every year. Far from trying to run the governmental force like an army, disregarding partisan affairs, as he had first tried to do, he turned from it all in disgust and permitted the Government to run itself. The king was not interested. The ministers had their way.

Then stink bombs were exploded, one after another.

There was the Whiskey Ring. The Federal Government had been cheated out of $1,650,000 within ten months. Two hundred and thirty-eight indictments were handed up. The leader, McDonald, once had entertained President Grant, and had presented Grant with that most acceptable of gifts, a pair of fast and beautiful carriage horses. The President's private secretary, General Babcock, was implicated, had been given a $2,400 diamond stud. Grant permitted Babcock to resign; and in the Senate Roscoe Conkling fought against his trial on impeachment articles on the technical ground that the Senate had no right to sit in judgment on an official who had already resigned and whose resignation had been accepted by the President. By a 35–25 vote, almost a party vote, Babcock was not convicted; but nobody doubted his guilt. Then he was given a sinecure as superintendent of the Lighthouse Board. Grant never deserted a friend, no matter how crooked.

In 1871 the District of Columbia had been put under territorial government. In the winter and spring of 1874 a congressional committee, investigating that government, turned over the case of the $700,000 DeGolyer wooden block paving contract. It seems that a matter of some $82,000 of this was dissipated in bribery. Nobody was punished; but the committee recommended a change of the form of government, which was made. Meanwhile the district was to be ruled by a transitional board of commissioners. The territorial governor, A. R. Shepherd, had been mentioned in the committee report as at least partly responsible for all the extravagance, corruption and oppression; but Grant placidly appointed him a transitional commissioner, and was amazed, and probably indignant, when the Senate rejected the appointment 36–6, one of the six being Roscoe Conkling the faithful.

The Secretary of War, Belknap, was caught red-handed selling Indian post traderships, in order to get bar-pin money for his wife. The House unanimously impeached him, but a few hours before the Senate could act President Grant consented to accept Belknap's resignation.

There was a howl of indignation when William A. Simmons was nominated collector of the port of Boston. The nomination was rejected, Senator Conkling not voting. Ben Butler, that fat, bald-headed, cross-eyed little vulgarian from Massachusetts, boasted to Judge Hoar that he'd forced the President to nominate Simmons, that he had a hold over the President. Hoar, a stern, unbending Puritan, took this tale to Grant in person: he begged Grant to deny it. Grant said not a word. He set his jaw and looked straight ahead. And after a long, terrific silence, the Judge tiptoed away, highly embarrassed.

THE President liked his job, and so did Mrs. Grant. When the Empress Eugénie was driven into exile, there was some talk of making Mrs. Grant the fashion czarina of the United States. She demurred. "In matters pertaining to good sense and fine taste, I rely upon Mrs. Fish. Say to her that you seek her presence by my direction." Mrs. Fish was the wife of the Secretary of State, and not so modest as Mrs. Grant. "I am glad the time has come when we shall have fashions of our own and not be dictated to by those who differ with us in the spirit of our institutions. This is a republic, not an empire or a monarchy. No woman, either at home or abroad, will be followed or allowed to set the fashions for this country. So far as I am concerned, the short, comfortable street dress. . . ."[2] American women continued to wear Eugénie styles; but it was a lot of fun to be an important hostess in Washington.

For undeniably the court was gay, whether on the Potomac or at the summer palace in Long Branch. The Grant dinners averaged $700 each, not counting the wines. The Grants liked to give dinners. They employed a steward at the White House—the first since the days of Dolly Madison.

BUILDING railroads was a marvelously profitable business. The Government granted you subsidies of millions of dollars and millions of acres of public lands. You were called a hero, a farsighted patriot. You awarded yourself building contracts, through junior clerks or office boys, just to keep the record straight; and made a lot of money. If you were really smart, you organized a holding company and made even more money than that. The Crédit Mobilier of America, originally the Pennsylvania Fiscal Company, was such an organization. It was formed, as has been noted, to take Union Pacific profits. And it did.

Oakes Ames, one of its officials, was elected to Congress from Massachusetts. He took with him to Washington ninety-three shares of Crédit Mobilier stock, which he distributed, in his own words, "where it will produce most good to us, I think," and he carried also a memorandum book which contained a list of fellow members who might be helpful.

The man approached was not asked for anything, specifically. He merely was given an opportunity to buy some Crédit Mobilier stock at a low price, without putting up any cash. The dividends were astounding,[3] and the stock paid for itself almost instantly; meanwhile, the Crédit Mobilier obligingly extended credit.

Roscoe Conkling was approached. He refused to have anything to do with the business. So did Blaine, and so did Bayard of Delaware, a Democrat, and Eliot of Massachusetts.

Others weren't so reticent, or so careful. Senator Logan subscribed for ten shares, and accepted a cash balance of $329 after the price had been subtracted from the first amazing dividend. Senator Wilson, Vice-President-elect, subscribed for twenty shares, in his wife's name. Garfield of Ohio, Dawes of Massachusetts, William D. ("Pig-Iron") Kelley of Pennsylvania, Allison of Iowa, took ten shares each. Boyer of Philadelphia, and his wife, took one hundred shares. Bingham of Ohio took twenty shares, and made a lot of money by holding on: most of the others, at the first whisper of scandal, rushed to return their stocks and all or the greater part of the dividend money. Vice-President Colfax, that sleek and smiling "Christian statesman," that pillar of the Methodist Episcopal Church North, explained that all his money came to him from a friend who just happened to mail it to him—an anonymous admirer, who didn't send checks, but cash. Brooks of New York, minority leader in the lower house, was a Government director of the Union Pacific, and so his one hundred shares—later he bought fifty more—were in the name of his son-in-law, Charles H. Neilson. Senator Patterson of New Hampshire held thirty shares and gleefully accepted all profits.

Of course, the whole thing was illegal from the beginning,

with the Government the principal cheated party. The scandal broke during a lame duck session, the members of which had raised their own salaries by $2,500 a year, making this retroactive for two years—which didn't put the public in a gentle mood.

Two congressional committees investigated; listened to the squirming-out-from-under stories; reported, at last, almost apologetically. Roscoe Conkling did not serve on either.

The report of the Poland committee was a whitewash, a masterpiece of evasion. The Wilson committee recommended a suit to recover Government funds unlawfully sequestered in the building of the railroad: such a suit, later brought in Connecticut, was lost by the Federal Government, and the Supreme Court sustained the decision.

Most of the congressional stockholders had hastened to turn in their stock and remit their profits, and were exonerated. Colfax and his story of the nameless benefactor were not even mentioned in the Poland report.[4] The House censured but did not expel Brooks and Oakes Ames. There was no other punishment, for all the fuss.

"It has been often asked how the managers of the Crédit Mobilier could be guilty of bribing men when nobody was guilty of being bribed," writes Senator Hoar. "But the answer is easy. The managers of the Crédit Mobilier knew that they had violated the law, and that an investigation would ruin their whole concern. The men who received the stock were in ignorance of this fact."

However, the public was more inclined to agree with Oakes Ames, who growled to a reporter the night the Poland report was brought in: "It's like the man . . . who committed adultery, and the jury brought in a verdict that he was guilty as the devil but the woman was innocent as an angel."

"Does anybody suppose," Oakes Ames added, "that such men were such fools they didn't know what they were buying?"[5]

NELLIE GRANT, nineteen, on May 21, '74, was married to an Englishman, Algernon Sartoris, who was twenty-three, in the East Room of the White House, which was decorated with tuberoses, spiræa, lilies-of-the-valley and other flowers. A rug sent by the Sultan of Turkey covered the dais in front of the east window, which was canopied by ferns and vines, and surmounted by a marriage bell made of white blossoms. Nellie wore white satin with point lace: it had cost $2,000. Algernon carried a rather startling bouquet of orange blossoms and tuberoses with a center of pink buds from which rose a tiny flagpole with a silver banner bearing the word "Love." There were eight bridesmaids in white corded silk covered with white "illusion," or tulle, with sashes of the same material arranged in loops from the waist down. Bessie Conkling was one of them, and a proud but stern father, watching her enter, nodded approval. He was ambitious for Bessie. The Marine Band played Mendelssohn's "Wedding March."

MEANWHILE, the South was being mishandled. Northern leaders were not pleased when the Johnson-organized state governments of the South sent back to Congress the same fire eaters who had done so much to cause and to carry on the war. They were still less pleased when in December, 1866, and January, 1867, state after state below Mason and Dixon's Line contemptuously turned down the proposed Fourteenth Amendment: it received not a single vote in the legislatures of Louisiana, South Carolina, and Mississippi, only one in Virginia, two in Georgia, three in Arkansas, ten in Florida, eleven in North Carolina. Rejection of this amendment might mean, probably would mean, a resumption of power at Washington on the part of the Southern leaders who, in ante-bellum days, whether regarded numerically, by population, or by taxable property or area, had enjoyed far more than their share of it.[6]

The South *must* be humbled! The carpetbag governments

resulted, and indescribable corruption and confusion. Not visiting Northerners alone, but also the local scalawags, were responsible for this. Nor were the scalawags themselves wholly blamable. There always had been a strong minority party in the South, but it had been kept in submission by the fire eaters, the brigadiers. Now, patted on the back by the Federal Government, and presently reënforced by the Negroes, it was coming into power—and determined to remain in power. There were "buckshot wars" in Alabama, Arkansas, Louisiana, when each of these states suffered under two crooked governments at the same time. Capitols were occupied, besieged, fought over; and of course the carpet-baggers, not always in vain, beseeched the Federal Government for help.

In the Southern states restored to the Union by 1868, 10 of the 14 United States senators, 20 of the 35 representatives, and 4 of the 7 governors had met their constituents for the first time either during or after the war; Governor Bullock had gone to Georgia from the North in 1859; all members of the two houses of the Alabama legislature paid a total of less than $100 in taxes in 1868; members of the South Carolina legislature paid only $635.23 in taxes that year, and 91 of them paid none at all.

A reaction was to be expected, and of course Washington was blamed. Long before the passage of the amnesty act of May 22, 1872, which enfranchised all but a few hundred whites, secret societies had been dabbling in terrorism. There had been such societies before and during the war—the Black Cavalry, Men of Justice, Home Guards, Heroes of America, Red Strings, Peace Societies, Constitution Union Guards, Pale Faces, White Brotherhood, Council of Safety, Seventy-six Association, Sons of Seventy-six, Order of the White Rose, White Boys, the White League of Louisiana, the White Line of Mississippi, the White Man's Party of Alabama, the South Carolina rifle clubs. . . . The Ku Klux Klan started in a small way, too. Quite as large and as important a post-bellum organization was the Knights of the White Camellia, which was formed in Louisiana and spread quickly through the deep South: its members were generally more substantial and conservative than the members of the Invisible Empire; but after 1868 or 1869 the better class began to get out of both organizations.

The act of April 20, 1871, gave the President despotic powers in the management of uprisings in the South. Grant, so far from being the military tyrant some of his enemies called him, was reluctant to use these powers in spite of all sorts of pressure brought to bear upon him by the desperate carpetbaggers. Pierrepont, his attorney-general, appealed to, decided that the act of April 20, 1871, the so-called Ku Klux Klan act, authorized the President to intervene only in "cases of an insurrection in any state against the government thereof"—though often enough it was difficult to tell which was the proper and legal government of a given Southern state. In other cases, Pierrepont decided, the power to put down an insurrection might belong to the Federal Government, though not necessarily to the President himself. The Ku Klux Klan act, he thought, made it "lawful" for the President to intervene, but not obligatory, or even justifiable, except where the state government already had exhausted its own powers. Grant sent troops to nine South Carolina counties in March, 1871, thereby causing a lot of hard feeling. Many other requests he turned down. Nor were the Federal troops themselves ever blamed, even by professional Southerners. It was generally agreed that the soldiers governed Southern states better than those states ever had governed themselves. It wasn't that. It was just the idea of the thing; for the South, defeated, was touchy, irritable.

Possibly the North had shown too much mercy? "It may well be doubted," thinks a recent writer, "if either the confiscation of the large estates in the South and the division of them among the negroes, or the execution of a few of the leading traitors, or both, would have left such bitterness in the breasts of the southerners as was actually left by the Reconstruction acts and their aftermath. It was certainly true that at the close of the war these leading traitors did not hope much better for themselves than a halter, and their countrymen at that time would not have been greatly disposed to regret such a fate to these authors of all their woes. As for the negro, he would have been benefited a great deal more by forty acres and a mule than he was by the ballot, and the former would have been conceded to him by his white neighbors with a great deal more grace than was the latter. Moreover, if he had forty acres and a mule, sooner or later he would have obtained the ballot, and under such circumstances as would have been of value both to himself and his country. It is notorious that the negro's disenfranchisement in the South at the present time is not due nearly so much to his color as to his economic dependence. Wherever he is the possessor of so much as forty acres of land he can have the ballot if he wants it."[7]

All guesswork, of course. But it is no guess that the wavering, off-again-on-again course eventually pursued by the Federal Government was unsatisfactory to all concerned, radicals and conservatives alike, Northerners and Southerners, Republicans and Democrats. The carpetbaggers and scalawags got their power, but they couldn't hold it; and they won for themselves the imperishable hatred of their neighbors. The Negroes got the vote, but for all the Fifteenth Amendment it soon was taken away from them. The South went solidly Democratic, and stayed that way, which was and is a bad thing for South and North alike. Economic recovery was delayed, and this delay hurt Northern merchants and manufacturers as much as it hurt Southern agriculturists.

It was during the two Grant administrations that the hard feeling was hottest, the misunderstandings most numerous; it was then that radical leaders were most ineffectual in their attempts to dictate terms to the South, and when they most

shamelessly waved the bloody shirt in an effort to stir Northern hatred; and it was then that Southerners, dripping with
self-pity, most bitterly blamed the North for all their woes.

NEVERTHELESS, General Grant himself continued to be popular—personally popular.

His administrations didn't escape censure; but this was
directed not so much at the President himself as at the men
behind the President, the dangerous, all-powerful Senate
clique. Conkling, Logan, Morton, Carpenter, Chandler—
these were the villains of the piece! And of these men it was
generally believed that Roscoe Conkling had the greatest
power with the President. Even *Harper's*, which called him
"the cleverest and most unshrinking courtier of an Administration under which the Republican party has been well-
nigh ruined," was obliged to admit that "it is undoubtedly
true that Mr. Conkling has declined more splendid offers of
official position than any man in our political history."[8]

He could have had a cabinet portfolio, any one; or an
ambassadorship. Salmon Chase died May 7, 1873, and nobody was astonished when Grant offered the chief justiceship
to Conkling. The Senator respectfully declined. The Supreme Court bench is a place for whitebeards who are almost
ready to die, for old fellows who care to end their days in an
atmosphere of interminable argumentation. Conkling preferred the storm and strife of the Senate. He told a friend
that on the Supreme Court bench he would constantly be
gnawing at his chains.[9]

Certainly he was at the height of his power, if not of his
fame. In the winter of '70–'71 he was offered a legal partnership in New York City which would have guaranteed him
$50,000 a year. He refused.[10] In January, 1873, he was re-
elected a United States Senator, without opposition.

XIX. There Was a Depression

GENERAL GRANT, on September 17, 1873, went to Philadelphia for the purpose of visiting his friend Jay Cooke, and also to place his son Jesse (on Cooke's recommendation) in a private school at Chelten Hills. He stayed with Jay Cooke that night, and he must have been very happy, for he loved estates like Ogontz. He thrilled to realize that he was the guest of the greatest financial power in the nation. He delighted to gaze upon the *porte-cochère*, the Italian garden (with a reconstructed ruined castle), the private theater, the art gallery and its three hundred paintings, the fifty-two rooms, dozens of servants. . . .

Jay Cooke himself seemed untroubled by reports coming into Ogontz by his private telegraph wire, and to Grant these meant almost nothing. There had been a big fire in Chicago a couple of years before, a big fire in Boston the previous year, and an exceptionally large crop of wars in various parts of the world. Foreign money markets, and notably that of Vienna, were not steady. On September 8 the New York Warehouse and Security Company had failed, and two days before Grant's visit Kenyon, Cox and Company had smashed. These firms had been deeply interested in railroad reorganization; and there were rumors that George Opdyke and Company, similarly involved, was on the verge of bankruptcy. Jay Gould had been bearing Western Union with considerable success, but Jay Gould always was up to something like that. Those Wall Street men were full of tricks. But smart—very smart! And one of the smartest of them all, one of the solidest too, the basic rock of the financial world, was the President's host.

So the President was well pleased as he sat and smoked cigars packed in Havana, in large glass boxes, especially for the great financier. The country was more prosperous than it ever had been; the Government was running nicely; and all, as far as U. S. Grant knew, was right with the world.

After breakfast the following morning, the eighteenth, they took a carriage to the station in Philadelphia. The President was going back to Washington. The private wire at Ogontz was busy again, and the news was disquieting, but Jay Cooke had kept this to himself. He knew how deeply he was involved in railroad reorganization, and how deeply his New York partners were involved in railroad iron. But he said good-by with a smile to his friend the President, and he drove to his old-fashioned, uncomfortable offices in Third Street between Chestnut and Walnut Streets. There he was handed a telegram announcing that his New York branch had closed its doors. He knew what that meant. He wept.

Soon afterward he recovered to close the main Philadelphia office, in which he sat, and to issue a short, formal, falsely cheerful statement which did no good at all. This was at eleven o'clock. The Washington office of Jay Cooke and Company was closed at twelve fifteen o'clock.

Wall Street was jammed: Western Union dropped ten points in ten minutes, and all railroad securities began to fall. Third Street was jammed: the crowds couldn't believe that Jay Cooke and Company *itself* had closed up, and a newsboy was arrested as a mischief-maker for shouting copies of an extra about the Big Crash. Fifteenth Street, Washington, was jammed: a criminal trial was stopped, and everybody rushed into the street for news.

The clerks toiled all that night in the draughty, gas-lit building in Third Street, but they toiled vainly. In New York, the Stock Exchange was moved, for practical purposes, to the Fifth Avenue Hotel, where the lobby and many of the rooms were crowded all night by white-faced brokers, while prices fell and fell.

THE real crash came the following day, Friday, September 19. There were many failures, many runs. A few loans were made at 1½ per cent per day, but for the most part money was not available at any price. Gold, and gold alone, went up. Western Union, which had been selling briskly at 92¼ a few days earlier, for all the bearing efforts of Jay Gould, sank to 45—with no takers. All railroads were down; for the railroads, insanely overcapitalized, had led the descent.[1] The First National in Washington, and in New York the National Bank of the Commonwealth, collapsed with a roar.

President Grant and his new Secretary of the Treasury, Richardson, went to New York and conferred with bankers. The Government agreed to buy in five-twenties at the market price, which released about $13,000,000 in greenbacks through the assistant treasurer at New York: it was like trying to stop a landslide with fence pickets.

On Tuesday, September 23, Henry Clews and Company suspended business. That same day the Rogers locomotive works at Paterson, N. J., laid off one thousand men. *This* first marked the difference between the panic of '73 and previous financial panics in this country. One thousand men laid off. And that was only the beginning.

Before this, the bankers and brokers had known hysteria, mismanagement, bad times. Before this, their fortunes had been lost spectacularly, within a short time. But that was their business: they were gamblers, nothing more, and they should expect to suffer as gamblers sometimes do. It was part of the game, for them, or should be.

But now it was different. Now great industries were financed from Wall Street, and when Wall Street was seized by a convulsion men all over the country who had been in no way responsible for that convulsion were made to suffer. It was more than a panic, it was a depression.

The New York Stock Exchange was reopened on Tuesday, September 30, after having been closed for seven and one-half business days. Clearing house certificates were put into use for the first time, in the Street. But thousands of men were out of jobs, and stayed out of jobs for months afterward, for years. Thousands of men were starving. The country had acquired a new class of citizens—a homeless, wandering population, always potentially dangerous—not merely loafers, petty criminals, but hungry, desperate men. The roads were filled with them. The American hobo had appeared; and though the public, with characteristic cruelty, has tried to make a comic character of him, he remains to this day a figure essentially tragic, as a homeless man must always be.

So it seems that Roscoe Conkling won his reëlection barely in time. Bribery and incompetence, nepotism, scandal, the memorandum books of yesterday and the black bags or tin boxes of today—these entertain the people, angering a few, but are readily forgotten. Not so hard times. Belknap, Babcock, Oakes Ames, Schenck, McDonald, Murphy, Simmons, Corbin, and many others of the sort might be criminally ignorant, or just plain criminal; but it is when a man loses his job that he changes his vote, and empty bellies have a greater effect upon the ballot box than platform speeches. The year 1874 was a big Democratic year.

In New York the Senator saw his friend General Dix renominated but badly defeated by Samuel J. Tilden. The Democrats even won the legislature that year. They won the lower house of Congress too, for the first time in more than a dozen years, almost getting a two-thirds majority. They fumbled with tariff reform for a short time, but dropped it in order to prepare for the Presidential election of '76, in which, they were jubilantly predicting, they would win complete power—both branches of Congress and the White House as well.

ALREADY there was talk of a third term for President Grant, and nobody encouraged it more than Roscoe Conkling, even though he too was frequently mentioned as a possible Republican candidate in '76. The "Cæsarism" cry had been

raised by the press almost as soon as Grant had won his re-
election, and now it was louder than ever. Democrats were
crying that Grant dreamed of making the nation an empire,
himself the emperor. This was ridiculous; but the fact didn't
diminish its campaign value. Still, even Republicans were
muttering that there might be such a thing as too much
Grant. Such talk, to Conkling, was treason. There was an
undercurrent of it at the state convention in September, and
a few anti-third term resolutions had been drawn for presentation; but the talk never was heard on the convention
floor itself.

THE anti-third term cry raised by the press must have
stimulated in Conkling an even greater resentment of that
institution. He never had liked newspapers, never had made
friends with reporters. Possibly it seemed to him like truck-
ling. Possibly his natural reticence was the reason. Or, again,
it may be that he hated the press because of its power—politically much greater in those times than it is today. Always
he was jealous of power in others.

Until the fight with Ellis Roberts, which this year burst
into full flame, he had enjoyed at least the nominal support
of the *Utica Herald*. Now he was without any journalistic
backing at all in his own city—and very little elsewhere—
until his friend Lewis Lawrence, the richest man in Utica,
started the *Daily Republican*. The *Republican* was intended
to be Senator Conkling's own organ. Lawrence brought
John F. Mines, a crack newspaperman from New York
City, to be its editor. Senator Conkling consented to submit
to an interview by Mines himself—and promptly upon publication raged that he'd been misquoted. This was characteristic of him. The reporter always was wrong, and he, the
Senator, was always right.

The *Utica Republican* lasted two years, and cost Lawrence a lot of money.

YES, he suspected power in others, distrusted them because of it. The men he fought were mighty men, or else men who pretended to be mighty. To the humble, the quiet, the unassuming, he could be charming—sometimes. His inherent nervousness, shyness, was a handicap. Parker tells a story he had from Governor Wells of Virginia:

Wells was in the Senator's parlor in Washington when a woman appeared with a request to have rescinded an order transferring her husband from Washington. The husband was in the Signal Service, and they didn't wish to move because they'd bought a house in Washington, and furniture, settled there, and liked it. Conkling said:

My good woman, what do you think I am elected Senator for? What do you think the people of the great Empire State sent me here to do, to represent them in the United States Senate and consider matters of importance to them and to the nation and help make laws, or to be an errand boy, running from department to department, from pillar to post, asking that routine orders should be rescinded, and little appointments made for New Yorkers? I wouldn't come here to do such work. I can do nothing for you. Probably the order is a good one, in the interests of the service.

The woman started away, weeping; but Wells called her back. Wells offered to take her to the Weather Bureau and arrange the matter, if the Senator would permit the use of his name. The Senator was not angry; instead, he seemed pleased. "Thank you, Governor. Do it for the poor woman. I cannot do such work, though, myself. I couldn't find words to talk in her behalf if I went there. Do that for me and you will do me a great favor."

He was thin skinned, for all the front. "He was haughty, imperious and often insulting with his social equals who differed from him, but soft and gentle as a summer breeze to subordinates and inferiors," wrote Senator Vest (whom he had snubbed), adding: "He had very few friends in the Senate." He never was able to forget his own dignity. "I mean always to measure utterances with extreme care if others are to be affected by them," he wrote to a friend, "& I am not willing except in the case of a few men to induce their being placed in positions of exposed trust upon my responsibility. . . . I think Mr. T. would serve you faithfully & this is all I should like to say."[2]

There are men alive in Utica today who remember with a grin the Conkling home-comings. The Senator, except on brass-band occasions, would dismiss his own carriage and seek out his friend Bill Dunn, who drove an express wagon; he would sit up front with Dunn, and laughing and arguing politics (Bill was a Democrat), they would ride to the big house in Rutger Street; sometimes they'd pick up a crowd of schoolchildren on the way; sometimes Bill would permit the Senator to drive.

But the same gentleman met hauteur in Washington, and met it with an intenser hauteur. He remained the fire eater, the man who should have been a Southerner, the man all Southerners hated, perhaps for that reason. Duel talk never died, never was given an opportunity to die.

Mr. President, this is not the place to measure with any man the capacity to violate decency . . . I have only to say that if the Senator—the member from Mississippi—did impute, or intended to impute to me a falsehood, nothing except the fact that this is the Senate would prevent my denouncing him as a blackguard and a coward. Let me be more specific, Mr. President. Should the member from Mississippi . . .[3]

Another senator, this one from Missouri, inspired:

Mr. President, personal courage, if it be true, does not blurt or swagger . . . and men eminent for the intrepidity and boldness of their character do not strut or perch themselves upon an eminence and boast of it, especially where it is not challenged. I have no wish—far from it—to put my courage or my dangerous capacities in hopeless competition with those of the distinguished Senator . . .[4]

And the Gordon incident caused weeks of talk.

General Gordon was from Georgia, a Confederate brigadier. Conkling, in the course of a tiff on the floor, had more or less called him a liar. "We will settle that hereafter," Senator Gordon said stiffly. "We will settle it here," said Roscoe Conkling. But Gordon said: "We will not settle it here, but elsewhere." This could mean but one thing; and again, as in pre-war days, Washington was abuzz with duel talk. Senators Hamlin and Howe acted for Conkling, Senators Ransom and McDonald for Gordon, and these men talked until after midnight, arriving at no decision. Next morning they met again, and talked further, and that afternoon they issued a statement assuring a breathless nation that there would be no meeting on the field. "It is not true that any communication passed between the parties," records the busy Ben Perley Poore, "although it is known that Mr. Lamar, of Mississippi, counseled General Gordon, and that Senator Jones, of Nevada, and General Phil. Sheridan were the advisers of Senator Conkling." Later, in Utica, Senator Conkling told a *New York World* reporter that Gordon and all Gordon's friends went about armed at all times. He sniffed. He was not afraid of Gordon or anybody else.[5]

POLITICALLY the man refuses to make a biographer's task easy by stepping into a numbered space, but insists upon remaining all by himself. Socially, too, it is difficult to indicate his position.

The Conklings were Best People in Utica. In Washington, too, the Senator (and Mrs. Conkling, when she appeared) had *entrée* to the houses of all the envied; the Senator, indeed, never ceased to be a parlor lion. Yet gradually the more severe, rarified intellectuals came to despise him. And

this influence should not be tut-tutted! Men like Godkin and
Curtis and Bowles, even men like Charles Sumner, were
easily sneered away from the platform, outmaneuvered in
convention or caucus, made fools of in the eyes of the practical fellows who saw jobs and votes and very little else; but
right or wrong, such men have a prodigious weight upon the
argument when posterity has retired to the jury room.

This from *The Nation* of October 4, 1877:

Stripped of the use of patronage and compelled to rely on
purely personal qualities for popular appreciation, Mr. Conkling would have appeared simply a *nisi-prius* lawyer of the second rank, possessed of a coarse and turbid rhetoric, destitute of
any wide culture or varied or thorough knowledge, but little interested in the pressing political questions of our own country
or the drift of events in others, and without the least constructive ability or ambition.

Unjust, but not uncommon. They all felt that way about
him—all the Harvardish disapprovers, the reformers, the
men of ideals. He didn't care. More: if you had endeavored
to comfort him with the assurance that this is, after all, a
democracy, and that he was more truly representative of the
people he was supposed to represent than were the *Boston
Transcript* crowd, he would have been furious! Who, they
were asking, is Roscoe Conkling? But he didn't hear them;
and the reason is that he was engaged in asking who, after
all, were Curtis and Bowles and Godkin? They called him a
demagogue, but he didn't, couldn't, take such opprobrium
seriously. Because (don't you see?) he believed that *they*
were demagogues.

FINANCIAL panics were nothing new, nor were bad business
years. They had come in regular succession, neatly spaced,
as inevitable as the seasons—1819, 1825, 1837, 1857—as
they have continued to come since: 1884, 1893, 1907, 1913,
1920, 1929. But it grew increasingly evident, as firm after

firm crashed, and bank after bank, that here was something more than a mere Wall Street disturbance. And things grew worse instead of better. Merchants and manufacturers, big and little and middle-sized, squealed in pain and turned angry faces toward Washington. Factories were closed, mortgages foreclosed, and men were made penniless and homeless. There were strikes, lockouts, boycotts; for at this time the history of American organized labor properly begins. The number of unemployed was estimated at 3,000,-000, an appalling figure. More than 450,000 immigrants, most of them ignorant and unskilled, entered the country in that year of 1873. Some of the Southern states, desperately in debt, bitter about the carpetbag governments which had just been overthrown, were threatening to repudiate their bonds: Georgia had already done so. President Grant didn't know anything at all about financial matters, and men declared, with some truth, that the new Secretary of the Treasury, Richardson, didn't know much more. Certainly there was no general confidence in the Federal Government. It was no use to look abroad for help; for Europe, wracked with war, was having its own depression. Germany, expanding, consolidating, was bleeding a beaten France; and English capitalists sobbed and wailed and cursed the day when they had sunk so much money into the Confederacy and American railroads.

As mosquitoes appear with the coming of night, the cranks emerged from remote, forgotten places; and each crank had a cure-all; so that soon the air was filled with talk about changing the currency. The sight is no strange one to Americans of today. A frightened Congress, assembling in regular session that December, was presented with more than sixty proposed remedies, all of them inflationary.[6] It was the supreme test for that rock-ribbed defender of sound money, Roscoe Conkling.

He had grown enormously in importance since the days when, a young congressman, he had opposed so vehemently the passage of the first legal-tender bill. But his opinions were the same. He had seen that original greenback bill open the floodgates, a second issue following in less than six months, a third in little more than a year. He had heard the cry that these were emergency measures, absolutely necessary to save the nation's financial structure, yet he was aware that it was the temporary deposits and certifications of indebtedness, and not the greenbacks, which in fact had tided the Government over the worst days, in February and March of 1862, and knew that the "entire issue of greenbacks bore a small and comparatively unimportant ratio to the total resources used to carry on the war."[7] He had witnessed the trouble fiat money had caused and was causing—the uncertainty, the confusion. He had helped to frame and to pass the contraction bill calculated to call in all greenbacks. And now he was more firmly than ever convinced that the dollar should be and must be worth a full 100 cents. Back to the wall, he waited for the onrush of cranks.

"SILVER DICK" BLAND was manufacturing the thunder which later was to be stolen by young William Jennings Bryan, and a not inconsiderable portion of Congress was clamoring for free silver. Other western nations, generally, thought less of this metal as a currency base. Great Britain had been on a single gold standard since 1798. France was buying in gold and disgorging silver, which went chiefly to the nations of the Far East. The International Monetary Conference at Paris in 1867 had been almost unanimous for a single gold standard, and probably would have adopted a resolution to this effect had it not been broken up by the Franco-Prussian War. Germany, which had been using only about 4 per cent gold currency, in 1870 started to sell silver and buy gold. The price of silver, in terms of gold, began falling in 1872, as the production enormously increased; and soon afterward the members of the Latin Union (the nations using the franc unit: France, Italy, Belgium, and Switzer-

land) suspended free coinage of silver, an example which was
followed promptly by Holland and all three of the Scandi-
navian countries.

The United States, too, quit silver—at least, in part. The
act of February 12, 1873, discontinued the coinage of the
silver dollar, though it continued the silver dime, quarter
and half-dollar. This was purely an act of realism, for in
fact silver had not been in general circulation, in dollar
form, for more than twenty-five years.[8] Nevertheless, and in
spite of the fact that the act, which had been almost three
years in passage, did nothing but recognize a condition
which had been obvious to everybody since 1849, Congress
now was dinned with the first howls about the "secret murder" of the silver dollar and accusations that the act of '73
had been "sneaked through." These howls were loud, too, and
terrifying, even before the smiling churchman came from
Nebraska to organize them into a national madness.

However, Senator Conkling never was greatly concerned
with the free silver agitation, for by the time it became truly
dangerous he was involved in another great political battle,
which occupied all his time and energies, and which eventually brought him to spectacular defeat. In the Congress of
1873–74 there were few members so foolish as to believe that
the demonetization of the silver dollar (for which Conkling
had voted) was responsible for the depression, and bimetallism still was a young issue, not strong, carrying no immediate threat. The Senator's big fight was against the Ferry
bill. It was around this bill that the inflationists of all sorts
rallied, hoping to make it the opening wedge.

The greenbacks, originally $400,000,000, had been re-
duced to $356,000,000 by the operation of the contraction
act, but at the time of the panic the Secretary of the Treasury had re-issued $26,000,000. Inflationists were clamoring
for more, more, more—the old cry. It was believed that the
re-issue of $26,000,000, admittedly an emergency measure,
was illegal; the Ferry bill proposed to legalize this, and also

to authorize the issuance of an additional $18,000,000, bringing the total back to $400,000,000. It was debated for four months.

Conkling was the only one of the Three Musketeers who fought this bill: Logan and Morton, conservatives though they were, truly believed that a little inflation was needed and that this inflation could be "controlled." Even Edmunds favored the Ferry bill, though not in its original form. Even John Sherman, who later was to reach for the Presidency on his record as a sound-money man, wavered now, and compromised. Senator Conkling had for support only one outstanding fellow Senator, his old enemy Carl Schurz.

Sherman's committee cut the sum from $400,000,000 to $382,000,000—in other words, recognized Richardson's act as legal but refused to favor any further inflation. The Senate, however, for all the protests of Conkling and Schurz, restored the full figure, and in this form the bill was passed April 6, 1874, by a vote of 29–24. Eight days later it passed the House, 140–102, and went to the President.

What would Grant do? Here was the great question, and a nation held its breath. It was certain that the inflationists would not be able to summon sufficient strength to pass the bill over a veto. But nobody ever did know what Grant was going to do next, and probably he didn't know himself. There was no secret about his ignorance of money matters, and in this decision, as in so many others, he would be guided by his friends.

Most of his friends were imploring him to sign, and a terrific pressure was brought to bear upon him. Schurz could be of no service here: Grant disliked him. The only member of the court party who stood for sound money at all costs was Roscoe Conkling.

Grant was told that a veto would ruin the country, and also that it would ruin Republican chances in 1876. He weakened. He used nine days of the ten allotted to him by the Constitution, and on the eighth night he wrote a message approving the bill; he read this message to his cabinet; but later he tore it up, and the next day wrote a veto message.[9]

Eventually it was agreed to legalize the *fait accompli*, Richardson's re-issuance of $26,000,000 in greenbacks. But no new legal tender was to be authorized. Inflation had been defeated.

That the passage of the Ferry bill would have ruined the nation's credit, today is almost unquestioned. And though this is not a matter of official record, few doubted then or have doubted since that one man alone was responsible for the veto. It was one of Roscoe Conkling's greatest services to his country.

XX. The Noisy Birthday

EIGHTEEN seventy-six marked the end of a century for the Republic of the United States of America, but not the end of the depression: there were 9,092 business failures that year, a record. All sorts of more agreeable records were established at the Centennial in Fairmount Park, Philadelphia, for this was also the year in which the United States formed the habit of staging world's fairs. Hundreds of thousands thrilled to see the biggest this and biggest that; only the art exhibit was a disappointment, for domestic painters did not glitter there, and the nation as a whole, in a new consciousness of the need for Culture, was offended because European countries did not see fit to send the works of their finest masters but contemptuously shipped third-class stuff.

But 1876 is most notable as being the year of the bitterest, dirtiest national election in our history, when the party system showed at its worst, and we came breathlessly close to a second, a calamitous and final civil war.

THE Senator's loyalty was absolute, and as long as there seemed a possibility that his friend U. S. Grant might get a third term, he refused to permit his friends to spread Conkling talk.

However, feeling against a third term was strong, and even the *New York Herald,* one of Senator Conkling's few friends in journalism, raised the cry of "Cæsarism." Few dared to say anything against Grant, the strong and silent man betrayed by false friends; few cared or dared to admit that he had made an unspeakably poor President; but there was much talk about his being now entitled to lay down the heavy burden of state and return to the quiet life for which he longed. Sheer buncombe. Grant, who in the White House loafed shamelessly, would have been delighted to be made President again. In the spring of '75 he had issued a foggy statement which left everybody wondering, a sort of I-do-not-choose-to-run statement. State, county, and municipal organizations everywhere were adopting resolutions opposing his reëlection.

In September of that year, when the New York State Republicans met in convention, Roscoe Conkling was not present. He seldom missed a state convention. This time, probably, he realized that even his power was not sufficient to keep an anti-third term plank out of the platform, and dignity, tugging his sleeve, kept him away from Saratoga. The Republicans needed a strong slate, and got it, but they had great difficulty persuading good men to run: there was an unavoidable analogy to rats and a sinking ship. The platform called for "a just, generous and forbearing national policy in the South . . . a firm refusal to use military power, except for purposes clearly defined in the Constitution," and it declared "unalterable opposition to the election of any President for a third term." In the campaign, Governor Tilden, the Democratic giant, drew a crowd of 25,000 in Senator Conkling's home town. The Senator himself made speeches in Albany, Buffalo, Utica, New York

City, and other places, and attracted good crowds, but he was careful to make no mention of a third term or of gentler treatment of the South.

When the House of Representatives at Washington, by a 233–18 vote, adopted a resolution expressing the opinion that a third consecutive term "would be unwise, unpatriotic, and fraught with peril to our free institutions," then even Senator Conkling was obliged to admit that Grant had no chance. Not until that time did he tolerate talk about his own candidacy.

How he felt about it, no man can say. He would do nothing, publicly or privately, to better his chances; and even his friends were puzzled. It was generally agreed that he was ambitious to be President, and some believed that he had refused the chief justiceship for this reason.[1]

It would have been bad politics for President Grant himself to issue an endorsement, since his friend and stout supporter, Oliver Morton, also was an aspirant. Nobody in Washington doubted that Grant's personal preference was Conkling; and had Grant been able to make this preference public, Conkling stock would have risen. But the hardheaded fellows who would attend the convention had no fear of Grant's merely private opinion.

No doubt General Sherman could have had the nomination, had he desired it, for his military popularity was second only to that of Grant. But the general, whose brother Senator John Sherman tried so hard to get into the White House, snorted in disgust at the very thought. "You need never fear that I will ever be infected with the poison of Presidential aspirations," he wrote to his wife that May, "on the contrary, the place has no temptations but quite the contrary. Let Blaine, Bristow and Conkling, trained in that school of scandal and abuse, have the office if they want it, each in turn. . . ." Blaine did want it, and so did Bristow. Blaine was clever, had many friends, but his name had been tainted by railroad scandals which he never had been able to

DOOMED

U.S.G.—"Everything is giving way, and I see no cause; yet it was very strong when I first sat here."

Andy J---n—"If that obstinate man could get where I am, he would soon discover the cause. Why, it's quite empty—cracked all over, and a large piece has fallen out of it!"

Liberals—"Those fellows thought our portion of it was of but little value. Now they find that when it was broken off the whole was so weakened that it must shortly come down with a crash."

CROSSING THE RUBICON

U.S.G.—"Well, there's time enough! Before Conkling gets half-way over, these Union League fellows will have chopped away his bridge from under his feet, and then maybe my plank will just reach across!"

explain away to the satisfaction of the nation at large; and the call now was for a candidate who would offset the administration record of corruption. Bristow was acceptable to the Better Element, but not otherwise powerful. Morton's hopes, for he came from Indiana, were chiefly geographical. There was also some talk of Charles Francis Adams, admittedly a commendable sort of person. But politicians like a candidate who will win, and as Blaine wrote to a friend: "No Adams ever yet headed a party without taking the life out of it. . . . The Republican party can be beaten under some candidate in 1876 and still have a future—but if it should win with Adams it would never breathe again."

The liberals did not tremble before the name of Conkling as they did before that of Blaine. Whitelaw Reid wrote to John Bigelow in January: "I don't believe his [Conkling's] candidacy is going to produce much effect. He has no strength outside of this State and not much in it. . . ." And Henry Adams told his friend Henry Cabot Lodge, "I feel little anxiety about Conkling. . . . But I do fear Blaine, because the Convention will see that we cannot deal with him easily. He will divide us. I feel no real hope about Bristow."[2]

The liberals, unchastened by the Greeley catastrophe, nevertheless decided not to bolt the party. Almost two hundred of them met in the Fifth Avenue Hotel on May 15 and adopted an address written by Schurz which intimated, without naming any names, that Blaine, Conkling, and Morton would be alike unacceptable.

A story about Blaine, unverified but quite possibly true, was circulated as convention time approached. He was supposed to have told Jere Black that he thought nothing of Morton's candidacy, that "Bristow has a great deal of strength among the people but it is not organized. . . . I don't see how he can possibly get a majority," that Conkling's candidacy was "absurd." Black asked: "Then is there anybody to be afraid of?" And Blaine replied: "Yes, there is—the Great Unknown."

THE March 22 New York State convention for election of national delegates adopted a resolution presenting "Roscoe Conkling as our choice for the nomination of President," though 113 of the 432 delegates stood with George William Curtis in opposition.

The Democrats, it now seemed certain, would nominate Samuel Tilden, Governor of New York. And Tilden would be a strong candidate. To be sure, he had no military record, but neither did any of the leading Republican possibilities. He was sixty-three years old, tall, thin, impressive in appearance. A wealthy bachelor, who lived in Gramercy Park among his books and pictures, he was supposed to be a master-mind, possibly because he so seldom appeared in public. Best of all, his name had been associated with reform: as governor, he had broken the corrupt, bipartisan Canal Ring, and to him was given most of the glory (more than he deserved, really) for smashing the Tweed machine.

Against such a candidate obviously it would be advisable to pit somebody whose name had not been associated with either of the Grant administrations. Nevertheless, in one sense this nomination would better Conkling's chances, for it would emphasize also the need for a Republican candidate who could carry New York State, which had given Tilden a majority of more than fifty thousand, a record, two years before.

THE Republican convention opened in Cincinnati, June 14. The New York delegates brought a large orchestra, wore bright blue badges, paraded in silk hats; they hired, complete, the Grand Hotel, and in front of that hostelry stretched a banner which read: "Roscoe Conkling's Nomination Assures the Thirty-five Electoral Votes of New York," and which, according to Conkling's fond biographer, was "more imposing than the banners of the delegates from any other State."[3]

The Senator himself never had attended a national convention, and he did not break his rule in 1876. It would not have been seemly. Ex-Mayor Opdyke of New York, visiting him at the Fifth Avenue Hotel, urged him to go to Long Branch and get himself an appointment to the Supreme Court. "He would not listen to it, but seemed to think he was surely destined to get nominated for the Presidency. I told him plainly that he was too high-toned a man to be a popular candidate for President."[4] It was precisely this argument which was used against Charles Francis Adams!

For all the silk hats, the badges, the most imposing banner, the parade, New York showed miserably at the convention. The Senator's interests were not well handled. His lieutenants were lost without him. Dignity and all, it would have been easy for him to direct the work, keeping the delegates in line, by wire. He didn't. He wrapped himself in his own sense of grandeur, and sat apart, silent; while his friends bargained clumsily.

General Woodford, placing the Senator's name in nomination, said that New York State honored all the candidates already before the convention, "but let us not nominate with our hearts but with our heads." He virtually admitted that the popularity and personal charm of James G. Blaine were far greater than those of Senator Conkling; but he iterated and reiterated that a candidate, to win, must carry New York State, and he said that Roscoe Conkling was the only Republican who could do so.

The speech, though well applauded, was shadowed by another. When Bob Ingersoll spoke, men gasped. And raved about it for years afterward.

Like an armed warrior, like a plumed knight, James G. Blaine marched down the halls of the American Congress and threw his shining lance full and fair against the brazen foreheads of the defamers of his country and the maligners of his honor!

Not an accurate description of the manner in which Blaine had tried to wriggle and lie his way out of the Mulligan letters charge—but it was exciting to hear, and men screamed with delight. It caused people to believe that truly great convention speeches might thereafter have some effect upon the balloting—a fallacy which, though it persisted for some years, resulted in only two other speeches which compare with Ingersoll's, one of them delivered by Roscoe Conkling in 1880, the other in 1896 by William Jennings Bryan.

The Bristow men, the reform element, abhorred the very name of Conkling. The Morton men resented his candidacy because it hurt Morton, who, had Conkling remained out of the race, probably would have won the White House endorsement. The Blaine men naturally didn't like him. So that the New York delegates, pledged to vote unanimously for the New York boss, found themselves almost uncourted—not at all the customary condition of New York delegates at a national convention. Only the supporters of Rutherford B. Hayes flirted; and Hayes was esteemed no more than a favorite son.

George William Curtis refused to vote for Roscoe Conkling—disregarding instructions, he didn't vote at all, though he seconded the nomination of Bristow—so that the Senator had only 69 of the 70 delegates from his own state. He picked up 30 scattered votes on the first ballot, most of them from the South. He ran fourth on that ballot. Blaine was an easy first, with more votes than any other two aspirants; Morton was second, Bristow third, and Hayes and Hartranft also ran.

Blaine led until the seventh ballot. Conkling's candidacy slipped slowly; so did Morton's, and Bristow's, and Hartranft's. But quiet little Rutherford B. Hayes crept up, until on the sixth ballot he slid into second place. Obviously it was Blaine, the favorite, or Hayes, the dark horse, the Great Unknown.

The New York delegation did not even take the trouble to withdraw Senator Conkling's name. He was forgotten in the scramble. One portion of the delegation, representing what was left of the Fenton machine, had been cheering Blaine from the start "to make things uncomfortable for Conkling rather than from a warm friendship for the man from Maine."[5] The seventh ballot showed 61 of the New York votes going to Hayes, 9 to Blaine. And Hayes won the nomination.

Conkling's humiliation was not yet complete. It was agreed, it had been understood, that the Vice-Presidency at least should go to New York; and the organization's official choice was Conkling's friend General Woodford. But another New Yorker, William A. Wheeler, a man who "very much disliked Roscoe Conkling and all his ways,"[6] was named by delegates outside of his own state, and his popularity was such that the Conkling delegates were obliged to withdraw Woodford's name. Wheeler won easily.

Soon afterward, the Democrats, as expected, nominated Samuel J. Tilden. Then, since Tilden was a hard-money Easterner, and a conservative, they selected Hendricks, a radical, soft-money Westerner, as his running-mate.

They made a curious pair, Tilden and Hayes. Each was a quiet, rather shy man whose personal acquaintanceship among the leading members of his party was inconsiderable. Neither was a good speaker.

Tilden's record was by far the more impressive. He was rich, a celebrated lawyer, a scholar. Certainly if not the noisiest, he was the most distinguished Democrat of his day.

Hayes, on the other hand, was nominated not because of what he had done, but rather because of what he had *not* done. This is now an established custom; but in 1876 some men still believed that a party should put forward its best statesman. There had been exceptions—as when the deserving Seward was defeated by an almost unknown Lincoln, in 1860. But even Lincoln was not picked for purely negative reasons. Hayes's greatest qualification for the candidacy lay in the fact that nobody had anything against him.

Hayes was a lawyer, and fairly successful. He had served in the Civil War, had been a colonel, had become a general, had been wounded: his military record was sound, if not spectacular. He had been Governor of Ohio, and a tolerably good governor at that. Once he had even served in Congress, soundlessly, briefly: almost nobody in Washington was able to remember him.

And when, having nominated him for the Presidency, Republicans crowded around for a look at him, they saw a man of average height, though somehow he seemed smaller; an affable, rather untidy fellow; a wonderful listener, quiet, canny. There was about him unmistakably the air of a country doctor. He could and did keep his mouth shut, though he never looked notably wise. He had been born of Scottish and English ancestry—not in a log cabin, alas, but in the first brick house in Delaware, Ohio. Still, he was as emphatically middle class as he was Middle Western. He liked lodges, and was an ardent G.A.R. man, favoring practically unlimited pensions for Union Army veterans. His opinions on other national issues nobody seemed to know.

It should have been a Democratic year. All the signs were there, and the portents. Tilden was a magnificent candidate, Hayes a very poor one, disliked and distrusted by some of the greatest leaders of his party. Much of the war feeling had died, at least in the North, where waving the bloody shirt no longer was a sure way to get applause. The money crowd knew little of Hayes, but they knew and trusted Tilden, the corporation lawyer, the sound-dollar man. The Republicans had disgusted and angered the country again and again. And, most important of all, times were hard.

Everything depended upon the South. Negroes still were supposed to be voters in the South, where "grandfather clauses" and the like had not yet been devised, and the voting machinery was in the hands of Republicans in the states still under carpetbag rule. But the South had methods of its own. Backed by Federal troops, the Negroes and their friends might prevail. But Federal troops couldn't be everywhere. In remote back-country places the word "bulldoze" was being added to the language—you gave a nigger a dose of the bull whip—a "bull's dose"—which taught him to keep away from polling places. South Carolina, Florida, Louisiana: these were especially in doubt.

SENATOR CONKLING's health was poor, a condition to which he was unaccustomed, and which might account in part for his pessimism. He didn't think the party could win. He despised Hayes, and was disgusted with the work of the convention. He sulked in his tent. Candidate Hayes wrote flatteringly to remind him of the almost miraculous effect of his Cooper Institute speech in 1872, and to request, almost to beg, that he take the stump in Ohio and Indiana. "The more meetings you can address, the better, but if you speak only in two or three large cities in each of the States named, and at Chicago, and at Milwaukee, I shall feel that you have placed the country and all of us under great obligations.'" Conkling's reply, if any, is not a matter of record. It is probable that he believed he had long since placed the country "and all of us" under obligations; and certainly he was reluctant to break a life-long rule by going out of New York State for a campaign.

It was esteemed a cheering sign when a Hayes-and-Wheeler banner was unfurled in Utica. And there was much joy in the party when, on the night of September 6, responding to a serenade, the Senator (though without once mentioning Hayes's name) promised to support the ticket.

He planned four great speeches, but he delivered only one of these. It was at the Utica Opera House, October 3.

There was much muttering, afterward, that he had betrayed his party. But all except his most unreasonable enemies eventually accepted the explanation that illness had caused the silence. The Senator was suffering from malarial disorders, and his eyesight was bad. His nephew publishes a convincing letter from his physician, testifying that he had strongly advised against even the Utica speech. On that occasion, the physician wrote, the footlights were dimmed for the Senator, but even so he was obliged to lean upon a table for support, and there were moments when the physician did not think he would reach the end.[8] After that, he could scarcely be expected to blind himself by making additional speeches—remember, a speech was a stupendous labor for him—for a man he abhorred. He remained for seven weeks in a dark room.

THE election itself was quiet. Even in Charleston, in New Orleans, though the voting was heavy, there were no riots. It was the quietest election day in the history of New York City, where nobody was killed.

XXI. Dishonors Were Even

FROM the beginning it looked like Tilden. The *New York Tribune*, which was being hysterically partisan to atone for its crime of defection in 1872, conceded early in the evening that the Democrats had won. So did the other papers, all over the country. All except the *New York Times*.

The *Times* was then Republican—severe, inclined to scold, but regular. Its managing editor, John Reid, who had spent some time in a Southern prison camp during the war, hated Democrats and never hesitated to say so; and the other editors, with a single exception, were more or less active members of the Republican party.

The first edition of the *Times*, which came out at about midnight, carried a story headed "A Doubtful Election." It was not yet prepared to concede a victory to Tilden, even though the other papers had done so, and even though Zack Chandler, the national Republican chairman, already had gone to bed in disgust. The *Times* pointed out that the Democrats, to win, would have to carry New York, New Jersey, and either Oregon or Florida. They had New York —final figures showed that Tilden had polled a record aggregate vote there—and almost certainly they had New Jersey. They were claiming Florida. As to Oregon, only one Associated Press dispatch had come through, by way of San Francisco, and that was vague.

The final edition of the *Times*, at six o'clock, said that the electoral vote seemed to be 184 for Tilden and 181 for Hayes, counting Oregon, South Carolina, and Louisiana for the Republicans, but that Florida's four votes were in doubt —that is, if the Republicans had carried Florida, then Hayes was elected.

Between those two editions, things had happened.

The man in charge of the Democratic national campaign finances, Senator Barnum of Connecticut,[1] had sent to ask the *Times* what reports they had on Oregon, Florida, South Carolina, and Louisiana; and the message caused Reid to do some thinking, and some figuring. If the Democrats themselves weren't certain, was the election really lost? At daybreak he went to the Fifth Avenue Hotel. In the lobby he encountered that handyman of the party, William E. Chandler, clad in a great coat and a heavy military cloak, with enormous goggles over his eyes: he had just arrived in the city, and carried a gripsack and a copy of the *Tribune* announcing Tilden's election. He and Reid went upstairs, awakened Zack Chandler, and began to scribble telegrams.

The telegrams were sent at the expense of the *Times*—because the national committee did not have an account with

Western Union, as the *Times* did—and they went to state leaders, who were asked "Can you hold your state?" and warned not to be "defrauded."

One electoral vote was at stake. Which meant one Presidency.

THOUGH the figures varied slightly, nobody questioned the fact that Samuel J. Tilden had received about a quarter of a million more votes than Rutherford B. Hayes. But here agreement ceased.[2]

The Republicans, to win, would be obliged to carry every one of the four doubtful states.

In Oregon they had won, but a technicality rose. One of the Republican electors, Watts, was found to be a postmaster, and thus ineligible to serve as an elector, and the Democratic governor decided that all votes cast for Watts were therefore void, and that the highest Democratic candidate had been elected—that is, that the state had elected two Republican and one Democratic electors. This, alone, would mean defeat for Hayes.

In South Carolina was one of those double state governments which were complicating affairs throughout the South, and feeling ran high. But by the middle of November it was ascertained that the state would be counted Republican—though the Democratic electors were planning to send in their vote too.

In Florida the Democrats claimed a majority of 90 or 113, the Republicans a majority of 45. Two of the three members of the returning board, which took evidence, were Republicans, and they proclaimed that Republican electors had been elected. Governor Stearns, a Republican, certified these electors. But the state attorney-general, who was a Democrat, certified the Democratic electors. The law said that the electoral vote must be certified and sent to Washington by December 6. Two sets were sent. On December 23 the state supreme court decided that the returning board had no judicial power and shouldn't have taken evidence in the cases of alleged fraud—of course everybody was crying fraud—and it therefore demanded a recount, which resulted in the election of Drew, a Democrat, as governor. There was a new returning board, too, which consisted of three Democrats and no Republicans, and which dutifully returned a majority of 87 votes for the Democratic electors. Drew certified this and sent it to Washington—a little late, January 19.

South Carolina and Oregon had each sent in two sets of electoral votes, and Florida sent in three.

The nastiest mess, however, was in Louisiana.

The popular vote in Louisiana, as in Florida, was unquestionably for Tilden. But again, the Republicans controlled the returning board, and cries of fraud rent the air. Louisiana's returning board consisted of four members, all Republicans, two of them Negroes. There should have been a fifth, according to the law, and he should have been a Democrat, but he had long since resigned and the other members of the board refused to name a successor or to permit the naming of one.

The four were not lovely to view. Kenner once had been a servant in a gambling house, but had been fired for stealing; and after that he opened his own brothel and faro bank. Anderson, poor at the end of the war, became a state senator and waxed very rich indeed: later he was to play fast and loose with both parties, but at the moment he was being a Republican. J. M. Wells held a lucrative sinecure as surveyor of the Port of New Orleans. Cassanave, a Negro undertaker, might have been honest (even the doubt made him unique here!) but he was ignorant, incompetent. The clerks employed by the returning board were all Republicans, and five of them were under criminal indictment at the time.

THERE was an eruption of investigating committees. The House, at Washington, was Democratic, the Senate Republican. Each appointed a committee to investigate matters at New Orleans. Each committee returned a minority and a majority report. The House committee's majority report was for Tilden, its minority report for Hayes. The Senate committee's majority was for Hayes, its minority for Tilden. The national Republican committee and the national Democratic committee also dispatched official investigators to the scene of the crime, and these men reported respectively for Hayes and for Tilden.

That there was dirty work, and a great deal of it, nobody doubted. It was found in both parties; as a popular saying had it "the dishonors were even."

The nation looked longest and hardest at New Orleans, where those four arbiters were trying to make up their minds how many Democratic votes they should cast out. Twenty-five prominent Republicans, among them Garfield and Sherman, arrived in that city November 12, to see if they couldn't help; and the next day more than twenty prominent Democrats arrived. These men were called "visiting statesmen." The phrase was meant to be acrimonious.

The Democrats asked that full publicity be given the hearings, but this was refused.

On November 27 the canvass of the uncontested parishes was completed. There were not many of these.

The board then heard more than three hundred witnesses, nearly all of them Republicans, who were summoned by a United States marshal at a cost of $10,000 to the Federal Government. When the hearing of evidence was completed, December 2, there were 4,500 pages of it. The four paragons had three days in which to weigh this, and to come to a decision. They went into secret session.

Doubtless they knew that they were being bought and sold. They were sold as Brooklyn Bridge is sometimes sold to visitors in New York City. A state senator offered them to Henry Watterson, one of the Democratic "visiting statesman."

"How much?" Watterson asked.

"Two hundred and fifty thousand. One hundred thousand each for Wells and Anderson and twenty-five thousand apiece for the niggers."

"Cheap as dirt. I don't happen to have the amount about me at the moment, but I'll communicate with my principal and see you later."

The senator took him seriously and accosted him a few days later, asking whether Sam Tilden had made up his mind!

There are dozens of stories like this, and the horrible realization is that they're probably all true.

The four men did curious things in that smoke-filled room. They cast out all the polls in East Feliciana and Grant parishes, though they hadn't remembered to take any evidence concerning the voting in Grant Parish. They cast out polls from 22 other parishes, a total of 69 polls complete. Twenty-five hundred ballots which contained votes for only 3 electors they counted for all 8 electors. They, or somebody acting in their behalf, did some extraordinary arithmetic, and when they emerged, blinking, a Democratic majority of 7,639 had been converted into a Republican majority of 3,437.

So much for the returning board. The governor, Kellogg, a carpetbagger, promptly issued certificates for the Republican electors, and the next day, December 6, the last day possible, these personages met at 4 P.M. to cast their solemn vote for President and Vice-President of these United States. Two, who previously had held Government jobs but had resigned to become electors, stayed away from the meeting until they were appointed to fill their own vacancies, and then they appeared and voted. In a crowd of cheats, nobody was trusting his neighbor. The election law of 1870 provided for the filling of such vacancies by popular election, but this didn't matter. The certificates were not properly endorsed, and new ones, signed December 29 and antedated December 6, in Washington, contained two forgeries; but this didn't matter either. The whole business was illegal anyway, and the only question was: Which set of electoral votes will be accepted? For of course the Democratic electors had met and sent in their own vote just the same.

The electors shall meet in their respective States, and vote by ballot for President and Vice-President, one of whom, at least, shall not be an inhabitant of the same State with themselves . . . they shall make distinct lists of all persons voted for as President, and of all persons voted for as Vice-President, and of the number of votes for each, which list they shall sign and certify, and transmit sealed to the seat of the government of the United States, directed to the president of the Senate;—*the president of the Senate shall, in the presence of the Senate and House of Representatives, open all the certificates, and the votes shall then be counted.*

Thus the Constitution. There is more; but nowhere does it say anything about what the President of the Senate should do if he finds himself confronted with two sets of votes from a given state. Should he himself decide which to count and which to ignore? The Republicans, in 1876 and 1877, said that he should, for the President of the Senate then was a Republican. Or should he call it a tie, and place the matter before the House of Representatives, as further provided in the Twelfth Amendment? The Democrats thought this was the way it should be done. The House was Democratic.

There were those who suggested that the whole matter be referred to the President, or to the Supreme Court, or to a court consisting of the President, the Chief Justice, the Speaker and the President of the Senate. The Democrats cried no. The President and a majority of the Supreme Court justices were members of the Republican party, like the President of the Senate.

Obviously it would do no good to place the matter before Congress. The Senate would count the Hayes electoral votes, the House the votes of the Tilden electors. But, suggested the Democrats, helpfully, why not put the question to a joint session and accept as final the vote of the majority? The Republicans were irrevocably opposed to this, for in the two houses put together there were more Democrats than Republicans.

And there was the problem of Congress' twenty-second joint rule, originally a partisan Republican measure but now favored by the Tildenites. It had been adopted in January, 1865, before the end of the war, when the problem of readmission of Southern states first came up. President Lincoln had recognized the temporary governments he caused to be established in Tennessee and Louisiana, but Congress had refused to recognize these or to count their electoral votes. Congress had passed a joint resolution, foreshadowing the long and bitter battle over reconstruction. It provided, in effect, that a state's electoral vote should not be counted until *both* houses of Congress had agreed to accept it. When it was feared that Lincoln wouldn't sign this (but he did, eventually), the twenty-second joint rule was hastily drawn and hastily adopted. It was the same as the resolution, except that it did not require the executive's signature.

Now since the Republicans, to win the Presidency, would be obliged to get the full electoral vote of each of the four disputed states, obviously the operation of the twenty-second joint rule at this time would elect Tilden. The Republicans insisted that this rule was not in force. It had been kept in force while Congress was battling with Andrew Johnson, of course, but it had standing, Republicans contended, only if voted in again by each house of each Congress.

A House committee hopefully compiled a record of all previous proceedings and debates touching on the count of electoral votes, and this was printed.[3] For all the good it did.

What was to be done? President Grant must quit the White House and Congress must be dissolved on March 4.

Should Grant be continued? Clearly that would be wrong: nobody, not even Grant himself, wished that. Should another national election be called? But by whom?

ONLY statesmen were bothered by those nice points. To the man in the street the whole thing was perfectly simple: Hayes had been elected—or else Tilden—depending upon which man you picked in what street. The country muttered, growled. Hard feelings, tucked in black forgotten corners after the close of the war, now emerged, to stalk the streets without shame—like prostitutes who appear the first day of a new and admittedly rotten city administration.

Letters, telegrams, all sorts of messages, poured in upon Hayes and Tilden, and each candidate was begged to proclaim his right to the Presidency.

Tilden was notoriously rich, so most of the men who would peddle cure-alls addressed themselves to him. For example, Henry C. Hall wrote December 27 that he had an answer to the whole difficulty. He argued that three separate and distinct bodies, the Senate, the House and the Vice-President (whom he evidently considered a body) must count the votes. He split a multitude of all-unresisting hairs to demonstrate that the Vice-President was not a member of or a part of the Senate. So, the Republicans would win if they only realized this, as he did. "Knowledge is power, and this particular knowledge gives me the power *to be silent and allow to you the Presidency*—to speak and give it *to Mr. Hayes,*" wrote Mr. Hall.

Now, who shall be President? On the Republican side as you well know the coffers of the Astors, the Stuarts, the Camerons and a hundred others are open for me to take almost as I will. Less knowledge than mine has brought men millions . . . I shall take the best offer of money that is made over one hundred and fifty thousand dollars. And I shall be secured the right to name during the whole time of the incumbency of the man to be elected the Postmaster of the City of Auburn, twelve places in the N.Y. Custom House not including the four highest. But I will not be bound until the money is paid and a written contract of terms is executed.

Ira Copeland of Brockton, Plymouth County, Mass., scenting the need for secret correspondence, wrote to offer an absolutely undecipherable cipher—"Not merely a cipher, but a system of ciphers; yea, a universal system." So did Dr. Von Berg, of 3840 Atlanta Street, Philadelphia, who used the letterhead of the Imperial German Commission for the Centennial Exhibition at Fairmount Park.

More startling was the suggestion of Dr. Mary E. Walker, contained in eight closely written pages mailed in Washington. "There is but *one course* left to you to win success, and that is with myself an actor in the 'drama,'" wrote she; "and there is no time to lose in the matter. . . . Follow my directions without delay, and get a straggling kind of a white wig, put some dark red paint on your face, *all over*, get some shabby clothes, and come to me and I will tell you all. Do not fail to get a poor red figured silk pocket handkerchief and crush it full of wrinkles and tie it over your head around your chin, and take a sleeping car so as to be here early in the morning. Have a shabby cheap umbrella for a cane, and come to me and I can manage everything for you here."

Some urged with song. The writer of this did not sign his name:

Come all you Democrats that's just and true,
Vote for Tilden and Hendrick too,
That is the best that you can do,—
They will wear the white and blue.

On Monday night it will never be
Forgotten to see
Our Democrats and their horses treading;
You'd think it was Napoleon going to Waterloo
The Black Republicans to subdue.

The Republicans will be all forgotten—
Like potato bugs they are almost rotten:
They will never revive again,
They must take another name to hide them from guilt and
        shame.[4]

HERE was an orthodox war fever. Each side furiously rejected all talk of compromise. Each declared that the other was wrong, was only bluffing, would back down at the last moment.

This was the Democratic attitude: Samuel J. Tilden had received a quarter of a million more votes than Rutherford B. Hayes, even after carpetbaggers and scalawags and niggers had done their worst with returns from the Southern states. Tilden clearly had been elected in Florida, in South Carolina, in Louisiana. The citizens of these states, at last permitted to vote freely, had favored him. Members of the returning boards, Black Republicans every one of them, had cast out as illegal the votes of just enough districts to swing the national and state elections to their party. Which insured Republican returning boards, nonrepresentative Republican state governments, for another two years. Which in turn insured the same thing for *another* two years. And so on. There was no reason why it should ever stop. The Democrats of the country, a majority of the people, must fight or be slaves.

This was the Republican attitude: The Southerners had been openly flouting the Fourteenth and Fifteenth Amendments. By one means or another they had prevented thousands of Negroes, legal citizens, from casting their votes. The southern fire eaters, the same men who had brought about the Civil War, were trying to bluster and bully their way back to power. If Negroes were not permitted to vote, but were counted as citizens and voters in the census, then each individual white Southerner would have a vote far more potent than that of an honest Northerner. This flagrant in-

justice would be even greater than it had been before the
war, when at least a Negro counted for only three-fifths of a
man. What had the war been fought for, anyway? And who
had won? Nobody denied that there had been intimidation,
there had been bulldozing, in many Southern districts. The
state returning boards had perceived these frauds, or some
of them, and had cast out the votes of certain districts. *State
boards* had done this, remember! Not the army. Not any
Federal officials. Now, for the Federal Government to step
in and set aside the work of the returning boards, go behind
the returns reported by those boards, would be a shrieking
invasion of states' rights—the very rights the Southerners
were forever blatting about. So!

NOT for the first time Americans were thankful that this is a
nonmilitaristic nation. A large standing army, inspired by
that impatience with civilian blundering which is characteristic of large standing armies, might have pushed itself forward to assume one of those positions of temporary control
which last as long as the armies can make them last. But
American officers kept their heads. "The army should have
nothing to do with the selection or inauguration of Presidents," Winfield Scott Hancock wrote to William Tecumseh
Sherman. "The people elect the President. The Congress declares in a joint session who he is. We of the army have only
to obey his mandates and are protected in so doing only so
far as they may be lawful."[5] And other generals seemed to
feel the same way about it.

But there were military men among the civilians too. They
were not feeble fellows mumbling in their beards about the
days when. They were everywhere, and active, men in the
fullness of life. The mayor of the town had been a colonel,
possibly even a general. The man across the street had been
a captain. The cobbler, the feed dealer, the livery man, the
grocer and butcher and barber, all had recently toted rifles.

Now they talked fight.

Henry Watterson told a large meeting that the Democratic party ought to send 100,000 men marching to Washington to insist upon the inauguration of Tilden; and Joseph Pulitzer, an inflammatory young Union veteran who followed him upon the platform, cried that those men should be "fully armed and ready for business."[6]

The candidates themselves maintained an admirable silence. Hayes remained in Columbus, Tilden in New York, in spite of all pleas that they go to Washington. Had either been a hot-head it is impossible to guess what would have happened. No large spark was needed.

The more excitable Democrats called Tilden's attitude spineless. Some of them think it so to this day.

Billy Hudson, pledged to silence, was the only newspaperman present when a deputation led by a prominent Southerner waited upon the candidate in his Gramercy Park home and bluntly proposed a serenade to which he should respond with an announcement that he believed himself elected President and was prepared to take his seat, come what may. Tilden listened, then conferred in whispers with his friend Charles O'Conor, and finally asked: "Would that not be an overt act of treason?" The leader spat out one word "that should not be printed here," and the deputation stamped off in disgust.

XXII. The Terrible Last Hours

WHEN President Grant was perplexed, which was often enough, he turned to his friends. One of his best friends, a man he believed knew as much about constitutional law as any other person in the country, was Roscoe Conkling. So now he turned to Conkling and asked him to frame legislation which would settle this matter.[1]

It was a lot to ask, even in the name of friendship. A lot to ask of one who had, as always, a pronounced opinion of his own, and who abominated compromise.

THE Senator was convinced that Tilden had been elected. He was careful not to commit himself in public, or to leave any written record of his opinion, but the testimony of others, enemies and friends alike, is not to be refuted; in private conversations he was outspoken.

His nephew avers that the Senator was at all times, even in thought, true to his party, but that he cogitated in this exalted strain: "There are charges of fraud made by each political party against the other; and there is some evidence in support of these charges. As a *Republican*, I prefer that the doubtful title should be given to the Democrats."[2] This is preposterous. Still, the Senator must have suffered mental agony. He was, after all, a Republican, who all his life had demanded party regularity. But he probably believed in the standing of the twenty-second joint rule, possibly in some of the other Democratic contentions.[3] His conscience said Tilden; and the Democrats, perceiving this, clustered around him.

A Utica man, a friend of the Senator, but a Democrat, on November 19 wrote this letter to "President Tilden":[4]

My Dear Sir

I have had an hour talk today with Senator Conkling, and I am happy to inform you he is sound as a bullet all through— He says of course he is desireous his party should succeed but if it is expected he will consent to succeed by fraud they are mistaken. He is sound on all the questions that will arise and means to act with our friends.

He is devoting himself to the law and means to hold ground with our friends in the Senate.

He asked me what position our people meant to assume and whether they meant to act upon the *good boy* principle of submission—or whether we mean to have it understood that Tilden

has been elected and by the Eternal he shall be inaugurated—
Thinks the latter course advisable the submission policy he dont
much believe in.

You may rely upon his *hearty coöperation.* I hope to see you
soon but I fear shall not be able to come down before the 1st of
Dec.

I dont know whether the Senator will unburden [unbosom?]
himself to Kernan but I know he is all right and I am corre-
spondingly hopeful and happy, as ever

> Yours truly,
> J. Thomas Spriggs.

It would seem conclusive—to anyone who did not know
how campaign workers, upon any evidence or none, soar to
dizzy heights of optimism when a doubtful election is involved. Senator Conkling always drew a sharp line between
his public and his private opinions. At the time of this interview with the overexuberant Spriggs, President Grant had
not yet asked him to work for a compromise.

Conkling knew and admired Tilden. Hayes he not only disliked, but distrusted. He was suspicious of the company
Hayes kept.

Hayes wrote in his diary December 5:

Yesterday Elwood E. Thorne and Francis A. Stout, of the
Republican Reform Club of New York, came here and had an
interview with me. The purport of their communication, written
and oral, was that New York was lost by coldness and neglect
(perhaps treachery) on the part of the New York managers of
the canvass—meaning Cornell [and] some of the Federal officers, generally, I suppose, friends of Conkling. Their facts were
not very conclusive, but tended to show a lack of hearty support.

Hayes's friend Garfield wrote from Washington a few
days later, warning him against this pair.

I think you ought to know that a persistent attempt has been made to lead the President to believe that you are going to ignore his friends in such a way as to imply a censure upon his Administration. I suspect that a part of this impression has come from the two New York gentlemen [Messrs. Stout and Thorne] who visited you the day we saw you. They came on to this city with us. I am informed that . . . they express their satisfaction with the prospect that the Senator and such as he will be ignored during your term. Now, I have no idea that anybody has any authority to speak for you on these topics. But I will say that Senator Sherman and I were not favorably impressed with the discretion of these gentlemen.

A few days after that, the nominee heard the other side. Sherman wrote that a Colonel Albert D. Shaw of New York would call with a letter of introduction, written at the request of Don Cameron and Tom Platt.

A studied effort has been made by influential men, mainly of the Democratic party, to poison the mind of Senator Conkling against you and your Administration, partly by assertions that you will be under the influence of Carl Schurz and Mr. Curtis whom he regards as his enemies, and partly . . . because he was not active in your support.

The Senator's health, Sherman wrote, was "much broken, and by reason of this he is more easily moved by such suggestions . . . you will see the importance of assuring Colonel Shaw that . . . the alleged hostility to Conkling has no foundation. He is undoubtedly a man of great ability and influence and we do not want either his opposition or cold reserve."

Shaw came, and talked "forcibly and [with] much feeling," Hayes informed his diary.

He fears that the apprehension that I am in the hands of the reform element of the Republican party will lose me in the Senate the friendship and support of enough Senators in the approaching struggle in the Senate to change the result of the

Presidential election, and bring in Mr. Tilden. Mr. Conkling has been committed against our present views on some of the legal questions now before the country—notably, as I infer, on the right of the Senate and House to pass on any returns of the Electoral Colleges. . . . He showed the reasons why Mr. Conkling took no active part in the canvass, that his health was broken, and his eyes required that he should remain in a dark room. He explained the bad faith of Curtis towards Conkling; of Bristow towards Conkling and Grant; of Morgan towards Conkling, etc., etc. He urged the appointment of Conkling (or rather his being offered the appointment) as Secretary of State.[5]

Mark this last. The Senator (assuming that Colonel Shaw's suggestion really came from him) wished to be *offered* the Secretaryship of State. He would refuse it, of course. He never had any interest in foreign affairs, and was not prepared to be second man in any body. But the offer would enhance his prestige. It would show men that Roscoe Conkling still was a power behind the throne.

He never was offered a cabinet portfolio, even unofficially.

The election was over, yet it remained necessary for the nominee to smile upon this person and that, to keep everybody pleased. A revolt within the party, even a small revolt, if led by some powerful figure, could throw the result of the election the other way. Hayes was cautious, as ever. And Conkling, as ever, was suspicious.

Under these circumstances it was natural for the Senator to hesitate when President Grant asked him to frame a compromise. But Grant asked it as a friend. So Conkling consented.

THE Electoral Commission bill was not Roscoe Conkling's own, though he probably had more to do with the framing of it than any other man. If it had carried a statesman's name, that name would be his.

It was a Republican, McCrary of Iowa, who first proposed in the House, December 7, that Congress form a joint committee to find some way out of the difficulty. His resolution passed the House December 14, the Senate four days later. It was agreed that the Senate was to appoint four Republicans and three Democrats, the House four Democrats and three Republicans.

Originally Senator Conkling was not appointed to this committee; but his friend Logan, who was troubled about his own reëlection and thought he should remain home in Illinois for the present, declined to act, and Senator Conkling was named then. Possibly this was done because Conkling was a "Grant man," like Logan. Possibly it was done at the request of Grant himself.

Sherman was alarmed. He wrote to Hayes:

The formation of the Senate committee gave us great solicitude, but the Vice-President, after consulting many Senators, thought it best to put Mr. Conkling in the place of Logan. My judgment was against it, but when pretty generally concurred in I did not feel justified in objecting further. The committee is now sitting daily. I have heard from the most reliable sources some indications of an unfavorable character, which I am only at liberty to communicate to you in like confidence. Mr. Conkling has openly stated in the committee his position that the President of the Senate has no right *to count* the votes, and that, as the case stands, he will not vote that you have either Florida or Louisiana. He may vote to allow the Supreme Court to pass upon these questions. This develops a danger that I anticipated, but perhaps it is no greater with him on the committee than in the Senate.[6]

The first meeting of the joint committee was on Saturday, January 12. The following day all but Springer of Illinois approved a plan for referring the matter to six Supreme Court justices, who would draw lots to eliminate one of themselves. Conkling especially urged Springer to consent to this, being eager to have the committee report Monday; but Springer preferred to wait.

Proposals like this—the drawing of lots, casting of dice, cutting of cards—were not unusual, and were made in all seriousness. This particular one Springer eventually refused to countenance. Conkling explained to the committee a few days later, in connection with a similar bill: "My idea was, in suggesting that four justices name the fifth, that one judge would say 'Here is Justice Field; why not take him?' Another 'Here's Judge Strong; why not take him?' But one is a Democrat, the other a Republican. Probably in the end they would say, 'Both are good men; put them in a hat and draw out one.' "

It would have been as fair a method as any. But Democratic and Republican die-hards alike opposed it. "I may lose the Presidency," Samuel Tilden said, "but I will not raffle for it."

No, the committee's work was not to be as easy as that. The bill it finally framed, which was presented in identical reports to the two houses a month after the appointment of the committee, "was fought over," Conkling later told a reporter, "not only section by section, but line by line and word by word."[7]

It called for a temporary tribunal which would settle all questions referred to it by Congress. The two houses should meet in joint session, as provided in the Constitution, and the President of the Senate should open the electoral certificates and announce the votes. Whenever a vote was objected to, everything pertaining to that vote would be handed over to the tribunal, or electoral commission, for decision. This decision could be upset only by a majority vote of *both* houses. Since it was unthinkable that both houses would agree upon any feature of this election, the bill practically would empower the commission to decide whether Tilden or Hayes was to be the next President.

The commission should consist of five members from each

house and five Supreme Court justices. It was understood—
though not specifically provided in the bill itself—that the
House was to appoint three Democrats and two Republicans,
the Senate three Republicans and two Democrats. This was
not important. The important fact was that there were only
two regular Democrats on the Supreme Court bench at the
time. It was specified in the law that these two would be members of the commission. It was further specified that two
regular Republican justices should be members. The fifth
and all-deciding justice was unnamed, but it was expected
that he would be David Davis of Illinois, a man technically
Republican but in fact highly independent.

THE agreement to recommend this commission, with everything depending upon David Davis, was greeted with howls
of disapproval by die-hards of both parties. "Judge Davis,"
said Senator Edmunds, "is one of those Independents who
stand always ready to accept Democratic nominations. It is
my observation that such men are generally the most extreme in their partisanship. I would rather intrust a decision
to an out-and-out Democrat." There were many others who
thought this way about it.

But what else was to be done? Rifle clubs were being
formed in the South, and in some parts of the North too. If
war came it would be no sectional affair this time. It would
be chaos. Officially neither the Grand Army of the Republic
nor the Democratic Veteran Soldiers' Association was involved, yet meetings of both these organizations were noisy
with threats. Men forgot they had sworn, at the end of the
Civil War, that such a thing never should happen again.
They said they didn't want to fight, but by God if they had
to, to get justice, they *would!* The framework of a Democratic military organization had been effected in eleven
states, and a commander-in-chief, "a man of national reputation," had been tentatively agreed upon.[8]

FROM the beginning there was prattle about a filibuster. The Democratic majority in the House was large, but the Republican majority in the Senate was dangerously small, and a few Senators, combining with the Democrats, could block acceptance of any commission decision. That is, if the compromise bill was passed.

Speaker Randall, who himself had once filibustered alone for seventy-two hours, heroically violated house rules and gaveled objectors to silence in his attempt to put the thing through. In the Senate, Conkling was the bill's greatest, almost its only prominent champion. He was magnificent in its defense.

Tall, well proportioned, with his vest opening down to the waist and displaying his full chest and broad shoulders to the best advantage, his hair tossed back from his massive brow with studied carelessness, his white and slender hands set off by spotless linen, he looked every inch a Senator. Before him, on his desk, were his notes, daintily inscribed on gilt-edged, cream-tinted paper; but he did not refer to them, having committed his remarks so thoroughly that many believed them to have been extemporaneous. His speech was pronounced by good judges as the greatest specimen of the "art which conceals art" that has ever been delivered in this country.[9]

Garfield, who was opposing the bill in the House, was not so friendly. He had slipped over to listen to the Senator. "He certainly is an able debater and his manners are very striking, though stagy. I was surprised at his mass of words in proportion to the ideas they contained."[10]

The Senator talked all afternoon. There was a dinner recess—and the Senator walked into a cloakroom and collapsed upon a sofa. His friends were alarmed. It was not like Roscoe Conkling to collapse. Senator Stewart supervising, a couple of porters assisted him out to a carriage; and in his rooms at the Arlington, after Stewart had sent for a physician, he was given an alcohol rub and a dose of quinine.

He did not attend the night session. His speech was to have been continued the next morning, but the Senate, after declaring a ten-minute recess out of courtesy, went on without him. Soon afterward he appeared, dramatically of course, and continued the speech. He talked until almost midnight. Then Morton, sitting in his seat, sweating profusely, spoke against the bill. Morton thought it unconstitutional. So did Blaine, the next speaker, who had been sworn in as a Senator only the previous day. So did Sherman. The session lasted until seven o'clock in the morning.

Eventually the bill was passed. Twenty-six Democrats voted for it, and only 1, a Northerner, against it; 21 Republicans were for it, 16 opposed.

THAT was January 25. The same day the Illinois legislature elected a United States Senator. "Black Jack" Logan, after a furious fight, was defeated. A combination of Democrats and independent Republicans unexpectedly threw the election to a compromise candidate—David Davis!

Davis promptly resigned from the Supreme Court.

The Democrats were frantic. They had placed great hopes on Davis because of his attitude in certain reconstruction matters. Nobody knows how he would have voted on the electoral commission. He never expressed any opinion, publicly or privately, and never was called upon to vote on any question involving the Hayes-Tilden election.

The understanding was patched up hastily. Justice Bradley, "Aliunde Joe" Bradley of New Jersey, was to take the place of Davis. He was the most nearly independent of the remaining justices.

The House passed the electoral commission bill the following day. The ayes included 160 Democrats, 31 Republicans; the noes 17 Democrats, 69 Republicans. It was really a Democratic measure, in each house.

THE Senate did not appoint Roscoe Conkling to the electoral commission. All sorts of reasons were given for this. He seemed a logical choice. Assuredly he could have had an appointment if he had asked for it. Nobody in Washington in those hysterical days, not even the President, not even the justices of the Supreme Court, escaped vituperation. Conkling got his share, possibly more than that. Just now his enemies were murmuring that he wished to remain off the commission in order to be able to lead a filibuster against the commission's decisions, and so, holding the situation in his well-kept hands, make terms with either the Democrats or the Republicans. In view of the work he had done in helping to frame the electoral commission bill, and afterward in getting it through the Senate, this is ridiculous. But nothing was too silly for belief in those mad weeks.

It is possible that the Senator, weak and tired, and in poor health, desired only to dodge additional responsibility.

THE formal counting of votes began February 1. They were opened in alphabetical order. Florida soon was reached, an objection was voiced, the matter was referred to the commission.

The commission's hearings were held in the Supreme Court chambers, with great solemnity. Some of the most expensive lawyers in the country were there to argue on this side or on that.

It was on February 7 that the commission decided it did not have the power to go behind the returns officially sent to Congress—that the Federal Government had no authority to invade the rights of states, no matter how patent the frauds involved. The commission decided that it must accept the first official returns, which were, of course, the Republican returns. If the election had been crooked, that was not the commission's business.

This decision, far more than any other one thing, cost Tilden the Presidency.

The vote was 8–7, with Justice Bradley voting with the Republicans.

The Louisiana question was reached February 12, that of Oregon February 20, that of South Carolina February 26— but by that time the Republicans were not even taking the trouble to present arguments.

By that time, too, in a room at Wormley's Hotel informal gatherings of Democrats and Republicans, of Tilden and Hayes representatives, were settling another matter of great importance.

The Democrats quite naturally wished to save something from the mess. The Presidency was lost to them, but there still was the question of the carpetbag governments in South Carolina and Louisiana. The Democrats had regained control in Florida, and they could regain control in South Carolina and Louisiana if the Federal troops were withdrawn. Then they would at least be free to keep the nigger in his place.

On the day the commission decided that Hayes was to get the electoral vote of South Carolina, the little group of men at Wormley's—Roscoe Conkling was not at any time associated with this deal—agreed that when Hayes got into the White House he would recall the Federal troops from the South. Afterward, Northern Democrats screamed that Tilden had been "sold" at Wormley's. This was not true. Tilden already had been defeated when the conference assembled. It wasn't a sale, it was a salvage agreement.

At the last moment the rumors increased in number and inanity, crackling through Washington like summer lightning, and Conkling's name was mentioned in every third or fourth one. It was reported again and again, but never with a splinter of evidence for support, that he was about to lead a grand filibuster, that he was going to block the count and force Congress to call a second national election, that he was (presumably by magic) going to keep Grant in the White House indefinitely. They were all frightened, the statesmen, and their nerves were shattered, so that they yammered like lunatics.

However, Whitelaw Reid, in a letter to William Evarts, who was one of the Hayes counsel before the electoral commission, reported this from the comparative cool of New York:

Mr. Conkling's friends here have been saying quite openly within a day or two, that he would yet be elected President of the Senate by a coalition with the Democrats, the completion of the count would then be prevented and he would then succeed Grant. I should attach no importance to this story were it not that some of his spokesmen are so positive about it. I think our friends ought to be very watchful on this point—especially if there should arise between now and Saturday any wrangling which should seem to make the election of a new President of the Senate necessary.[10a]

On the day the *Tribune* editor spread this blather upon paper—Thursday, March 1—the two houses of Congress assembled for the finish of the count. In sheer, hot idiocy the buzzing then surpassed all that had gone before. Filibuster, filibuster, filibuster. Who's got the filibuster? Everything would be stopped, jerked to a dramatic halt, just before the finish line. Who would do this? who would perform this miracle? Why, Conkling of course! People said that Conkling would do it because he didn't like Rutherford B. Hayes. Conkling would pull the whole business up short. He would throw the country into a turmoil. But where was Conkling? Nobody could find him.

As a matter of fact, the Senator was in Baltimore visiting friends that night.

At four o'clock on the morning of March 2 the President of the Senate announced that Rutherford B. Hayes had been

elected President of the United States of America—by one
vote.

OF course there were a million more stories. One of the favorites involves our Senator and the sprightly Kate Chase
Sprague. It would be fun to believe this. It is told in many
versions. This is Colonel McClure's:

> The Senate was carefully canvassed, and enough Republican
> votes were marshalled to throw the vote of the Senate in favor
> of Tilden on the Louisiana issue if Conkling would lead in sup-
> port of that policy, and it was understood that he had agreed
> to do so. When the crucial time came Conkling did not appear
> at all, and the anti-Hayes Republicans, being without a leader,
> fell back to their party lines and gave the vote of the State and
> the Presidential certificate to Hayes. It is an open secret that
> Conkling resolved his doubts as urged by Mrs. Sprague, who
> thereby avenged the defeat of her father in the Democratic
> nomination 1868, that had been accomplished by Tilden; and
> thus Tilden lost the Presidency, to which he had been elected by
> a popular majority of over 250,000.[11]

A charming story. It has an Old World flavor. Also it
reminds irresistibly of a certain Biblical tale, and Conkling
was bulky enough to suggest Samson.

To be sure, the story libels a couple of citizens, for Delilah
too is concerned. It libels her common sense. It makes her
not only selfish and vindictive, not only a shameless, unpatriotic seducer of senators for the settlement of personal
grudges, but also a damned fool. It makes Conkling a
damned fool too, and a traitor, and a liar.

Tilden didn't block Chase's nomination in 1868, though it
is possible that Kate Chase Sprague believed at the time that
he did. Chase would have lost that election if he *had* been
nominated: nobody could have defeated Grant then. Eight
years later Conkling toiled long and hard to persuade Congress to pass the compromise bill he had toiled long and hard

to frame. When Congress had passed that bill, when Justice
Bradley had voted with the Republicans on the question of
going behind the returns, most emphatically of all when the
matter of carpetbag governments had been settled quietly in
Wormley's—after that even Roscoe Conkling couldn't have
blocked the election and inauguration of Hayes if he had
wished to do so.

In many respects our Senator was none too admirable, no
glittering hero. He probably did sleep with a lot of women.
Though financially honest, surely he was a political crook—
a domineering, thundering, bluffing boss, a bully, a tyrant.
Unquestionably he did tell his fellow solons, with what
Henry Adams called "the Websterian or Conklinian pom-
posity," that in an opponent's argument "there is not one
substantial averment which has not been pulverized," and it
is true that his speeches were very, very long. He was essentially parochial. He was not a really great man, certainly
not a great statesman. But when he helped to make and to
pass the electoral commission bill of 1877 he helped to avert
another civil war; and it's a pity that at precisely this point
in his career someone like Colonel McClure should assert that
he would have undone all this work if his woman hadn't
called him off.

XXIII. Cheers for the Champion

MARCH 4 was a Sunday, and the Hayeses, particularly Mrs. Hayes, did not believe in doing
things on Sundays. The previous night the
Grants had entertained at dinner—thirty-six
covers, and gallons of wine—and a little before this function
began General Grant with his son Jesse had led General
Hayes into the red room, where Chief Justice Waite swore
him in as the new President.

There was a formal inauguration Monday, but even this was kept very quiet—no parade, no ball, and the bands did not play. Which was both appropriate and prophetic, for we never had a less exciting President.

RUTHERFORD B. HAYES went about his duties beaming and nodding. He seemed to be having a quiet good time, all by himself. Every morning he took setting-up exercises; after each meal staidly he walked a certain distance through the halls; his nap followed regularly upon his regular afternoon drive. One cup of coffee at breakfast, one cup of tea at lunch, but with dinner nothing stronger than water. He didn't smoke, and he didn't chew, and he didn't use swear words.

Nobody at the White House during those four years ever partook of alcoholic liquids. Nobody was offered any. President Hayes was no fanatic—he refused to vote for a state prohibition amendment in Ohio in 1883 and warned the Methodist Church that it should keep out of politics. Until his marriage he had sometimes taken a glass of spirits. After that event he drank only wine. But after his inauguration he didn't even drink wine.

At the time of his marriage, too, he had quit the Protestant Episcopal Church and joined the Methodist Episcopal Church, of which Lucy was a member.

Inevitably it was said that Lucy and not Rutherford was running the government. This wasn't true; but Lucy *did* run the White House, her proper province. "Lemonade Lucy"—she enraged some, amused most. Feminists and prohibitionists adored her. The W.C.T.U solemnly proposed to erect a fountain in her honor, but when Rutherford said he thought a portrait would be nicer, his wish was carried out. George W. Cable, enraptured, wrote of her:

> That woman's hand that puts away the cup
> Is fair as Joan's with the sword lifted up.

The new Secretary of State, Evarts, almost succumbed to

panic. It was without precedent, it was highly disturbing, this Mohammedan proscription of liquor! It might have grave diplomatic consequences! He persuaded Lucy to relent just once, at the first formal banquet under the new administration, when the Grand Duke Alexander Alexandrovitch and the Grand Duke Constantine were entertained. What, he cried, would these Russians think of us if we offered them only water? But thereafter Lucy stuck to her determination to keep the place dry. And Evarts subsided, licking his diplomatic wounds—until once when a friend asked about a White House dinner, and the secretary snarled: "Oh, it was a brilliant affair! The water flowed like champagne."

She was a determined woman, Lucy. The first college graduate ever to be First Lady of the Land, she was dark haired, handsome, sturdy, a capable hostess, pitilessly wholesome. Fashions meant little to her if they happened to be foolish, as most of them were at that time. No frizzly false hair for Lucy! no monstrous, rickety bustles; no long trains, and certainly no *décolleté* necks! There was a lap dog craze in the land, but Lucy didn't have a lap dog. She believed in bringing her children up right, too. Every evening after dinner they were herded into the red room for hymns and Stephen Foster ballads, then into the blue room for family prayers, then into the library to prepare their lessons for the next day at school—and finally, good and early, they were sent to bed. They were taught to respect the Sabbath, too, as was their father. The Hayeses went to Foxall's old Foundry M.E. Church; and in the afternoon, back in the White House, they would entertain a few friends by passing out hymn books and clustering around the harmonium, which Lucy played.

Rutherford had a tolerable if apologetic baritone. He was methodical in all desk matters, and loved to fuss with papers. He kept a diary and innumerable scrapbooks. His favorite authors were Emerson, Hawthorne, Scott, Lincoln, Howells, Byron, Browning, and Edwin Arnold. He was a nice little man; and everybody who didn't happen to find him politically distasteful, liked him a lot.

His latest biographer, Eckenrode, has suggested that Hayes resembled Calvin Coolidge. This is unjust to Hayes. Each man was smallish, quiet, cautious, and seemed in his exalted position vaguely ludicrous. A dark horse, each had been made President for negative, not positive reasons. Each too had about him some quality which Americans like to call "homespun"—whatever that means.

But Coolidge, a high priest of the *status quo*, was adored by the Republican Old Guard; and by the people, while he was in office, he was absurdly overrated. The Old Guard's equivalent of the Hayes administration, Blaine, Conkling, Cameron, Logan, despised the President, whose good qualities were not appreciated by the general public. Coolidge took things easy; Hayes was a hard worker. Coolidge, utterly hard-boiled, never made an appointment from any but the strictest organization motives; but Rutherford B. Hayes cherished certain quaint Ideals about appointments. No reformer in the orthodox sense, no raver, no shouter of demands, Hayes nevertheless was convinced of the wisdom of civil service regulation. He did rash things with his appointing power. He refused to give Blaine's friend, William P. Frye,[1] a position in the cabinet, and thereby earned Blaine's enmity. He refused to proffer Conkling the state portfolio but instead gave this to a man Conkling disliked, Evarts. Through Evarts, too, and not through the Boss, he offered another Conkling enemy, George William Curtis, the St. James's Ambassadorship. He knew how Morton and Logan and other Middle West Republican powers disliked Carl Schurz, but he made Schurz Secretary of the Interior. Conkling had let it be known that he would like to see his friend Tom Platt made postmaster general, but Hayes appointed David M. Key—a Tennessean! a Confederate army veteran!

Sometimes there was even something childlike about this President, as when, in the days when civil service reform still was a pet of cranks, he announced that "Party leaders should have no more influence in appointments than other equally respectable citizens."[2] Imagine Coolidge saying that! Yet Hayes was perfectly serious. The statement was not contained in a showy speech, but in a carefully prepared executive order.

It was this matter of civil service, this Presidential tendency to make on-merit-only appointments, which caused the rift between Rutherford B. Hayes and the most puissant leaders of his party. They hadn't wanted Hayes very much in the first place, and they thought that now that they'd given him the Presidency the least he could do was keep his reform propensities in check. Already he had done much to weaken the party by ending the carpetbag era in the South. For with the troops withdrawn, the Negroes no longer would be permitted to vote and the South would become solidly, indisputably Democratic. And one of Hayes's first official acts was withdrawal of the troops from the immediate vicinity of the Louisiana State House. This was a virtual recognition of Nicholls as governor—though the same returning board which had counted in the Republican Presidential electors had counted out Nicholls, a Democrat, declaring the Republican Packard elected. Packard was governor just so long as the Federal soldiers were there. Without them, he didn't have a chance. Yet if the state really had voted for Hayes, then certainly it had voted for Packard too? Indeed, Packard had received about 1,000 votes more than the Hayes electors.

The same thing happened in South Carolina. The same blatant inconsistency. But Hayes had his obligations, whether incurred at Wormley's or elsewhere, and he lived up to them.

CIVIL service regulation was a new idea in Hayes's time, an English experiment, and the American public, traditionally conservative, shied away from it. Organization politicians, of course, abhorred it. "Snivel-service reform," Conkling said. And why not? After all, he and those like him lived upon their ability to dictate appointments. The organizations from which they derived their power were shored up by patronage. Without jobs to distribute, how could state leaders be expected to keep their home machines going? And if those machines did not function smoothly, how could they, the Republican leaders, be expected to win elections? Look: there was that English examination in which applicants for some minor clerkship were asked what five rivers empty into the Caspian Sea. Now, which was more important—that Government clerks should know things like this, or that state leaders should be permitted to retain and control the organizations they had built up and through which they were keeping the Republican party in power?

It was all very well for literary Unitarians like Curtis, water-sipping Methodists like Hayes, to have ideals about the service of the public; but since when had ideals meant majorities? "Party leaders should have no more influence in appointments than other equally respectable citizens." For God's sake! Had anybody ever before heard anything quite so silly as that? It should be chanted with uprolled eyes, while Lucy played an accompaniment on her harmonium.

Instinctively Roscoe Conkling hardened against the Hayes administration. He didn't like the man himself. He "never spoke of him in public or private without a sneer."[3] He never really believed that Hayes had been properly elected President, and in private conversation it was his habit to refer scaldingly to "Ruther-*fraud* B. Hayes" or "His *Fraudu*lency the President"—the italics being his. His suspicions and jealousy had been aroused by the placing in high positions of such men as Evarts and Schurz, and by the frequency with which the President consulted Curtis of *Harper's*. He knew that here was an enemy, and he prepared to fight.

And instinctively he was accepted as the champion. "Politics for the politicians" might have been, though it wasn't, the slogan of those who rallied around him. He was the leader, the absolute leader, of the most populous and most important state. More than any other one man he would feel the effects of civil service reform.[4] His stake was the greatest; his abilities, his masterful use of the weapon scorn, peculiarly fitted him for leadership in this battle.

AFTER the election dust had settled he went to Europe, for his health. The trip wasn't important, but the return was. New York City then was not accustomed to carefully planned welcome-home celebrations, and the unknowing found it curious that this one, easily the biggest on record at the time, was tendered to a personage essentially unpopular, and in an "off" political year.

The chartered steamer *Thomas Collyer*, gayly bedecked, and stocked with ample provisions (there was a heavy fog down the bay, and the officeholders, facing the prospect of a long wait, wished to be prepared against colds) sailed from the foot of West Twenty-fourth Street at eight thirty o'clock on the morning of Friday, August 11. It touched at the North German Lloyd dock in Hoboken, and the welcomers learned that the *Neckar* had passed Fire Island at eight o'clock. The fog was lifting. They stopped at Governor's Island and picked up a band.

Off Sandy Hook the German ship was sighted, and Rans von Volkenburg's brass cannon boom-boomed many times, while whistles were blown, bells rung, the band played "Hail to the Chief," and according to one reporter:[5] "The passengers on board the steamer *Neckar* looked with wonder and surprise upon the demonstration."

He stood on the bridge, very erect, smiling a regal if

rather chilly smile, and waving a little American flag. And when the officeholders swarmed aboard, and greeted him with speeches of welcome, he replied in exactly sixty words (counting four first person singulars), which was unlike him, but effective. Even informally he was careful to evade talk about politics, though he condescended to relate "many humorous incidents of his journey on the other side of the ocean, and gave the impression to his listeners that he had not become a great admirer of the Old Country."

Opposite Governor's Island the steamers *Seneca* and *H. M. Welles*, one with a band, both with four-pounders, hove to for additional salutes. Then came a flotilla of more than thirty tugboats. It was one of the most exciting days the harbor had ever known, and certainly the loudest, inasmuch as "forty steam-whistles, three cannons, four steamer bells, and two bands can make a good deal of noise when judiciously operated." Also, the refreshments hadn't been wasted.

At two o'clock the *Neckar* was warped at Hoboken, where Mayor Pangborn welcomed home the Senator in the name of New Jersey. The hero graciously replied that, aside from New York, there was no state he would rather have welcoming him than the great state of New Jersey.

This matter attended to, the Senator was taken aboard the *Thomas Collyer*, which proceeded for a short sail up the river before it docked at the foot of West Twenty-fourth Street. There were so many persons who wished to see the Senator about so many things.

A carriage took him through cheering throngs to the Fifth Avenue Hotel. The porch and corridors, and Madison Square in front, were crowded with members of the Grand Old Party, who continued to talk about civil service, some of them confidently predicting that the Senator would scotch that snake without delay, while others knowingly whispered that he was planning to "go easy at first."

At eleven o'clock that night the square was jammed,

though "there was a marked absence of the men known as Morgan-Weed Republicans, and also a general absence of the leading men of the Union League Club." Gilmore's Band (fifty pieces) was on the porch, playing "Swanee River," when the Senator made his appearance on a balcony.

His speech was cautiously unpolitical. France was praised for her art treasures, but the German voters were not forgotten, and the Senator reminded his audience that these very art treasures of France were monuments to the clemency and inherent kindliness of conquering Germans who had permitted them to stay there. Americans were assured that the Old World, though it might have more traditions than the United States, was woefully backward in most other respects. England, in particular. "English hotels would seem sadly behind the times here; indeed, they would not be endured. Telegraphic service is inferior to ours. Railway service in general is destitute of facilities, comforts and conveniences which here are matters of course everywhere." And finally there was a boost for General Grant.

It was one o'clock in the morning before the crowd began to quit Madison Square.

Then a few days were spent in conferences. The excitement had subsided swiftly, and when on Monday morning Senator Conkling took a train for Utica there were only three or four friends to wave him good-by. "He entered the depot satchel in hand, the same as any other passenger, took his seat in the drawing-room car and then quietly awaited the departure of the train."

However, there was a reception, with music and fireworks, in Albany; another in Schenectady; and at Little Falls the vanguard of the Utica greeters boarded the train.

Utica did herself proud that night. Practically everybody assembled in Bagg's Square at eight-thirty, and there was a parade along Genesee, Hopper, and Rutger Streets to the

Conkling house, which was decorated with Chinese lanterns and lighted by locomotive lamps.

The Senator was a different man. Laughing, talking rapidly and loudly, he romped from group to group in a perfect frenzy of sociability. Some nervous reaction, possibly, from the strain of the New York greeting and all the work which had followed it; or perhaps it was a genuine boyish pleasure, a welling-up of emotion at the sight of old friends and associates. He was a man of moods, after all, and this particular mood, though it was rare, was not without precedent. He was more than exuberant, he was hysterical; and persons who didn't know him well assumed that he was drunk. But he wasn't. At least, not with wine.[6]

He made them a speech, still avoiding politics, and related again some of his amusing adventures. The depression? They should see conditions in Europe! They didn't know what a depression was! And finally he praised General Grant.

He didn't know then, he couldn't know, that here was the wrong turn in his career. He never looked back, never bent; he wouldn't take advice. He was not able to understand what had not yet become clear to many another politician—that the public really desired civil service reform, the clamor for which was to become too loud for any man or group of men to shush. After seven years of absolute power, faced now by so unimpressive an opponent as Rutherford B. Hayes, and with the cheers of thousands ringing in his ears, he couldn't suppose that he was leading a cause doomed to defeat. *He* would not falter! Even if his army deserted behind him, *he* would march on! As the Uticans drifted back to their homes that night, and servants went around putting out Chinese lanterns and collecting glasses, the Senator, going to bed, could scarcely be expected to know that exactly this was to happen soon.

XXIV. The Keystone Endangered

THE keystone of the New York political edifice was the customs house. Who controlled that controlled the state—a fact of which Thurlow Weed was well aware when he grabbed it in September, 1864[1]—and without it no Republican leader could hope for long to keep the boys in line.

The customs house was a bowl overflowing with the heady punch of patronage. Offering all sorts of opportunity for graft, it spouted scandal with the regularity and spectacular force of a well-advertised geyser. Expected to be rotten, it obliged.

Tom Murphy, whose appointment as collector had raised such a storm of protest, had admitted to investigators that "There were certain people who had to be taken care of. . . ." And Moses Grinnell waded through another pool of muck. For instance, both these collectors dealt with Colonel Leet. Leet, once a member of Grant's staff, had profited to the tune of $50,000 a year through warehousing contracts, though he had made no investment of his own, and had not even found it necessary to quit Washington. Incidentally, all this time he was drawing the pay of a colonel in the regular army *and* of a War Department clerk.

Senator Conkling himself had moved an investigation of the New York customs house on December 18, 1871. But that was before he got control of it.

He got control March 14, 1872, when his friend Chester Arthur was made collector and that other sturdy Conkling man, Alonzo Cornell, was appointed naval officer.

Thereafter the Senator did not approve of investigations of the New York customs house.

But one was in progress. Indeed, there were commissions at this time investigating the customs houses in New York, New Orleans, Philadelphia, and San Francisco, though the

New York house, by reason of the vast business it handled, was much the most important of these. The New York commission handed in a series of reports, six of them, extending from May 24 to November 1 in this year of 1877, and none of them was pleasant reading for the Senator.[2]

The commission found all sorts of petty inefficiency, petty bribe-taking (though it made no specific charge against anybody), playing of politics, carelessness, etc., etc., and calculated that one-fourth of the revenue was lost to the Government because of these conditions. It recommended a 20 per cent reduction of the force.

Hayes, meanwhile, had promulgated an executive order—which for all its resounding periods was no more than a statement of personal policy—against Federal officeholders taking an active part in politics; and it was made clear to Cornell that he was expected to resign either as naval officer of the port of New York or else as Republican state chairman. He refused to give up either job.

On September 6 the President asked for the resignations of Arthur, Cornell, and Sharpe, the surveyor, another Conkling man. They all refused to resign.

Two dear enemies, Hayes and Sherman, the Secretary of the Treasury, had started all this fuss, and the Senator was in an ugly mood when the Republican state convention assembled in Rochester, October 4. His puppet, Tom Platt, opening the convention, announced that the whole question of civil service reform had been "magnified to unseemly proportions" and had become a "shibboleth" that "nauseated the public." He called Evarts a "demagogue" and spoke of the "Pecksniffs and tricksters" who fought the state Republican organization.

It was an angry speech, a startling speech to come from so mild-mannered a fellow; but nobody doubted its inspiration. Anyway, it was no more than a curtain raiser.

The platform mentioned President Hayes in a dim, watery way, but said nothing about the recent electoral contest. George William Curtis offered an amendment asserting that "the lawful title of Rutherford B. Hayes to the Presidency is as clear and perfect as that of George Washington." Why Curtis thought that such an amendment was needed is not apparent. His amendment went on to praise the President for his moderate Southern policy (not, however, mentioning the Treaty of Wormley's) and his work for civil service reform. And Curtis, in offering this, though he remained at all times the smiling, dapper gentleman, the friend of Lowell, Bryant, Sumner, the graduate of German universities, the women's suffrage worker, the lecturer on such topics as "The Duty of Educated Men"—Curtis did not fail to use this opportunity to wallop the Boss, as he had been doing for years in the pages of *Harper's*. Nobody, he said, "unless intoxicated with the flattery of parasites, or blinded by his own ambition," could hope to carry New York State for the party while standing opposed to the national administration. He overstepped the mark a little when he ventured to ask why it was that Senator Conkling, who controlled the appointment of Federal judges, always seemed to win his cases in Federal courts. Even so, even without this below-the-belt punch, Curtis was asking for it.

He got it. Tom Platt was in the chair, and this was the Senator's convention. The Senator had been waiting for Curtis "as the American fleet waited for the Spanish at Santiago."[3] He took the platform.

Slowly he began, reminding the convention that it was assembled to conduct state business, not national business. But:

Who are these men who, in newspapers or elsewhere, are cracking their whips over me and playing schoolmaster to the party? They are of various sorts and conditions. Some of them are the man-milliners, the dilettante and carpet knights of politics, whose efforts have been expended in denouncing and ridiculing and accusing honest men . . .

That "man-milliners" produced a howl of laughter. Everybody remembered that *Harper's* had recently started to run fashion articles.

Some of them are men who, when they could work themselves into conventions, have attempted to belittle and befoul Republican administrations and to parade their own thin veneering of superior purity. Some of them are men who, by insisting that it is corrupt and bad for men in office to take part in politics, are striving to prove that the Republican party has been unclean and vicious all its life . . .

By this time everybody in the hall had stolen at least one look at George William Curtis, who, according to Chauncey Depew, seated next to him, was muttering: "Extraordinary! What an exhibition! Bad temper—very bad temper!"
The Senator warmed to his task.

Some of these worthies masquerade as reformers. Their vocation and ministry is to lament the sins of other people. Their stock in trade is rancid, canting self-righteousness. They are wolves in sheep's clothing. Their real object is office and plunder. When Dr. Johnson defined patriotism as the last refuge of a scoundrel, he was unconscious of the then undeveloped capabilities and uses of the word reform . . .[4]

He didn't look at Curtis. He didn't have to.
"Some of these new-found party overseers . . . forget that parties are not built up by deportment, or by ladies' magazines, or gush. . . . The grasshoppers in the corner of a fence, even without a newspaper to be heard in, sometimes make more noise than the flocks and herds that graze upon a thousand hills. . . ."
Just in case there *should* be any question of whom he meant:
"For extreme license in criticism of administrations and of everybody connected with them, broad arguments can no

doubt be found in the files of the journal made famous by the pencil of Nast."

He asked why all this pother about supporting Hayes? Hadn't New York helped to nominate him, in the first place?

"Even the member from Richmond was, I believe, in the end prevailed upon, after much difficulty, to confer his unique and delicate vote also."[5]

There was more of it, and more. It *was* the convention, that speech. Afterward half the delegates went home—for the Senator wasn't scheduled to speak again, so why linger? —and the other half occupied less than an hour with the task of nominating the Conkling candidates.

Incidentally, the convention defeated Curtis' resolution, 311–110.

THE speech created an extraordinary sensation. It was a masterpiece of spleen, the Senator at his bitterest-best; and for years afterward men talked about it and quoted it with tears in their eyes, but all the while laughing; men boasted of having heard it, as later men were to boast of having heard Bryan's "Cross of Gold" effusion. There is no doubt that the Senator's personal appearance and his manner of delivery had much to do with his effectiveness as an orator, and this speech, like his others, made a much more profound impression upon those who heard it than upon those who merely had read it after the event. Even Curtis himself admitted this in a letter to a friend:

It was the saddest sight I ever knew, that man glaring at me in a fury of hate, and storming out his foolish blackguardism. I was all pity. I had not thought him great, but I had not suspected how small he was . . . Conkling's speech was carefully written out, and therefore you do not get all the venom, and no one can imagine the Mephistophelean leer and spite. I have many letters. Oh, dear! how much I prefer these quiet hills, and how I am driven out on the stormy seas![6]

The Best People were indignant, and seemed to consider it unsportsmanlike of such a big strapping fellow as the Senator to pounce upon neat little, cherubic little George William Curtis.

But this was absurd. Even supposing that politics have anything to do with sportsmanship, Curtis, for all his appearance, for all his quiet charm and lovable manner, was no suckling babe. He knew what he was doing. He had not been "driven out on the stormy seas"—he'd gone there of his own volition, with his eyes wide open. True, Conkling in classing his opponent among the "man-milliners, the dilettante and carpet knights of politics" had hit him in his weakest spot; but since when has this been anything but good tactics? Conkling had been effective but not unfair. He had not made any unjust accusation comparable to that of Curtis when he expressed wonder at the ease with which the lawyer who dictated appointments to the Federal bench won his cases in Federal courts.

Nor had the editor injured the Senator only then. Indeed, in spite of appearances, and for all the popular version of the story, Conkling had not been stung to reply by this single taunt. He had not even known that it would be made, when he prepared his own speech.[7] No, Curtis had been baiting the Senator for months, for years; in editorial after self-righteous editorial he had exacerbated the Senator with that sort of abuse which is cheered by the Best People when one of their own directs it against a professional politician but is deplored as vulgar when the politician responds in kind. Not only the editor's own pen, but also the pencils of Reinhart and Nast, who worked under his orders, had been used, without any thought of "sportsmanship," against Roscoe Conkling.

For all his exclamations of dismay, too, Curtis rallied from the shock, and a few days later he helped to stage a protest mass meeting in New York City. "The audience was large and of the best quality," *The Nation* reported, "and Mr. Dwight's speech and Mr. Curtis's were both good; but we are bound to say, nevertheless, that we do not believe that the demonstration will have any great effect or be much heeded by the Conklingites."[8]

In this *The Nation* was right. Apparently Conkling, when he returned to Washington for the special session, was stronger than ever. Actually, however, he had weakened his own leadership.

This was not at first evident. But thoughtful Republican leaders, though they might be amused at the confusion of Curtis, were not so pleased with the slap at Rutherford B. Hayes. They might not like Hayes—most of them didn't. But Hayes was a Republican, and for more than three years would be President of the United States. It didn't pay to tilt against a man like that. It didn't pay openly to insult the President, openly to sneer at so great and so rapidly growing a force as the civil service reform movement. The Senator had pleaded for harmony, but by this he meant that everybody else should bury personal differences and think as he himself thought. He was splitting his own party with his arrogance, his refusal to compromise. Indisputably, now, he was fixed in the public imagination as the champion and spokesman of the anti-administration, anti-reform forces. The people were looking upon him not as a lawyer who had taken to politics, but as a politician who sometimes practiced law; and the gulf between these two conceptions, in this country where politics are regarded as inevitably dirty, is incalculable.

It was certain that the Senator would not retreat from his position, or conceal his feud against civil service reform under some high-sounding name. The Senator just didn't do things like that.

In displaying his strength, too, he had shown his weakness. He had no new weapons in his armory. He was magnificent, granted, but he was repeating himself. Never before

A LEADER WITHOUT A FOLLOWING

THE NEW OFFICIAL DOORKEEPER

Conkling—"Well, just at this moment, I feel as though I was a bigger
man than old Hayes!"

had he looked so splendid when he rode into the lists, and never before had he used with such marvelous effect the lance of invective, the battle-ax of scorn; so that the crowd behind the barriers cheered and cheered him. Yet the sober ones who lingered after the crowd had gone buzzing home, observed that when the dust settled the saintly little challenger, dazed perhaps, panting, with badly dented helm, still remained in saddle. There had been no *coup de grâce*. George William Curtis caught his breath, dusted and polished his nimbus, and was ready to fight another day.

CONGRESS reassembled with everybody talking about the Hayes-Conkling controversy. The President had offered Chet Arthur the Consulship at Paris, a very lucrative post then, if he would resign as collector of the port; but Arthur refused. "He is a gentleman," *The Nation* pointed out primly, "and gentlemen are supposed to be very sensitive about staying in places where they are not wanted."[9] Nevertheless, Chet Arthur stuck. No doubt he did so at the command of the Senator.

Roscoe Conkling had seen the Senate defy one President of the United States in the matter of removals from office, and possibly he supposed it could be done again. But the Senate of 1877 was a different body from the Senate of ten years previous; the whole atmosphere on Capitol Hill was different; and Hayes, though not popular, was not generally hated and distrusted as Andrew Johnson had been.

The tenure of office act still was on the books, but it had been modified at the motion of Conkling himself, for the benefit of President Grant, in 1869.

Late in October President Hayes removed the three high officials of the New York customs house and appointed in their places Theodore Roosevelt (father of T.R. and a prominent member of the Republican reform wing in New York) as collector, L. Bradford Prince as naval officer, and E. A. Merritt as surveyor. These nominations were sent to

the Senate October 28, and were referred to the committee
on commerce. Roscoe Conkling was chairman of the committee.

He stalled. He could have returned a prompt report
against the nominations, but he did not wish to do this. He
petitioned the Senate for permission to ask Secretary Sherman why Arthur and Cornell had been removed. This permission was granted, and the question asked. Sherman's reply was long and warm, but not notably enlightening. Senator Conkling had a defense, ostensibly framed by his friend
Chet Arthur, which was read into the record.[10] His committee, near the end of the session—it was on Friday, November 30—decided to report unfavorably on the Roosevelt-
Prince-Merritt nominations. Even then, Conkling did not
hand up the report. He waited a little, until the close of the
special session, thereby making it necessary for Hayes to
submit the nominations again, to the regular session.

Hayes was not frightened. He said in his annual message
to the regular session that when he needed senatorial advice
in the matter of removals and appointments, he would ask
for it. He renominated Roosevelt and Prince and Merritt.

The public, sick of all this, was asking whether the Senate
and the President didn't have anything better to do than
squabble about a few wretched sinecures. But Conkling took
it with the utmost seriousness. He was fighting for an abstract political principle, which is not like fighting for a
friend's job. He was convinced by this time that the whole
business was a plot to wrest his leadership from him—and it
is possible that he was right. Rutherford B. Hayes appeared
to be expending a disproportionate sum of energy upon the
mopping up of New York State, while the rest of the grand
investigation of customs houses was coming to nothing. Boston, possibly the worst, was not being investigated at all. In
Baltimore the President had turned out one set of officials
but had replaced them with a set certainly no better.

So why, Roscoe Conkling cried, pick on him?

Letters, petitions, telegrams, swamped the White House. Fifteen of the seventeen New York Republican members of Congress called to beg the President to retain Arthur, Cornell, and Sharpe. Sharpe, the removed surveyor, early in December withdrew his petition for reinstatement, thereby making the matter a shade less complicated. In the new session, Burnside, an administration man famed for his whiskers, had replaced Conkling's friend Jones of Nevada on the commerce committee; but the Senator still was able to get a 6–2 vote against Roosevelt and Prince. The committee reported unanimously in favor of Merritt. Merritt, though a close friend of Reuben Fenton, seems never to have been objectionable to Conkling, who was willing to support him once Sharpe had withdrawn.

Conkling submitted the report next day, December 12, and from two o'clock in the afternoon until six o'clock in the evening the battle raged. It was an executive session; and from it senators withdrew red faced and sweating. The Democrat Kernan, New York State's other senator, fought hard for confirmation of the Roosevelt and Prince appointments. Conkling insisted that the evils complained of had already been corrected, at the instigation of Chet Arthur himself; that all prominent members of the New York bench and bar and most of the prominent merchants had placed themselves on record as approving Arthur; that the removals constituted nothing but a personal attack inspired by Evarts.

The Merritt appointment was confirmed without a division. The Roosevelt and Prince appointments were rejected 25–31.

"The action of the Senate was indefensible" and "a gross breach of public duty," thought Sherman.[11] In private conversation the secretary's language was much stronger. He could think of nothing good to say about Chester Arthur and Alonzo Cornell—at least, not until two years later when he went to New York to speak for the Cornell gubernatorial candidacy, which was being managed by Arthur. He had some difficulty explaining that, and was obliged to fall back upon an old favorite, a chestnut growing rottener every year: "We must carry New York next year, or see all the results of the war overthrown and the constitutional amendments absolutely nullified."[12]

So Arthur and Cornell stayed in. But was the fight finished? No, indeed. Theodore Roosevelt died February 7, thereby subtracting himself from the controversy; but that summer, when Congress had adjourned, the quiet, smiling, apologetically persistent Rutherford B. Hayes removed Arthur and Cornell "for the good of the service" and appointed Merritt collector, Silas W. Burt naval officer, and General Charles K. Graham surveyor.

Then there was nothing to do but wait until Congress got back to Washington again.

XXV. The Taste of Defeat

RUTHERFORD and Lucy celebrated their silver wedding anniversary not on the day itself, for that was a Sunday, but the day following. Old Dr. McCabe, who had come all the way from Ohio, married them in the blue room, as twenty-five years and one day earlier he had married them in Columbus. Lucy wore the same dress—white brocade with a wide, straight skirt trimmed with tulle and with a white silk fringe—the same white slippers and long white gloves, the same silver comb in her now liberally silvered hair. Laughing a little, she confessed that she had been obliged to let the gown out a bit at the waist. Everybody wept. The United States Marine Band played Mendelssohn's "Wedding March."

Inevitably, Roscoe Conkling (who did not attend this ceremony) must have been reminded of a gayer wedding at the White House a few years earlier. Bessie had been a bridesmaid at *that* wedding, and the Senator had watched her come in. Now Bessie was disappointing him, planning to marry a young fellow from Philadelphia, a fellow named Oakman. Good family and all that, but the Senator didn't approve of him. The young man was studying railroads, working his way up from the bottom, and not infrequently would appear in public in dirty, greasy overalls. This was no way for a gentleman to behave—at least, not any gentleman who aspired to the hand of Roscoe Conkling's only child.

Annoyingly, Mrs. Conkling favored the match. The Senator was very bitter about this.

STILL the depression raged, and it was estimated that 3,000,-000 men were out of work. The number of tramps increased. The newly arrived immigrants, vexed at finding that American streets weren't paved with gold after all, became ugly. There was a rash of strikes upon the industrial epidermis—not the comparatively polite paper strikes we have nowadays, but violent, noisy affairs. The words "blacklist" and "boycott" appeared, and the phrase "closed shop." Private detectives appeared too,[1] and company guards, and union representatives, and scabs—all new. People began to hit one another on the head, and to shoot one another, to burn and wreck things.

Worst of all was the great railroad strike of '77, which started when the B. & O. directors, taking the lead in a move to break the powerful Brotherhood of Locomotive Engineers (it included in its membership conductors, trainmen, and trackmen, more than 50,000 in all), announced a flat 10 per cent cut. Then B. & O. trains were seized, the Governor of Maryland called out the entire militia, President Hayes dispatched 250 regulars to Martinsburg, West Virginia. But the men were starving, the tramps with nothing to lose were looking for trouble, and a flash of bayonets was not enough. Guardsmen were mobbed in Baltimore, chased from house to house, trapped in the station—and the station was fired. In Cumberland other guardsmen were rushed, beaten.

The strike spread north, jumping the international boundary, and the Canada Southern workers walked out. It spread west, jumping the Mississippi, causing all sorts of disturbances along the Missouri Pacific and the St. Louis, Kansas City, & Northern. Nine persons had been killed in Baltimore. In Pittsburgh twenty-five were killed and scores hurt. Six hundred and fifty soldiers were besieged in a round-house, and carloads of burning coke were pushed against the building, setting it afire. Eleven more were killed in Reading, and there was a Buffalo riot, prompting the governors of Pennsylvania and New York to call out the whole militia. Ten were killed in Chicago, more in St. Louis.[2]

John Milton Hay, who had married money, was busy managing his father-in-law's interests in Cleveland while the father-in-law was abroad. Hay wrote him on July 24:

Since last week the country has been at the mercy of the mob, and on the whole the mob has behaved rather better than the country. The shameful truth is now clear, that the government is utterly helpless and powerless in the face of an unarmed rebellion of foreign workingmen, mostly Irish. . . . The Army has been destroyed by dirty politicians, and the State militia is utterly inefficient. . . . It is probable that the strike may end by the surrender of the railroad companies to the demands of the strikers. This is disgraceful, but it is hard to say what else could be done.

There was a single consolation, but a significant one. "One astonishing feature of the whole affair is that there has been very little fall in stocks."[3]

Nor were dividends cut. The immensely overcapitalized railroads held firm, and the strike collapsed as suddenly as it had started. The country, recovering from its panic, was angry.

Of course Hayes was blamed. Everybody in Washington

was blamed. The administration had done nothing about the depression, practically nothing about the riots. People didn't even have the spirit to talk about prosperity being just around the corner; and the following year, 1878, showed another record for business and bank failures.

THE never-to-be-satisfied *Nation*, on January 10, 1878, tartly asked:

Have the bankers observed that their "Senior Senator," the only one belonging to the party in power, has not during the last nine months of anxiety and alarm once opened his mouth about the danger with which the country is threatened by schemes of repudiation and adulteration, or given the smallest sign either in public or private of knowledge of or interest in them?

If a shade severe, this was, unexpectedly, true. Currency legislation was the most important matter before the Federal Government at the time, yet with the passing of Grant from the White House Roscoe Conkling appeared suddenly to have lost all interest in this. He remained a hard-money man, like Hayes himself, but he did nothing about it except vote at the proper times. His enemies, inevitably, though not altogether with justice, shouted that it was evidence of the smallness of the man that he took no part in the debate over the Bland-Allison silver act, being absorbed in the task of retaining his own leadership.

It is curious—this abrupt falling-off of interest in money matters. It may be that the Senator supposed the battle for a sound currency already won, believed the crisis had been surmounted with Grant's veto of the inflation bill of 1874, and in spite of the fact that the Greenbackers could claim about 1,000,000 votes, really thought that because both major parties were certain to straddle the question the true danger was past. Or it may be that he did believe his fight for a Federal hands-off policy in regard to state boss-ships a more important matter than the silver content of the dollar.

IN almost everything but the dispute about the New York customs house he was to be found laboring and voting for administration measures. In January, 1879, he led the opposition to the Chinese immigration bill, which was passed but vetoed, and later he helped to bring about confirmation of a treaty which accomplished the same purposes for which the bill had been designed but did so without breaking a national promise. In April and June of 1879 his was one of the strongest voices against the army appropriation bill. The Democrats had both houses of Congress then, and the Southern influence was making itself felt. To the original bill was tacked a rider prohibiting the use of the army at elections, and for this reason Senator Conkling opposed it.[4] The bill was passed, but vetoed. The Democrats then succeeded in putting through a separate bill prohibiting army attendance at the polls, but this too was vetoed. Then the original appropriation bill was taken up again and a clause inserted providing that none of the money should be paid to Federal troops used as policemen at state elections. Conkling realized that Hayes, because of the wording of his veto messages, would be obliged to sign this, and he made a tremendous effort to have it defeated. But the House Republican leader, Garfield, was determined to have the appropriation bill at all costs, and he blocked the Senator's move to call a joint Republican caucus. The bill passed both House and Senate— though Conkling was able to keep all but one Republican senator, Burnside, in line against it—and reluctantly Hayes signed it, and the soldiers got their held-up pay.

The Senator, too, took an active part in the campaign of 1878, and stumped his state in behalf of the national bank. As always, he refused invitations to speak outside of New York, but he worked hard there—not for the administration as such, for he seldom mentioned the President, but for the Republican party.

Dr. White remembers him in this campaign, remembers that he

had a sledge-hammer way which broke down all opposition, and he exulted in it. One of his favorite tactics, which greatly amused his auditors, was to lead some prominent gainsayer in his audience to interrupt him, whereupon, in the blandest way possible, he would invite him to come forward, urge him to present his views, even help him to do so, and then, having gradually entangled him in his own sophistries and made him ridiculous, the senator would come down upon him with arguments—cogent, pithy, sarcastic—much like the fist of a giant upon a mosquito.

Garfield, running for reëlection, but sure of his own Ohio district, made a short speaking trip through western New York in behalf of the party. He followed Senator Conkling in several places, and at Elmira the two met and talked for half an hour. "Conkling is very strong," Garfield wrote in his journal afterward, "a great fighter, inspired more by his hates than his loves; desires and has followers rather than friends. He will be of more service in a minority than in a majority. In his long service he has done little constructive work."[5]

This last is a familiar criticism. Detractors of the Senator constantly were reminding their audiences, or readers, that no great piece of legislation bore the Conkling name. And this, of course, is true. To Thad Stevens went most of the praise and blame for the work of reconstruction. Sherman got all the glory for the hard-money victory. The electoral commission bill, surely one of the most statesmanlike measures ever adopted by an American Congress, might well have been called the Conkling bill; but it wasn't. Alfred Conkling has described his uncle as "not an originator, but a moulder of legislation. . . . It may be said that during his last seven years in the Senate, no other member of that body has, since the time of Webster and Clay, exercised so much influence on legislation."[6]

Nor was there anything new in the assertion that Conkling's *métier* was opposition. Acrimony befits a minority, and the Senator always was brilliant in attack. But opposition calls for patience too, and good humor, and the Senator had none of these. Moreover, his whole political existence had been as a member of a dominating faction. During the war and for some years thereafter, the Republicans had been supreme. The Senator was not accustomed to real resistance—pauseless, organized, untiring resistance. It seemed to him treason, or at least insubordination, and he was infuriated by it.

Nevertheless, and whether he liked it or not, he was a member of the minority now. For '78 was a Democratic year. The followers of Jefferson saw their majority in the House slightly reduced, but they gained control of the Senate.

THE Democrats, so many of whom were veteran martyrs, with both houses under control, for the first time in almost twenty years, proceeded to poke up the Hayes-Tilden election scandal—which was the one action needed to close Republican ranks.

They held up the army appropriation bill for a long time, eventually winning their point. A New York representative, Clarkson N. Potter, introduced a bill calling for an investigation of the '76 elections in Louisiana and Florida. The Republicans fought this in vain. As was the case with every question connected with that election, the vote was strictly along party lines. The Republican senators in caucus appointed a committee to see what could be done about it. A member, Hoar of Massachusetts, framed a strong statement of the Republican case, asserting that Hayes was in the White House to stay and that any attempt to unseat him would mean civil war. This was almost as stupid as the Clarkson bill which provoked it, for it was certain to lead to nothing but hard feeling. Yet every member of the committee had approved it, informally, when Senator Conkling came to the meeting late. The statement was read to him. "He opposed the whole plan with great earnestness and indignation, spoke with great severity of President Hayes, and said that he hoped it would be the last time that any man in the United States would attempt to steal the Presidency."[7]

The matter was dropped.

THERE were plenty of intelligent men to argue both sides of the silver question, but when he criminally ignored another great national problem Roscoe Conkling was in fashion. Until Cleveland, the pension legislation, like the tariff, inspired some speech making but almost no real congressional work.[8] You were for pensions—unless you happened to be a Southerner, in which event you were against them—but you didn't stop to ask questions. Possibly you feared the soldiers' vote, the growing power of the G.A.R. (which like the American Legion was organized as a nonpolitical body, and which like the American Legion didn't live up to its good intentions); or possibly you were just careless. With Conkling, apparently, it was just carelessness.

In the seventy-one years between the founding of this republic and the outbreak of the Civil War the Federal Government had spent about $90,000,000 in military pensions, exclusive of administrative expenses, besides giving away 65,000,000 acres of very cheap bounty land.[9]

There was practically no opposition to the act of July 14, 1862, which produced the only system of military pension laws in force until July 27, 1890. It established a Bureau of Pensions, and it has applied to survivors of all wars after March 4, 1861 (excepting the World War), whether in the navy, army, or marines, whether they were regulars, militiamen, or volunteers, and provided pensions for men permanently hurt as a direct consequence of performance of duty, and also for the widows, children, and other dependents of those who died in actual military or naval service or who died after the close of hostilities from causes to be traced directly to injuries received or diseases contracted during such service.

The first commissioner of pensions, in his first report, predicted that the sum needed to carry out this law would never exceed $7,000,000 a year. He could not know what was to happen. By 1870 the Government was spending $29,000,000 a year; in 1880 it spent $57,000,000; in 1890 it spent $106,-000,000. And this was only the beginning.

The act of July 4, 1864, began the process of increasing the pensions in cases of shocking disabilities.

In February, 1873, the law was "liberalized" without serious opposition, and the discretionary power of the administrators greatly increased. This power was still further increased by the act of August 27, 1888.

Grant, of course, had approved all pension legislation. And Hayes was enthusiastic. Hayes later told himself in his diary:

As to pensions I would say our Union soldiers fought in the divinest war that was ever waged. Our war did more for our country than any other war ever achieved for any other country. It did more for the world—more for mankind—than any other war in history. . . . No soldier who fought in that war on the right side nor his widow nor his orphans ought ever to be forced to choose between starvation and the poorhouse.[10]

Only two members of the Hayes cabinet, Schurz and Sherman, objected to the increases.

It was the Cummings Arrears Bill which really opened the floodgates. Hard times and the increases had caused large numbers of veterans to wonder why they hadn't applied for pensions. "Veterans' lawyers" infested Washington then as they do today, and the G.A.R. was beginning to organize its monstrous lobby.

The Cummings Bill provided that veterans or their dependents who applied for and were granted pensions would receive all back payments for which they never had asked, precisely as though application had been made promptly upon the return to civilian life. In other words, a man whose lawyer could convince him that his ailments might be a result of his war service fourteen or fifteen years earlier, and who could get a pension on the basis of this claim, would receive back payments for all the years in which he hadn't been troubled by the said ailments at all and during which he never had thought of asking for a pension. The results, some of them, were astounding. There was, for example the case of Mrs. Mary A. Van Etten, whose husband, an uninjured veteran, was drowned in 1875, ten years after the close of the war, when a buggy he was trying to drive through a swollen stream—in spite of warnings—was upset. Ten years later, in 1885, the widow applied for a pension with full arrears for twenty years, on the ground that the death was directly attributable to war service: her husband, she contended, could have swum ashore if it hadn't been for his rheumatism, which had been contracted in the war. She got the money, too! And so did hundreds of others, thousands of others, with claims not a whit less foolish than this one.[11]

The pension laws not only cost the Government incalculable millions of dollars directly: they occupied weeks, months, even years of Congressional and executive time. The waste was appalling.

All this got its true start with the passage of the first arrears bill, the Cummings Bill. Properly examined, properly equipped with teeth, it might have done little harm. This was the time for some careful senator or representative to study the matter, to foresee and to warn loudly against the evils which would result from passage of this bill as introduced. But nobody did. It was passed with large majorities; and gleefully the "veterans' lawyers" and the G.A.R. lobbyists came to the realization that they could ask for almost anything they wished, and get it.

THERE were some slight last-minute misgivings. Senator Saulsbury did ask Ingalls of Kansas, chairman of the committee on pensions, to give the Senate a notion of how much money the bill would mean. "We ought not to vote blindly on this matter," Saulsbury announced. Ingalls, who five years later, while arguing for a bill to repeal the time limitation on arrears, was to shout: "I do not care whether it costs one million or one thousand millions: I am pushing this matter simply upon its abstract justice!"—Ingalls in 1879 was rather less reckless:

Mr. President, in 1876, when a similar measure was pending before the Senate, I addressed a communication to the Commissioner of Pensions and asked him for information in regard to the amount which would be required to make the bill operative. . . . I do not know that it will be necessary to read specifically the annual amounts, but up to the 1st of January, 1876, the Commissioner reports that there were 16,454 invalid cases to which the limitation of the section applied, and the estimated amount of arrears at that time was $9,529,775. The number of widows and dependents was 5,145. The amount required to pay the arrears of those would have been $3,887,334; making a total at that time of $13,417,109. There have been three years since that date, and of course I can only estimate what amount would be required since this computation was made; but taking the estimate for 1875 as an average, my judgment would be that to this sum should be added not less than five million dollars for claims since allowed to which the limitation now applies. Of course these estimates are very largely in the nature of surmise, because we cannot tell until the bill is put practically in operation exactly what will be required.

It would have been a fitting moment for somebody to anticipate Alice with the exclamation: "If any one of them can explain it, I'll give him sixpence. *I* don't believe there's an atom of meaning in it!" Instead, the senior Senator from New York asked:

Making in all how much, as the Senator has it there?
Mr. Ingalls: Making in all, up to the 1st of January, 1876, the sum of $13,417,109, and that amount I should judge would be increased by not less than $5,000,000 up to the 1st of January, 1879.
Mr. Conkling: Which makes about $19,000,000?
Mr. Ingalls: I should judge somewhere from eighteen to twenty million dollars, in round numbers. Of course it is impossible to make anything like an accurate calculation upon a matter of this kind.[12]

And this closed the discussion. Four senators voted against the Cummings Bill, but Roscoe Conkling was not one of them.

THE first howl rose over the fact that the bill did not provide any appropriation. Sherman wailed that there would be no money to put the law in operation: anyway, it would certainly create a deficit. The pension bureau held up all cases affected, pending further congressional action. Soft-money cranks, just when it had begun to look as though the nation was about to shake off the greenback Old Man of the Sea at last, began babbling about the need for another $50,000,000 of legal tender. Possibly it was this threat which roused Roscoe Conkling to a sense of the importance of the situation. Or possibly he thought that he had been fooled. Anyway, he began to take some interest in pension legislation—now that it was too late. An appropriation bill, as amended by the Senate, greatly limited the operation of the arrears bill. It set July 1, 1880, as the last date for filing of applications if arrears were expected; and it carried an appropriation of $25,000,000 for arrears up to the time of the passage of the Cummings Bill, January 25, 1879, and $1,800,000 for the fiscal year ending June 30—that is, arrears from January 25 to June 30. What would happen after that was something for John Sherman to worry about. Even in its amended form, Pension Commissioner James A. Bentley calculated that the Cummings Bill would ultimately cost the nation $150,000,000. In fact, it was to cost, directly and indirectly, many times that sum.

Senator Conkling, angry, read from the record Ingalls' long and foggy answer to the Saulsbury question, and he seems to have realized at last that he didn't understand this —that none of the other senators had understood it, that probably Ingalls himself didn't.

Mr. Conkling: Will the Senator allow me once more to ask, because I am stupid, I confess I do not yet understand him, did the Senator mean that $19,000,000 would be the cost of the arrears of pension bill, or did he mean that it would cost up to that date, to wit: January, 1879, $19,000,000 and leave an indefinite cost afterward?

Mr. Ingalls: That was what I said, and of course it was what I meant, because the arrears of pension bill provided for the removal of the limitation, and what would be required of [for?] those who thereafter made application could no more be calculated or estimated than one could calculate the number of birds that will fly through the air next year.

Mr. Conkling: Then if the Senator will allow me, I shall apologize I think sufficiently for my misunderstanding by reading the question which he answered: "Mr. Saulsbury: I should like . . ."

[He read it all.] Listening to the Senator from Kansas in response to that question I understood, and I think naturally and excusably, that he was answering that and telling us the total amount, as far as could be estimated, covered by the bill, and not telling us merely that without reference to the whole amount, up to a certain date, probably, nineteen millions would be paid out under it.[13]

Yet for all this indignation, the barn door remained unlocked and there were many, many horses still to be stolen. The deficit Sherman was moaning about never materialized, for the following year showed an unexpected increase in tariff revenues; men looked around, and couldn't find the depression at all; capital, made dizzy by the sudden release, gayly started another ride for another fall; and pension lobbyists perceived with joy that the real fun was only beginning. The country was prosperous again! Let the politicians spend all they wished, for the country was prosperous!

DEFENSE of the abstract political principle was not going well. Arthur and Cornell had been removed, and Merritt, Burt, and Graham appointed in July, 1878. On December 3, the day after Congress reassembled in regular session, the Merritt-Burt-Graham appointments were submitted to the Senate. Roscoe Conkling, whose committee on commerce remained the same, was not present, so consideration was postponed. The Senator didn't appear until the tenth. On the twelfth his committee met, but only five members were there, so nothing was done about the nominations. By the twentieth, when Congress adjourned for the holidays, the committee still had not acted. The committee met again January 7, 1879, but again it did nothing about Merritt and Burt and Graham.

There had been no change in the personnel of the committee on commerce, and there is little doubt that Senator Conkling, had he wished to do so, could have smothered these nominations. But such action would not have restored Arthur and Cornell; it would only have resulted in the continuance in office of Merritt and Burt and Graham; it would have been, for Conkling, an admission of defeat.

January 15 there was an executive session of the entire Senate, and the president of that body read a long letter from John Sherman. It repeated the charges against Arthur and Cornell, but contained nothing new. Conkling successfully fought a motion to have this letter made public, and carried a motion to have it submitted to his committee for investigation and to give Chet Arthur a chance to reply. The following day the committee met, but it did nothing—probably because, as the *New York World* said, Senator Conkling wished first to be certain of his own reëlection.

January 24 the committee reported against the nominations of Merritt and Burt but made no mention of Graham, and three days later, at another executive session, it reported favorably on Graham and submitted the Arthur and Cornell answers to the Sherman letter.[14]

All this was bad for the party. It was not, as administration spokesmen asserted, a battle of reform against bossism, but merely a sordid fight for patronage, for political control of the most important state. Nobody pretended that Merritt and Burt would give the New York customs house a better administration than Arthur and Cornell. It is probable that most of the senators believed with Vest, a member of the commerce committee, that Senator Conkling was being "badly treated." Their inclination was to support him, for he represented the dignity of the Senate, he represented an established Republican organization, strong party discipline. The boss was an inevitable evil—if indeed he was an evil at all—and New York appeared to be satisfied with Roscoe Conkling, who at least stood upon clear ground and had nothing hypocritical about him. Moreover, the real reformers, the true zealots, were beginning to see that an administration which had started so well, from their point of view, in fact was not notably sincere about this whole business; and Curtis' friend Cary raised a typical sob of disillusionment when he expressed a conviction that civil service reform was "a subject which has gone . . . on its way to dusty death in the pigeon-holes of Mr. Hayes's Cabinet."[15]

The Senate Democrats, pleased with things, decided in caucus to oppose confirmation of the Merritt and Burt nominations. It would widen the rift, they hoped.

The following day at still another executive session Senator Conkling abruptly announced himself in favor of prompt action. Undoubtedly he wished to gather his Democratic votes while he might. Senator Mathews moved for consideration on Monday (this was a Wednesday) hoping to give the administration forces a chance to repair breaks, but Senator Conkling succeeded in having the motion changed to Friday.

The Friday executive session lasted four bitter hours. A message from the White House enclosed a long rebuttal from Sherman. Senator Conkling submitted a supplementary statement by Arthur. His fellow senator from New York, and fellow townsman, Kernan, submitted a petition from the Democrats of the New York State senate. Conkling unexpectedly read a petition *for* confirmation signed by a large number of New York legislators, forty-six of them Republicans, and then read telegrams from twenty of these men protesting that they had signed that petition only because they thought he wished them to do so. Evidently something at home had slipped, and the Senator had been obliged to speak sharply. Mathews moved for postponement until Monday because of new evidence, and in spite of the Conkling opposition this motion carried.

The Democrats were wavering in their original determination to oppose confirmation. Their party discipline at this time, their respect for caucus decisions, was not nearly so firm as that of the Republicans; and probably the Senator had foreseen this wobbling; probably it accounts for his about-face in the matter of prompt consideration.

Monday there was still another executive session. It started at one o'clock, and continued until eight. Conkling submitted one more Arthur statement. The Democrats were breaking away from him, and, no longer eager for promptness now, he moved that the whole matter be referred back to his committee. He talked for two hours, and it was a speech of exceptional bitterness, even from him. He scoffed at the contention that Hayes and Sherman really were trying to do anything to better the public service. He read many communications from members of the administration party to Chester Arthur, as collector, asking him to give jobs to friends.

But this thing had gone too far. It was splitting the party, holding up legislation, raising yaups of protest from press and public, and worst of all threatening members of both houses with a summer or part of a summer in Washington. The Senator's motion was brushed aside, the nominations at last were voted upon. Twenty-five Democrats and fifteen Republicans voted for confirmation, seven Democrats and twenty-three Republicans voted against confirmation.

The Senator was beaten. Jubilant Democrats demanded clamorously that all the proceedings, and particularly the letters Conkling had read, be made public. It would be a lovely scandal. The Senator angrily refused, stuffed the letters into a pocket, stalked out.

Four days later the nomination of General Graham was confirmed without any opposition. Nobody ever had objected to that nomination, anyway.

XXVI. He Was a Gambler

HE was down only figuratively. Defeat seemed only to stiffen him, increase his arrogance. He knew that a pack of political wolves padded close behind him—not snarling, as wolves are supposed to do, but following in watchful silence, with the hope that he would forget their presence—watching and waiting for him to stagger, to stumble. But he walked straight, without hesitation, and held his head high. Editor Brockway wrote: "Take half a dozen men from that body [the Senate] and Mr. Conkling had more brains than all the rest put together." Surely the Senator agreed. Nor did he forget that, after all, and in spite of unthinking popular criticism, the United States Senate really was as it is today the most august and most distinguished legislative body in the world.

The Senate was his own. He belonged to it, or it belonged to him, by something akin to divine right. Once, in the course of the debate on the army appropriation bill, April 24, 1879, he had been speaking for half an hour when General William T. Sherman appeared in full regimentals. General Sherman was the highest ranking officer in the army, and except for Grant carried more prestige than any other military figure in the country. Senator Conkling greeted him affably. "Good morning, general. I'm glad to see you here. Take that seat." He pointed to an empty chair in the front row on the Democratic side, and a rather startled visitor moved into this while the Senator continued his speech. "He welcomed General Sherman to the Senate Chamber as a private gentleman would receive an invited guest to his home," recorded one awed spectator, "and ignored entirely the existence of the Senate or its presiding officer."[1]

He told a story to a reporter who cornered him one night in the Fifth Avenue Hotel, and who noted that "the reddish tints in his whiskers and hair are still very noticeable amid the gray." Ben Hill had encountered him in the street: "Senator, I am obliged to give you notice that I have filed an application for your seat when you are compelled to leave it. I don't say that I personally hope it will be empty; but in case it is—and that now looks probable—I have put a caveat on it." A smiling Senator replied: "Mr. Hill, there have been five applicants for my seat, and they are all dead or disappointed. I don't know that I hope you will have as bad luck."[2]

When the time came, mutterings of discontent were stilled by the awful Presence. Cæsar turned, the blue-gray eyes flashed, and the wolves, forgetting all about a contemplated meal, hastened to lick the beautifully polished Conkling boots.

The Greenback movement, a movement indeed, had come east. Quitting Ohio, its original stronghold, it gave the genial Major McKinley a chance to get into Congress. In Massachusetts it boosted that tubby little demogogue Ben Butler back into the national House of Representatives. In New York it cut deeply into the Democratic vote, so that the legislature, in 1879, was predominately Republican again, and the election of a Republican senator was certain. Who else could this be but Roscoe Conkling, the Voice? Who else would dare aspire to that seat? George William Curtis was grievously disappointed; his after-the-fact cheeriness gave a dull sound, creating no echoes. "But the unanimity of action does not imply unanimity of feeling. The vital spirit of the Republican party is the spirit of reform and progress. Of that spirit Mr. Conkling has never been, and can never be, a representative leader."[3] The fact remained that for the third time, and without one officially audible grunt of dissent, Roscoe Conkling was elected to the United States Senate.

BESSIE married that Oakman lad after all; and though the bridegroom, recently made assistant to the D. L. & W. district superintendent at Utica, no longer might be seen with the grime of toil upon his person, the Senator was unforgiving. Thereafter he referred to Oakman only as "Mrs. Conkling's son-in-law."

But then, the cold gray house in Rutger Street was by this time little more than a legal residence. The Senator was spending most of his days in Washington or in New York, where he conducted such law cases as he had time for; and in both of these cities his life was that of a bachelor. He still could gather with the somewhat pompous and paunchy "boys" who played poker upstairs at Harvey's; he still glittered as a glass of fashion, attracting all eyes, when he stalked through the lobby of the Fifth Avenue Hotel; and the stories of his affairs with women persisted.

However, the scandal tales remained vague. They were no more than whispers. The press then, though not addicted to the use of 96-point streamer heads, "cosmographs," double column boxes, and other modern refinements, was quite as eager as the press today to print details of hideous happenings in high places; and the press was almost unanimously hostile to Roscoe Conkling. Notwithstanding, there was never a public charge of improper personal conduct made against the Senator. Indeed, now and then some fair-minded editor even took it upon himself to shush angrily at the dirty-story repeaters; and once Conkling found himself writing a stiff but obviously sincere note to Whitelaw Reid of the *Tribune*, thanking him for such a defense, "all the more gratifying because I had no reason to expect you to concern yourself in the least in my behalf in any affair whatever."[4]

But at their worst, these were no more than minor irritants. The Senator's mind was occupied by greater things—and chiefly by the problem of regaining his one-time prestige as a power-behind-the-throne. There must be no more accidents like Rutherford B. Hayes. What the country needed was another term of General Grant, and the Senator meant to see that it got this. Nor would he take any chances with a blundering, vacillating New York delegation. This time he would go *in person* to the national convention! He would supervise the job *himself!*

HAYES wouldn't run again. This fact was a well of consolation to the practical politicians all through the bleak years of 1877–80. The President had long ago announced that he favored a six-year term and no reëlection, and with characteristic doggedness he stuck to this belief. Not only was he stepping aside, but he did not advance any favorite of his own; he didn't lend the weight of his position to any aspirant.

But if there was no White House candidate, there was assuredly a Treasury choice. As early as the previous summer Secretary Sherman had dined his fellow Ohioan, James Abram Garfield, and afterward, in the course of a long carriage drive through Maryland, had mentioned significantly that he was not ambitious to step from the cabinet into the senatorship which would soon be open for somebody. He needn't have been so secretive. Garfield, who was to get that senatorship himself, was perfectly aware, as was everybody else in national politics, that Sherman wished to be President. And eventually, after other talks, Garfield consented to be his campaign manager.

Blaine's ambition too was an open secret, for all his protestations. "I will never again fight an aggressive battle," he wrote his friend Whitelaw Reid, December 10, "horses cannot drag me into it, and as you well know I am literally doing nothing in the matter. . . . I enjoy my place in the Senate and unless the deuce comes to be counted as the ace in Maine I can hold it indefinitely. Why then should I fret to get into a doubtful contest?" He pointed out that he would only have been in his early fifties if elected in 1876, and "Frank Pierce once told me that God Almighty had permitted no torture to be invented so cruel as the life of an Ex-President; in fact, as he said to Gov. Shaw, 'there is nothing left for him but to get drunk.' As I have no taste for liquor even that resource would have been cut off from me."

He had confided to Garfield in April of '79 that he deemed the nomination of Grant "impossible." The following month, however, in the course of a long walk around the grounds of the Naval Observatory, he had told Garfield that he then believed the Grant nomination "quite probable," and was planning to run only because he thought himself the best stop-Grant possibility. "On the whole I think that Blaine is now more confident of the nomination than I have ever known him," Garfield wrote in his journal April 14. "I like Blaine, always have, and yet there is an element in him which I mistrust."

Others felt the same way. Personally Blaine always enjoyed an immense popularity; yet so many of the men who liked to spend time in his company, felt, for some reason they could not quite explain, that it would not be proper to put such a man in the White House. There was something vaguely disgusting about his fondness for money and for millionaires. And while nobody ever was to prove any dishonesty against him, always there were hints, there were whispers. . . .

Morton was dead, and Bristow had retired; but there were Edmunds, and Washburne, whom the reformers rather favored, and Windom, and sundry others; and of course Roscoe Conkling's friends were urging him to run.

But Conkling would not tolerate such talk while his friend U. S. Grant had a chance.

THE Grant stock was higher than ever. He was, first of all, the general: he was the man who had made a sensational success as director of the late carnage, and this fitted him to be a peace executive. Inexplicably, for the depression had started in his second administration, his name was associated with prosperity. After four years of the Hayes uncertainties, the silence and supposed strength of Grant had a tremendous appeal. The fact that he was more than a merely national figure had recently been emphasized when kings and emperors and mikados and suchlike had bobbed before him, and dukes and earls and barons had fought for a look at him, while he made his trip around the world. This was incalculably flattering to the vanity of a democratic nation. The whole world had been huzzaing Grant; and should his own country fail to cheer? The general landed in San Francisco in September, 1879, and his trip east was one long frenzy of applause. People shrieked, shouted, and sobbed Grant's name; people waited for hours at obscure railroad stations to cry him on his way; they wined and dined him, and made all sorts of speeches at him, and presented him with almost everything conceivable; people stepped on one another's toes and jabbed one another in the ribs and punched one another's faces for the privilege of getting close enough to have one peek at the soundless bearded hero.

It is true that some said that Grant was drunk during much of this time. But such remarks were not new, and not important.

It is true that some sneered at the whole triumphant journey as stage-managed, press-agented. This, however, was not the case. Indeed, his more sagacious friends had urged the general to postpone his return to this country, so that the echoes of the clamor would still be ringing throughout the nation when the national convention assembled. But he was tired, and wished to be rid of be-ordered potentates, banquet menus, city keys. From a sheerly political point of view he came back much too soon. There was time for a revulsion of feeling. "The ovation business," as the *Atlantic Monthly* perceived, "palled upon the public taste."[5]

The prejudice against a third term, not so evident then as it has become since, nevertheless was considerable.[6] Even the reformers were frightened, the "man-milliners." George William Curtis and his followers were firmly set against a third term. John Milton Hay was pessimistic. He wrote to his friend Whitelaw Reid that the movement could no more be stopped by a sober, serious presentation of facts than a yellow fever epidemic could be stopped by a brass band. And though Grant said nothing, indubitably Grant wished to get back into the White House. For didn't Mrs. Grant wish it, and wouldn't the general "rather offend forty million people than Madame"?

SHOUTS and cheers are not enough; but Grant had plenty more than these. Working for him was the most powerful group of political bosses in the country, a triumvirate of czars: Logan of Illinois, Don Cameron, who had succeeded his father Si as ruler of Pennsylvania, and Roscoe Conkling.

In Conkling's instance it was much more than a service to a friend. The Senator, apparently supreme, in fact was fighting for his political life.

On the surface all was tranquil. Conkling had no rival, and his word was law: there was no appeal from his decision. But underneath it all the party had for several years been split in New York State; and now that the two factions had names the real battle came into sight.

Names make such a difference! A group of men controlling a party in a given city, or county, or state, do well enough so long as they are known collectively as an "organization," but once the public has formed the habit of calling them a "ring" or "machine" the end is near. More, if they are so foolish as to permit themselves to be called by a *specific* name, then certainly they are doomed to unceasing reproach. Tammany is the classic example. The greatest blunder the rulers of that organization ever committed—and they have made, through the generations, some astoundingly stupid mistakes—was when, in the first place, they permitted themselves to be plastered with a name. It has been a can tied to a dog's tail. Even if Tammany were today to become honest and decent and efficient, the name would persist and because of it righteous noses would be turned away from a stench departed.

Many, many of the nicknames for political factions originated in New York—Conscience Whigs, Silver-Grays, Woolly-Heads, Hunkers and Barnburners, Locofocos, Scratchers, Hardshells and Softshells, Copperheads, Feather-Heads, Know-Nothings. . . . Though there can be no certainty, and lesser personages have squabbled about it with the shrill passion of men who snatch at what might prove a shred of accidental immortality, Senator Conkling himself has generally been credited with invention of the terms Stalwart and Half-Breed.

He was a Stalwart. He was, indeed, *the* Stalwart. And as

all who were not his absolute slaves were his enemies, those were Half-Breeds.

It is possible to understand why men go to war, stupid and futile and disgusting though war may be. It is easy to sympathize with and even admire the men who become martyrs to their religious beliefs, though one may not share those beliefs. But about political battles of the past, purely local, factional fights, compressed like so many flat flowers in the book of time and no longer giving out any odor or bearing the smallest resemblance to their original shape of loveliness —about these the loftiest brow and the lowest contract in perplexity. Why all the pother? What made these men so excited, so long ago? With no great issue involved, why did they tear their hair and beat their breasts, thump speakers' stands so that the ice-water pitchers leapt, and why did they call one another such hard, hard names?

The term Stalwart quickly came to have a national application—came to be fixed upon those men who recently were known as the Republican Old Guard, and who still more recently have been sneered at as the Rugged Individualists— though this latter comparison is not altogether fair. Also there were men in Washington who were called Half-Breeds; and in Washington, indeed, were fought some of the hottest battles of this war. Yet the war itself was essentially a New York affair.

Today it is incomprehensible. For it was bitter. It broke up old friendships, and even families, setting brother against brother, father against son. It caused men all over the state to rant for the Senator or against him. It inspired men who never before had given a serious thought to James G. Blaine now to cheer Blaine as their absent and none-too-enthusiastic leader—only because Blaine was the most conspicuous among the Conkling enemies.

It was not a reform fight, though members of the Better Element, always negligible but just now rather noisy, and always eager for a change, any change, were to be found in the ranks of the Half-Breeds. It was not a struggle of giants for leadership of the state, for Conkling had no real rival: nobody had the temerity to reach for his scepter.

It seems to have had something to do with Conkling's own personality, and in an even more blurry sense with the whole idea of bossism. It was the ins against the outs, an ancient struggle deprived of its customary rules and good-nature. Half-Breeds and Stalwarts. . . . You would have supposed that the fate of civilization depended upon it, the way they fought.

The Senator's own attitude was clear enough. He was a gambler, playing for all or nothing. If Grant were made President, he, Conkling, would be the most powerful political figure in the country. With the Federal patronage again in his grasp, he could club dissenters back into line, and all rebellion would end.

Moreover, Grant would serve only one term—nobody, not even the Senator himself, dreamed of a *fourth* term! At the end of those four years, then, it was quite possible that the White House would be found naming the next nominee. Blaine never had enjoyed the Grant favor. Logan wasn't of Presidential caliber, and didn't pretend to be. Morton was dead now. There could only be Roscoe Conkling.

If, on the other hand, Grant were defeated— But the Senator did not consent even to contemplate this possibility.

XXVII. With Colors Flying

AGAINST a man like James G. Blaine you could not get started too early. The Pennsylvania state convention for the selection of delegates to the Republican national convention was held in Harrisburg, February 4. There was much Blaine sentiment, but Don Cameron did his work well—he was a more finished boss than his father Si—and the convention voted 133–113 for Grant and for unit rule. In other words, Pennsylvania was solid for Grant.

It was Conkling's turn next, and his task was more difficult. His opposition was stronger, for one thing. The close vote at Harrisburg was discouraging. And the Germans, then highly important citizens, particularly in New York and Wisconsin, inclined to liberalism and hated even a hint of despotism: they were unbudgingly opposed to a third term.

The state convention was held in the Utica Opera House, February 25. Charles Emory Smith, with his ruddy cheeks and sparkling eyes, was chairman. He was editor of the *Albany Evening Journal,* and once he had been Reuben Fenton's secretary; but he was nothing if not a practical politician—he later became postmaster general—so now he was a Conkling man, and dutifully opened the convention with a reference to "the never vanquished hero of Appomattox."

Young Isaac Hunt was a delegate from Jefferson County, who had been working against the unit rule. The Senator had not failed to watch these little outcroppings of the independent spirit here and there; and when young Hunt, all a-tremble at the honor, first was presented to the great man, in the Mansion House lobby amid a great crowd, there was boomed at him: "You have a strange way of running your politics in Jefferson County!" In the circumstances it scared the young man half out of his wits; but it didn't change his opinion, or his vote.[1]

In the Senator's home town tickets should go only to the faithful, but the Half-Breeds this year persuaded the printer to strike off many extra tickets and by using these they packed the balcony. When the clerk, reading a report of the resolutions committee, hesitated at a difficult word, somebody up there precipitated a demonstration by shouting "Hurrah for Blaine!" The Senator, pale with fury, administered a classic rebuke. Head back, his eyes flashing with Olympian fire, majestically and very slowly, he quoted Walter Raleigh's line:

"The shallows murmur, but the deeps are dumb."[2]

It silenced, as it delighted, the gallery. Thereafter the work of pledging for Grant was not interrupted. But the vote was a mere 216–183, not at all impressive.

Nevertheless, the Senator would not tolerate anything but an iron-bound unit rule. "What is the use of a delegate? Is it a man to go to a convention representing others, and then determine as he individually prefers what he will do? Let me say frankly that if any man, however much I respect him, were presented to this convention who would prove recreant to its judgment, I would never vote for him as a delegate to any convention." The Stalwarts deliberately asked the opponents of unit rule—who had the Senator's threat ringing in their ears—whether they would be bound by the resolution; and the answer, if reluctantly given, was affirmative.

So New York State was in line, and fastened there. Soon afterward Logan followed with Illinois, neatly wrapped for delivery. The spontaneous popular demand for a return of Grant was making headway, inch by inch.

Some silence followed. Then Judge Robertson, on May 6, almost three months after the convention, publicly announced that he intended to vote for Blaine, pledge or no pledge. The *New York Times*[3] expressed a belief that this "tardy revolt" was dictated by "self interest," inasmuch as "the pliant politician from Westchester had chafed under a sense of disappointed ambition ever since the defeat of his nomination for governor in 1872"—a defeat for which he blamed Conkling. Still, here was open defiance. It raised echoes. The independents began to get independent again, and Curtis wrote in *Harper's*[4] that Roscoe Conkling had "tricked" the delegates into a pledge which the convention had had no authority to exact. Woodin said that since he personally was not able to vote for Blaine, because of the pledge, he would send his alternate to the national convention and direct *him* to vote for Blaine; and Birdsall and Sessions, going further, announced from the floor of the state senate that Blaine would get their own votes.

CONKLING had yet his ultimate weapon. He could make a speech.

The whole country was waiting to hear that speech, too. For the Senator, as he'd promised, was preparing to attend his first national convention—along with Chet Arthur, Governor Cornell and James D. Warren he had been elected a delegate-at-large—and of course he was slated to place Grant's name in nomination. It would be a great event. The West, the country as a whole, had not yet heard the Conkling voice. Just at that time there was a general conviction, probably inspired or stimulated by Bob Ingersoll's "plumed knight" speech of '76—which, however, had not brought about the nomination of Blaine—that orations might conceivably affect convention votes. That is, if they were great orations. And Conkling's would be great: nobody doubted it.

The convention was held in Chicago, in June, and it was as much fun for the public, and promoted as much hard feeling, as though it had been a Democratic affair. Colonel McClure, something of a connoisseur of national conventions, for he had attended every one since 1848, believed that the Republican conventions of 1860 and 1880 were easily the greatest in ability and leadership. "As compared with these two, all subsequent conventions were tame."

It is not true that all Republican Presidential nominees since the Civil War have been selected by a few men in a smoke-filled hotel room at midnight. Surely this was not the case in 1880—and not simply because Senator Conkling would not tolerate cigar smoke, but even more because he wouldn't tolerate any dealing with the enemy. He was for

Grant, and he was for nobody else under any circumstances whatever.[5]

THE Conkling-Logan-Cameron machine was a masterpiece, and well-oiled throughout, but even these skilled engineers could not keep away all the tossers of monkey wrenches. In fact, they were sadly outnumbered. Don Cameron was chairman of the national committee, and he tried hard and long to keep the permanent chairmanship of the convention away from Senator Hoar, the Sherman-Blaine choice. But Hoar got the job. Cameron sat all one morning refusing to entertain a motion which would instruct Hoar against acknowledging the unit rule; in the afternoon he was told "informally, and in a rather veiled fashion" that the committee would get a new chairman if he didn't behave; and again, though not until he had sounded the sergeant-at-arms on the possibility of keeping his seat by force, he was obliged to submit.[6]

Garfield was chairman of the rules committee, which after a three-hour session decided against the unit rule. A Conkling member, General Sharpe of New York, led the minority which framed a separate report. Frye, a Blaine friend, moved that these reports be submitted before the report of the credentials committee, since the latter wasn't ready. Sharpe objected. Garfield, always trying to be conciliatory, and probably certain that the unit rule cause was lost anyway, agreed to hold up the rules committee reports—though he pointed out that the convention as a whole could call for them any time it wished.

There was a lot of jockeying about these reports, the Blaine men, led by Henderson of Iowa, working for quick adoption, the Grant men, in this headed by Logan, bitterly opposing such a course.

"Our work here still drags its slow length along, through more passion than there was at Chickamauga," Garfield wrote to his wife. "I have seen nothing like it in politics."[7]

But the report of the credentials committee on Illinois saw the defeat of the Grant bloc anyway. "Black Jack" Logan had operated his steam roller too noisily, and the committee refused to take his dictation. The convention adoption vote was close, 387–353. The vote against unit rule itself was somewhat wider, 449–306. It was followed by a resolution providing that when any delegate took exception to the correctness of his state vote as cast by the delegation's chairman, the president of the convention should insist upon a roll-call vote of the individual members of the delegation. For nobody trusted anybody else in this fight.

The unit rule was broken. It was the greatest defeat the Grant group could possibly have suffered. It cost Grant, immediately, indisputably, 17 New York votes, 23 from Pennsylvania, and 10 from Illinois.

If it had not been for this decision, if the Conkling-Logan-Cameron plan had succeeded, it is almost certain that Grant would have been nominated, possibly on the first ballot. Which might have resulted in a split, and another convention: anyway, there were the usual threats.[8]

GRANT stayed at home, that being Galena, Illinois, and smoked cigars, and said nothing. He was in the hands, the very busy, efficient hands, of his friends.

Sherman stroked his beard and bit chunks of skin from the inside of his mouth, while he wondered whether James A. Garfield was the right choice for manager after all. A clever man, Garfield. But Sherman couldn't help wondering . . . and worrying. He was a gloomy soul at best; and he desired the nomination so ardently that it hurt.

Blaine, for all his insistence about not wishing to be nominated, had arranged to have a private telegraph wire, a most extraordinary expense in those days, direct from the convention hall to his own home in Washington.

There, on the field, Roscoe Conkling's was easily the most pointed-out figure. For a man who never before had attended a national convention, even as a spectator, he was doing himself remarkably well. He was lodged in fine style at the Grand Pacific Hotel. He was gaped at when he ate breakfast there, gaped at wherever he went. Breathless whispers whirled and eddied behind him like tobacco smoke as he stalked from place to place. His silence in the presence of reporters, his fondness for quiet little talks in corners, made him a man of mystery. His entrances into the convention hall itself were masterfully timed, invariably effective. Again and again, when the Senator appeared at a nicely chosen moment—the hall being filled, the opening, tedious business almost concluded—he was cheered like a conquering hero. And this was not merely from the galleries, which were not notably either pro-Grant or anti-Grant, but from the floor as well. Head high, looking neither to right nor left, he would stride down the center aisle to his seat in the first row; and there he would listen with chin-up dignity, not turning, while Chet Arthur, Ben Tracy, Edwards Pierrepont, Tom ("Me-too") Platt, Charles E. Cornell, the pale undersized alternate for his father the governor, General Sharpe, Levi Morton, and the others, in their proper order, respectfully, even reverently, leaned over his chair and whispered requests for instruction.

It was, to be sure, more than a shade exasperating when on the second day, while the Senator was speaking in connection with a minor matter, a recess motion, James Abram Garfield entered the hall and was greeted by applause which interrupted this speech.

But for the most part, the Senator had no cause for complaint about applause. Nobody attracted half so much attention. No other man controlled half as many votes. In the limelight, and back in the corridors and committee rooms as well, it was "his" convention.

Yet this was not enough. He must have Grant.

A small and unimportant setback, which, however, must

have hurt the Conkling vanity, occurred when he offered a
resolution proclaiming it to be the sense of the convention
"that every member of it is bound in honor to support the
nominee, whoever that nominee may be; and that no man
should hold a seat here who is not ready so to agree." This
seemed harmless enough—even commendable as a harmony
move, in view of the certainty that the convention, whatever
its outcome, would leave hard feeling somewhere—and it was
carried by a vote almost unanimous, 716–3. But the Senator
went too far when he followed it with a second resolution declaring "the delegates who have voted that they will not
abide the action of the convention do not deserve and have
forfeited their votes in this convention." This brought a
howl of protest, led by Garfield. That man Garfield! The
three negative votes, all from West Virginia, were Blaine
delegates. The Senator was obliged to withdraw his motion.

WHEN his time came, the Senator paused for a dramatic
interval. Then he moved forward, stepped easily upon a reporters' table almost in the dead center of the hall, and
stood there, all six feet three of him, head back, his left
thumb hooked in a waistcoat pocket, his great shoulders, his
flashing gray eyes, his beautiful beard and the Hyperion
curl in the middle of his forehead, fascinating a silent, utterly breathless multitude. Another dramatic pause—and he
opened with verse:

> *When asked what state he hails from,*
> *Our sole reply shall be,*
> *He comes from Appomattox*
> *And its famous apple-tree.*[9]

It was a full ten minutes before he could continue. The
mention of Appomattox (though surely they might have expected it!) had rendered the delegates insane with enthusiasm. Conkling waited, perfectly poised, until the last echo

had chased itself to nothingness. Then he delivered The Speech.

Men babbled and gibbered about it for years afterward. Every word, perfectly enunciated, reached every person in the hall; finished, polished phrases, exquisitely balanced periods, all were delivered in the manner of a master. There was no wildness, no hurry. Emotion there was, sometimes,

BORROWED PLUMES—MR. JACKDAW CONKLING
EAGLE—" Perhaps you would like to pluck me."

but nothing maudlin: it was restrained emotion. Sometimes there was sarcasm, too, as men had expected, but the Senator did not wield rhetorical bludgeons aimlessly and angrily.

"In obedience to instructions which I should never dare to disobey. . . ." But he did not look at the dissenting New York delegates, the men who planned to break their state convention pledge. He didn't have to do so.

Mostly it was about Grant:

. . . perils and emergencies will search in vain in the future, as they have searched in vain in the past, for any other on whom the nation leans with such confidence and trust. Never having had a policy to enforce against the will of the people, he never betrayed a cause or a friend, and the people will never desert or betray him. Standing on the highest eminence of human distinction, modest, firm, simple and self-poised, having filled all lands with his renown, he has seen not only the high-born and the titled, but the poor and lowly in the uttermost ends of the earth, rise and uncover before him. . . . Vilified and reviled, ruthlessly aspersed by unnumbered presses, not in other lands but in his own, assaults upon him have seasoned and strengthened his hold upon the public heart. Calumny's ammunition has all been exploded; the powder has all been burned once; its force is spent; and the name of Grant will glitter a bright and imperishable star in the diadem of the republic when those who have tried to tarnish that name have moldered in forgotten graves and their epitaphs have vanished utterly.

Not all scintillating phrases, either. There was a careful review of Grant's record. There was a warning:

No, gentlemen, the need that presses upon the conscience of this Convention is of a candidate who can carry doubtful States both North and South. And believing that he, more surely than any other man, can carry New York against any opponent, and can carry not only the North, but several States of the South, New York is for Ulysses S. Grant.

Nor were Blaine and Sherman forgotten. Certainly not Blaine!

Without patronage and without emissaries, without committees, without bureaus, without telegraph wires running from his house to this Convention, or running from his house anywhere else, this man is the candidate whose friends have never threatened to bolt unless this Convention did as they said. He is a Republican who never wavers. He and his friends stand by the creed and the candidates of the Republican party. They hold the rightful rule of the majority as the very essence of their faith, and they mean to uphold that faith against not only the common enemy, but against the charlatans, jayhawkers, tramps and guerrillas—the men who deploy between the lines, and forage now on one side and then on the other.

When it was finished, even the men who hated him cheered him.

GARFIELD spoke for his friend John Sherman. Here was no stammering novice, though it was not easy to follow Conkling on the stand.

"I have witnessed the extraordinary scenes of this Convention with deep solicitude," he began sadly. "As I sat in my seat and witnessed this demonstration, this assemblage seemed to me a human ocean tossed in tempest . . . but I remember that it is not the billows but the calm level of the sea from which all heights and depths are measured. . . . Gentlemen of the Convention, your present temper may not mark the healthful pulse of our people. When your enthusiasm has passed, we shall find below the storm and passion that calm level of public opinion from which the thoughts of a mighty people are to be measured. Not here, in this brilliant circle, where . . ."

Senator Conkling snorted, rose. "The man's making me seasick!" His voice was considerably louder than a whisper.

He left the hall, not on tiptoe; and Garfield talked on and on.

Balloting started the fifth day. There was a great deal of guessing as to what Senator Conkling would do about the New York minority. Passionately he believed that they were pledged to vote as one for Grant, despite the convention's smashing of the unit rule, yet if as delegation chairman he cast the state's entire vote for the general it was certain that somebody would cry for and be granted a roll-call.

He stilled this talk when he told the convention that he thought it best to have the New York delegates vote individually. A few hearts beat more rapidly at this, and a few throats got tight. It would mean that the rebels must announce their dissent to the whole world, and this would not be easy with the blue-gray eyes of the Boss, unspeakably cold, such a short distance away.

Birdsall of Queens County was the first Blaine man. He had declared on the floor of the state senate that he would vote for Blaine. He did so, too. But he did it in a low voice, and afterward he sat down in a hurry, his face flaming. There were hisses. But others gained courage; and by the time Robertson cast his vote, loudly, firmly, without any hesitation, there were some cheers.

Fifty-one of the New York votes went to Grant on that ballot, 17 went to Blaine, 2 to Sherman.

The first ballot showed: Grant 304, Blaine 284, Sherman 93, Edmunds 34, Washburne 30, Windom 10; whole number of votes 755; number necessary for choice 378.

Grant and Blaine both picked up a little after that; Sherman stayed about the same; Edmunds, Windom, and Washburne fell off a bit. The balloting went on and on, day after weary day, with no important change. Conkling did not demand a roll-call of his state after the first ballot, but reported unchangingly: "Two delegates are said to be for Sherman, seventeen are said to be for Blaine, and fifty-one

are for Grant." It was unfortunate that he was obliged to
recognize these traitors, but it was his duty and he did. The
West Virginia chairman, not friendly since that foolish resolution about the three West Virginia votes, used to mimic
him: "One delegate is said to be for Grant and eight are
known to be for Blaine."

On the seventeenth ballot Dennis McCarthy, state senator
from Onondaga, switched his vote from Grant to Blaine.
Otherwise the delegation remained unchanged.

IT became increasingly apparent that neither Blaine nor
Grant could get the necessary 378. Grant's vote wavered between 302 and 313, and Blaine's was always a little less than
that. Sherman's did not increase.

Clearly it would be a dark horse; and now the real bargaining began. Conkling would have none of it. He was no
political huckster, to haggle and wave his hands, to promise
this for that, tinkering, tampering, making surreptitious
exchanges. He'd get Grant if he had to smash the party wide
open.

Sherman seems not to have been considered, though some
talked of his campaign manager, Garfield. The three lesser
aspirants had each his proponents, but nobody was willing
to start a real movement toward any of them.

Grant, said Senator Conkling. Nobody else but Grant.
There must be "no angle-worm nomination," said he, doubtless thinking of Rutherford B. Hayes.

No man was in a stronger position for bargaining. He
could not, it is true, throw all the Grant votes to another
candidate, but he could easily throw enough to start a stam-
pede. The delegates were getting tired, were willing to vote
for almost anybody who might win. Conkling could have
made almost any deal he wished—could have clinched for
himself and his friends almost any ambassadorship or cabinet position his fancy suggested. But he wouldn't stir from
his position. And he made it clear, as he had done at Utica,

that any man who broke away from Grant, with whatever excuse, could expect the life-long enmity of Senator Conkling. Grant it must be. Nobody else.

There was even some talk of making *him* the dark horse—and on the thirty-first ballot he did get one vote—but he sniffed at this. Boutwell, one of those present, and a pretty shrewd judge, believed that there was "never a moment of time when such a result was possible."

It was on the thirty-fourth ballot that the break came. The last state to report, Wisconsin, unexpectedly plumped its 16 votes into the lap of James Abram Garfield. That worthy rose to protest that he was not to be considered as a— But Hoar, the chairman, ruled him out of order. On the next ballot Grant had 313 votes, Blaine 257, Sherman 99, Edmunds 11, Washburne 23, Windom 3—and Garfield 50.

This was enough. No remarkable perspicacity was needed to see who would be the winner. All the non-Grant votes from New York State swung swiftly to Garfield, along with many, many others. The thirty-sixth ballot showed: Grant 306, Blaine 42, Washburne 3, Garfield 399.

Sherman didn't get anything. His manager had won.

Senator Hoar asked for a motion to make the nomination unanimous. Roscoe Conkling, erect, austere, made that motion. It was sheerly a formality, yet in him it was almost sportsmanship—the last he was to show. For inside he boiled. The convention was proclaimed a moral victory for Senator Conkling, but he had no interest in such victories. After the first break, a preconvention break which he esteemed nothing less than perfidy on the part of those who would not respect the state convention pledge, his ranks had held. While the Blaine men had broken, sensing the end, and with the Sherman men, and the Washburne and Edmunds and Windom men, were scampering helter-skelter for the Garfield bandwagon, the Grant phalanx, headed by a chief who was the tallest and most rigid of them all, firm in defeat, went down with colors flying. Three hundred and six of them stood on the burning deck whence all but them had fled (it was by no coincidence that the Senator's favorite poem was "Casabianca") and they spent the rest of their lives rather tiresomely congratulating one another because of this fact. One, Chauncey I. Filley,[10] went so far as to have 306 Grant medals struck, and he distributed these: they bore not only the much publicized number, but also the words "The Old Guard," and thereby gave Republican reactionaries, when the term Stalwart was outworn, a new title.

As though a little frightened by what it had done, instantly the convention arranged to nominate some New York Stalwart for the Vice-Presidency. The Senator did not seem interested. General Woodford, his friend, was approached by the Garfield men, and he went to Roscoe Conkling. "I hope no sincere friend of mine will accept it," Conkling told him. The Senator didn't think a man like Garfield could win, and "the question is, whom shall we place upon the altar as a vicarious sacrifice?" Woodford declined the honor.

But it must be a New Yorker, a Conkling man, a Stalwart, somebody who would stand for everything Garfield opposed while opposing everything for which Garfield stood.

If not Woodford, then perhaps Levi P. Morton, the banker? He had all the qualifications. Would he accept?

It seems probable that Morton would have accepted gladly (he was actually to get the Vice-Presidency eight years later, under Benjamin Harrison), but the Boss was not pleased. "If you think the ticket will be elected," he said coldly, "if you think you will be happy in the association, accept." Morton replied humbly that he had greater confidence in the Conkling judgment than in his own. The Senator said: "Governor Boutwell of Massachusetts is a great friend of yours. Why don't you talk with him?" Boutwell, consulted, advised against acceptance, so Morton declined.[11]

Well then, what about Chester Arthur? General Sharpe had suggested him when the Garfield camp begged for *some-*

body, and Chet was acquiescent. The Senator, absent at the time of this decision, was angry when he learned about it; but then it was too late. Chet Arthur was nominated—by the national Half-Breeds who had kicked him out of the New York collectorship as an incompetent.[12]

AFTER this the Democratic national convention, held in Cincinnati, seemed polite, dull.

The Democrats had persistently kept before the public the assertion that Tilden had been elected President but had been cheated out of his office. It had been taken for granted, almost until the last month, that Tilden would be nominated in 1880.

But as the time approached Tilden's chances dimmed. The habitually bellicose esteemed him spineless because he had refused to "fight for his rights" in 1877, whatever the cost (Claude Bowers hasn't forgiven him to this day!) Tammany, somewhat stronger now, was his natural, unforgiving foe. The notorious cipher dispatches published by the *New York Tribune* had made it seem certain that somebody very close to Tilden, possibly with Tilden's knowledge and consent— though this never was proved—had been trying to buy the electoral college in 1876. A Republican Federal court had postponed hearing of the charges of income tax evasion against him from January, 1877, to April, 1880, finally dropping them altogether.

Tilden showed strong at the state convention, which adopted the sternest unit rule resolution on record: "In case any attempt is made to dismember or divide the delegation, or if delegates countenance such an attempt by assuming to act separately from the majority, or fail to co-operate with such majority, the seats of such delegates shall be deemed to be vacated." This, however, was partly because of the behavior of the Republican rebels, partly for fear of reprisals from Tammany, which had taken a bad beating in this convention. It was no indication of enthusiasm for Tilden. "His

[Tilden's] personal popularity vanished with his reputation for lofty statesmanship," observed the *Atlantic Monthly*, and "there cannot be said to be any element in any State that feels the slightest disposition to hurrah at the mention of his name."[13]

Even so, the smart of the '76 defeat still was sharp, and Tilden might have got the nomination if he had tried. He didn't. He had retired from Gramercy Park and active practice, to his country place at Graystone-on-Hudson, and was reported to be in poor health—another factor against his nomination. Certainly he was silent. Nobody, not even his close friend and biographer Bigelow, knew whether he would accept the nomination if it were offered to him. "He probably did not know himself."[14]

There was some talk of Senator Conkling's brother-in-law, who had retired to Deerfield to lead the life of a country gentleman, but Horatio Seymour informed a friend that if he had to choose between a funeral and a nomination he'd pick the funeral.[15]

He wasn't called upon to make this choice, nor was the old man at Graystone asked for a decision. The Democrats unexpectedly, and most unwisely, behaved like a majority party, stole a Republican trick, and nominated General Winfield Scott Hancock, an amiable, good-looking fellow with an excellent military record, who, however, had not at any time given anybody the slightest reason to suppose that he was of Presidential caliber.

Senator Conkling had little interest in this. He believed the campaign lost to the Republicans already, and he'd gone on a fishing trip—with Chet Arthur.

XXVIII. Politicians Are Tradesmen

JAMES ABRAM GARFIELD was a likable, even a lovable sort of chap. He was tall, very handsome, with bright gray eyes, and hair that was dark brown with hints of red; he stood erect, chest out, head back; he had a muscular neck, high cheek bones; he impressed you as being packed with good health, though in truth he suffered all his life with indigestion. There was that in his manner which today we would call Y.M.C.A.-ish, or Boy Scouty; yet he took a drink now and then, loved to play billiards, and enjoyed a good dirty story.[1] He was an active Mason. The phrases "old fellow" and "old boy" were frequently on his lips. He laughed a lot.

He was intelligent, and was perhaps the best read man in Congress. His was an unpausing inquisitiveness; and whenever a new subject excited his interest he would scurry to the Library of Congress and gulp every book on that subject immediately available. However, he was not profound.

The Stalwarts have branded him as a hypocrite, which is not altogether fair. If there could be such a thing as an *unconscious* hypocrite, a hypocrite *unawares*, then he was one; but usually he meant what he said, at the time he said it. He looked firm, very sure of himself, but his spirit swarmed with doubts. Aware that hesitancy lent him a bad appearance, he tried to avoid it, to be definite, assured; and this resulted in a succession of amazing inconsistencies. His life, supplemented by his correspondence and his journal, as edited by the friendly Theodore Clarke Smith, makes this clear. No Viennese motive-prober is needed. It was always difficult, often impossible, to know what James Abram Garfield would do next; but the man himself, now, is easily understood.

He was lazy as a boy, but became a hard worker. He met Lucretia Rudolph in 1852, reached an understanding with her in 1854, was formally engaged in 1856, and became married in 1858, and all this time he was worrying whether marriage was the right thing for him, and writing her letters in which he described in detail his mental agonies and his doubts. He was a college graduate, had been a teacher and a preacher, with rarefied ideals which easily dissolved, leaving no trace. The youth considered politics revolting, dirty, the law too crassly material for him to touch; yet he became a lawyer and a politician and was not in the least affiliated with reform in either profession—quite the contrary! He knew nothing about the army, about arms, and was not even an amateur hunter, but political pull, when the war broke out, had obtained for him a colonelcy, then a generalship, and he was leading a brigade, a lone command, when first he came under fire. The experience was exhilarating, and for a time he had no doubt as to his ability as a soldier. There was a story current of a Western boy who was asked on his first day in school whether he could read, and replied that he reckoned he could as soon as he got the hang of the schoolhouse. Garfield, the general, did not even make this qualification. While he cooled his heels in Washington, fretting at the delay, at the political entanglements which prevented him from getting another and better command without loss of time, he subscribed to the popular feeling among amateur Marlboroughs of the time: "If the Republic goes down in blood and ruin," he wrote to a friend, "let its obituary be written thus, 'Died of West Point.'" He then was studying the career of Frederick the Great and trying to make up his mind whether to write a critical biography of that warrior. Yet a little later, when he got a good post as chief-of-staff for Rosecrans, a West Pointer among West Pointers, he was all respectful attention. There was such a thing as useful experience after all, and such a thing as the military art. When they found themselves, rather unexpectedly, with a battle on their hands (it was Chickamauga) he forgot much of this, and rushed in where the angel Rosecrans feared to tread; but it was all right, and ended happily, for he emerged a sure-enough hero.

He first thought the House "a rabble of men who hasten to make weathercocks of themselves." He became the weathercock supreme, a man with an uncannily keen scent for majorities. He seems never to have realized this. He believed himself a conscientious independent. When he decided to vote against the Johnson impeachment resolution he wrote to Burke Hinsdale, "It may, and probably will, cost me my political life," but the vote was 108–57, and his political life never had been threatened. To Hinsdale too he confided his opinion of Lincoln as "a second-rate Illinois lawyer," though after Lincoln's death there was no spellbinder more fulsome in praise of that person—"Gifted with an insight and a foresight which the ancients would have called divination, he saw, in the midst of darkness, the logic of events and forecasted the result. . . . He was one of the few great rulers. . . ." Even in this he was probably with the majority! He didn't think much of Grant as a President, and in December, 1871, was writing to a friend that he hoped somebody else would get the nomination the following year, for he looked forward "with positive dread to the work that will be required on the stump next fall, to defend him [Grant] from the criticisms which will certainly be made." To another friend, the following summer, he wrote: "In my interior view of the case, I would say Grant was not fit to be nominated and Greeley is not fit to be elected." But on March 5, 1877: "No American has carried away greater fame out of the White House than this silent man who leaves it today."

For one who was so reliable a party worker, so sturdy a wheelhorse, Republican leader of the House for so many years, he was singularly scary about his own constituency. His district did not waver, but he did. In 1876, when there was everything to indicate a Democratic landslide, he was "very greatly distressed about my future" and feared that

he had come to "the parting of the ways." He was reëlected
by a vote of almost 2 to 1. Though canny enough several
times to dodge attempts to make him governor of Ohio—it
would have been a come-down for a man of his position in
the House—he hesitated pitifully about being a candidate
for the Senate. He was certain to win, but he paused. He was
a little afraid of the Senate. Yet his election was a walk-over.

Such a man and Senator Conkling were natural enemies.
The leader of the gallant three-o-six, who from his peak of
disdain had watched that undignified scramble of Sherman
and Blaine delegates for the bandwagon, well knew—as indeed did everybody else—that Garfield would parrot his
friends and that his closest friend would probably be the
senator from Maine. Conkling scorned advice, assistance;
but Garfield floated in it, carried with the current but sincerely believing himself a swimmer. Conkling abhorred fa-
miliarity, shrank from all intimate contact, could not even
endure another's foot or hand on the chair in which he sat;
but it was Garfield's abominable habit to take a man's elbow
as he walked or talked with him, or even to throw an arm
over his shoulders.

"Sensitive as a girl," Platt thought the Ohioan, and Jere
Black remembered that he would rush into trouble with "the
horns of a bull and the skin of a rabbit." These descriptions
might have been applied to Conkling, with equal accuracy.
But no other similarity between the two is evident.

From the beginning the Senator distrusted James Abram
Garfield. He believed that many of the nominee's friends already had launched a scheme to root out forever the Conkling power, to topple the Conkling throne. Those friends,
while always prepared indignantly to deny that Garfield was
weak, continuously offered him props; they rushed to his
side, and stayed there, with words of good counsel; they
shored him up, and stood close around to shield him from
harm.

"It was my theory," wrote Murat Halstead, "that he needed a good deal of admonition; that he had a tendency to sentimentalism in politics that called for correction; that he required paragraphs to brace him up in various affairs; that he lacked a little in worldly wisdom, and maybe had a dangerous tendency to giving and taking too much confidence. . . ."

"First of all," Whitelaw Reid cautioned him, "I beg of you to make no promises to anybody."

"Beware of your own generosity!" came from John Milton Hay. He predicted a victory in November, but: "It will pay you to keep a cheap friend to drone continually in your ear, 'It was *you* who were nominated at Chicago and elected by the people.' "

So it went. Friend after friend. "Don't listen to advice from anybody—except, of course, from me." James Abram Garfield listened to them all.

He made a wonderful candidate. In the first place he enjoyed the advantage of having been born in a log cabin—even though he hadn't lived there long. He never had split rails, but he had done something almost as exciting when he worked on a canal boat—briefly, and rather as a lark—but this didn't matter—"From Tow Path to the White House" unfailingly thrilled. He was a general. He came from Ohio too, though this was not so important, for the winning party was only just forming the habit of electing Presidents from Ohio. He had been touched a bit by scandal (he had voted for the salary grab of 1873, though he'd hastened to change his vote when frightened by the hue and cry; he had been mixed up in the DeGolyer contract business, and was one of the Congressmen who had purchased and then hurriedly got rid of a little Crédit Mobilier stock) but there was nothing which couldn't be explained away. Aside from Conkling he had no puissant enemy. Somewhat curiously he was acceptable not certainly to any real reform group but to the Better Element. The very fact that Conkling despised him in some strange manner raised him in their eyes. He would, at least, take advice. The Better Element had plenty of it to give.

There was no real issue, no serious difference between the parties. The Democrats had nominated Hancock largely because of his record as a Union soldier; but they might have spared themselves that trouble, for the Southern question was dead, dissolved into nothingness by the simple process of ignoring the Fifteenth Amendment. There was some vague talk about the tariff: Hancock said something about its being a local issue after all.

Hancock was all right, nobody had anything against him, but he wasn't a politician, he wasn't a showman, he could give no reason for a change. And he was utterly without experience in national affairs. An unkind campaign pamphlet gives the story. It is white and has eight pages. The cover: "A Record of the Statesmanship and Political Achievements of General Winfield Scott Hancock, regular Democratic nominee for President of the United States, compiled from the Records." You open—and every page is a dazzling blank, except the last, upon which is gleefully printed the word "finis."

IT was not considered dignified for a candidate to do much stumping, and Garfield conducted what today we would call a front-porch campaign. He stayed on his farm at Mentor, Ohio, and let the nation come to him. It came in the form of school children, senators, business men, suffrage workers, prohibitionists, and hot crowds of people who might be classed as more or less mere. It came carrying banners, presenting petitions, giving all manner of fantastic and useless gifts, reciting speeches, singing songs, even quoting poetry. It came climbing fences, trampling grass and flowers, shouting and cheering and whistling too. It came singly and in groups large and small, and it came by district, by crank-notion, by organization, by profession, sometimes even by appointment.

Young Stanley-Brown, the candidate's personal secretary, for some time carried on unassisted in a small, one-story building near the farmhouse, but later it became necessary to call in professional stenographers and the like. Garfield himself stayed in his second floor rear room as much as possible, but he was constantly being called downstairs to greet the Fisk Jubilee Singers (September 30), to shake hands with the 400 members of the Young Men's First Voters Garfield and Arthur Club (October 8), to beam upon 1,000 Cleveland business men who appeared in a thirteen-car special train (October 15), to listen to an address in German, a translation of which had been sent to him in advance (October 18), to hurrah with the members of the Lincoln Club of Indianapolis, 500 strong in linen dusters and three-cornered hats (October 19). . . . Frequently the guests were so important that it was necessary to urge them to stay the night. The farmhouse wasn't big. Stanley-Brown and the Garfield children often slept in the attic, occasionally even in the barn. The Mentor station was only one mile away, but Painesville, the nearest express stop, was seven miles. Every neighbor who had a horse and some sort of vehicle delightedly went into the hacking business: they were miffed when a good-natured railroad agreed to stop its trains right on the farm, so that the candidate's visitors needed only to walk a few hundred yards up a lane and through the barnyard.

ALL this was fun, and the candidate enjoyed it, but he did not permit it to blind him. Tramping, cheering visitors didn't change votes. The fact remained, indisputable, that unless he carried New York he could not win the election. He couldn't carry New York without the assistance of Roscoe Conkling.

In his letter of acceptance Garfield was cautious. He touched carefully the Southern question, slid over monetary legislation without scratching any paint from his keel, was vague and studiously orthodox in the matter of the tariff but said nothing about reform, waxed fearlessly outspoken about the need for Federal regulation of Mississippi River traffic, commended the Hayes administration for settling the Chinese immigration question by treaty, and suggested the need for some sort of civil service commission but hastened to add that this should be a legislative, not an executive matter. The Stalwarts must be placated, at all costs. "To select wisely from our vast population those who are best fitted for the many offices to be filled, requires an acquaintance far beyond the range of any one man. The Executive, therefore, should seek and receive information and assistance of those whose knowledge of the communities in which the duties are to be performed best qualifies them to aid in making the wisest choice." There! Could they complain about that? Well, they could and did. They said bluntly that they weren't asking for foggy generalities but for definite, unmistakable promises concerning their share of the patronage.

Garfield appointed former Governor Jewell of Connecticut his national chairman. Jewell had been on bad terms with Grant when a member of the Grant cabinet, and the Stalwarts were angry. To quiet them Logan was permitted to name the national secretary, and he selected Senator Dorsey, a Stalwart, who made the matter clear in a letter to the nominee July 26:

I repeat with all the earnestness I have, that in my judgment it is a duty which you owe to yourself and to the Republican party to be here [in New York] on the 5th of August regardless of what Mr. Jewell says or Mr. George William Curtis or Mr. Anybody else . . . I insist that a conference with Governor Cornell and Senator Conkling is an absolute essential to success in this campaign. I have been told within the last four or five hours that when this question was suggested to you, you made the natural inquiry as to what these people wanted to see you about. My reply to that is that they want to know whether the

Republicans of the State of New York are to be recognized
. . . or whether the "Scratchers" and Independents and
"feather-heads" are to ride over the Republican party of this
state as they have for the last four years. They not only want
to know that but they intend to know it and they can only be
satisfied by a personal conference with you . . . I believe that
a discussion of thirty minutes with the persons named will settle
for all time the doubt that exists in their minds. What we want
is the State of New York . . . I wish you would telegraph me
immediately when you will start and how you prefer to come.

It was annoying. So much depended upon that angry
man! A disgusted friend wrote to Halstead: "They all stand
around and watch Conkling as little dogs watch their master
when he is in a bad mood—waiting for him to graciously
smile, and they will jump about with effusive joy." Another
wrote:

A strong letter was written urging Conkling, in the most flattering way, and appealing to him in the most humble manner, to
come to Ohio and deliver a speech in the Cincinnati Music Hall,
and promising no end of thousands of people and bands and
guns and things . . . I opposed sending such a missive, advo-
cating such a simple and cordial invitation as it is customary
to extend to a leader and honest, earnest party man. But they
looked upon me (probably rightly, too) as a fool. . . . And
now, Jewell writes that he has not dared to give the letter to
Conkling yet, as he has not "deemed any moment yet as oppor-
tune." . . . Dorsey humbly and piously hopes Conkling can be
induced to make a speech in Vermont, and if the Almighty hap-
pens to take the right course with him, he may condescend to
come to Ohio.

But for the present the Senator stayed where he was.
They had heard his terms, through Dorsey. He would be the
mountain, and Garfield must be Mohammed. Garfield, worried, was wobbling. Whitelaw Reid, after reporting that
Conkling was "behaving like a spoiled child," wrote: "I

don't believe in running after the malcontents. Let them run after you. More than enough was done for conciliation when Arthur was taken. They can't help themselves, and, if they could throw away the State they dare not. They want promises about office. They haven't any right to them. Nobody has." Others had the same advice to give. But Garfield's chief concern from the beginning was not whether to go or not to go, but how he could go without appearing undignified. This was at last arranged for. There would be a large conference at the Fifth Avenue Hotel—not a mere putting of heads together with Conkling and perhaps a few of his henchmen, but a big affair which Blaine and Sherman and George William Curtis would attend, like so many seconds grimly come to see that their principal got fair play. That would make it seem all right. A board of strategy meeting, a powwow of national leaders. It would not look like a deal, then.

He got a bit panicky at the last minute. "My dear friend, you must stand by me," he wrote to Blaine.

Many of our friends who have written me think there are evidences that a few leaders in New York meditate treachery and say that the visit will either prevent it or so develop it that the country will understand it and place the responsibility where it belongs . . . I want you to find the exact situation, if possible before I arrive. I want you to know how large a force C has behind him and just what the trouble is.

So eventually he went. They all went, except Conkling. "Where is my Lord Roscoe?" the candidate asked, laughing, but nervous. They waited and waited. And at last, giving him up, they went about their business.

Just what that business was we don't know. But it is tolerably certain that specific promises were exchanged. The Conkling lieutenants were not the sort of men to be soothed and quieted with sweet-flowing generalities. They thought in terms of jobs; and if the conference was satisfactory to them

—as it appeared to be, they all said it was—we may be sure that the Conkling machine interests were promised good protection.

We don't know, either, why Senator Conkling didn't appear. Tom Platt and Alfred Conkling say that it was because the conference was arranged without consulting the Senator in the first place—from fear that he would object—by anxious lieutenants who wished to have the favor of the new administration. When the Senator learned of this, a few days before the conference, too late to stop it, he refused to be present in person, fearing the cry of "Deal! deal!" He remained in the home of his brother Frederick, where the servants were instructed to say he wasn't in. Tom Platt and Alfred Conkling are not ordinarily good witnesses, but this explanation seems rational. The Senator loathed publicity, which hurt his dignity. Moreover, he must have known that Platt and Crowley and the rest were hard bargainers, men unlikely to fret about matters of dignity, men, in short, much better fitted for this work than was the Senator himself.

Whitelaw Reid, in a letter to Garfield August 15, offered a different explanation:

Briefly stated it was George William Curtis that drove him away from the conference; not Blaine or Sherman. These it would seem he could have stood, but the idea of "conferring" with Mr. Curtis was too much for him. Payn, Platt and others of his close friends have talked to him with great plainness, not to say severity. His answer is that he is in the hands of his friends and will do whatever they ask. They have already asked that he speak first here [New York], then in Indiana and Ohio, and they are thinking of asking that he also go to Maine. This last, I suspect, would be a hard dose to take, and I doubt whether it will be pressed upon him.

PROMISES are everything in politics, where you cannot hold a man to a written contract. Political ethics in this country are

and always have been high—as high, at least, as those of
most professions, far higher than those of business. Promises
are political currency, the media of exchange; for politicians
are tradesmen, like most of the rest of us, in spite of that
horrific association of words, in spite of the George William
Curtises and their women's-club ideals. A good politician is
reluctant to give a promise, but once it's given he sticks to
it. If he doesn't, he is, or should be, ruled out of the frater-
nity, like a gambler who has welshed on a debt.

The Republican organization of New York State was satisfied with whatever it was promised in the Fifth Avenue
Hotel. We don't know just what that was, but it convinced
Conkling. He took the stump, and his lieutenants too were
active. They didn't like Garfield, and didn't trust him, or the
men behind him; but once they knew where they stood, they
carried out their end of the contract. Tom Platt, who was
Republican state chairman, wrote to Federal officeholders—
this was by no means a custom confined to New York—telling them that they would doubtless consider it a "privilege
and a pleasure" to contribute to the campaign fund. Levi
Morton put aside his banking business and devoted his talents to raising a national fund, with New York, as always,
giving the lion's share. Arrangements were made to have the
nominee greeted noisily at railroad stations on his way back
west through New York. A parade of 50,000 in New York
City, and similar demonstrations elsewhere in the state, were
promoted without delay. The machine had started to manu-
facture enthusiasm, and it was a mighty efficient machine.

And the Senator addressed 20,000 persons in the Academy of Music, burying the hatchet (if not very deep) with
what was for him good grace. He spoke for three and one-
half hours, and the speech was printed and widely distributed as a campaign pamphlet.

A candidate, if he be an honest, genuine man, will not seek
and accept a party nomination to the Presidency, Vice-Presi-

dency, or Congress, and after he is elected become a law unto himself. Few things are more despicable than first to secure elevation at the hands of a party, and then in the hope of winning pretentious non-partisan applause, to affect superior sanctity, and meanly to imply that those whose support and confidence were eagerly and deferentially sought are wanting in purity, patriotism, or some other title to respect.

He knew his Garfield! And feeling as he did about him it was not easy to be enthusiastic. There was almost no mention of the Mentor farmer. "That he [Garfield] is competent to the duties before him, there seems to me no reason to doubt." Thereafter he turned to Chet Arthur, and praised him to the skies.[2]

Nobody insisted upon the Maine speech. Really, it would have been too much to ask that the Senator go to talk in Blaine's territory. Garfield was worried about Maine, for the Democrats there had combined with the Greenbackers, and the moral effect of an early election is strong: at least as early as 1840 men had been prattling as-Maine-goes-so-goes-the-nation. Garfield was worried too about his own state of Ohio and about Indiana. His own state because the Sherman people didn't like him much for getting a nomination he had been instructed to get for Sherman. Some said, and some men say to this day, that it was a clear case of treason, and that all the time, though pledged to Sherman as Sherman's manager, General Garfield was working for himself— that he had "sneaked in."[3] Certainly the Stalwarts believed this, or pretended to believe it. There is no proof of the charge, and the strong probability is that it was untrue. Senator Hoar, who was in the chair at the convention, believed that Garfield was perfectly sincere when he rose to object to the votes given to him at the close of the thirty-fourth ballot. "I recall the incident perfectly. I interrupted him in the middle of his sentence. I was terribly afraid that he would say something that would make his nomination impossible, or his acceptance impossible, if it were made. I do not believe it ever happened before that anybody who attempted to decline the Presidency of the United States was to be prevented by a point of order, or that such a thing will ever happen again." Hoar was no fool, and Garfield wasn't a good actor.

As to Indiana, there, like Maine, the election was early, and the result in doubt.

So would the Senator speak in Ohio and in Indiana? The Senator didn't like it, but he consented.

The first meeting, and the biggest one, was at Warren, where he shared the program with his friend General Grant. "It is his [Conkling's] first visit to Ohio," Garfield wrote eagerly to a friend on the arrangements committee, "and everything ought to be done to give him the most generous welcome and make it understood that it is his meeting." And it was, indeed, "his" meeting. He spoke for more than two hours, and General Grant spoke for seven minutes, and neither of them so much as mentioned the name of James Abram Garfield.

"Conkling is a singular compound of a very brilliant man and an exceedingly spoiled petulant child," the candidate wrote to that same friend, Harmon Austin, afterward. "For myself I do not care to be praised, but it was a narrow and unmanly thing on his part to make such a manifest effort as he had done in Ohio to avoid mentioning the head of the ticket in any generous way."

Nevertheless, that Warren speech was of incalculable assistance to the farmer of Mentor. Forty thousand persons heard it, and the whole country heard *about* it.

After the meeting there was a luncheon at the home of Senator Perkins in Warren, and there was a surprise. One Mark Hanna, a business man who fooled around with politics on the side, was in charge of transportation for the Grant-Conkling party. At the luncheon he said suddenly to Grant: "General, it has been arranged that we return to Cleveland by way of Mentor, and if you propose to stop and see General Garfield we shall have to start in a very short time." Grant did not change expression, but Senator Conkling glared. The question had been publicly put, and the Senator was obliged to fall back upon insincerities about the weather and the late hour. He was told that the Erie had agreed to route the special train through Mentor, giving the party time to visit Garfield and yet reach Cleveland for the night meeting. Grant burst into speech. "We'll go," he said. So they went.[4]

THE policy of "open covenants openly arrived at" never has been popular among the men who run governments. Publicity spoils so many nice plans; and as often as possible the ways of the politician, even when not notably evil, are dark. And quiet.

We don't know what happened at Mentor when Roscoe Conkling arrived that evening in a downpour of rain, but the public, which didn't know either, instantly began talking about a "treaty."

It seems highly improbable that there ever was such a treaty. There are other, more logical ways to account for the Conklinian activity, which in fact had already started anyway. He had recovered from his fit of temper caused by defeat at the Chicago convention. He was beginning to believe that the Republicans did have a chance after all—there was a weak Democratic candidate, and in the Senator's own state "Honest John" Kelly, the Tammany boss, had angered the German Democrats by nominating a ticket made up mostly of Irishmen. Garfield was so conciliatory, so eager to win, that it was yet possible that he might hand over to the Senator what the Senator so desperately needed—the Federal patronage in New York. It was possible that all was not yet lost. Besides, there had been that meeting at the Fifth Avenue Hotel, which, if it had done nothing else, at least had salved the Senator's lacerated pride. But it is impossible to

believe that the conference did not also result in some specific agreement. If there was any Stalwart–Half-Breed understanding in this campaign, certainly it must have been a
"Treaty of Fifth Avenue" rather than a "Treaty of Mentor."

All those present denied it. The Senator, indeed, seems to
have feared that he would be trapped in a room alone with
the candidate, thus giving rise to "treaty" talk. Alfred Conkling says that his uncle took extraordinary pains to prevent
this, and says also that Garfield greeted the Senator ef-
fusively, running down the steps (seemingly in disregard of
the rain) with arms outstretched, almost with tears in his
eyes, shouting "You have saved me!" Tom Platt, in the
Autobiography a newspaperman wrote for him years later,
repeats this tale. Boutwell in his *Reminiscences* declares that
Conkling informed him that he had not been alone "one minute" with Garfield, "intending by that care-taking to avoid
the suggestion that his visit was designed to afford an opportunity for any personal or party arrangement." In a
letter written in 1924 to Professor Smith, Garfield's biographer, Stanley-Brown, the secretary, denies both the story of
the warm greeting ("You have saved me!") and the story of
the "treaty." "I was present during the entire period of the
meeting and there was never a moment when the Conkling
group were closeted with the General nor was there ever presented any opportunity for such a bargain. It was a deliberate lie." And Garfield himself, that night, simply wrote in his
journal—never intended for publication—"I had no private
conversation with the party but the call was a pleasant and
cordial one all around."

Common sense, which to be sure never enters into the repe-
tition of political anecdotes, likewise rejects the tale of the
treaty. The Conkling-Grant party was at Mentor for only
about an hour. A good portion of this time must have been
occupied with shaking hands. Mrs. Garfield made them sand-

wiches and coffee. A crowd of some two hundred neighbors pushed in to see an ex-President, and Garfield, as host, surely must have been present throughout this not-brief business.

Nevertheless, the public went right on talking about the "Treaty of Mentor."

THE Senator stumped hard. He made speeches in Cleveland, Cincinnati, Indianapolis, Lafayette, Richmond (Indiana), and Terre Haute.

He was blue on his return to New York. After all, what was there left for him? Only humiliation. This man Garfield might smile today, when he needed the Conkling tongue, but what would he do tomorrow? Blaine was riding the top horse, and the Senator never even considered any suggestion that he make his peace with Blaine.[5] There seemed not a doubt that he would catch steel between the shoulder blades some time soon after March 4, if Garfield did get elected. The new President would have the excuse that he couldn't desert the eighteen New York delegates, the eighteen pledge-breakers, who had leapt aboard his bandwagon at the last moment. He would insist that these fellows, all rebel leaders, be recognized in the distribution of the patronage.

"Have you any faith in Garfield?" Tom Platt asked him.

The Senator made a wry face.

"Not much, but we will try him out."[6]

His spirits were low, for he was a moody fellow always. He was tired of fighting. Also, he was in debt. To make this trip he had returned $18,000 in retainers, including one advance fee of $10,000, and his nephew estimated that in traveling and other expenses he had spent an additional $11,-000.[7] There must have been a great temptation to retire as champion, to go into the active practice of law and make some money.

But he continued with the campaign in the most important state of all, his own. He spoke in Albany, Oswego, Utica (twice), Rochester, Buffalo, Lockport, Jamestown. . . .

IT was a close election, yet oddly unexciting.

The Greenback-Democratic combination carried Maine. The Republicans won Ohio and Indiana. More important still, they won New York, where a shift of only 10,517 of the 1,103,945 votes cast would have given Hancock the Presidency.

The electoral vote was 214–155. However, in the total popular vote of 9,218,251, Garfield had a majority of only 9,464.

XXIX. Advice to a Farmer

NOW the Senator was not certain of his position. Everything depended upon the undependable Garfield. If Garfield fully recognized the Conkling leadership, then at least the Senator would be no worse off than he had been before. But if Garfield, now safely elected, decided to fight—

It was not like Garfield to fight. But he had the example of Hayes in front of him, knew how Conkling could make a President seem a fool; and though he was afraid of Conkling, he was determined, with the stubbornness of a man inherently weak, to show the public that he was *not* afraid. Besides, he was surrounded by men who didn't like Conkling, all talking.

Two major tests loomed. It was understood that one member of the new cabinet would be a New Yorker. And a new senator was to be elected in January—a Republican successor to Kernan, for the Republicans now had both houses of the legislature.

Conkling stayed aloof from the senatorship scramble. It seems probable that he would have liked to see his friend Levi P. Morton get the post, but he understood, as did the other Stalwarts, including Morton himself, that because of his Herculean services as a fund-raiser in the campaign, Morton was to be made Secretary of the Treasury. It was for this reason that Morton did not enter the contest.[1]

The two chief aspirants were Conkling lieutenants, which might have been the reason for the Senator's neutrality. Tom Platt was conducting his own campaign, with the aid of his friend Louis Payn. Governor Cornell too supported him. But General Sharpe, Tom Murphy, John F. Smyth, and other Stalwart worthies were back of Richard Crowley of Niagara, and Chet Arthur himself was Crowley's manager. It was a race within the clan, exclusively a family fight, and nobody looked for outside interference.

Chauncey Depew spoiled this. And back of Depew was a meddler from Maine, already getting things ready for his friend the President-elect.

Depew wrote in his memoirs:

I was called to a meeting in New York, where Mr. Blaine . . . was present. Mr. Blaine said that administration managers had made a thorough canvass of the legislature and they had found that I was the only one who could control enough anti-organization votes to be elected, and, therefore, General Garfield and his friends had decided that I must enter the race.

Or, as he had put it earlier, when interviewed by the historian Alexander: "Blaine, representing Garfield, came to New York and asked me to enter the contest for the purpose of securing the election of a senator who would support the Administration. That was the reason why I became a candidate."

Now certainly the Half-Breeds didn't think Chauncey Depew could win. But his independent strength, combined with the Democratic vote, would be enough to prevent either of the two Stalwart aspirants from getting a majority. Until Depew got out, neither Platt nor Crowley could be elected, and therefore Depew could withdraw on his own terms.

James G. Blaine was taking the fight into Conkling's own territory.

MEANWHILE, it began to look as though Morton might not get the Treasury after all. The givers of advice, at any rate, were against this. John Hay was made indignant by the very thought, and wrote to his friend Whitelaw Reid: "Conkling did not carry New York, as you know, and it would be a fatal error for Garfield to abdicate at the start. There is infinitely more reason why you should name the New York member than why R.C. should."

It was a bewildering business, and the man in Mentor seemed to be trying to do right by all concerned. He went to Washington for five days, ostensibly to dismantle his I Street house. He ate with the Rockwells, Ingersoll, Sherman, Senator Edmunds, Levi Morton, Evarts, the President and Lucy Hayes, General Schenck. . . . Morton, whom he had sent for, told him that New York expected the Treasury. He seemed dismayed at this information. He breakfasted with Blaine, November 27, and they agreed that Blaine should be made either Secretary of State or Secretary of the Treasury. Sherman, at dinner, said he wouldn't object to being dropped from the cabinet: he wished to get back into the Senate anyway.

Soon after the return to Mentor, Governor Cornell, Louis Payn and Dick Crowley came calling. They urged the appointment of Morton as Secretary of the Treasury.

A few days later Senator Dorsey wrote, quoting Senator Conkling as saying that he desired to support Garfield's administration as he had supported Grant's,

and with an impressiveness for which he is distinguished, he said "There are two ways of dealing with your peers to secure their coöperation and friendship. One is to crush them out and the other is to consolidate them. I am not a rival of Garfield's, Grant is not a rival of Garfield's. I desire to be his friend and am more than anxious to stand by him, not halting or half-hearted but as I stand by men. No man can create a rival of Garfield four years hence except Garfield himself. If he has one, he alone is responsible for it." I cannot convey to you the manner, earnestness and power with which this expression was made. It was intense to the highest degree.

So the terrible Conkling was coming to terms? It must have made pleasant reading. The letter went on:

In the conversation which continued he said that, if, upon further reflection, the General [Garfield] thought it unwise to give New York the Treasury, he wished he would say so distinctly so that there would be no mistake about it and then they would know better what to do. He hoped that there might be some place in the cabinet arranged so as to save the self-respect of the man who believed that he had been offered the position of Secretary of the Treasury and, at the same time, consolidate the party in New York.

Garfield tentatively put Morton down as Secretary of the Navy, but this position Morton, doubtless at the bidding of the Boss, refused.

It was no simple task, this making of a cabinet. So much geography was involved! Garfield wrote in his journal January 16: "If I were compelled to make a cabinet today, it would read: State Department, Blaine; Treasury, Knox or Allison; New York, James or Morton; Pennsylvania, McVeagh; Indiana, Harrison; Illinois, Lincoln; South, Phillips (?) or Morgan."

UNTIL Garfield, a President-elect had thought of his secretary-to-be only as a sort of glorified clerk. But Garfield realized how important the post might be.

"The man who holds that place," he wrote to Whitelaw Reid, "can do very much to make or mar the success of an administration. The position ought to be held in higher estimation than Secretary of State."

Reid presumably suggested his dear friend John Hay, who had been one of Lincoln's secretaries. Hay had come up in the world since that time, and now was rich, independent. Garfield, offering him the post, was careful to stress the importance he placed upon it, and to assure Hay that the President's secretary should hereafter be a personage of considerable dignity. But Hay wouldn't hear of it. "The contact with the greed and selfishness of office-seekers and bull-dozing Congressmen is unspeakably repulsive," he wrote. "The constant contact with envy, meanness, ignorance, and the swinish selfishness which ignorance breeds needs a stronger heart and a more obedient nervous system than I can boast."

Still, Hay had Garfield's interests at heart. He wrote to Reid: "I hope you will go to Mentor before very long—not for any special interest, but simply because this is the time when G. is making the future of his administration. Deadbeats and office-seekers there will be in plenty—but he needs to talk occasionally with a strong, disinterested friend, who knows men."

Reid didn't go, but he kept his hand in.

He wrote excitedly to Walter Phelps:

In deepest confidence, the head of the Cabinet is fixed. Mr. Blaine has been offered the Secretaryship of State and has accepted, and it is mutually agreed that nobody but their wives shall know it for some weeks or months yet. . . . Next, as to you. It is agreed . . . that you are to have the Italian mission. You are to take Italy because the climate suits you and because the classical surroundings will specially interest you.

Allison is much talked of for the Secretary of the Treasury. There seems a chance for Depew on the Senatorship. Platt and Morton are both keen, but Conkling doesn't decide. I'm to go to Albany Sunday night, to tell our friends that they'll be defended if they defy Conkling and that they won't lose the good graces of Garfield. Over this last we've had a dinner here to-night, Blaine, Depew, Robertson and some others, and they've only just left me.

The secret which was to have been confided only to wives and to friends who required Italian skies and classical surroundings, soon was everybody's. It never had been much of a secret anyway. The stupidest had from the first predicted that Blaine would get whichever portfolio he most desired.

Indeed, Blaine already was representing the administration. Especially in New York. He had induced Whitelaw Reid to publish a "by authority" editorial stating that the President-elect would take no part in the coming senatorial election, but adding: "The incoming administration will see to it that the men from New York and from the other states, who had the courage at Chicago to obey the wishes of their districts in the balloting for president and who thus finally voted for Garfield, shall not lose by it."[2]

Reid reported to the man at Mentor:

It really looks as if we had a chance to carry. At any rate we shall show that Mr. Conkling doesn't own the State. Half his strength at present consists in the belief, which his friends are everywhere inculcating, that he is to control your administration absolutely, and that all its patronage will be wielded against the men who dare to oppose him.

There is absolutely no change in his feeling or that of his people toward you. They mean to confront you with the two Senators from the State, and to demand the entire patronage of the State. In a word they mean to be your masters, and when you submit they will like you well enough. But they don't trust you; even their common mode of alluding to you shows their feeling. It is always "this man Garfield."

A FIGHT for the speakership threatened in January, just before the senatorial election, but the anti-Conkling group was weak and had no good candidate, and General Sharpe won easily. Working for his friend Crowley, he tried the old trick of withholding committee appointments, but he was severely rebuked for this, and it made no difference in the election.

Tom Platt was a shrewd man. He went to Depew and asked him why he was running. "I told him frankly that I was in it to see, if possible, that the senator-elect should support the administration. He said: 'Very well. I will do that.'" So there was a conference, attended by Depew, Robertson, Senator Woodin, and a few others, who formally, delightedly —for they knew Platt wouldn't break his word in a matter of this sort—listened to his promise to support the administration. Woodin asked: "Does that statement cover appointments?" Platt said that it did. "Even if Judge Robertson's name should be sent in?" Platt said yes, even then. Woodin chuckled. "We can trust Platt. When he's elected senator we shall not need a stepladder to reach his ear." So Chauncey Depew pulled out in Tom Platt's favor, and Platt won on the first ballot.[3]

"A dwarf on stilts," grunted William Allen White. And perhaps he was. But he'd promised! he'd promised! Whitelaw Reid reported to the man at Mentor:

The inside facts as to the Senatorial election are these.
Platt had the most alliances with us, and our people made excellent terms. He gave me personal pledges which ensure not only fair but friendly general treatment. To Depew he pledged himself that—
1. He would countenance no effort at crushing or ignoring the Chicago bolters.
2. He would not oppose their getting either from State or Nation their fair share of patronage.
3. He would not oppose their confirmation, if any of them should come before the Senate, but on the contrary would do all in his power to help it.
4. He would help in the prompt confirmation of your Cabinet

—even in so extreme a case as the possibility of its containing the name of Judge Robertson—though much opposed to such a nomination.

5. He would do all he could (not much, probably) to keep Conkling reasonable.

Really, young Whitelaw Reid was having a wonderful time filling the Greeley shoes. It was so much fun putting it across an old stuffed-shirt like Roscoe Conkling! You looked a daring hero, a public benefactor too, because you were defying the terrible Boss.

Certainly "we" were playing against the Boss every trick the Boss himself ever had used, and a few more. Could it be that the Boss at this hour was repeating grimly to himself the Biblical passage about he who liveth by the sword, by the sword shall he perish—or however it goes? But this was not likely. The Boss had too many other things to think about just then.

THE President-elect resembled some poor fellow who finds it agony to write a letter, and who, having penned "Dear Oswald:—" chews a pencil for the next hour or two. Only with Garfield it was a matter of months.

He had started. There it was: "State, Blaine." But now the task began to get hard.

Don Cameron proposed his brother-in-law, McVeagh, for attorney-general, and this Garfield wrote in—and kept there. Cameron also suggested that Robert Lincoln, son of the martyred President, be given some portfolio; and the President-elect considered this a good idea. Just *what* portfolio he didn't know. But there'd be one. There'd be one left over, probably.

The Treasury comes after State on the list, and just as the first sentence of a letter is the hardest to write, after the salutation's put down, so Garfield suffered most about the future Secretary of the Treasury. He was inclined to think well of Allison, or John J. Knox. Allison came from Iowa, and—he'd just remembered this—there had to be somebody from Iowa, which state, solidly Blaine at Chicago from the beginning, had become solidly Garfield at least as soon as any of the others.

Sherman favored Windom first, Allison second, but he thought better and better of Knox as the weeks wore on. Blaine thought Allison all right, but was strongly opposed to Windom. "Any darned fool . . . can spend money." The President-elect seems never to have cogitated upon Morton as a Treasury possibility. What he had against Morton isn't clear. He was prepared to give the New York Stalwart almost any other portfolio at his disposal. It might have been the Wall Street taint—Morton was an original Morgan partner. But bankers, since the end of the depression, no longer were the objects of suspicion and hatred they'd been in 1873–79. Probably Garfield wished to recognize the silver men of the West. They were strong, and didn't like Wall Streeters. And Allison had sponsored the free silver bill in the house.

A couple of Ohio congressmen, McKinley and Townsend, called to speak a good word for Allison. So did Kirkwood of Iowa, though he questioned Allison's silver stand. Allison himself was at Mentor on January 16; he was vague, but the President-elect got the impression that he'd be satisfied if either Wilson or Kirkwood, both Iowa men, got the Treasury. Blaine didn't think Wilson would do—he'd been out of public life too long.

But what about Levi P. Morton?

In the middle of January Morton himself, in a rather plaintive letter, pointed out that he'd lost the senatorship, which had been the great aim of his heart, just because he understood that Garfield was going to give him the Treasury. He reminded that the two senators, the Vice-President-elect, the governor of New York, and "nearly all" the members of the legislature and the New York congressmen, were in favor of his appointment. He hinted that these fellows would start exerting a little pressure soon.

They did, too. Edwards Pierrepont called, pressing the Morton claim. General Grant wrote, suggesting that Morton "or some one friendly to Senator Conkling" should get the Treasury. Alonzo Cornell and Tom Platt were in the farmhouse for three hours one night, talking Morton. "I wrestled with them as best I could," the President-elect wrote to his wife, who was visiting the Whitelaw Reids in New York.

She had a suggestion, characteristically feminine:

Mr. Reid told me this morning that Morton had been very ugly in his talk about you, using the expression that seems to be so gratifying to the Conkling clique, "That Ohio man cannot be relied upon to stand by his pledges." And said that Mrs. Don Cameron said, with a toss of her head, after Mrs. Morton's outburst of indignation over the New York Senatorial election, "O, Mr. Morton will be taken care of, if General Garfield does as he agrees to do." You will never have anything from these men but their assumed contempt, until you fight them *dead*. You can put every one of them in his political grave if you are a mind to and that is the only place where they can be kept peaceable.

But Garfield wasn't prepared to go that far. He was wondering if he couldn't possibly satisfy the Conkling crowd by tossing it the Postmaster Generalship. Wouldn't they like that? That was a nice job. Perhaps Tom James— But Blaine and Sherman, with much feeling, all said that James in the cabinet would be nothing but a tool for Conkling, and a spy.

What about C. J. Folger, the New York State Chief Justice? *There* was a good man! But the Conklingites replied that Folger was needed at home, and what about making Morton Secretary of the Treasury?

The President-elect must have got a little panicky at this time, for he actually proposed to Blaine that it might be possible to settle the whole matter by including Roscoe Conkling himself in the cabinet! To be sure, Conkling would not accept anything less than the Secretaryship of State, and this had been promised to Blaine, but as one friend to another, in an emergency like this—

Blaine replied hastily: "His appointment would act like strychnine upon your administration—first, bring contortions and then be followed by death."

Besides, there were so many others to warn against Conkling. The givers of advice. Sherman, for example, in this letter January 23:

I know him well, and while I concede his ability as a party leader and debater, I think him greatly over-rated in other respects. His egotism is unbounded. He is sensible to criticism and ridicule. He never interests himself in anything but personal antagonisms, he never rises above a Custom House or a Post-Office. As an able Republican and the recognized leader of a great state where bosses seem to be necessary, he is entitled to consideration and full recognition but, if you ever yield to him so that he thinks you fear him, he becomes overbearing. He treats his New York friends like lackeys. Your great office will enable you, without loss of self-respect, to make advances to him to do what seems best and proper to conciliate him. . . . If that fails, then the only way is to give him blow for blow.

The matter was dropped.

On February 3, a trifle dizzy, Garfield recapitulated in his journal. He found that he had Blaine, McVeagh, Lincoln (Logan was to approve this appointment a week later, making it all right, for Robert Lincoln, like his father, was from Illinois) and Benjamin Harrison (who, however, the very next day was to decline to act). The Treasury still troubled him, and the Interior, and the Southern member, but most of all the New York member.

Inspired, he wrote to Conkling, invited him to Mentor.

The Senator took eleven days to reply, another five days to come. But he did come.

This time it was no disguised conference, but a straight, heads-together talk, lasting six hours. Yet it seems to have accomplished nothing. Conkling had no word to say afterward, though he did not appear to be angry. Garfield burst into writing, as usual.

In his journal: "I had a full conversation on the cabinet and kindred subjects. His knowledge of men is fuller and more accurate than I had expected and, in the main, his judgment is sound. He appeared to be frank and friendly. Urged the importance of recognizing New York and thought Morton would do well in the Treasury."

To Blaine: "The conference was conducted in excellent temper. He really made no demand, but strongly urged the fitness of Morton for the Treasury. He said he believed it would be better all around, to appoint no cabinet officer from New York than to take one for a minor place."

To his friend Hinsdale:

The Senator has come and gone and we had not less than six hours' conference which was very frank on both sides; and I think the sense of independent self-respect in each was enhanced by it. On one side, information, suggestions and argument, but no demands; on the other, listening, questioning, comparison of views but no promises. I think much better of him than I expected and I shall be surprised if he has not carried away the same impression.

THE relative importance of cabinet portfolios varies. There were no commerce or labor departments in 1880. American foreign relations were trifling, yet the prestige of the place, its immense dignity, the fascination it exercises upon even the most sophisticated statesmen, who thrill at the thought of writing letters to kings and emperors, made the Secretaryship of State the most desirable. The Treasury always has been and always will be of incalculable importance. A pre-Sherman Act nation was not greatly concerned with the attorney-generalship. The Interior was then a position of great power, for the gypping of the redskin was just getting well under way, and there were vast tracts of Government land still to be distributed. The head of the Post Office Department was by the very nature of his situation a powerful controller of patronage, and earnest manipulators reached for that place avidly, though the postmaster general was not quite what he has since become—a sort of Secretary of Practical Politics, manager of the President's pie counter.

But the Army and Navy were empty honors. The militia still was a militia, not a National Guard, and the standing army itself was of petty proportions: the nation had suffered from more than enough of army during the four years of the war. Captain Mahan was working on but had not yet published his monumental treatise on this country's need for far-flung coaling stations and more and more and more battleships;[4] if people didn't talk about disarmament, neither did they talk about rearmament; Manifest Destiny was an excuse yet unconceived; in short, though there *was* a United States Navy, nobody but its own officers took it very seriously.

The Stalwarts made it clear that they were not to be placated by a gift of the Navy. The President-elect offered that portfolio to Justice Folger, February 19, but Folger, four days later, declined to accept. The President-elect offered it, definitely now, to Morton, and followed this note by another, begging Morton to reply by wire—for it was February 28.

Whitelaw Reid, almost delirious with joy, wrote on March 1 to the Miss Mills whom he intended to wed as soon as it was safe to leave Garfield for a little while: "Morton has accepted the Navy. So we have carried our exact point there, and Conkling is at once utterly foiled and left without any cause of quarrel."

But the young editor cheered too soon.

The Boss of New York was in the home at 14th and F

Streets, which he shared as bachelor quarters with Chet Arthur, when he learned about Morton's acceptance. He was wild with rage. He wired for Tom Platt, in New York, explaining the situation—"our unwise friend is making a great deal of trouble for us"—and then dispatched Arthur and John H. Starin to fetch Morton. They found the banker in bed with a chill. But a chill was no excuse, when the Boss had issued a summons! Starin, who had once been a druggist, mixed him a brandy and quinine, administered this, and with the Vice-President-elect helped him to get into his clothes and over to "The Morgue."[5]

New Yorkers in Washington called Conkling's quarters "The Morgue." It was an uncheery place, and nobody liked to be ordered there. The Boss was not in the habit of summoning his vassals in order to bestow praise upon them.

Morton got back into his bed at four o'clock that morning—they'd awakened him at one—and Garfield had for breakfast a letter withdrawing acceptance of the Navy portfolio.

Tom Platt, arriving next morning, found the Senator and Chet Arthur at breakfast. The meal finished, all three went to the Riggs House, where Garfield was staying. They were granted an audience promptly, and were closeted with the President-elect for more than an hour. What was said, or done, we don't know. It might be that the Senator quoted some of the more sonorous portions of the Garfield acceptance letter. He might have reminded Garfield of the work the New York organization had done in the campaign. Probably he suggested that it was hardly fair to make a cabinet appointment from New York without consulting at least one of the senators from that state, or the governor, or one of the more prominent legislators or congressmen. Certainly he was indignant at finding a newspaper editor managing this appointment. We know that he complained about "the tall young man from New York," for Garfield, a few days later, repeated this complaint "with a chuckle" to Whitelaw Reid.

But whatever the Senator said, it made no difference to the cabinet formers. Morton's withdrawal had changed everything again, so Blaine wrote a new slate that day, which included Thomas James for postmaster general. And Blaine sent for Whitelaw Reid, who was running the *Tribune* from Washington in this crisis. The messengers sought Reid "at the hotel, the office, the State Department, Hay's house, and pretty much everywhere," until finally they located him at the White House. He was hurried to the Blaine residence, was closeted with Blaine in extraordinary session—the servants had been instructed to tell visitors there was nobody home—and so learned about the new scheme. He wrote about it to Miss Mills that night.

I went first to Garfield's, talked it all over with him, and then telegraphed James to come on, on the night train. I'm a little afraid of it yet, but it looks as if the plan would work. The policy is to detach James from Conkling and make him feel that he owes his appointment to that.

Thomas James always had been a Conkling follower. He had been appointed by Grant at the recommendation of the Senator, and was decidedly an ornament to the machine. Even the Half-Breeds admitted that he had given the New York City post office the best administration of its history; his reforms were everywhere applauded.

James obeyed the telegram, took the night train, and at eight o'clock in the morning was pounding upon Whitelaw Reid's door, getting that busy man out of bed. Reid's assigned task, as he related to Miss Mills later, was to keep this fellow from the sight of such as might recognize him and tell Conkling he was in Washington. He explained the situation to James, and took James to Blaine's house. They got Blaine out of bed. He was delighted. They all went to see

Garfield. It was more difficult here, for usually office-seekers get up earlier than Half-Breed statesmen, and of course the quarters of the President-elect were surrounded; but they got James through without raising a murmur. They introduced him to Garfield, who until this moment hadn't even met the man.

Next I had to get Platt, and make him say that, while Conkling had nothing to do with this, and knew nothing of it, and had refused to recommend James or even mention him, he could not object with any reason, which he (Platt) fully approved. This I did,—taking Platt up and asking the questions myself in Garfield's presence. G. is greatly pleased . . . he asked me to keep James as quiet as possible and to get him out of town on the afternoon train. It's done.

By now it was March 3, a day of cold rain, followed by a light snow. Allison caused a final flurry by accepting the Treasury, and then at the very last minute withdrawing his acceptance.

The sun was out by noon, and the streets were dry before the end of the parade. The ball that night in the new National Museum was a grand success. The guests consumed 1,500 pounds of turkey, 100 gallons of oysters, 3,000 biscuits and rolls, 50 hams, 200 gallons of chicken salad, 50 gallons of jelly, 250 gallons of coffee, 15,000 cakes, 250 gallons of ice cream, 300 pounds of butter. . . . Mrs. Garfield wore light lavender satin with point lace, and a cluster of purple pansies at her throat.

March 4, even though the cabinet was still uncompleted, dawned fair and warm. It was perfect inauguration weather. James Abram Garfield read his address before taking the oath of office. Immediately behind him on the stand was the towering figure of Roscoe Conkling—a fact upon which everybody commented.

The President talked to Windom for an hour after the

ceremony, and Windom at last agreed to act as Secretary of the Treasury.

LEMONADE LUCY had caused the White House billiards table to be carried up to the attic, and had used that space to enlarge her conservatory, but James Abram Garfield had the table brought back. He was an excellent billiards player.

Mrs. Garfield wished to have the interior redecorated, so the President sent to the Library of Congress for copies of all available books on the subject, and started to study these.

A new administration had begun.

XXX. As of Thunder

THE hush, really, was terrifying; and statesmen scanned the heavens for a bolt expected. Yet the Senator seemed earnestly intent upon keeping the peace. His position immediately behind Garfield at the inauguration ceremony was generally taken to be a peacemaking gesture. When the nomination of James as postmaster general came up, he moved that it be confirmed promptly and without the usual reference to a committee—a minor politeness, but significant. His enemy Evarts was nominated a commissioner to the International Monetary Conference, but the Senator immediately and without comment voted to confirm this nomination as well. His vote was "aye" also when Henry G. Pearson was nominated postmaster of New York City, and when Levi P. Morton (he had to be remembered in *some* way!) was nominated Minister to France.

But though he was quiet, even affable, he never believed in Garfield's sincerity. He didn't trust the man behind Garfield. Boutwell told him Blaine had said that Roscoe Conkling and his friends should receive fair consideration in the matter of the New York appointments. The Senator snapped: "Do you believe one word of that?" Boutwell said yes, he believed Mr. Blaine. The Senator said "with emphasis" that *he* didn't.

Garfield was not big enough for his job. He resembled the youthful George III of England, whose doting mother was wont to admonish him: "Be king, Georgie, be king." He was an experienced though not a brilliant politician, but he was appalled by the "Spartan band of disciplined office-seekers who drew papers on me as highwaymen draw pistols," and he was pathetically eager to please everybody.

March 20 he invited Senators Conkling and Platt to a conference on New York appointments. Platt wrote that he was obliged to go to New York and asked that no action be taken until his return; but Conkling appeared, and from three o'clock in the afternoon until five-thirty he and the President conferred.

"If it had been with General Grant it couldn't have been more agreeable," the Senator told his friend Gorham.

The following day he sent a note to the President saying never mind about waiting for Tom Platt to get back. This was like him. And the President didn't wait, but on that very day sent a list of five appointments to the Senate. They were: Stewart L. Woodford, U.S. attorney for the southern New York district; Louis F. Payn, U.S. marshal for that district; Asa W. Tenney, attorney for the eastern district; Clinton D. MacDougall, marshal for the northern district; and John Tyler, collector of customs at Buffalo. All were incumbents and all were Stalwarts, tried units of the Conkling machine.

Though there was no reason in the world why these men shouldn't have been continued in their jobs, the journalistic howl of rage which greeted this action was very loud indeed and just the sort of noise calculated to make President Garfield lose his head. "A complete surrender," cried the *New York Times*. Of course the givers of advice were indignant

and alarmed; and James G. Blaine was closeted with the
President from 10 P.M. until almost midnight.

Next morning, while the Senate was in session, a communication from the White House was placed before Vice-Presi-

THE SPOIL–ED

NEW YORK (*meaning business*) [to Conkling and Platt]:
"I know what you DO want!"

dent Arthur. He read it, turned it down to a certain point, and sent it to his friend Senator Conkling.[1] Conkling knew at a glance that the bolt had been hurled. For the President had nominated Judge Robertson collector of the port of New York.

A newspaper correspondent who was sitting next to the Senator, had a peek. "That ought to mean a fight?" The Senator stated: "The nomination is the result, sir, of a perfidy without parallel. It should never be confirmed by an assemblage of American Senators—or gentlemen." Then he refused to talk any more.[2]

THE guinea-pig had growled, had ground its teeth, was behaving like a bulldog. Stalwarts, Half-Breeds, Democrats, all politicians alike were flabbergasted. For this was an act of the most astounding courage, a deliberate invitation to fight. It was more than that—it was a sudden and terrible invasion of neighboring territory.

There is little doubt that the Senator had become reconciled to the prospect of Robertson's getting some post of honor, preferably a diplomatic post. But his appointment as collector, a position at that time absolutely necessary for political control of New York State, was astounding.

Moreover, the message to the Senate gave no reason for the appointment, no explanation of why General Merritt, installed as a reform collector in the first place, should be moved out. The message appointed Merritt Consul-General at London; General Badeau was moved from that position to a less desirable one as Minister at Copenhagen; Cramer was moved from Copenhagen to Switzerland; while the Swiss chargé d'affaires, Nicholas Fish, presumably was to be dropped without a word of farewell.[3]

Badeau and Fish and Cramer were Grant appointees, friends of the former President, and excepting Cramer were New Yorkers. They had not been consulted about the shift.

Merritt, another New Yorker, hadn't been consulted. Grant hadn't been consulted. And of course Tom Platt and Roscoe Conkling hadn't.[4]

It is even possible that James G. Blaine hadn't been consulted. Politicians and newspapermen instantly leapt to the conclusion that Blaine was behind the whole business. Possibly they were inclined to make more than a Machiavelli of the man from Maine, who was, after all, only human. They found his fine Italian hand everywhere. But this was so like him! and so unlike James A. Garfield! It was known that Blaine had been closeted with Garfield for two hours the previous night. He protested that he had not known a thing about the appointments, and Garfield said the same thing, but very few believed them.

It was an act of high political strategy, brave, farsighted, utterly ruthless. Men simply couldn't believe that Garfield had conceived and executed it alone.

Conkling had nothing left to do but fight. He represented the Stalwart tradition of loyalty to friends at whatever cost. He represented General Grant. But even without this, even supposing that a man of his character would be willing to accept such an insult in silence, his whole political career was at stake. There couldn't be any backing out now. He must resist or be ruined.

GARFIELD might have been startled by what he had done, a trifle dismayed, but now that the issue was opened, he would be stubborn.

In the long run, if he sat tight he would win. Not because he was a stronger man than any of the Senate leaders, for he wasn't. Not because he had the assistance of Blaine, valuable though that was. Not because he had public opinion on his side—the public at this stage of the war didn't really give a damn. But because he was President, a new President.

A recently inaugurated President of the United States is

a most powerful potentate indeed. With four years ahead of him, with most or all of his appointments yet to make, he is almost unbeatable.

The New York State legislature, eager for peace at any price, on March 24 passed a resolution favoring confirmation of the Robertson appointment. The Senator was furious.

"What does it mean?" Gorham asked him of the appointment.

"I don't know. All we ask is to be allowed to win in New York, and it's hard enough to do at the best."

Postmaster General James came storming into the executive presence, fuming about Robertson, threatening to resign. Garfield put an arm around him, talked him out of it.

Senator Allison rather unexpectedly appeared in the Conkling cause. Garfield was pleasant, but promised nothing.

Tom Platt and Thomas James handed the President a written remonstrance, signed by them and by Senator Conkling and the Vice-President. It was pigeon-holed without comment.

When John Hay, now living in Washington, read a letter from his friend Whitelaw Reid, prodding the President with remarks about the boastings of the Conkling adherents in New York, Garfield snapped: "They may take him [Robertson] out of the Senate head-first or feet-first: I will never withdraw him!"[5] And on April 3 he went for another long carriage ride with John Sherman, who was back in the Senate and who now agreed to lead the fight for confirmation.

The Senate, consisting of 76 members, was divided 37–37, the other two being not easily classified. Davis of Illinois was an independent Republican elected by Democrats, and Mahone of Virginia was an independent Democrat elected by Republicans, which made things rather confusing. The Republicans had been able to organize the Senate only because of Chet Arthur's vote as Vice-President. And when the Republicans, flirting with Mahone, backed his man for sergeant-at-arms, the indignant Democrats filibustered in force, and all business was stopped.

"Nothing doing," an unnamed Democrat was reported to have said to Whitelaw Reid, and later to Blaine. "We're not going to help you tear down Conkling in New York while you're building up Mahone in Virginia."[6]

So through no fault of his, Conkling was popularly blamed for holding up the nation's affairs because of a wretched personal quarrel about patronage.

THE party suffered, the nation suffered, and compromises were offered by such spokesmen as Tom Platt and Chet Arthur and Tom James. But Garfield stood firm.

Platt suggested that Robertson be made federal district attorney for the southern (New York City) district, and proposed to "pull out" General Woodford by a promise of Rome. When it was learned that Rome had been promised to Walter Phelps, the Reid friend who craved classical surroundings, Platt suggested Portugal instead. This would leave the field free for Robertson to accept the attorney-generalship of the southern district—if Robertson would consent to accept it, and if Garfield would consent to offer it in the first place. But Garfield wouldn't.

Logan dined at the White House, and talked and spluttered; but Garfield kept smiling, shaking his head.

Tom Platt, who was in a peculiarly embarrassing position because of his pledge to support the appointment of Robertson to any office,[7] tried to talk Robertson himself into requesting the President to withdraw his name. But of course Robertson refused. "Under no circumstances will I ask President Garfield to withdraw my nomination . . . nor will I consent to its withdrawal . . . the withdrawal of my name at his instance would make him Conkling's abject slave for the residue of his term," Robertson wrote to Whitelaw Reid. The editor inclosed this in a letter to President Garfield. "This shows how absolutely you are master of the situation," he wrote encouragingly. "Conkling will every month become more and more powerless. I really believe you have him where there is a chance to make an end of him."[8]

On the night of April 14 the Vice-President pleaded with the President, asserting, with utter truth, that Robertson's appointment and confirmation would split the party in New York, smashing the whole organization.

"Of course I deprecate war," the President wrote to Reid, who seemed always able to instill fighting spirit into him, "but if it is brought to my door the bringers will find me at home."[9]

In his journal, April 26, the President recorded that he had talked with "about twenty senators" concerning Robertson. It is probable that they all urged him to withdraw that appointment. The senatorial attitude was clear enough. Even those who didn't like him were obliged to support Roscoe Conkling.[10] He represented the dignity of the Senate. He represented the tradition, the unwritten law rather, of "senatorial courtesy," whereby senators would vote for a nominee only after endorsement by a fellow senator from the state involved. They were jealous of this privilege, and it was only human that they should be.

A conciliation committee was appointed, with H. L. Dawes as chairman, and Roscoe Conkling addressed this committee for two and a half hours.

"I had heard him in all his great efforts since he entered Congress, more than twenty years before," Senator Dawes has recorded, "but I had never heard anything which equalled this effort for flights of oratorical power—genuine eloquence, bitter denunciation, ridicule of the despised faction in New York and contempt for its leader."

Conkling finished with: "I now say to you and through you to those whom it most concerns, that I have in my pocket an autograph letter of this President . . . which I pray God I may never be compelled in self-defense to make public; but if that time shall ever come, I declare to you, his friends, he shall bite the dust!"

The committee "was left in a great state of excitement." It called upon the President the following night, and begged him to withdraw the Robertson nomination. He was told about the mysterious letter, but "seemed unalarmed."

"Oh, you allude to a letter Conkling is saying that he has of mine and which he represents to be a pretty bad one. I know what it is and have a copy of it." He treated the whole matter lightly and as of no consequence . . . took the letter from his pocket and handed it to me. Upon perusing it I discovered that it was one of those indiscreet letters, like the Jay Hubbell letters, which he had written during the presidential campaign, aiding the efforts to collect from clerks and other government officials subscriptions to campaign expenses.

Dawes urged the President to publish it himself, but at this moment Blaine came in and Garfield handed him the copy of the letter: "Here, Blaine, is where I have been slopping over again." Blaine advised against publication, so of course it wasn't published.[11]

It is well that a President of the United States should not submit to blackmail. But his behavior here was less admirable than it seems. It wasn't bluff, assumed indifference: he really didn't attach much importance to that letter: his political conscience was of the toughest. However, the incident shows Senator Conkling at his worst.

The letter was not mentioned again.

THE next night Dawes was back at the White House, and argued for two hours—in vain. A few days later, May 2, the Republican senators appointed a committee of safety which recommended that a majority of Republicans in the upper house decide the order of executive business, including "contested nominations." It was distinctly a threat, and there is little doubt that Conkling was behind it. It said to the President: "Unless you listen to us in the matter of appointments, we will reserve the right to postpone confirmation indefinitely." This, at least, is the way the press took it; for by now the press, at least, and possibly the public too, was on the President's side. The merit of his attitude has nothing to do with it: unless he be a good deal of a fool, or patently a rascal, any American President in a battle with either or both houses of Congress is likely to have the sympathy of the public.

Dawes, representing the Senate in general, with Senator Hawley, waited upon the President that night. They settled nothing. Garfield wouldn't budge.

The following day, however, the President seemed to weaken a little. At least, for the first time he consulted his cabinet on this matter.

The day after that the senatorial deadlock over the Mahone business was broken.

The day after *that*, May 5, President Garfield unexpectedly withdrew the names of the five Stalwarts he had reappointed attorneys and marshals and Buffalo collector in New York. Again there was a great gasp. Letters and telegrams of congratulation poured into the White House, the pro-Garfield press was delighted, and the givers of advice chortled with joy at this added show of battle spirit. For here the President was telling the Senator: "Either you take Robertson or you get nothing at all!"

GARFIELD wrote to Murat Halstead: "Conkling, after ten years of absolute despotism in New York . . . got the elephantiasis of conceit . . . a plain, old-fashioned case of sore-head."

Grant, who seldom became outspoken about anything, wrote to General Badeau: "Garfield has shown that he is not possessed of the backbone of an angle-worm. I hope his nominations may be defeated."

And Whitelaw Reid, from New York, continued to send letters to the White House repeating every absurd Stalwart story, every silly boast of irresponsible Conkling fanatics, as though it were a solemn and indisputable truth. Whitelaw Reid was near victory, and he cried again, with rising fervor: "Be king, Georgie!"

THE appointment probably would pass the Senate, now that the Democrats had been mollified in the Mahone matter. But Republican senators generally were most reluctant to vote one way or the other. They would have preferred to see the matter settled out of court, avoiding scandal. On May 9 there was a caucus, at which Roscoe Conkling was amazingly conciliatory. Edmunds moved that the Robertson matter be put over until December, and Conkling supported this motion in a long speech. The motion was withdrawn to save it from defeat. Conkling proposed a face-saving device which stirred little interest: Robertson should be confirmed with the preliminary agreement that he decline to accept the position. The caucus finally adopted a resolution to delay consideration for the present. This was not satisfactory to anybody.

At the next caucus, May 13, the Senator was very angry. He had not been able to get any agreement with the Democrats, and it was apparent now that the matter would soon come to a vote, and that Robertson's appointment would be confirmed.

THAT scrawny, imperious, astounding old Scotsman, Bennett *père*, had recently died, and the *New York Herald* was being run from Paris or where-not by his even more astounding son, a half-Irish, half-mad, and wholly unpredictable young drunkard. The editor, Connery, literally didn't know whether this tyrant was in Europe, Asia, or Africa at this time—indeed, it is altogether possible that Bennett *fils* himself didn't know—but "I remembered how he had directed

me, in a sweeping way, to oblige and help the Senator whenever opportunity offered." So Connery went to Washington
to see what he could do.

Chet Arthur was alone in The Morgue, and Connery first
heard the Vice-Presidential version, which of course was the
Senator's too:

Garfield has not been square, nor honorable, nor truthful with
Conkling. It's a hard thing to say of a President of the United
States, but it's only the truth. . . . Long ago we heard that
Garfield said he intended to "break" Senator Conkling by showing special favor to the Half Breeds. We were told that the
president deemed it necessary to humble Conkling's pride—that
he would first break and then conciliate him.

When the Senator himself appeared he spoke for two solid
hours. Connery enjoyed every minute of it—and believed
that Chet Arthur did too, notwithstanding the fact that
Arthur undoubtedly had heard it all before—"Conkling all
the time pouring out beautifully rounded periods without
halt or hesitation, with the grace and earnestness of a finished actor on the stage."

At Mentor, it seems, the Senator had asked the then President-elect what he had against Folger, and Garfield, muttering something about a whiskey drinker, dropped that subject and invited his guest to have some tea.

"Tea! tea!" Conkling cried, walking the floor. "Tea!"

It seemed to render him especially furious. The editor and
the Vice-President listened reverently.

" 'Reward! reward!' Reward, sir, for treacherously betray-
ing a sacred trust!" He threw on the floor a clipping of the
pre-inaugural *Tribune* editorial (January 3, 1881) in which
it was stated, obviously with authority, that the administration would not permit the New York rebels to suffer—
though much more than this was implied.

What was the meaning of that article? What was the meaning of it, sir, if not to give me timely warning that the men who

had voted faithfully for Grant—the men who clung to their pledges and honor—need expect no quarter from the administration, while the men who had basely violated their pledges by abandoning Grant for Garfield and thereby turned the tide of voting in favor of Garfield, were to be rewarded for their treachery? "Rewarded! rewarded! Recognition! reward! compensation at the public's expense! The administration will foment no quarrels." Bah!

It was very wonderful, and it made a profound impression upon Editor Connery, but it didn't change a single vote.

NOBODY, not even Roscoe Conkling, could stop confirmation. Press and public were angry, impatient, remembering the squabbles of the Hayes administration. Not only the smaller politicians at home, but also men like Governor Cornell, were frightened; for they saw that Garfield was going to fight, and they couldn't survive a fight with another President. It would kill them, smash their organization. If Garfield refused to move, Senator or no Senator they must crawl to Garfield.

And Garfield did refuse to move. So did Robertson.

May 16 there was a terrific crash as of thunder, followed by an eagerly echoing "pip." The crash was Roscoe Conkling: "I hereby resign from the United States Senate!" The echo was Tom Platt valiantly squeaking: "I do too."

XXXI. The Bullets of an Assassin

THE sun rose next day promptly on time—4.53 o'clock in Washington, 4.36 o'clock in New York —and though there was some rain, though the day was cloudy and chilly,[1] the heavens did not fall and it was soon apparent that the world had not come to an end.

AT first it was supposed that Senator Conkling had acted in a fit of pique. Headstrong, quick-tempered, always ready to cut off his nose, his chin, or any other feature in order to spite his face—it was, men held, just like him. If he couldn't be captain of the team he wouldn't play. Clearly he had been unable to block the confirmation—which occurred two days later, with only one senator, Conkling's faithful friend Jones of Nevada, voting against it—so he had thrown down his toys and stamped out of the nursery.

But was this all? Could it be possible that the Senator, like William of Orange, was prepared to fight it out in the last ditch?

He had owned the New York legislature, had controlled it, but never had paid much attention to it. But what if he demanded that it reëlect him (and Tom Platt) to the United States Senate? Would anybody dare to disobey him? deliberately vote against him? Both houses of the legislature were Republican, and even Whitelaw Reid's paper admitted that the Boss had a majority in each.[2]

If Conkling and Platt, after resigning in specific protest against the Robertson nomination, were triumphantly reelected, sent back to Washington—then what could Garfield and Blaine say or do?

FOR some time there was uncertainty. Conklingites in Albany sent wire after anxious wire to the Boss, but received no reply.

Nor was there anything in the letter of resignation itself to give a hint of future conduct. Conkling had written to Chester Arthur in his official capacity of presiding officer of the Senate: "Sir: Will you please announce to the Senate that my resignation as Senator of the United States from the State of New York has been forwarded to the Governor of the State? I have the honor to be, with great respect, your obedient servant—" Tom Platt's message, almost identical, was no longer. The clerk read Conkling's first, and not until he was half through with Platt's did senators, beginning to understand what had happened, rush to the desk for a look.

Not more than three or four personal friends had known that this was to happen, though the letter to Cornell, signed by both senators, had been sent by mail two days previous, May 14. It was dignified, commendably cool:

THE LOST HEAD

Grant attempting to replace Conkling's head.

We have not attempted to "dictate," nor have we asked the nomination of one person to any office in the State. Indeed, with the sole exception of the written request set forth above [the formal remonstrance submitted by Arthur, Platt, James, and Conkling, and embodied in full in the letter of resignation] we have never even expressed an opinion to the President in any case unless questioned in regard to it. . . .

With a profound sense of the obligations we owe, with devotion to the Republican party and its creed of liberty and right, with reverent attachment to the great State whose interests and honor are dear to us, we hold it respectful and becoming to make room for those who may correct all the duties we have misconceived.

We therefore inclose our resignations. . . .

Reporters scurried back and forth, gleaning expressions of dumbfoundment. Some senators spoke of the resignations as "an exhibition of petulance that is unwarranted by anything that has occurred," the *Times* correspondent learned, and "nearly every senator approached upon the subject condemned the course of Messrs. Conkling and Platt"—but begged not to be quoted.[3]

Platt, of course, later insisted that he himself had first proposed resignation.[4] It is possible that this is true, though nobody at the time believed it. Alfred Conkling says that his uncle had been wishing to resign anyway, for months.[5]

State Stalwarts were panicky. Fighting a new national administration was unthinkable, but so was fighting the Boss. Somebody sent a "handsome floral ship" to Judge Robertson's desk in the state senate by way of congratulation. Governor Cornell shook his head, privately admitted that he didn't like the whole business, but refused to be quoted. He had, before the resignations, dared to send the Senator a telegram recommending that the fight against Robertson be given up—so that hereafter he was an enemy in the Senator's eyes: he was "the lizard on the hill" in the Senator's conversation. The legislature that Friday adjourned early for the week-end, and the members hurried home to see what their constituents thought about it all.

Conkling remained silent, in Washington.

Saturday he took a train for New York, and that night, and far into the next morning, he sat in a suite in the Fifth Avenue Hotel while Stalwart after Stalwart slipped in to see him, using the Twenty-third Street entrance in order to avoid reporters. He was making up his mind.

Next afternoon he drove to Chet Arthur's home at 123 Lexington Avenue. The Vice-President was there, and General Sharpe, speaker of the assembly, Tom Platt, Police Commissioner French, Charles M. Denison, Arthur B. Johnson of Utica, John Smyth, Louis Payn, Assemblyman Carpenter, and the faithful Senator Jones of Nevada. What to do? The Senator made a speech.

His greatest desire at this time was to make a *real* speech, before thousands. Instinctively he fell back upon oratory, his best weapon.[6] He desired a mass meeting in the city. He would put his case before the people.

"I have not tried to steal the Collectorship," he cried. "I have tried to keep it in the hands of the man who has a right to it until his term expires, but I am the man accused of being a thief. I am accused of grabbing for patronage. I have simply tried to prevent others from succeeding in their grab for patronage."[7]

Understandably it made him angry that people called him an office-snatcher. From the beginning of his congressional career he had held himself aloof from the scramble for jobs. A few jobs, yes—those he really needed in order to keep his machine oiled—the key positions to which any state boss should be entitled—but nothing more.[8] Yet here he was being made to seem the arch-villain of that monstrosity, the Spoils System! Merritt, appointed as a reform collector, had been replaced by Robertson for sheerly political purposes;[9] yet by the law of black and white, which admits of no grays, Conkling was the grabber, Garfield and Blaine the defenders of civil service! He must explain this to the people; he must set himself right, before actually retiring to private life; and how to do this better than by a great speech?

They talked him out of it. He must go to Albany, they said, and persuade the legislature to reëlect him. *This* must be his vindication.

Finally he consented. It was an unfortunate decision.[10]

THE train arrived at two o'clock Tuesday afternoon—a few minutes early, but there was a good crowd anyway. He walked to the Delavan House, smiling right and left, calling greetings. Gone was the God-damn-you stare. "The ex-Senator never was more cordial than today. He put up with the most tiresome of men without shrinking . . . nothing could have been more gracious than his manner."[11] There were cheers for him in the lobby, and cheers for Grant, for the gallant 306, even for Tom Platt—though some unfeeling person in the back afterward yelled "Me too!"

He nodded and smiled his way up to Room 57. He did everything but bow.

This was all in the best regal tradition. The haughtiest of princes have unbent when their power was threatened—but usually, like Roscoe Conkling, too late. Still it seemed wrong. It did not make a good impression. For the first time, men who had feared or hated him began only to feel sorry for him.

HE returned to New York City a few days later. Things were very quiet around the Fifth Avenue Hotel. A few of the standbys were there, but nobody fawned upon Roscoe Conkling.

Men were saying that he was beaten, already. Stalwarts were breaking loose.

"I will not indulge in prophecies with half a dozen cable lengths between us," John Hay wrote to Whitelaw Reid, who was honeymooning in Europe while Hay ran his paper for him, "but to speak of certainties, Roscoe is finished. That Olympian brow will never again garner up the thousands of yore. Of course we shall have a bad state of things for a while and shall almost certainly lose the State next fall. But that will be after your return, and I can charge it to *my* leaving the Tribune.

"The whole thing has been a freak of insanity on the part of a man who has lost sight of his true relations with the rest of the world. It was the logical result of the personality of Conkling and the workings of the Boss system."[12]

Garfield wrote in a letter: "—if our friends in N.Y. have the requisite sense and pluck they can end his hateful career as a politician."[13]

Conkling went back to Albany.

HE must have suffered acutely. He saw everybody.

—any man, let him be ever so dull, or never so much opposed to Conkling's re-election, could, by speaking the word, be accorded a private interview with him, and command his time for a half-hour, an hour, or longer, while the ex-Senator would most graciously, explicitly, confidingly unfold to him the secret bitterness and misery which he had been made to suffer at the hands of a hostile administration.[14]

His friends tried to arrange a caucus. The caucus committee refused to issue a call, and busy Tom Platt himself wrote a call and started his campaign to get a majority of the Republican legislators to sign. "I know he's against our return," he told Brigham in trying to persuade Brigham to speak to his partner, an assemblyman, "but you can surely convince him that if we are to be beaten we're entitled to be beaten in the good and ancient form—the form by which we were originally chosen." The partner finally signed the call, but remarked that it wouldn't do any good.[15]

Conkling always had been fond of caucuses. He thought in terms of party organization, party discipline. He believed that if he could face the Republican legislators *as Republicans*, off the floor, they would not dare to vote against him. Tom Platt thought that too. But they didn't get their caucus.

The Half-Breeds were striving for adjournment, but the Conklingites were able to block this.

Chauncey Depew was a candidate, and again by request. "Mr. Blaine came to New York and insisted upon my entering the canvass, and that I was the only one who could get the whole of the anti-organization vote. . . . With the Democrats voting for their own candidate, and the anti-organization men voting for me, it was impossible for any one to have a majority. The fight was most bitter." Depew and Blaine were both railroad men, Depew outspokenly and by actual employment. Depew, a handy friend to have, knew his way around in Albany, for he was a member of what was then called the Third House. He represented the New York Central, and as such naturally was familiar with members of the legislature. He was a very good fellow, and made a strong candidate. There were whispers, sometimes shouts, of bribery in connection with his candidacy; and there was even, later, an official investigation; but nothing came of it.[16]

Cornell refused to be a candidate, though some of his friends voted for him again and again. He had not seen Conkling. He must have heard what Conkling was saying about him, but he was not angry; that silent hulk wasn't easily moved to anger. He had made an exceptionally good governor, and if he had entered the race as a Stalwart compromise candidate it seems quite possible that he could have defeated Platt and won election to the long term. But he refused to do this. The Boss had said it must be Conkling and Platt, and Alonzo Cornell still was an organization man. Conkling, angry, convinced that he had been betrayed, would not go to the governor, or send for the governor, and of course the governor could do nothing without a word from the Boss. It was a most unfortunate situation. Privately

Cornell urged his friends to vote for Conkling and Platt, but publicly he was not able to do anything. Conkling never forgave him.

BALLOTING started May 31, in joint session, and continued week after weary week. It was an exceptionally hot summer. Tom Platt led for the long term, on the first ballot, as Roscoe Conkling led for the short term, but after that each was second or third, sometimes lower. There were never fewer than nine candidates for the long term, seldom fewer than seven for the short term. The Democrats, in spite of all sorts of dickering, didn't break.

Tom Platt nipped here and there, smiling, furtive, full of important little whispers. Roscoe Conkling stayed in Room 57, Delavan House, and writhed in his humiliation. He had tried everything he knew. He had endeavored to make a deal with the Democrats, as indeed had the Half-Breeds.[17] He had smiled upon people, shaken people's hands, listened to people's opinions. He had even gone so far as to write personal notes to men he knew, asking if they would do him the favor of waiting upon him at such-and-such time in his room. This was his low point; and the politicians themselves, sentimental persons always, no matter what their votes, felt the pity of it. Brigham tells a story—

He was talking to Senator Davenport and some other men in the Delavan lobby when a note came to Davenport from Roscoe Conkling upstairs. Davenport read it, sadly shrugged. "The sooner it's over, the better." He quit the group in the lobby. Half an hour later he was back, shaking his head. "Boys, that's the most embarrassing interview I ever had. You know, I've been brought up on Conkling. But when he put it to me plain I had to tell him I approved of his resignation but didn't approve of sending him and Platt back to fight the administration."

Week after week. Neither Platt nor Conkling rose again to the top. Eighty-one votes were necessary to elect, at first.

After the first ballot Conkling never got more than 39, Platt never more than 36.

It was the burning deck act again, with fewer Casabiancas. Moreover, it didn't seem so glorious this time. The *Times* said angrily that "the blind, unreasoning obedience of the Conkling guard is robbed of all pretensions to heroism by its absolute idiocy."[18]

Then two unexpected and shocking things happened. One of them was funny, but the other was a tragedy. To Conkling both were tragedies.

A COUPLE of Half-Breeds got a stepladder and used it to look over the transom of Tom Platt's hotel room, and they saw Tom in bed with an unspeakable female. Tom was an elder of the Methodist Episcopal Church, an enthusiastic singer of psalms and hymns, a passer of collection plates. It was too good to keep—if, indeed, the Half-Breeds ever had thought of keeping it.

Now of course this had nothing to do with Platt's qualifications to be a United States senator. But it was very, very funny, and almost everybody in Albany knew about it soon afterward. Sooner or later some editor was going to find the nerve to publish it. If it became officially public it would kill Platt's chances, and there were some breathless days while men tittered and watched the papers for a reference to the "stepladder committee." It came July 2, a mercilessly hot day. The *Albany Argus* and the *New York World* took the chance, telling the story delicately but unmistakably. Tom Platt called in Lou Payn and instructed him to withdraw his name, for he knew when he was beaten.

Platt announced, of course, that he was doing this in order to help the candidacy of his dear friend Senator Conkling. In fact, it hurt Conkling; but what else was there to do? Conkling, who had agreed to run only on the understanding that Platt too should be supported by the organization, is-

sued a statement saying that he much regretted to hear that
his friend Senator Platt was withdrawing from the contest.
There was much public talk about harmony and the good of
the party, but the talk in private concerned other things,
and echoes of that prodigious tittering still hung in the air
—until, that same morning, the second thing happened.
Then Conkling and Platt and all the rest of them were
shoved off the front pages with a sickening push.

JAMES ABRAM GARFIELD, after the resignations, had sent
back to the Senate the names of three of the five Stalwarts,
appointing Half-Breeds in place of Payn and Tyler. These
nominations had been confirmed. Curiously, Garfield was
praised as magnanimous because he did not shut out Conkling entirely; but the realists in the party, and notably
Blaine, argued that if he was going to fight at all he should-
n't, against a man like Conkling, pull his punches. "Some
blunders are worse than crimes," Blaine wrote in a passionate note to the President. "I fear this is one."[19]

But Garfield and Blaine continued to be the best of
friends. They were together, chatting gayly, on that morning of July 2 while Tom Platt was elsewhere engaged in
getting his name withdrawn. They were going to Williams-
town, where the President was to attend a class reunion.
Sundry other cabinet members and their wives already were
seated in the special train, and still others of the party were
coming up in the rear. The President and his Secretary of
State entered the Pennsylvania station in Washington at
9.20 o'clock.

A man with a revolver stepped forward and fired twice at
the President. One bullet grazed an arm, the other chipped
the spinal column and split two ribs.

The President fell, not bleeding much, but unconscious,
and apparently dead. They took him into the railroad office,
and a little later, after he had recovered consciousness, to

the White House. Physicians examined him and shook their heads. No use to probe for the bullet. He was as good as dead anyway.

Roscoe Conkling was in Albany at the time, and could prove it. Besides, the assassin didn't run, but stood there waving his revolver and shouting: "I did it and I want to be arrested. I am a Stalwart and Arthur is President now"— or words to that effect: nobody was certain, in the excitement. His gun was taken from him. In the other hand he held a letter addressed to General Sherman, requesting a military guard around the prison in which he would be placed. "I have just shot the President," the letter said. "I shot him several times, as I wished him to go as easily as possible. His death was a political necessity. I am a lawyer, a theologian and a politician. I am a Stalwart of Stalwarts." There was another letter in one of his pockets, addressed to nobody in particular: "The President's tragic death was a sad necessity but it will unite the Republican party and save the Republic. . . ." From another pocket they took a recent issue of the *New York Herald,* folded to a marked editorial in which President Garfield was taken to task for his treatment of Roscoe Conkling.

Charles J. Guiteau wasn't a "lawyer, a theologian and a politician." He was an obscure office-seeker, unknown to any responsible leader of the Republican party, or to any other person of consequence. He had been gently ushered out of the White House several times, after babbling of his need to see the President about a job. Today, almost certainly he would be pronounced a lunatic. In 1881 he was rated just inside of the technical, legal border of sanity, and was classed as an "eccentric." They put him in jail, where his conversation didn't make much sense, and a year later, after a trial, they got around to executing him. He kept saying that he was a Stalwart and that he had killed Garfield only in order to make Chester A. Arthur President.

ARTHUR (it was rather undignified for a Vice-President of the United States, but the Boss had spoken) was in Albany campaigning for Platt and Conkling. When he heard the news he hurried to Washington.

Conkling sent to the White House a message of regret, formal, like all his letters, but doubtless sincere: he must have been profoundly shocked. From that day he began to get threatening letters. If the President dies, the letters said —most of them—*look out!* Excepting Guiteau, possibly not even excepting Guiteau, for nobody paid much attention to the assassin himself, Conkling was the most hated man in the country. As in all his fights, there had been so much that was *personal* in the battle between him and Garfield. It hadn't been a Stalwart–Half-Breed war so much as a single duel. And Conkling, originally cast for the villain's rôle, now was hopelessly settled there. It would do no good to try to explain. Even one of his speeches would not be effective.

In the balloting he rose from third to second place (not counting the Democratic candidate). Shock or no shock, it seemed highly probable that Chet Arthur soon would be President of the United States. The Conkling stock rose. Recently the Half-Breeds at Albany, surer of themselves, had been trying to arrange a conference of Republican legislators, in effect a caucus; the Stalwarts had been opposed to this, and now they were more firmly opposed. Why not? It was understood that sooner or later there probably would be some compromise and one Stalwart and one Half-Breed would be elected to the Senate. But if Arthur was President, and the Federal patronage practically pledged to the Stalwarts, there was no reason why that faction shouldn't get both senatorships. They temporized, reading the bulletins from the White House bedside. It was deplorable, but it was politics.

The *Tribune*, always enterprising, sent a man out to West New Brighton, Staten Island, to ask George William Curtis his opinion of the shooting. Curtis attributed it to the Spoils System. "In the event of President Garfield's death, what do you think would be the policy of Vice-President Arthur?" he was asked. "I presume," he said, "that if Mr. Arthur should become President, in his ignorance and inexperience he would be compelled to rely on some one more capable than himself. Obviously that person would be Mr. Conkling, and he would be the controlling influence of the administration."[20] Everybody else presumed the same.

Next day the *Tribune* editorially denied that it had ever called Roscoe Conkling a murderer. But "when a child, in its mad rage, kicks over a table, upsets a lamp, sets the house on fire, and burns people to death, nobody supposes that the child intended murder. Mr. Conkling has been acting like a child in a fit of passion."

The President began to rally, and Conkling dropped to fourth place. Physicians found that the second bullet had torn away a portion of the spinal column but had not actually touched the spinal cord itself. They couldn't locate the bullet, and didn't dare to go looking for it. It is customary to describe prominent persons who are dying slowly as "putting up a gallant (or valiant) fight." James A. Garfield really did. His physical courage was magnificent, and he was the perfect patient. He took a gay interest in his own case, read books on anatomy, studied the charts of his condition and discussed these with the doctors, chuckled over the unsuccessful search for that chunk of lead . . . he even wished to debate with his friend General Swaim the probable velocity of the bullet at the instant it entered his body! The nation worshiped him, now. He continued to improve; and Conkling dropped to fifth place in the balloting.

IN the city of Albany, muggy and sticky and hot, the long fight dragged on. There wasn't even much public interest in it any longer. Sixty-two Republicans signed a caucus petition, but the call specified that one Half-Breed and one Stalwart candidate should be picked, and the Stalwarts objected to this with loud cries. The ex-Senator was in this thing to stay, and caucus or no caucus, murder or no murder, he would see it through. He could do nothing less. It was not possible for him to retreat, smirking, as Tom Platt had done, or to compromise. "He will never surrender or give up so long as there is any possible way out of it," one of his friends told a reporter.[21]

The caucus was held, nevertheless. This was July 8. Congressmen Miller and Lapham were selected for the long and short terms, respectively. Miller, a tall, stern man with a blond mustache, was a Half-Breed. Lapham had been a Stalwart, and still was rated as such—but not by Roscoe Conkling. For had not Lapham deserted? Was not Lapham one of the first rats to quit the sinking ship? Conkling cried bitterly: "That man must not reap the reward of his perfidy!" But nobody was paying much attention to what Conkling cried.

Chauncey Depew dropped out "in the interest of harmony." He wasn't needed any longer.

July 12, before the forty-third ballot was taken, the Conkling men were trying to get another caucus called. Lapham was too much to ask! But the ballot was taken, with Lapham and Miller on top. They were on top the next day too, in the forty-fourth ballot, though there was no decisive change. July 15 the Conkling men and the Democrats tried to push through an adjournment motion, and failed. At the beginning of this contest the Conkling men had been strong enough to defeat such a motion. Now they were wishing they hadn't. Possibly they could elect a legislature which would be kinder to the Boss.

July 16 Miller was elected. Lapham—it was the forty-eighth ballot—was within 5 votes of election. Only 73 were necessary now, and he had 68, Potter, the Democrat, had 47, Conkling had 29, Evarts had 1. The others had dropped out after the caucus.

General Sharpe switched to Lapham. Sharpe was one of those who in the Lexington Avenue conference had urged Conkling to go to Albany and stand for reëlection.

Conkling went to Washington, called at the White House. He did not see the wounded man—almost certainly he had not expected to do so—but he left a formal message of good wishes.

When he returned to New York he took Chet Arthur with him. Chet didn't like it much.

Lapham gained a vote on the fifty-first ballot, July 20. It was incredible! It was unthinkable that any other man should have Roscoe Conkling's seat in the United States Senate! The legislators were going home in disgust. The old guard was almost down. July 23, on the fifty-fifth ballot, Lapham had 63, Conkling 28.

Lapham was elected on the fifty-sixth ballot. The election was made unanimous by giving him the votes of all the Republicans present, a total of 93. This was to show the public that there was real harmony in the party, this unanimous business. It was an old stunt of Roscoe Conkling, the ex-Senator. You remember?—Conkling, the former Boss.

XXXII. Most Successful, as a Lawyer

WHEN they told the President he murmured, "I am glad it is over. I am sorry for Conkling. He has made a great mistake, in my judgment. I will offer him any favor he may ask, or any appointment he may desire."[1]

Likely enough Garfield meant this. There was nothing vindictive about the man. Had he lived, it is probable that he would have made a "broken" Conkling some flattering offer—which Conkling would have refused.

But Garfield didn't live. He suffered nobly and well, while

the nation prayed for him, following the bulletins from day to day. August 26 and 27 he was sinking badly. He survived that crisis; but it was decided to take him out of Washington to the seashore, as he himself wished; so on September 6 he was carefully carried into a special train, and hurried to Elberon, N.J. The night of September 19 was an anniversary of the battle of Chickamauga. Eighteen years earlier, to the hour, Garfield, as Rosecrans' chief-of-staff, had been writing dispatches in feverish preparation for the second day of fighting. Now, in Elberon, he clutched his heart. "It hurts here!" General Swaim rushed to him with a glass of water. The President drank some of it, but cried afterward: "Swaim, can't you stop this? Oh, Swaim!" Then he died.

THE threatening letters to Conkling increased. He paid them no heed. No longer, now, could he hope to explain himself. "How can I speak into a grave?" he would cry. "How can I do battle with a shroud? Silence is a duty and a doom!"[2]

He kept his word, too. It is almost unbelievable that a politician of his glint and prominence should retire so spectacularly into private life—and not write a book about it. But Conkling wrote no book, not even a magazine article; nor did he engage any newspaperman or literary hack to do this for him under his own or any other name. No doubt there were large money offers, for statesmen's autobiographies were popular then, and most of Conkling's associates had written, or were writing, or were to write, their own versions of things. The nation has heard them—Weed, Blaine, Grant, Edmunds, Childs, Schurz, Hoar, McCulloch, Platt, Sherman, Stewart, Welles, Vest, Watterson, White, Butler, Depew, Greeley, and all the others—but it has not heard Conkling. The only biography of the man, published after his death, was written by his adoring nephew, Alfred Conkling. It is incomplete, inelegant, poorly edited, preposterously, almost hysterically one-sided; and the widow, even more reticent than her husband had been, abhoring personalities, censored it energetically before publication.

WRITES White: "It was a common saying at that time among those who knew him best, 'Chet Arthur president of the United States! Good God!'"

They underrated the man. Nobody ever pretended that Chester Alan Arthur was great—but how few among our Presidents, whether elected or installed, *have* been! Arthur at least was no fool. He was a Phi Beta Kappa (he had been graduated from Union College, Schenectady, N. Y., at the age of eighteen), and a lawyer, a teacher, most emphatically of all, a gentleman. He was a six-footer, good looking, quiet, affable. His whiskers were beautiful. He wore "nobby" clothes with an air—light blue ties, trousers the color of vanilla ice cream, dazzling waistcoats. Most talked about of all were his hats. He went in for high, bell-crowned, broad-brimmed "plugs" made of white beaver in the rough—the sort of hat nobody but a dandy of great courage and unquestioned taste could wear, as Arthur did, with success. He even had a valet, a negro named Aleck.

Chester Alan Arthur looked over the White House and roundly declared—it was his first astounding display of independence—that he wouldn't live in such a place. This was no affectation. The White House was in bad shape, though most of its previous occupants had been so delighted at getting into it that they hadn't noticed this, or hadn't cared. The furniture was soiled and worn; the china chipped, mismatched; the rugs were thready; the storerooms and attic were crammed with leftovers no President's family had ventured to throw away. Arthur lived in a hotel, and called for a new deal in decoration. There was an auction sale, and a total of $3,000 cash was realized, so that the place could be made decent. Twenty-four wagonloads of stuff were taken out of the White House! Souvenir hunters had a wonderful time. There was a portmanteau which once had belonged to

Abigail Adams, a battered silk hat and a pair of trousers so worn that even Abe Lincoln had refused to wear them any longer. . . . There was the sideboard Mrs. Hayes had caused to be relegated to the attic. Sideboards meant only one thing in those days. The Washington saloonkeepers chipped in to buy this one, and stocked it with everything conceivable, and gave it back to the new President, who accepted it with a smile. What Lemonade Lucy thought we don't know.

It was significant, this clean-up. Men were learning about a new Chet Arthur. Incidentally, men no longer were calling him "Chet"—not to his face. They no longer were slapping his back, twice. He took his new job seriously, and made a much better President than anybody had expected. Old-time Stalwarts grumbled and cursed, but the nation as a whole, if not loud in applause, clearly was pleased.

Before Garfield's death Chet Arthur had taken orders from his Boss. He had labored in Albany like any ward worker. It was undignified, and he hadn't liked it, but he had done it.[3] But now he was the President, sir.

He worked. He vetoed one of the earliest rivers-and-harbors pork-barrel bills. He asked Congress for territorial government in Alaska, for preservation of the national forests, tariff reform, a large navy, an interstate commerce law, currency reform, national aid to education, clarification of the Presidential succession and electoral count provisions of the Constitution, legislation for Chinese exclusion, encouragement of shipping—even for civil service reform! This does not mean that he accomplished much. But he did his best, which, axiomatically, is all any man *can* do. He had inherited an unfortunate Government, split and spattered by the passions of war, by corruption under Grant, by the rage-provoking scandals of the 1876–77 election dispute, the party squabbles of the Hayes administration, and recently the Stalwart–Half-Breed war which had roused extraordinary hatreds not only in New York but all over the country. The machinery was rusted, unreliable. During the months while Garfield was engaged in dying very few wheels had been made to turn. President Arthur was a tolerably good mechanic, and a skilled wielder of the oil can; but the job called for a master engineer, and he wasn't that.

He was no showman, and hated publicity. Much of his real work of persuasion was done late at night, at the quiet little suppers for which the White House became famous. Decanters, some glasses, cigars, and a few congressional leaders seated around a table and willing to listen—this was Arthur's system. He talked late, and rose late.

Rutherford B. Hayes, who had retired to Spiegel Grove, Fremont, Ohio, where he answered letters, attended G.A.R. and Odd Fellows meetings, dedicated things, served as honorary chairman of uncountable committees, raised chickens, went to class reunions, interested himself in prison reform— Rutherford B. Hayes shook a sad head over the doings at the White House, "liquor, snobbery, and worse,"[4]—but Chester Arthur had selected his own path and he followed it.

CONKLING? It was assumed that Conkling would be given a good cabinet post—the cabinet members, of course, all had offered to resign and all had been asked to stay where they were, please, for a little while—and that he would control this administration as he had controlled those of Grant.

Only his closest friends, and they were not many, knew and believed that he did intend to stay out of public life and make some money. The public never believes a thing like that. The public, with good reason, thinks of retiring politicians as it thinks of retiring stage stars or opera singers: they are always to be counted upon for just one more final appearance. But Conkling meant it. He wasn't going to try to show Chet Arthur how to run the country. He had but a single request to make of Chet. He looked for one thing, and one thing only—the removal of Robertson.

Not long after the inauguration they met—it was like old

times—in a room in the Fifth Avenue Hotel. Anybody's guess is good. They were there, undisturbed, from nine o'clock at night until four o'clock the next morning. A few weeks later there was another conference, this one at the White House. They were closeted for five uninterrupted hours. A reporter saw the ex-Senator at the Washington station just after that conference. His face was almost black with rage, and his eyes glittered.[5] For Robertson remained collector of the port of New York. Chester Arthur was going to be king.

ROSCOE CONKLING opened a law office.

"No man, however strong," wrote Henry Adams in one of his more confident moods, "can serve ten years as schoolmaster, priest, or Senator, and remain fit for anything else."

When Henry Adams is not uncertain of himself he is not sound. And sometimes when he essays an epigram he becomes, for all the charm of his style, just plain silly.

Despite a pauseless but always fashionable stoning of derision, the United States Senate since the earliest days of the republic has attracted many men of great ability. Roscoe Conkling is one of them; and his case alone would be sufficient to puncture that cocky statement in the *Education*. People had been thinking of him only as a politician, and they had rather forgotten, even if he himself hadn't, that he was a good lawyer.

Utica was too small. New York City was his field now. And he would not be a mere criminal attorney, or one to dazzle juries in damage cases, but a corporation counsel. This was in the first full dawn of American corporations, when millions were being hurled madly in all directions and competition was terrific. The ex-Senator might have accepted all sorts of lucrative partnerships, but characteristically he decided to go it alone. He opened an office, two small rooms on the third floor at 31 Nassau Street. His health was none too good. He used to work mornings, quit at noon, walk up to the Fifth Avenue Hotel, his home, for the exercise. He disliked street cars, and loathed the new elevated; for all close contact with crowds made him shudder; but he always had been a good walker.

Soon he got the Northern Pacific account. Then Jay Gould came a-knocking—Jay Gould, "Mephistopheles," that mild-mannered little cutthroat of Wall Street, that most dangerous, most hateful of all the period's robber barons. Among other properties Gould just then owned, almost accidentally, the *New York World,* and soon Roscoe Conkling found himself defending that ancient enemy in two libel suits, which he won. The young tinkerer Thomas A. Edison came. He brought a lot of business. Collis P. Huntington— Joseph Choate called him "the Jay Gould of the Pacific Coast," though in fact he was living in New York at this time[6]—came with more railroad work. Huntington and the former Senator became close friends.

His fellow lawyers esteemed him highly.

It is safe to say, I think, that during these last seven years of his practice, he received a larger professional income than was ever paid, in the same length of time, to any other lawyer in this country. Something, doubtless, is to be credited to personal admiration and personal devotion, but, in the main, his unprecedented success was due to the fact that he was deemed by those having great interests at stake to be as great a power at the bar as he had been in public life.

But

his substantial withdrawal from the Bar during this period of twenty-two years, covering his life from the age of 29 to 51, took the very heart and marrow out of his professional career. It did this in more senses than one. It not only deprived him of much of the wholesome discipline which his ardent and exuberant nature so much needed to compact his faculties and steady and clarify his judgment, but it had the usual effect of relaxing

the habit of close legal reasoning, and sometimes clouding the
very point which he sought to irradiate.[7]

Cookingham believed that "had he devoted his entire life
to the study and practice of law, he would have ranked as a
lawyer among the foremost that the country has ever produced."

Another thought: "He had the art, in exciting interest
and attention, of a skilful book reviewer, who leaves his
reader full of curiosity to see the book itself."[8]

And another: "His pride was too deep, his bearing too
haughty, his opinions and methods too firm, his shirt and his
speech too clean, for a successful leader in American politics. As a party leader he was overthrown more by his own
inordinate pride than by anything else."[9]

Perhaps. Yet as a practitioner at the bar he only stirs the
admiration of lawyers, but as a politician he should interest
any American citizen. He was successful, because he made a
lot of money—he had been penniless when he resigned from
the Senate,[10] but quickly and easily he became rich. As a politician he was a failure, yes. But failures fascinate long after
the stories of great success, pushed upon us from all sides,
become tiresome. Failures are more instructive, easier to understand; they don't scintillate, blinding the spectator, but
glow in a way that warms.

WHEN Ward Hunt retired from the United States Supreme
Court, in February, 1882, President Arthur nominated Roscoe Conkling to fill the vacancy, and the Senate confirmed
this. But Conkling declined to accept. It is true that the
President was virtually obliged to appoint a New Yorker,
for Hunt came from that state (Supreme Court justices are
not supposed to be appointed this way, but they are), and
Conkling was a logical choice. Still, the appointment seemed
a gesture of friendliness. Conkling's letter of refusal was polite, but it was final. He and Arthur no longer were friends.

Conkling often went to Washington, but not to visit at the White House. He went quietly, avoiding reporters when it was necessary to do so—they never had bothered him much anyway, for he was notoriously close-mouthed with them— and he kept away from Capitol Hill. He was not among those present, February 27, 1882, when James G. Blaine scored a peculiarly Conklinian triumph with his memorial address in honor of the late James A. Garfield, martyr. Chester Arthur was there, and Senators Lapham and Miller, and all the members of both houses and of the cabinet; and they wept, even the hardest of them, when they heard Blaine.

As the end drew near, his early craving for the sea returned. The stately mansion of power had been to him the wearisome hospital of pain, and he begged to be taken from its prison walls, from its oppressive, stifling air, from its homelessness and its hopelessness. Gently, silently, the love of a great people bore the pale sufferer to the longed-for healing of the sea, to live or to die, as God should will, within sight of its heaving billows, within sound of its manifold voices. With wan, fevered face, he looked out wistfully upon the ocean's changing wonders; on its far sails, whitening in the morning light; on its restless waves, rolling shoreward to break and die beneath the noonday sun; on the red clouds of evening, arching low to the horizon; on the serene and shining pathway of the stars. Let us think that his dying eyes read a mystic meaning which only the rapt and parting soul may know. Let us believe that in the silence of the receding world he heard the great waves breaking on a farther shore, and felt already upon his wasted brow the breath of the eternal morning.

ROSCOE CONKLING fought on, or rather, now, quarreled on. No longer was he very glorious. He was a prosperous corporation lawyer with some unsavory but rich clients, retaining still enough strength to be vengeful when he fancied the sweet taste of revenge in his mouth, but accepting no public responsibilities. Thousands of Stalwarts looked to him for leadership, but he refused to lead: he was done with leading. He didn't attend the state convention of '81, and the Half-Breeds had their own way, Miller being elected temporary chairman and Depew permanent chairman. The party lost both branches of the legislature, for the first time in twelve years. There was no Boss. There had been no chance to train a boss, groom a boss, while Conkling sat on the throne.

He didn't forgive Cornell for the governor's passivity in the senatorial contest. He did not enter officially into the crooked state convention of 1882, but it was known that he was secretly working against Cornell, who had wished for, and worked for, and deserved a renomination. Not only was Conkling against the governor, but so also was Jay Gould with his suitcases filled with cash, and the President himself, who was quite as annoyed as Conkling at the Cornell do-nothingness in the senatorial contest, and who whipped the postmasters into line shamelessly. Instead of Cornell, Charles J. Folger was nominated. A good man, an excellent man; but the convention itself had been such a scandal that many of Folger's friends urged him, in vain, to refuse the nomination.

It was frequently charged that Conkling's opposition to Cornell was accountable to the fact that the governor had vetoed an elevated railroad bill Jay Gould had purchased from the legislature.[11] It is possible that this was true, but unlikely. Personal reasons always counted most with the Senator; and Gould was quite capable of doing his own dirty work.

In any event, Folger was swamped by a Democrat hitherto almost unknown, the mayor of Buffalo, Grover Cleveland, a large and coarse man, shaggy, slow, unimaginative, stubborn, who didn't owe anything to anybody. Cleveland's majority was a record in New York, and this fact won him a Presidential nomination two years later.

"The Republican party being now a burst bladder," Henry Adams wrote to a friend, "I am going back to it to give it respectability, since I can give it nothing else."[12]

It didn't need Henry Adams. It needed a boss. Eventually it got one, in New York, but only after some years, losing years. And the one it got was—Tom Platt! That prideless little fellow, laughed at everywhere, grew himself a handsome set of chin whiskers, and went right on whispering and whispering. He was canny, determined, unhampered by scruples. As president of the United States Express Company he had great influence among the farmers and small merchants of the southern tier of counties, those along the line of the Erie Railroad, for he was able to do them many favors or to hurt them. So he spaded and scraped and wheelbarrowed, soundlessly, tirelessly, until at last men began to defer to him. Remembering Conkling, he didn't try to be haughty, domineering—it would only have made him look ridiculous anyway—but soon won a reputation for quite different behavior and came to be known as the Easy Boss. He got back into the Senate, an old man by then, and ruled from rooms in the Fifth Avenue Hotel, as Conkling had done before him—Thurlow Weed had used Room 11 at the Astor House—and under his soft, apologetic suzerainty it came to be called the Amen Corner. What he said went; but he said it so gently! He made governors and "conferred" with them about running the state. Theodore Roosevelt was one—a rather troublesome one at times, so Tom Platt tried to kick him upstairs by making him Vice-President, and thus unexpectedly found himself hailed as a Warwick. But all this was years later, when Roscoe Conkling, who meanwhile had quarreled also with Platt, and with Jay Gould, and with others, was dead. And even then it was obvious that the day of the great New York bosses was gone. Alexander Hamilton, De-Witt Clinton, William L. Marcy, Silas Wright, Martin Van Buren, Thurlow Weed, Roscoe Conkling—these fellows were giants, and the very pronouncing of their names is like a roll of political drums. Tom Platt does not belong among them. He never was anything but an eager little echo.

XXXIII. They Were All Dying

NOW he was able to relax somewhat, talk with a few friends, drink a bit. He was a personage still, and pointed out, for he was unique as an honest man and almost painfully proud of this fact.[1] He attended dinners of the New England Society, affairs noted for their brilliant speeches. He was often seen in the bar at the Hoffman House, then owned by Ed Stokes, the man who had killed Jim Fisk in a quarrel over a woman (Fisk was keeping the woman, who in turn was keeping Stokes, so it is a little difficult to understand why Stokes did the shooting, more difficult still to understand why he was acquitted), in the company of such famous conversationalists as John Chamberlain and Tom Ochiltree.[2] He frequented the New York Club at Broadway and Twenty-fifth Street, and sometimes was to be seen at the Union League Club. Many nights he might be found in the library of the city bar association in Twenty-ninth Street, preparing a case with all the earnestness of a newly admitted youngster.

Occasionally he went to Utica, but the visits were brief. He would appear, sometimes unannounced, of a Friday afternoon, and perhaps would stay the week-end, or perhaps he would leave the next morning. When it was known that he was coming Bill Dunn would be at the station with his old baggage wagon, and then the ex-Senator would wave off the carriage from Rutger Street and ride home with Bill, talking of old times.

In the summer of '83, with Mrs. Conkling and some friends, he made a flying trip to Yellowstone National Park, just opened to the public. Henry Villard, president of the Northern Pacific, lent them his private car. The name of the former Senator was the first to be written upon the Mammoth Springs Hotel register.

But for the most part he saw little of his wife, still less of his daughter and "Mrs. Conkling's son-in-law." Appearances were kept up, as always; there was no breath of scandal; and legally Roscoe Conkling remained a resident of Utica, though in fact he was a New Yorker. That fall, when he moved his offices to a bigger place in the United Bank Building at Wall Street and Broadway, he brought his law library down from Utica. At about the same time he quit the Fifth Avenue Hotel for a home of his own in West Twenty-ninth Street next to the Association of the Bar of the City of New York building.

THERE was a case he argued in the Supreme Court in Washington[3] which harked back to the days of Thad Stevens and a nation still in turmoil, and which excellently illustrates the difference between the Conkling legal and political minds. It was one of a series of cases, started with the first Slaughter House litigation,[4] which subsequently flooded the highest tribunal, and which "today are among the main sources of the Supreme Court's business."[5] Conkling, representing the Southern Pacific Railroad, advanced the startling argument that the court in deciding the Slaughter House cases had misconceived the intent of the framers of Section I of the Fourteenth Amendment to the Federal Constitution:

All persons born or naturalized in the United States, and subject to the jurisdiction thereof, are citizens of the United States and of the State wherein they reside. No State shall make or enforce any law which shall abridge the privileges or immunities of citizens of the United States; nor shall any State deprive any person of life, liberty, or property, without due process of law, nor deny to any person within its jurisdiction the equal protection of the laws.

The Committee of Fifteen, of which he himself had been a member, had designed that section as much for the protection of white people as Negroes, he said. The word "person" was placed in juxtaposition with the word "citizen," true, but the two were not synonymous: "person" had its ordinary juristic meaning, and therefore included artificial persons, that is, corporations, as well as natural persons. And so the Supreme Court had the power to overrule state legislation which tended to deprive corporations of their rights under the Fourteenth Amendment.

This extraordinary argument he backed with selected readings from the journal of the Committee of Fifteen, which he carried with him into the court. He was careful to omit names, for he himself had consistently voted against the section in question, the first.[6] It was, in fact, the only one of the five sections in which he had shown a great interest, though his objections were of a purely technical nature.

The significance of his point cannot possibly be overestimated. It was the Washington "in" the corporations had all this time been seeking. It was a club to be used against lawmakers intent upon curbing corporate power.

He carried the point, too. The case itself was dismissed as having become moot, but Conkling had shown the way. Great corporations were just coming into existence, and so, of course, were great corporation lawyers, who all owe Roscoe Conkling a debt of incalculable value. They followed him, hammering at his point until it was definitely established, until the Supreme Court had taken unto itself an absolute veto power over state legislation affecting the great industrial combinations. They went to Washington in droves, those sleek men with briefcases, blandly and continuously protesting that corporations were "persons" within the meaning of the Fourteenth Amendment. They overspilled all sorts of state attempts to control them. And so the trusts grew and grew. . . . They jumped state lines. They laughed at legislatures, and went to Washington with cries of alarm, loudly invoking the "due process" clause. And the learned justices obliged.

Immediately after the Civil War this business of getting

the principle of *laissez faire* firmly established as the law of the land began; and by the end of the century the Supreme Court literally was hearing these cases by the hundreds, and the great industrialists were learning what a wonderful instrument is the injunction.

It is not contended that Roscoe Conkling was the first to argue that a corporation is a person. But he was easily the most important of the early champions of the trusts. He did more than any other man to establish this doctrine. His dramatic production of the journal of the reconstruction committee, his prestige as a former member of that committee, really gave fellow lawyers something to work with. The Rockefellers and Huntingtons and Goulds, were they alive to their obligations, would keep fresh flowers on Conkling's statue all the year round.

Moreover, the San Mateo case affords another interesting view of the workings of the Conkling legal mind. When the Senator was representing the people of New York he helped to frame legislation designed for the protection of the civil rights of Negroes, and for nothing else whatever.[7] But now, when he was representing the Southern Pacific Railway, he decided that he and his fellow members of the Committee of Fifteen had framed the amendment in order to permit corporations to appeal to the highest tribunal in the land. That was, of course, the very last thing the committee members had in mind. Roscoe Conkling as a statesman would have confessed as much. As chief counsel for the Southern Pacific he was out to get what he could for his friend Collis P. Huntington—and incidentally for every trust builder in the country. The client makes all the difference.

JAMES G. BLAINE was about to make his third and most impressive reach for the Presidency. Many men were talked about as possible Republican nominees—Edmunds, Logan, the two Shermans,[8] Hawley, Postmaster General Gresham—

but there were only two strong aspirants, Blaine and Chester A. Arthur.

Arthur wasn't above using the postmasters, but he had behind him a creaking, rusted machine. He had made a reasonably good President, but at best he was not big enough for the office. He didn't have a small fraction of Blaine's political genius.

Even so, with Roscoe Conkling behind him he might have won.[9] But Roscoe Conkling was out of politics.

Blaine, who was seldom fooled in any matter like this, knew his vulnerability. "I can't carry New York State," he wrote to Halstead.[10]

People still were suspicious of Blaine, more suspicious than ever. Not only habitual reformers but also straight and faithful party men warned against him. He was too clever. There were too many business deals he couldn't explain. Veteran cleaners like Curtis and Schurz, and newly arrived moralists like Theodore Roosevelt and Henry Cabot Lodge, alike were declaring that they would not support such a fellow.

At the convention Conkling's name rose only as a negative force, when Townsend of Pennsylvania, placing the name of Chester Arthur in nomination, denied that Arthur was a machine man and cited the fact that "Roscoe Conkling has given his whole influence against Mr. Arthur." Tom Platt was one of those who made seconding speeches for Blaine, "believing as I do that his turn has come."[11]

Blaine was nominated.

The following day the *New York Times* announced that "defeat will be the salvation of the Republican party." It thought Blaine represented "the average of Republican principles and purposes, of Republican honor and conscience, as they are now." The *Times* always had been regular, but it had solemnly warned the party that it would not continue to be so if Blaine were nominated—and it has kept its word to this day. As its historian points out, though the

Times had not really married the Republican party to reform it, certainly it was entitled to expect something less murky than Blaine. "To one who studies the evidence of that struggle in the columns of the papers for those years (1872–84) there is apt to be suggested the simile of a loyal wife doing her best to get along with a scandalously dissipated husband."[12]

Nor was the *Times* alone. The *Chicago Tribune* and the *Cincinnati Commercial*, which formerly had opposed Blaine, supported him after the nomination; Whitelaw Reid's paper, determined never again to be involved in a bolt, was enthusiastic; but a host of other normally Republican journals all over the country turned against him—the *Springfield Republican*, in New York the *Post* and the *Herald*, in Boston the *Transcript*, the *Herald*, the *Advertiser*. So did such strong magazines as *The Nation, Puck, Harper's.* Andrew White, young Roosevelt and his friend Henry Lodge, Hamilton Fish, Governor Robinson of Massachusetts, stuck to the party. Edmunds made a single campaign speech, but never mentioned the candidate's name. John Hay thought Blaine was marvelous.[13] But Curtis, Schurz, Henry Ward Beecher, Thomas W. Higginson, Josiah Quincy, Bristow, Charles F. Adams, Jr., and other powers broke away. They were commonly called Mugwumps, sometimes Ishmaelites, political hermaphrodites, soreheads, Pharisees, goody-goodies, assistant Democrats—and one shudders to think of what Roscoe Conkling might have done to them in a single speech, if Roscoe Conkling had been interested.

"Blaine," writes Herbert Agar positively, "was the only man ever nominated to the Presidency in spite of the fact that the public knew perfectly well he was dishonest. Garfield was thought to have been dishonest, but only in the mildest sort of way; Blaine was known to have been dishonest, and on a good scale."

This isn't fair. Nobody ever proved anything crooked against James G. Blaine, and thousands of citizens were prepared to punch jaws in defense of his integrity. But the fact is indisputable that there were ugly suspicions, and a Presidential candidate should be a Cæsar's wife.

The contrast with Grover Cleveland made him seem the shadier, for here was one unquestionably, almost unbelievably honest. "—the country was sickening for an honest man, and the fact that New York State had a Governor who meant what he said attracted as much attention as if it had a Governor with feathers."[14] Even more attention, however, was attracted at the Democratic national convention by the fact that Cleveland had carried New York by a record majority of almost 200,000 just two years earlier. Cleveland was nominated. Being a new Easterner, a hard-money man, and an independent, he was given a running-mate, Hendricks, who was an old-time Westerner, a soft-money man, a machine politician.

Ben Butler bobbed up, ranting, scheming, causing worriment. He had flirted with Tammany, hoping vainly to get the Democratic nomination; but he was nominated by the Anti-Monopoly party and by the National party, the legatee of the Greenback party. Everybody feared him. The Democrats contended that the Republicans had an understanding with him, and the Republicans said the same thing of the Democrats. There was afterward much disputation as to which party he hurt and which he helped. However, there is no doubt about the influence of the Prohibition party candidate, a fighter, John F. St. John of Kansas. Irked because he wasn't taken seriously, he went East and struck in vital places, and struck hard, and it was the Republicans who suffered. He polled 150,305 important votes, as compared with the 10,305 cast for Neal Dow, the Prohibition candidate of 1880. Thereafter both major parties were politer to Prohibitionists.

THE campaign was the dirtiest in the history of the country. There was no issue,[15] but only name calling.

The key states were New York, New Jersey, Connecticut, and Indiana, but especially New York. Grover Cleveland stayed in Albany most of the time. Blaine stumped extensively through the East and Middle West.

"Can Conkling be induced to speak for us?" Blaine wrote anxiously to a friend, shortly after his nomination. "It would be an immense thing for us. How can he be induced to do it?"[16]

How indeed? Like so many other former associates, Blaine evidently believed it impossible that Roscoe Conkling really was out of politics permanently. And nobody knew better than Blaine the campaign value of that fiery tongue. There is no doubt that fancy offers were made to Conkling, and that he was given at least a promise of restoration to the United States Senate if he would make "two or three speeches."[17] A delegation of Blaine workers waited upon him at his office one day, and made him a flattering offer. It was a great moment in Conkling's life. No doubt he even smiled as he rose.

"Gentlemen, you have been misinformed. I have given up criminal law."

THE *Buffalo Evening Telegraph* really started the muck flying when it broke the story of Maria Halpin. She was a widow with two children, who was working in a Buffalo dry-goods store when she met and had an affair with the bachelor Grover Cleveland. Their son, Oscar Folsom Cleveland duly acknowledged, was born September 14, 1874, and was sent to an orphan asylum March 9, 1876, when a court decreed that his mother, who was drinking herself into madness, was incompetent to care for him. Unblushingly the Republicans smeared these facts, and others affiliated with them, or imagined, all over the land. Fathers of daughters were asked whether they would care to have a man like that in the White House, and the nation was rehearsed in a monotonous but effective marching song, thumped out everywhere, and written upon fences:

> *Ma, ma,*
> *Where's my pa?*

To which waggish Democrats would sometimes respond:

> *Going to the White House—*
> *Ha, ha, ha!*

Cleveland frankly admitted the truth of the charge. He had been providing for both mother and child, and hadn't even seen the mother in eight years. That didn't matter. Clearly it was necessary to fight dirt with dirt; so the Democratic strategists did some dredging in forgotten sewers, and emerged, all a-grin, with a story to the effect that James G. Blaine had married Mrs. James G. Blaine only three months before the birth of their first child. This lie was denied. It had been a full year before, the Republicans retorted. And the Republicans bammed the bass drum again and restarted the chant:

> *Ma, ma,*
> *Where's my pa?*

Betting was even. Despite all attacks upon him, Blaine had an enormous personal following, and he was a master campaigner. Almost anything would tip the scales. And several things happened, close together. There was the visit of the Prohibitionist, St. John, who concentrated on New York State, where he was to get 25,016 votes. There was the notorious "millionaires' dinner" to Blaine in New York City, attended by all the principal Wall Street highwaymen, from which reporters were excluded but which the *World* (no longer owned by Gould) gave to the public in the form of a terrifying cartoon spread clear across its front page. There was the incredibly stupid "rum, Romanism and rebellion" speech of the Reverend Mr. Burchard. There was—it is by no means too small to overlook—the letter in the *Utica Daily Press.*

That letter, in the October 24 issue, on the editorial page, was addressed to Republicans everywhere and was signed by 146 prominent Oneida County Stalwarts. It set forth seven reasons why the signers were not going to vote for Blaine. The reasons were the usual ones—"His prostitution of his official position in his most influential station as Speaker of the House of Representatives, to his own private gain and emolument," his dubious behavior in connection with the Mulligan letters and similar matters, his lack of statesmanship and failure to be identified with any great act of public benefaction, the effect of this negative course in blocking progressive measures, his mysteriously acquired wealth, his excess of ambition, his dangerous and ignorant policy as Secretary of State. "We cannot . . . give up our convictions or surrender our manliness at the mere behest of party."

The letter, which Roscoe Conkling did not sign, and which contained no direct or indirect reference to Conkling, was extensively quoted (and misquoted) as evidence that the former Senator was opposed to Blaine. A Utica correspondent, cornering Conkling in his West Twenty-ninth Street apartment next day, "engaged in legal writing" and enjoying a "dry smoke," found him affable but with absolutely nothing to say.[18] It was generally reported that he himself had written the letter, and many persons believe so to this day. It is possible, but not probable. Conkling was not underhanded. Certainly he was not ambitious to return to politics, and so would have no reason for being eager to keep his record clear; and while he probably preferred Cleveland to Blaine, if he had wished to do anything about this preference he would have added his signature to the letter. The context of the letter gives no clue. Conkling had a distinctive speaking style, but no distinctive literary style; and there is nothing unusual about this letter except the circumstances under which it was published—and its effect.

EVEN the weather, in New York, went against Blaine. It rained all day, keeping upstate Republican farmers from the polls.

Cleveland carried New Jersey, Connecticut, Indiana. And New York? Blaine could still win if he carried New York. For three days the result was in doubt and the nation held its breath. Finally it was announced, to cries of fraud from the *New York Tribune*, the *Utica Herald* and other die-hards, that Cleveland had carried New York by from 1,043 to 1,049. It was just sufficient to make him President.

Garfield, in 1880, had carried Oneida County by 2,053. Blaine lost it by 19 votes.

THERE was a blaze of publicity for the ex-Senator, a bath of public applause, which however did not tempt him back into politics, in the Broadway Franchise investigation of 1886. Undoubtedly he did a brilliant job of it. Even that grizzled Tammany smasher Sam Tilden, moldering at Graystone, paid him a compliment on his work.[19]

The Broadway Surface Railroad Company obtained from the board of aldermen a franchise to operate from Fourteenth Street to Bowling Green. The total bribe was half a million, which was not notably high for those days—a rival company had offered $750,000 but this was to be part cash and part bonds, and the aldermen decided that $500,000 straight cash was safer.

After a time aldermen began going to Canada and Mexico, very quietly. The state senate had started an investigation, through a special committee, which engaged Roscoe Conkling and his friend Clarence A. Steward as counsel.

It was not a difficult job, but it was sensational, and Conkling performed his part in a thorough, competent manner, holding the front pages for weeks together. The charter was revoked, twenty-one bribery indictments were handed up, and one man, Jacob Sharpe, the head of the street car company, actually was sent to jail.[20]

HE was comparatively young, and men still talked of him as a Presidential possibility, but he gave them no heed. He was very successful, and very lonesome. "Black Jack" Logan died, and he attended the memorial service—the only time he entered the Senate chamber at Washington after his resignation. Chet Arthur succumbed suddenly to apoplexy in his Lexington Avenue home. Garfield was dead. Greeley and Thurlow Weed and Reuben Fenton were dead. Back in Fremont, fuzzy little Rutherford B. Hayes went on being honorary chairman of organizations, and tut-tutting the woman's suffrage movement, and all unheard boosting for some manner of union with Canada. And General Grant died.

Grant had fooled with a Mexican railroad project which came to nothing, and then he had gone into Wall Street with a man named Ferdinand Ward. Grant in Wall Street! Of course Ward, something of a genius and completely a scoundrel, desired the general as a partner only because of his name. The general went to the office sometimes, and sat there smoking cigars, and said nothing and did nothing—while Ward raised money on whispered promises that certain firms were going to get lush Government contracts by means of the general's influence. On Sunday night, May 4, 1884, Ward telephoned that unless the Marine Bank had $150,000 first thing in the morning, the firm of Grant and Ward would crash. It was the first time the general knew there was anything wrong. He went to W. H. Vanderbilt and raised $150,000 on his personal, unsecured note. But the crash came anyway, Tuesday.

"I don't see how I can ever trust any human being again," said poor Grant.[21]

He had a cancerous throat and was in great pain. He wrote his memoirs, which cover only his military and not his political career, and these were to make fabulous sums of money and eventually to clear his estate of debt. He had just finished them when he died, July 23, 1885. He was buried with unprecedented pomp.

When Oliver P. Morton had died, Senator Conkling delivered the formal eulogy in the Senate chamber:

"Death is nature's supreme abhorrence. The dark valley, with its weird and solemn shadows . . . is still the ground which man shudders to approach. The grim portals and the narrow house seem in the lapse of centuries to have gained rather than lost in impressive and forboding horror. . . ."[22]

Morton had been the first of the Three Musketeers to go, Logan the second, and Roscoe Conkling was to be the last. Conkling alone outlived the man they had served.

XXXIV. He Walked Alone

ONE Saturday, in Rutger Street, Mrs. Conkling told him that the housekeeper's little nephew, Phil Brannigan, had recited creditably at the Utica Free Academy an extract from one of the Conkling speeches. She had become interested in the boy and was having him to the house that afternoon to repeat the performance in the presence of the author.

The boy came, with many misgivings, and dressed in his Sunday suit. He was thirteen years old.

I can see it all now. Mr. Conkling standing at the corner of an immense fireplace, with his elbow resting on the marble mantelpiece; I on the opposite side of the room, and Mrs. Conkling in a big chair beside the Senator. I remember that at the start I was much more nervous than the day before on the Academy rostrum, but a smile from Mrs. Conkling gave me courage and I tried to put into the speech as much as I could of what I thought he had done when he delivered it. When I was through

Mr. Conkling not only complimented me highly but pulled out his wallet and handed me a new crinkly one-dollar bill, which to me in those days seemed like all the money in the world. The Senator was kind enough to say that I had something worth while and added that he was going to keep track of me and make a lawyer out of me. I have no doubt this would have happened, for Mrs. Conkling told me many times afterward that her husband more than once spoke of the incident and asked how her little friend was coming along.[1]

But an act of God intervened, and Phil Brannigan became not a lawyer but a publicity man.

THERE was no sunshine in or around New York City on Sunday, March 11, 1888, but the day was warm, windows were open, and everybody went to church, agreeing that winter was over. The Weather Bureau forecast was "fair and warmer." It rained some in the afternoon, and gutters were swollen with chocolate-colored water, but the thermometer never went below 34.4 and once it rose as high as 46. Wild geese were seen flying north.

The Weather Bureau, to be sure, put up a cold wave signal at 6.50 o'clock that evening, but nobody paid much attention.

At 10 minutes after midnight the rain turned to snow, and the snow continued until 3.40 o'clock Wednesday morning. The temperature, meanwhile, dropped and dropped, and the wind went mad.

It seems that a cyclone had started west of the Mississippi River, roughly from Arkansas to Wisconsin, and had proceeded east. It split into two portions: one, going through Ontario and Quebec, lost itself in the north Atlantic; the other, getting as far south as Georgia, swung around the end of the Appalachian range and swept north. While this cyclone was engaged in quitting Dixie, New Jersey and New York and New England were getting the anti-cyclone from the west, which was bitterly cold. When the cyclone and the anti-cyclone met, strange and terrible things began to happen, and a garrulous generation was given its greatest single weapon against children- and grandchildren-to-be.[2]

Even on the charts it is one of the most amazing things of its kind—a great arched line-squall more than one thousand miles long, moving east at a speed of six hundred miles a day, and extending from the Great Lakes and northern Vermont to northern Cuba. An immense trough of low pressure between two ridges of high, instead of the usual circular or oval storm area, it formed elongated north and south isobars.

The snow was fine, cutting. The wind, from the northwest, was without mercy. Forty-eight miles an hour was the maximum velocity recorded; but from three until ten o'clock that Monday morning it was impossible to get an official reading because the Weather Bureau's anemometer wire had been snapped and could not be repaired.

The actual fall in the 53½ hours was 20.9 inches, or more than twice as much snow as had fallen all that winter, but this figure gives no conception of the difficulties travelers met. For the wind continued high, and the soberest observers reported drifts of fifteen and twenty feet. It was almost impossible to walk. A few hacks took to the streets, the drivers charging anything they could get and in some cases forcing whiskey down the throats of their horses in order to keep them alive. Surface cars struggled for a little while, and then stopped: many of them were literally buried. The Third Avenue Elevated Railway, not then electrified, ran a few trains downtown—one car each, with two or even three dinkey engines pushing it—but these too were stalled. In one of them, helpless between stations, were thirty men; but though they could not get down, they were so fortunate as to be in front of a saloon, and hot toddies were hoisted to them by means of a pail and a length of cord, so that the men remained tolerably happy for the fifteen hours of their captivity, and even were heard to sing. Sturdy little boys with ladders went from place to place letting people down out of second-story windows; generally they charged (this being in the days before Boy Scouts) fifty cents the descent.

Roscoe Conkling went to his office.

But he had little to do when he got there. The lower Broadway section was almost deserted. Of the 1,100 members of the Stock Exchange, only 30 appeared, and most of those lived in Brooklyn Heights and found it a comparatively simple matter, and even rather fun, to walk across the East River, which was frozen solid.

The head of the local Weather Bureau, Elias B. ("Farmer") Dunn, also lived in Brooklyn. He boarded a truck, but it was stalled, and so he walked across the river and to his office in the five-story Equitable skyscraper at 120 Broadway, where he collapsed. A benign Government later transferred him to Florida, and he spent the rest of his life explaining that Sunday, March 10, when the famous "fair and warmer" forecast was issued, had been his day off.

The city was in darkness, utterly isolated. "Trains!" Chauncey Depew snorted when some inane person asked him whether the New York Central was going to maintain its service. "Why, we don't even know whether we've got a railroad left!" There *were* trains, of course, but they didn't move. No less than sixteen of them were stalled between Yonkers and Grand Central.

Earmuffs sold for $5 a pair. Milk, when it was obtainable at all, went for $1 a quart. Newspapers brought anything the boys cared to ask: one copy of the *Times* reached the Hoffman House, where hundreds were marooned, and was auctioned at 40 cents.

Thousands went forth, but few returned—at least, not until the next day, or even Wednesday. The barrooms were crowded, and your credit was good almost anywhere. One hustler hung a sign outside of his Bowery establishment: "A free drink of whiskey to anybody that needs it and has not got the money to pay for it. Come in if you need it. Steve Brodie." Many went in.

Macy's harbored hundreds. Mattresses and bedclothing were spread on the floors.

About three hundred slept in Grand Central Terminal, or else played euchre in the waiting room.

Even the braves of Tammany trembled, remaining at home. Only seventeen appeared at a regularly scheduled meeting that night, and they did nothing but talk about the weather—until Tony Pastor invited them upstairs to watch the show and to double the audience.

Henry Irving and Ellen Terry did "Faust" and later "Midsummer Night's Dream" before a handful at Daly's. Exactly five persons presented their tickets at Niblo's Garden, but the actor-manager, Daniel E. Bandmann, put on "Dr. Jekyll and Mr. Hyde" just the same.

P. T. Barnum had staged a parade Saturday, and the Greatest Show on Earth was to open Monday night at Madison Square Garden before a record-breaking throng. A few newspapermen, none of them too sober, did get there. P.T. rewarded them with expected fluids, and then ordered the show to go on as usual; but before the night was over many of the professional clowns were in the spectators' seats watching the newspapermen, who did things in the ring. It was a lot of fun, and everybody voted P.T. a jolly good fellow.

ROSCOE CONKLING had an opportunity, early in the afternoon, to hire a hack at the modest rate of $50, but he refused. At about five o'clock he started up Broadway on foot. It was the only way to go.

But he was used to walking. He liked walking, alone.

His breath froze, and his whiskers resembled the prism chandeliers in fashion just then. Upright, shoulders back, long legs swinging, he churned through the drifts. What to him was the greatest Blizzard in Manhattan's history? The wind shrieked around him, buffeted him; but he was accustomed to noisy resistance, and scorned it. The snow, which had turned to hard sleet, hissed and stung his face, burning him. He walked on.

From Wall Street to Madison Square is about three miles. Roscoe Conkling, a very fast walker, made it in three hours. In the Square was a freak of the storm—a tiny patch of earth, holding not a particle of snow, though surrounded by high drifts, and supporting a sign which said sternly: "Keep Off the Grass." He walked past this. He walked into the New York Club at Broadway and Twenty-fifth Street. And there he fell flat on his face.

He didn't crumble, he didn't collapse. He fell full length. For he was that kind of man.

TUESDAY was much the same as Monday. Nothing moved. Here and there somebody struggled home, or to another bar. Here and there a corpse was dug out of the snow. The snow still fell, though it was not as heavy, and the wind at one time reached fifty-seven miles an hour.

On Wednesday there was a little sunlight, though there was also a little more of the snow. The mercury climbed as high as 40.9, though the day's minimum was 12.9. The *Sun* was delighted with its scoop: it had learned, by way of London, England, that Boston also was snowbound. Hudson River ferries were moving a little, though trains remained motionless.

Thursday was warmer, and the snow had ceased. All over the city were huge bonfires, and people were scattering rock salt and thawing things out with hot water. Trains were being operated, though hesitantly and certainly not on schedule. Friday there was a blessed thaw. And by Saturday, which was St. Patrick's Day, things were almost normal, except for the conversation.

The Blizzard cost some twenty or twenty-five millions of dollars in property damage. Twenty persons were frozen in New York City, though the true death list certainly was much longer than this, for scores of babies died of malnutrition because of the milk famine, and scores of men, among them our Senator, succumbed soon afterward to internal complications brought about by exhaustion.

IT is customary to say that Roscoe Conkling was killed in the Blizzard of Eighty-eight.

In fact, he rested for a time; but he went back to his office as soon as it was possible for him to get there. He worked for more than two weeks, and worked hard.

It was not until April 4 that he took to his bed. Dr. Fordyce Barker and his assistant, Dr. Adlerton, who had been attending him, called into consultation Drs. Agnew, Delafield, and Sands.[3] Members of the family were summoned. The Senator had a bad ear abscess, probably caused by overexertion during that walk from Wall Street to Madison Square. The physicians feared that the inflammation might reach the brain.

The first real public alarm was sounded April 9. The Hoffman House Annex, at 9 West Twenty-fourth Street, was cut off from the main part of the hotel, and nobody was even permitted to ring the bell. The Senator, in the central room of his suite, had a temperature of 103½, a pulse of 100, and he was in hideous pain. At four o'clock that afternoon the physicians performed an operation to free an outlet for the suppuration formed in the abscess, in the hope of confining the inflammation to the region of the ear and preventing it from getting to the brain membranes.

The following day he was delirious, and couldn't recognize Mrs. Conkling or his old friend Judge Shipman. They were feeding him milk with a spoon. Early in the afternoon he sprang out of bed and paced the floor wildly for a time, resisting all attempts to quiet him.

His temperature was normal the next day, and he got some sleep. He recognized Mrs. Conkling. But he weakened in the afternoon.

April 12 there was a rumor that he was dead, and the

street outside was crowded. This day and the next his condition was about the same, and he still occasionally paced the floor. They give him a little champagne with his milk, but nothing else. April 13 he wouldn't permit them to change his head bandage. The man was mad with pain, and had all a madman's strength. Clarence Thomas, his nurse, was not strong enough to hold him down, and the head porter of the Hoffman House, lusty Mike Toole, a great friend of the Senator, was called in; even Mike, whom the Senator didn't recognize, wasn't strong enough, with Thomas; and eventually they were forced to give him ether. It rained all that day, but there were hundreds of anxious callers. And this was true, too, of the next day, Sunday.

On Monday, April 16, Mrs. Conkling received this wire, among others: "Citizens of Utica, irrespective of party, are on bended knees tonight imploring Almighty God that He will spare to his family and his country that greatest living statesman, the Hon. Roscoe Conkling."[4]

His condition became worse, and the next day it was not necessary to give him ether, for Toole and Thomas were able to hold him down while the bandage was changed. Œdema set in. He muttered continually, and recognized no one. He suffered muscular contractions of the legs and arms. Dr. Barker, shaking his head, told reporters that he probably wouldn't survive the night. And he didn't. He died at two o'clock in the morning.

THE day of the funeral services, April 20, there was an unceasing rain, a heavy rain, and the wind was cruel. Seventy-five policemen held back the crowds at the Hoffman House while a simple oaken coffin covered with broadcloth was carried out. Regular Episcopal services were conducted by Reverend Dr. Morgan Dix at Trinity Chapel in West Twenty-fifth Street. The choir sang the Senator's favorites, "Rock of Ages" and "Abide with Me." Afterward, Undertaker Bevans dismissed the police escort, for Mrs. Conkling did not wish to attract attention; and the *cortège* went over Twenty-fifth Street to Fifth Avenue, up the Avenue to Forty-third Street, and across to Grand Central, where a special train awaited them: it consisted of a baggage car, two drawing-room coaches, and Chauncey Depew's own private car, which he had turned over to the widow of an old and honored political enemy.

Of course there were great crowds in Utica. The body lay in state in the Rutger Street house for only an hour, and the services in Calvary Church were brief and simple; there was no sermon. Burial was in Forest Hill Cemetery, with only members of the family and a few close friends present. There was a wreath sent by Grover Cleveland.

Another great conservative, another old-fashioned statesman, his brother-in-law Horatio Seymour, sleeps near him in the same plot. It is in a remote part of the cemetery. The Conkling grave is marked by a simple rectangular piece of granite; on the side facing the roadway it bears only the words "Roscoe Conkling"; on the opposite side are engraved his name and dates and the name and dates of his wife.

"HE had not only the courage of his convictions," the *World* announced, "but, that rarer quality among public men, the courage of his contempt."

Bob Ingersoll said the same thing, though less briefly, in a memorial address before the New York legislature, preceding passage of the customary resolution:

He walked a highway of his own, and kept the company of his self-respect. He would not turn aside to avoid a foe—to greet or gain a friend. In his nature there was no compromise. To him there were but two paths—the right and wrong. He was maligned, misrepresented and misunderstood—but he would not answer. . . . He was one of the classic mould—a figure from the antique world. He had the pose of the great statues—the pride and bearing of the intellectual Greek, of the conquering Roman, and he stood in the wide free air, as though within his veins there flowed the blood of a hundred kings. And as he lived he died. Proudly he entered the darkness, or the dawn, that we call death. Unshrinking he passed beyond our horizon, beyond the twilight's purple hills, beyond the utmost reach of human harm or help—to that vast realm of silence or of joy where the innumerable dwell. And he had left with us his wealth of thought and deed—the memory of a brave, imperious, honest man, who bowed alone to death.

The Senator would have enjoyed listening to that.

Bibliography

IT would be natural to suppose that Roscoe Conkling left carefully arranged letters and papers, copies of speeches, prepared statements, defenses. He didn't. Lesser and greater statesmen saw to it that their desks were in order and accessible to biographers—if indeed they did not consult those biographers while still alive, or else indulge in autobiography. But Conkling, scorning explanations, apologies, bequeathed us almost nothing. The material upon which his nephew built an incomplete and biased biography, soon after the Senator's death, was found tucked away in remote places, forgotten; and anyway it was mere scraps, memoranda, first drafts of speeches, clippings, unimportant letters. Even this much has apparently been destroyed. The Senator's only direct descendant, a grandson—Walter Oakman who now lives in Cazenovia, N.Y.—does not have so much as an autograph. Mr. J. F. Jameson, chief of the Division of Manuscripts of the Library of Congress, informs me that he has made "more than one attempt" to find manuscript material of Conkling, but without success. The Senator didn't write well. Such few letters as I have been able to unearth are stilted, unenlightening, and of no possible interest to the average reader. Some of the Conkling letters among the Greeley Papers, in the Ford Collection at the New York Public Library, are quoted in the text. At that same institution the Tilden Papers and the Lincoln Letters have yielded a few relevant items. Newspapers, in particular those of New York City, have helped greatly. So too have such magazines as *Harper's, Atlantic Monthly, North American Review, The Nation,* etc., in their editorials and signed articles. The House Documents and Senate Documents, and the *Congressional Globe* and later the *Congressional Record,* have been used extensively. A vast number of campaign pamphlets have been examined, but they are generally untrustworthy. Conkling died in 1888. His intimates were never many, and for the most part they were men older than he. There are few men alive today who remember him well. I have talked to many who heard him speak, or who shook his hand, but I have been unable to find many men who really knew the man. I have particularly to thank Mr. J. Phil Brannigan of Utica, Judge Isaac Hunt of Adams Center, N.Y., and Mr. Johnson Bingham of Des Moines,

Iowa. Of published sources and authorities the most useful were Alexander's *Political History,* Badeau's *Grant in Peace,* Beale's *Critical Year,* Blaine's *Twenty Years,* Boutwell's *Reminiscences,* Chadsey's *Struggle between President Johnson and Congress over Reconstruction,* Conkling's *Life and Letters,* Cortissoz' *Whitelaw Reid,* Depew's *Memories,* Dunning's *Reconstruction,* Flack's *Adoption of the Fourteenth Amendment,* Greeley's *Recollections,* Haworth's *Hayes-Tilden Election,* Hudson's *Random Recollections,* Kendrick's *Journal of the Joint Committee of Fifteen,* Mathews' *History of the Fifteenth Amendment,* McCulloch's *Men and Measures,* Mitchell's *Business Cycles* and his *History of the Greenbacks,* Platt's *Autobiography,* Schurz's *Reminiscences,* Sherman's *Recollections,* Smith's *Garfield,* Thayer's *John Hay,* Welles' *Diary,* White's *Autobiography,* and Williams' *Rutherford B. Hayes.*

ADAMS, CHARLES FRANCIS. Charles Francis Adams. Cambridge, Houghton Mifflin Co., 1900.

―― Pensions—Worse and More of Them. *The World's Work,* December, 1911, January and February, 1912.

ADAMS, HENRY. Letters of Henry Adams, 1858–1891. Ed. by Worthington Chauncey Ford. Cambridge, Houghton Mifflin Co., 1930.

―― The Education of Henry Adams. Cambridge, Houghton Mifflin Co., 1927.

AGAR, HERBERT. The People's Choice, from Washington to Harding: A Study in Democracy. Cambridge, Houghton Mifflin Co., 1933.

ALEXANDER, DEALVA STANWOOD. A Political History of the State of New York. New York, Henry Holt & Co., 1909. 3 vols.

―― Four Famous New Yorkers. New York, Henry Holt & Co., 1923.

ANDREWS, E. BENJAMIN. The United States in Our Times. New York, Charles Scribner's Sons, 1903.

ATKINSON, EDWARD. Veto of the Inflation Bill of 1874. *Journal of Political Economy,* December, 1892.

BADEAU, ADAM. Grant in Peace: A Personal Memoir. Hartford, Conn., S. S. Scranton & Co., 1887.

BALCH, WILLIAM RALSTON. The Life of James Abram Garfield. Philadelphia, Hubbard Brothers, 1881.

BANCROFT, FREDERICK, and DUNNING, WILLIAM ARCHIBALD. A Sketch of Carl Schurz's Political Career, 1869–1906. In Schurz's Reminiscences, vol. III. New York, The McClure Co., 1908.

BARNES, THURLOW WEED. Memoir of Thurlow Weed. Cambridge, Houghton Mifflin Co., 1884. 2 vols.

BARRETT, DON C. The Greenbacks and Resumption of Specie Payments, 1862–1879. Cambridge, Harvard University Press, 1931.

BARRY, DAVID S. Forty Years in Washington. Boston, Little, Brown & Co., 1924.

BEALE, HOWARD K. The Critical Year: A Study of Andrew Johnson and Reconstruction. New York, Harcourt, Brace & Co., 1930.

—— The Tariff and Reconstruction. *American Historical Review,* January, 1930.

BEER, THOMAS. Hanna. New York, Alfred A. Knopf, 1929.

BELLOWS, HENRY W. Civil-Service Reform. *North American Review,* March, 1880.

BENEDICT, ERASTUS CORNELIUS. The Presidential Election: An Open Letter to Hon. Roscoe Conkling, Senator. New York, 1877. (Pamphlet.)

BIGELOW, JOHN. Mr. Tilden's War Record. New York, 1876. (Pamphlet.)

—— The Life of Samuel J. Tilden. New York, Harper & Brothers, 1895. 2 vols.

BLACK, JUDGE J. S. The Third Term: Reasons Against It. *North American Review,* March, 1880.

BLAINE, JAMES G. Life and Character of James A. Garfield, President of the United States. Memorial address pronounced in the Hall of Representatives, Washington, February 27, 1882. Washington, Government Printing Office, 1882.

—— Twenty Years of Congress: From Lincoln to Garfield. Norwich, Conn., Henry Bill Publishing Co., 1893. 2 vols.

BLAINE, MRS. JAMES G. Letters of Mrs. James G. Blaine. Ed. by Harriet S. Blaine Beale. New York, Duffield & Co., 1908. 2 vols.

BLISS, DR. D. W. The Story of President Garfield's Illness. *Century Magazine-Scribner's Monthly,* December, 1881.

BOLLES, ALBERT SIDNEY. The Financial History of the United States from 1861 to 1885. New York, D. Appleton & Co., 1886.

BONNER, JOHN. The Great Gold Conspiracy. *Harper's New Monthly Magazine,* April, 1870.

BOUTWELL, GEORGE S. Black Friday: September 24, 1869. From the Standpoint of the Secretary of the Treasury under Grant's First Administration. *McClure's Magazine,* November, 1899.

—— Blaine and Conkling and the Republican Convention of 1880. *McClure's Magazine,* January, 1900.

—— General Grant's Administration. *McClure's Magazine,* February, 1900.

—— Reminiscences of Sixty Years in Public Affairs. New York, McClure, Phillips & Co., 1902. 2 vols.

—— The Impeachment of Andrew Johnson. *McClure's Magazine,* December, 1899.

BOWERS, CLAUDE G. The Tragic Era: The Revolution after Lincoln. Cambridge, Houghton Mifflin Co., 1929.

BREEN, MATTHEW P. Thirty Years of New York Politics. New York, published by the author, 1899.

BRIGHAM, JOHNSON. Blaine, Conkling and Garfield: A Reminiscence and a Character Study. Des Moines, Iowa, published for The Prairie Club, 1915.

BRISBEN, GEN. JAMES S. The Early Life and Public Career of James A. Garfield. Philadelphia, Hubbard Brothers, 1880.

BROCKWAY, BEMAN. Fifty Years in Journalism. Watertown, N.Y., Daily Times Printing and Publishing House, 1891.

BRUMMER, SIDNEY DAVID. Political History of the State of New York during the Period of the Civil War. New York, Columbia University Press, 1911.

BURGESS, JOHN W. Administration of President Hayes. New York, Charles Scribner's Sons, 1916.

—— Reconstruction and the Constitution, 1866–1876. New York, Charles Scribner's Sons, 1911.

BURTON, THEODORE E. Financial Crises and Periods of Industrial and Commercial Depression. New York, D. Appleton & Co., 1902.

—— John Sherman. Cambridge, Houghton Mifflin Co., 1906.

BUSBY, L. WHITE. Uncle Joe Cannon: The Story of a Pioneer American. New York, Henry Holt & Co., 1927.

BUTLER, BENJAMIN F. Autobiography and Personal Reminiscences of Major-General Benj. F. Butler: Butler's Book. Boston, A. M. Thayer & Co., 1892.

CARY, EDWARD. George William Curtis. Cambridge, Houghton Mifflin Co., 1895.

—— The Administration and Civil-Service Reform. *The International Review,* March, 1879.

CHADSEY, CHARLES ERNEST. The Struggle between President Johnson and Congress over Reconstruction. New York, Columbia University Press, 1896.

CHILDS, GEORGE W. Recollections. Philadelphia, J. B. Lippincott Co., 1891.

CLEMENCEAU, GEORGES. American Reconstruction, 1865–1870, and the Impeachment of President Johnson. Ed. with Intro. by Professor Fernand Baldensperger, trans. by Margaret MacVeagh. New York, The Dial Press, 1928.

CLEWS, HENRY. Forty Years in Wall Street. New York, Irving Publishing Co., 1908.

COLEMAN, CHARLES H. The Election of 1868: The Democratic Effort to Regain Control. New York, Columbia University Press, 1933.

COLMAN, EDNA M. White House Gossip, from Andrew Johnson to Calvin Coolidge. Garden City, N.Y., Doubleday, Page & Co., 1927.

CONKLING, ALFRED R. The Life and Letters of Roscoe Conkling. New York, Charles L. Webster & Co., 1889.

CONKLING, EGBERT S. Record of Descendants of Daniel Conkling, 1751–1874. Brooklyn, N.Y., 1904. (One of twenty typewritten transcriptions by the author is at the New York Public Library.)

CONKLING, IRA BROADWELL. The Conklings in America. Washington, Charles H. Potter & Co., 1913.

CONKLING, ROSCOE. America, Germany, France: The Administration Vindicated. Washington, F. and J. Rives and Geo. A. Bailey, 1872. (Pamphlet.)

—— Congress and the President: The Political Problem of 1866. Speech delivered at Mechanics' Hall, Utica, N.Y., September 13, 1866. (Pamphlet.)

—— The Extra Session of 1879: What It Teaches and What It Means. Washington, 1879. (Pamphlet.)

—— The Issues of 1880. Speech by Senator Conkling at the Academy of Music, New York City, September 17, 1880. New York, Cromwell Press, 1880. (Pamphlet.)

—The Issues of the Day. Speech by Senator Conkling at Cooper Institute, New York City, July 23, 1872. (Pamphlet.)

CONNERY, T. B. Secret History of the Garfield-Conkling Tragedy. *Cosmopolitan Magazine,* June, 1897.

COOKINGHAM, HENRY J. Recollections of the Oneida Bar. Utica, N.Y., privately printed for the Oneida Historical Society, 1903.

COOLIDGE, LOUIS A. Ulysses S. Grant. Cambridge, Houghton Mifflin Co., 1917.

CORTISSOZ, ROYAL. The Life of Whitelaw Reid. New York, Charles Scribner's Sons, 1921. 2 vols.

CORWIN, EDWARD S. The Twilight of the Supreme Court. New Haven, Yale University Press, 1934.

Cox, JACOB DOLSON. How Judge Hoar Ceased to Be Attorney-General, *Atlantic Monthly,* August, 1895.

CRAWFORD, J. B. The Crédit Mobilier of America: Its Origin and History. Boston, C. W. Calkins & Co., 1880.

CROLY, HERBERT. Marcus Alonzo Hanna: His Life and Work. New York, The Macmillan Co., 1923.

CROOK, COL. WILLIAM HENRY. Memories of the White House. Compiled and edited by Henry Rood. Boston, Little, Brown & Co., 1911.

—— Through Five Administrations: Reminiscences of Colonel William H. Crook, Bodyguard to President Lincoln. Compiled and edited by Margarita Spalding Gerry. New York, Harper & Brothers, 1910.

DANGERFIELD, ROYDEN J. In Defense of the Senate: A Study in Treaty Making. Norman, Okla., University of Oklahoma Press, 1933.

DAVENPORT, JOHN I. The Election Frauds of New York City and Their Prevention. New York, published by the author, 1881.

DAVIS, ELMER. History of the New York Times, 1851–1921. *New York Times,* 1921.

DAVIS, WILLIAM WATSON. The Civil War and Reconstruction in Florida. New York, Columbia University Press, 1913.

—— The Federal Enforcement Acts. In Studies in Southern History and Politics. New York, Columbia University Press, 1914.

DAWES, HENRY L. Garfield and Conkling. *Century Illustrated Monthly,* January, 1894.

DENNETT, TYLER. John Hay: From Poetry to Politics. New York, Dodd, Mead & Co., 1934.

DEPEW, CHAUNCEY M. My Memories of Eighty Years. New York, Charles Scribner's Sons, 1922.

DEWEY, DAVIS RICH. Financial History of the United States. 9th ed. New York, Longmans, Green & Co., 1924.

DODGE, MARY ABIGAIL (GAIL HAMILTON). Biography of James G. Blaine. Norwich, Conn., Henry Bill Publishing Co., 1895.

DOUGHERTY, J. HAMPDEN. Constitutional History of the State of New York. 2d ed. New York, Neal Publishing Co., 1915.

DUNNING, WILLIAM ARCHIBALD. *See* Bancroft.

—— More Light on Andrew Johnson. *American Historical Review,* April, 1906.

—— Essays on the Civil War and Reconstruction, and Related Topics. New York, P. Smith, 1931.

—— Reconstruction, Political and Economic, 1865–1877. New York, Harper & Brothers, 1907.

—— The Second Birth of the Republican Party. *American Historical Review,* October, 1910.

ECKENRODE, H. J. Rutherford B. Hayes: Statesman of Reunion. New York, Dodd, Mead & Co., 1930.

EDMONDS, FRANKLIN SPENCER. Ulysses S. Grant. Philadelphia, George W. Jacobs & Co., 1915.

EDMUNDS, GEORGE F. Another View of the Hayes-Tilden Contest. *Century Illustrated Monthly,* June, 1913.

FAULKNER, HAROLD UNDERWOOD. American Economic History. Rev. ed. New York, Harper & Brothers, 1931.

FICKLEN, JOHN ROSE. History of Reconstruction in Louisiana. Baltimore, Johns Hopkins Press, 1910.

FIELD, DAVID DUDLEY. The Vote That Made the President. New York, D. Appleton & Co., 1877. (Pamphlet.)

FIELD, OLIVER P. The Vice-Presidency of the United States. *American Law Review,* May-June, 1922.

FISH, CARL RUSSELL. The Civil Service and the Patronage. Cambridge, Harvard University Press, 1920.

FLACK, EDGAR HORACE. The Adoption of the Fourteenth Amendment. Baltimore, Johns Hopkins Press, 1909.

Fleming, Walter Lynwood. The Sequel of Appomattox. In The Chronicles of America, vol. XXXII. New Haven, Yale University Press, 1919.

Ford, Worthington Chauncey. *See* Adams, Henry.

Foulke, William Dudley. Life of Oliver P. Morton. Indianapolis, The Bowen-Merrill Co., 1899. 2 vols.

Frankfurter, Felix and Landis, James M. The Business of the Supreme Court: A Study in the Federal Judicial System. New York. The Macmillan Co., 1927.

Fry, Gen. James B. The Conkling and Blaine-Fry Controversy, in 1866: The Outbreak of the Life-long Feud between Two Great Statesmen. New York, A. G. Sherwood & Co., 1893.

Fuess, Claude M. The Life of Caleb Cushing. New York, Harcourt, Brace & Co., 1923. 2 vols.

Fuller, Robert H. Jubilee Jim: The Life of Colonel James Fisk, Jr. New York, The Macmillan Co., 1928.

Garner, James W. Southern Politics Since the Civil War. In Studies in Southern History and Politics. New York, Columbia University Press, 1914.

Gerry, Margarita Spalding. *See* Crook, Col. William Henry.

Giffen, Robert. The Case against Bimetallism. 3d ed. London, George Bell & Sons, 1895.

Glasson, William H. Federal Military Pensions in the United States. Ed. by David Kinley. New York, Oxford University Press, 1918.

Gorham, George C. Roscoe Conkling Vindicated. His Controversy with Mr. Blaine, 1866; His Resignation from the Senate and the Causes That Led to It, 1881. New York, 1888. (Pamphlet.)

Gosnell, Harold Foote and Merriam, Charles Edward. The American Party System. Rev. ed. New York, The Macmillan Co., 1929.

—— Boss Platt and His New York Machine. Intro. by Charles E. Merriam. Chicago, University of Chicago Press, 1924.

Grant, Jesse R. In the Days of My Father: General Grant, in collaboration with Henry Francis Granger. New York, Harper & Brothers, 1925.

Grant, U. S. Personal Memoirs of U. S. Grant. New York, Charles L. Webster & Co., 1886. 2 vols.

GREELEY, HORACE. Recollections of a Busy Life. New York, J. B. Ford & Co., 1868.

GRESHAM, MRS. MATILDA McGRAIN. Life of Walter Quinton Gresham, 1832–1895. Chicago, Rand McNally & Co.. 1919.

GRESHAM, OTTO. The Greenbacks; or, The Money That Won the Civil War and the World War. Chicago, The Book Press, 1927.

HACKER, LOUIS M. and KENDRICK, BENJAMIN B. The United States Since 1865. New York, F. S. Crofts & Co., 1932.

HALE, EDWARD EVERETT, JR. William H. Seward. Philadelphia, George W. Jacobs & Co., 1910.

HALL, CLIFTON R. Andrew Johnson, Military Governor of Tennessee. Princeton, Princeton University Press, 1916.

HALSTEAD, MURAT. The Defeat of Blaine for the Presidency. *McClure's Magazine,* January, 1896.

—— The Tragedy of Garfield's Administration: Personal Reminiscences and Records of Conversations. *McClure's Magazine,* February, 1896.

HAMILTON, J. G. DEROULHAC. Reconstruction in North Carolina. New York, Columbia University Press, 1914.

—— Southern Legislation in Respect to Freedmen, 1865–1866. In Studies in Southern History and Politics. New York, Columbia University Press, 1914.

HART, ALBERT BUSHNELL. Salmon Portland Chase. Cambridge, Houghton Mifflin Co., 1899.

HARTLEY, REV. ISAAC SMITHSON. Roscoe Conkling. *Magazine of American History,* August, 1888.

HAWORTH, PAUL LELAND. Reconstruction and Union, 1865–1912. New York, Henry Holt & Co., 1912.

—— The Hayes-Tilden Election. 2d ed. Indianapolis, Bobbs-Merrill Co., 1927.

HAY, JOHN MILTON and NICOLAY, JOHN G. Abraham Lincoln: A History. New York, The Century Co., 1917. 10 vols.

HAZARD, ROWLAND. The Crédit Mobilier of America. Providence, R.I., Sidney S. Rider, 1881.

HENDERSON, GEN. JOHN B. Emancipation and Impeachment. *Century Illustrated Monthly,* December, 1912.

HIBBEN, PAXTON. Henry Ward Beecher: An American Portrait. New York, George H. Doran & Co., 1927.

HOAR, GEORGE F. Autobiography of Seventy Years. New York, Charles Scribner's Sons, 1903. 2 vols.

HOLLISTER, OLVANO JAMES. Life of Schuyler Colfax. New York, Funk & Wagnalls Co., 1886.

HOLT, W. STULL. Treaties Defeated by the Senate: A Study of the Struggle between President and Senate over the Conduct of Foreign Relations. Baltimore, Johns Hopkins Press, 1933.

HOUGH, CHARLES M. Due Process of Law—Today. *Harvard Law Review,* January, 1919.

HOWELL, CLARK. The Aftermath of Reconstruction. *Century Illustrated Monthly,* March, 1913.

HUDSON, WILLIAM CADWALADER. Random Recollections of an Old Political Reporter. New York, Cupples & Leon Co., 1911.

HUNT, GAILLARD. The President's Defense. *Century Illustrated Monthly,* January, 1913.

INGERSOLL, ROBERT G. Memorial Address on Roscoe Conkling. Delivered before the New York State Legislature (includes a sketch of Conkling's life, and tributes of public men and of the press). Albany, N.Y., James B. Lyon, 1888.

JAY, JOHN. Civil-Service Reform. *North American Review,* September-October, 1878.

JONES, ROBERT L. History of the Foreign Policy of the United States. New York, G. P. Putnam's Sons, 1933.

JOSEPHSON, MATTHEW. The Robber Barons: The Great American Capitalists, 1861–1901. New York, Harcourt, Brace & Co., 1934.

KASSON, JOHN A. A Veto by Grant. *Century Illustrated Monthly,* April, 1897.

KENDRICK, BENJAMIN B. *See* Hacker, Louis M.

—— The Journal of the Joint Committee of Fifteen on Reconstruction. New York, Columbia University Press, 1914.

KING, GEN. CHARLES. The True Ulysses S. Grant. Philadelphia, J. B. Lippincott Co., 1914.

KINLEY, DAVID. *See* Glasson, William H.

LANDIS, JAMES M. *See* Frankfurter, Felix.

LANG, LOUIS. *See* Platt, Thomas Collier.

LAUGHLIN, J. LAURENCE. Political Economy and the Civil War. *Atlantic Monthly,* April, 1885.

—— The History of Bimetallism in the United States. 4th ed. New York, D. Appleton & Co., 1898.

LIGHTNER, OTTO C. The History of Business Depressions. New York, The Northeastern Press, 1922.

LODGE, HENRY CABOT. William H. Seward. *Atlantic Monthly,* May, 1884.

LONN, ELLA. Reconstruction in Louisiana, After 1868. New York, G. P. Putnam's Sons, 1918.

LOWELL, JAMES RUSSELL. Political Essays. Cambridge, Houghton Mifflin & Co., 1888.

LYNCH, DENIS TILDEN. Grover Cleveland: A Man Four-Square. New York, Horace Liveright, Inc., 1932.

MACVEAGH, MARGARET. *See* Clemenceau, Georges.

MARBLE, MANTON. A Secret Chapter of Political History. New York, 1877. (Pamphlet.)

MARTIN, EDWARD SANDFORD. The Life of Joseph Hodges Choate. New York, Charles Scribner's Sons, 1920. 2 vols.

MARTIN, EDWARD WINSLOW. *See* McCade, James D.

MATHEWS, JOHN MABRY. Legislative and Judicial History of the Fifteenth Amendment. Baltimore, Johns Hopkins Press, 1909.

McBAIN, HOWARD LEE. DeWitt Clinton and the Origin of the Spoils System in New York. New York, Columbia University Press, 1907.

McCADE, JAMES DABNEY (Edward Winslow Martin, pseudonym). Behind the Scenes at Washington. New York, Continental Publishing Co., 1873.

McCALL, SAMUEL WALTER. Thaddeus Stevens. Cambridge, Houghton Mifflin Co., 1899.

McCLURE, ALEXANDER K. Our Presidents, and How We Make Them. New York, Harper & Brothers, 1902.

McCOWN, ADA C. The Congressional Conference Committee. New York, Columbia University Press, 1927.

McCULLOCH, HUGH. Men and Measures of Half a Century. New York, Charles Scribner's Sons, 1889.

McELROY, ROBERT. Grover Cleveland, the Man and the Statesman. New York, Harper & Brothers, 1923. 2 vols.

—— Levi Parsons Morton: Banker, Diplomat and Statesman. New York, G. P. Putnam's Sons, 1930.

MERRIAM, CHARLES E. *See* Gosnell, Harold F.

MITCHELL, WESLEY CLAIR. Business Cycles. In Business Cycles and Unemployment, report by National Bureau of Economic Research Made for the President's Conference on Unemployment. Chap. I. New York, McGraw-Hill Book Co., 1923.

—— A History of the Greenbacks. Chicago, University of Chicago Press, 1903.

MOODY, JOHN. The Railroad Builders. In The Chronicles of America, vol. XXXVIII. New Haven, Yale University Press, 1920.

MOORE, COL. W. G. Notes of Col. W. G. Moore, Private Secretary to President Johnson, 1866–1868, with Intro. by Prof. St. George L. Sioussat. *American Historical Review,* October, 1913.

MORTON, OLIVER P. Presidential Nominations. *Atlantic Monthly,* April, 1884.

MUZZEY, DAVID SAVILLE. James G. Blaine: A Political Idol of Other Days. New York, Dodd, Mead & Co., 1934.

MYERS, GUSTAVUS. History of Tammany Hall. New York, Boni & Liveright, 1917.

NEVINS, ALLAN. Grover Cleveland: A Study in Courage. New York, Dodd, Mead & Co., 1933.

—— The Emergence of Modern America, 1865–1878. New York, The Macmillan Co., 1927.

NICOLAY, JOHN G. *See* Hay, John Milton.

NORTHRUP, MILTON HARLOW. A Grave Crisis in American History: The Inner History of the Origin and Formation of the Electoral Commission of 1877. *Century Illustrated Monthly,* October, 1901.

OBERHOLTZER, ELLIS PAXSON. A History of the United States Since the Civil War. New York, The Macmillan Co., 1926. 5 vols.

—— Jay Cooke: Financier of the Civil War. Philadelphia, George W. Jacobs & Co., 1907. 2 vols.

OGILVIE, J. S. The Life and Death of James A. Garfield. New York, J. S. Ogilvie & Co., 1881.

ORCUTT, WILLIAM DANA. Burrows of Michigan and the Republican Party, a Biography and a History. New York, Longmans, Green & Co., 1917. 2 vols.

OTIS, HARRISON GRAY. The Causes of Impeachment. *Century Illustrated Monthly,* December, 1912.

OWEN, ROBERT DALE. The Political Results from the Varioloid. *Atlantic Monthly,* June, 1875.

PARKER, DAVID B. A Chautauqua Boy in '61 and Afterward. Ed. by Torrance Parker, Intro. by Albert Bushnell Hart. Boston, Small, Maynard & Co., 1912.

PEACOCK, VIRGINIA TATNALL. Famous American Belles of the Nineteenth Century. Philadelphia, J. B. Lippincott Co., 1901.

PEIRCE, PAUL SKEELS. The Freedmen's Bureau: A Chapter in the History of Reconstruction. Iowa City, University of Iowa Press, 1904.

PLATT, THOMAS COLLIER. The Autobiography of Thomas Collier Platt. Compiled and edited by Louis J. Lang. New York, B. W. Dodge & Co., 1910.

POORE, BEN: PERLEY. Perley's Reminiscences of Sixty Years in the National Metropolis. Philadelphia, Hubbard Brothers, 1886. 2 vols.

PROSCH, THOMAS W. The Conkling-Prosch Family. Seattle, Press of the General Lithographing & Printing Co., 1909.

RAMSDELL, CHARLES WILLIAM. Reconstruction in Texas. New York, Columbia University Press, 1910.

REID, WHITELAW. After the War: A Southern Tour. Cincinnati, Moore, Wilstach & Baldwin, 1866.

RHODES, JAMES FORD. History of the United States, from the Compromise of 1850 to the McKinley-Bryan Campaign of 1896. New York, The Macmillan Co., 1920. 8 vols.

ROGERS, JOSEPH M. How Hayes Became President. *McClure's Magazine,* May, 1904.

ROOD, HENRY. *See* Crook, Col. William Henry.

ROOSEVELT, THEODORE. Theodore Roosevelt: An Autobiography. New York, The Macmillan Co., 1913.

ROOSEVELT, ROBERT BARNWELL. Speech of Hon. Robert B. Roosevelt, Delivered at Rockville Center, Long Island, Thursday Evening, October 15, 1872. New York, Journeymen Printers' Co-operative Association, 1872. (Pamphlet.)

Russell, Charles Edward. Blaine of Maine: His Life and Times. New York, Cosmopolitan Book Corporation, 1931.

Schurz, Carl. Reminiscences of Carl Schurz. New York, The McClure Co., 1908. 3 vols.

Seitz, Don C. Horace Greeley. Indianapolis, Bobbs-Merrill Co., 1926.

—— Joseph Pulitzer: His Life and Letters. New York, Simon & Schuster, 1924.

—— The Dreadful Decade. Indianapolis, Bobbs-Merrill Co., 1926.

—— The James Gordon Bennetts. Indianapolis, Bobbs-Merrill Co., 1928.

Seligman, Edwin R. A. The Income Tax: A Study of the History, Theory, and Practice of Income Taxation at Home and Abroad. New York, The Macmillan Co., 1910.

Sherman, Gen. William T. Home Letters of General Sherman. Ed. by M. A. DeWolfe Howe. New York, Charles Scribner's Sons, 1909.

—— Hon. James G. Blaine. *North American Review,* December, 1888.

Sherman, John. John Sherman's Recollections of Forty Years in the House, Senate and Cabinet. Chicago, The Werner Co., 1895. 2 vols.

Shipman, William D. A Brief Memorial Sketch of Roscoe Conkling as a Lawyer. Vol. 48, no. 24. Association of the Bar of the City of New York.

Shores, Venila Lovina. The Hayes-Conkling Controversy, 1877–1879. Northampton, Mass., Smith College, 1919.

Sioussat, St. George L. *See* Moore, Col. W. G.

Skinner, Dr. Charles H. A Memorable Senatorial Contest. *State Service Magazine,* January, 1920.

Smalley, E. V. Characteristics of President Garfield. *Century Magazine–Scribner's Monthly,* December, 1881.

Smith, Charles Emory. How Conkling Missed Nominating Blaine. *Saturday Evening Post,* June 8, 1901.

Smith, Harry Edwin. The United States Federal Internal Tax History from 1861 to 1871. Cambridge, Houghton Mifflin Co., 1914.

SMITH, THEODORE CLARKE. Life and Letters of James Abram Garfield. New Haven, Yale University Press, 1925. 2 vols.

SMITH, W. ROY. Negro Suffrage in the South. In Studies in Southern History and Politics. New York, Columbia University Press, 1914.

SPARKS, EDWIN ERLE. National Development, 1877–1885. New York, Harper & Brothers, 1907.

SPAULDING, ELBRIDGE G. History of the Legal-Tender Paper Issued during the Great Rebellion. 2d ed. Buffalo, 1875.

STANTON, HENRY S. Random Recollections. New York, Harper & Brothers, 1887.

STANWOOD, EDWARD. A History of the Presidency from 1788 to 1897. Cambridge, Houghton Mifflin Co., 1898.

—— American Tariff Controversies in the Nineteenth Century. Cambridge, Houghton Mifflin Co., 1903. 2 vols.

—— James Gillespie Blaine. Cambridge, Houghton Mifflin Co., 1905.

STEBBINS, HOMER ADOLPH. A Political History of the State of New York, 1865–1869. New York, Columbia University Press, 1913.

STEWART, WILLIAM H. Reminiscences of William H. Stewart of Nevada. Ed. by George Rothwell Brown. Washington, Neale Publishing Co., 1908.

STODDARD, HENRY LUTHER. As I Knew Them: Presidents and Politics from Grant to Coolidge. New York, Harper & Brothers, 1927.

STOREY, MOORFIELD. Charles Sumner. Cambridge, Houghton Mifflin Co., 1900.

STOUGHTON, E. W. The Third Term: Reason for It. *North American Review,* March, 1880.

STRONG, THERON G. Joseph H. Choate. New York, Dodd, Mead & Co., 1917.

STRYKER, LLOYD PAUL. Andrew Johnson: A Study in Courage. New York, The Macmillan Co., 1929.

TAUSSIG, F. W. The Tariff History of the United States. 8th ed. New York, G. P. Putnam's Sons, 1931.

TAYLOR, HANNIS. The Solid South, a National Calamity. *North American Review,* January, 1909.

THAYER, WILLIAM ROSCOE. Life and Letters of John Hay. Cambridge, Houghton Mifflin Co., 1915. 2 vols.

THOMAS, DAVID Y. Southern Political Theories. In Studies in Southern History and Politics. New York, Columbia University Press, 1914.

THOMAS, HARRISON COOK. The Return of the Democratic Party to Power in 1884. New York, Columbia University Press, 1919.

THOMPSON, C. MILDRED. Carpet-baggers in the United States Senate. In Studies in Southern History and Politics. New York, Columbia University Press, 1914.

—— Reconstruction in Georgia: Economic, Social, Political, 1865–1872. New York, Columbia University Press, 1915.

THOMPSON, HOLLAND. The New South, Economic and Social. In Studies in Southern History and Politics. New York, Columbia University Press, 1914.

TILDEN, SAMUEL J. Letters and Literary Memorials of Samuel J. Tilden. Ed. by John Bigelow. New York, Harper & Brothers, 1908. 2 vols.

TRUMAN, MAJOR BENJAMIN C. Anecdotes of Andrew Johnson. *Century Illustrated Monthly,* January, 1913.

TUCKERMAN, CHARLES K. Personal Recollections of General Grant. *Magazine of American History,* August, 1888.

—— Personal Recollections of President Johnson. *Magazine of American History,* July, 1888.

VEST, G. G. A Senator of Two Republics: Personal Recollections. *Saturday Evening Post,* August 8, 1903.

WADE, STUART C. Concklin or Conkling Family of East Huntington, L.I., N.Y., 1900. (Typewritten transcript by the author of original letters, at the New York Public Library.)

WARREN, CHARLES. The New "Liberty" under the Fourteenth Amendment. *Harvard Law Review,* February, 1926.

WARSHOW, ROBERT IRVING. Jay Gould: The Story of a Fortune. New York, Greenberg, Inc., 1928.

WATTERSON, HENRY. Colonel Watterson's Rejoinder to Ex-Senator Edmunds. *Century Illustrated Monthly,* June, 1913.

—— Marse Henry. New York, George H. Doran Co., 1919. 2 vols.

—— The Hayes-Tilden Contest for the Presidency: Inside History of a Great Political Crisis. *Century Illustrated Monthly,* May, 1913.

——— The Humor and Tragedy of the Greeley Campaign. *Century Illustrated Monthly,* November, 1912.

WELLES, GIDEON. Diary of Gideon Welles. Cambridge, Houghton Mifflin Co., 1911. 3 vols.

WERNER, M. R. Tammany Hall. New York, Doubleday, Doran & Co., 1928.

WHEELER, EVERETT P. Sixty Years of American Life. New York, E. P. Dutton & Co., 1917.

WHITE, ANDREW DICKSON. Autobiography of Andrew Dickson White. New York, The Century Co., 1907. 2 vols.

WHITE, HORACE. The Life of Lyman Trumbull. Cambridge, Houghton Mifflin Co., 1913.

WILLIAMS, CHARLES RICHARD. The Life of Rutherford B. Hayes, Nineteenth President of the United States. Cambridge, Houghton Mifflin Co., 1914. 2 vols.

WILSON, JAMES HARRISON. The Life of Charles A. Dana. New York, Harper & Brothers, 1907.

WINSTON, ROBERT W. Andrew Johnson: Plebeian and Patriot. New York, Henry Holt & Co., 1928.

WOODBURN, JAMES ALBERT. The Life of Thaddeus Stevens. Indianapolis, Bobbs-Merrill Co., 1913.

WOODWARD, W. E. Meet General Grant. New York, Horace Liveright, Inc., 1928.

WOOLLEY, EDWIN C. Grant's Southern Policy. In Studies in Southern History and Politics. New York, Columbia University Press, 1914.

——— The Reconstruction of Georgia. New York, Columbia University Press, 1914.

Notes

See also Addenda, page 429

I

1. A distinguished example is the late Roscoe Conkling ("Fatty") Arbuckle.

2. *See* the biographies by Captain Jesse, Barbey d'Aurevilley, and Lewis Melville. The popular belief that Brummel originated fashions probably was brought about by the Clyde Fitch play.

II

1. *American Law Review,* July–August, 1888.

2. Rev. Isaac Smithson in the *Magazine of American History,* August, 1888. *Dictionary of National Biography,* Vol. XVII. In this chapter the facts about Conkling's early life, and in this and the next chapter the facts about his upstate law cases, except when another authority is specifically cited, are from *The Life and Letters of Roscoe Conkling,* by the Senator's nephew, Alfred R. Conkling. But I have not leaned heavily upon this work in the writing of later events. Alfred Conkling, almost the only source of information about his uncle's early life, was a hero worshiper, and his book is a prolonged shout of praise.

3. Quoted from the memorial volume published by the New York State Legislature after the death of Senator Conkling.

4. This in a letter to Alfred R. Conkling, quoted in *Life and Letters,* p. 54.

5. "It would be a safe estimate to make that, out of the twenty-four hours of the day, he worked eighteen." Cookingham, *Recollections of the Oneida Bar,* p. 33.

6. Shipman, *Roscoe Conkling as a Lawyer,* in the twentieth annual report of the Association of the Bar of the City of New York, 1890.

7. *Education of Henry Adams,* p. 104. Adams' quotations, unless otherwise labeled, are from the *Education.*

8. Andrew Johnson in a letter to Major Truman, his secretary. *See* article by Truman in the *Century Magazine* of January, 1913. Andrew D. White wrote in his *Autobiography* of Greeley's "broad, smooth, kindly features as serene as the face of a big, well-washed baby."

9. He never got it back. Seitz, *Horace Greeley,* pp. 46–47.

10. There are several versions of the story, and according to some Conkling owed his congressional nomination entirely to his physique. It seems unlikely.

III

1. Thaddeus Stevens was hated by all good Southerners. On this day (December 6, 1859), besides raising a point of order against Gilmer, he addressed the House only once, but then it was with his usual bitterness, and resulted in a scorching tiff with Crawford, a Southern hothead. There are various versions of what happened then. This is the official one: "During the above colloquy, members from the benches upon both sides crowded down into the area, and there was, for a time, great confusion and excitement in

the Hall." *Congressional Globe* (36th Cong., 1st Sess.), Pt. I, p. 24. When the staid and cautious *Globe* goes as far as this, it may be assumed that there was in fact something like a riot in the House that day.

2. Conkling voted for Sherman, who was to become one of his most active enemies. Burton, *John Sherman,* p. 62.

3. *New York Post,* January 14, 1860.

4. *Congressional Globe* (36th Cong., 1st Sess.), pp. 233–236 appendix.

5. A compromise proposal providing for the adoption of a series of constitutional amendments, forbidding slavery in all federal territory north of 36° 30' while permitting it in territory south of that line; forbidding congressional interference with slavery in the District of Columbia and with the domestic slave trade, and prohibiting future constitutional amendments that might interfere with slavery in any state.

6. Barnes, *Memoir of Thurlow Weed,* p. 271.

7. Conkling, *Life and Letters,* pp. 107–108.

8. Alexander, *Political History of the State of New York,* II, 334–335.

9. Stanton, *Random Recollections,* p. 218; Alexander, *Political History of the State of New York,* II, 366; Brockway, *Fifty Years in Journalism,* chap. XLIV.

IV

1. Quoted in the *Life and Letters,* from which the entire account of this trial is taken. Mr. Clark, a few months later, read a paper on the case before the New York Academy of Medicine; and this was published; but I have not been able to procure a copy of it.

2. Later reports showed the loss to be much smaller; but Conkling was giving the best information available at that time. *Congressional Globe* (37th Cong., 1st Sess.), Pt. I, pp. 189–191. For a good description of the debate which followed, *see* Blaine, *Twenty Years of Congress,* Vol. I, chap. XVII.

3. Nicolay and Hay, *Abraham Lincoln: A History,* V, 150.

4. Nicolay and Hay, *Abraham Lincoln: A History,* V, 202–217.

5. McCall, *Thaddeus Stevens,* p. 216.

6. For the nation was, for all practical purposes, on a monometallic standard. "In discontinuing the coinage of the silver dollar, the act of 1873 thereby simply recognized a fact which had been obvious to everybody since 1849. It did not introduce anything new, or begin a new policy . . . Silver . . . had not been in circulation [in the United States] for more than twenty-five years." ". . . the real demonetization of silver in the United States was accomplished in 1853. It was not the result of accident; it was a carefully considered plan deliberately carried into legislation . . . the act of 1853 tried and condemned the criminal; and, after twenty years of waiting for a reprieve, the execution only took place in 1873." Laughlin, *History of Bimetallism,* pp. 92, 80.

7. Elbridge G. Spaulding, Buffalo banker, head of the ways and means subcommittee which framed the legal tender acts, probably was the man who convinced Stevens of the need for these acts. "The bill before us," he told the House, "is a war measure, a measure of *necessity* and not of choice, presented . . . to meet the most pressing demands upon the Treasury." *Congressional Globe* (37th Cong., 2d Sess.), p. 523. Earlier, he had written to Isaac Sherman: "The treasury-note bill . . . is a measure of *necessity* and

not one of *choice*. . . . We will be out of means to pay the daily expenses in *about thirty days."* Spaulding, *History of the Legal-Tender Paper Money issued during the Great Rebellion,* pp. 17–18. Yet it was forty-eight days after this when the act was passed, thirty-four more before the first of the notes were issued. Mitchell, *A History of the Greenbacks,* p. 73.

8. Burton, *Life of John Sherman,* pp. 100–101.

9. *Congressional Globe* (37th Cong., 2d Sess.), pp. 615, 634.

10. Of course it opened the floodgates, as Conkling had predicted. A few men even then dreamed of "controlled inflation"—though they didn't use that very phrase—and virtually all of its supporters insisted that the first legal tender act would be the last. But there was a second within six months, a third a little more than a year after that.

11. An example of his memory was his speech at the Academy of Music in New York City during the 1880 campaign, when, again, he used notes for effect only. It took him four uninterrupted hours to deliver that speech. On the stage near him sat John Reed, of the *New York Times,* who held in his hands the proofs which had been set up in advance and which filled ten small-type columns of the *Times.* Reed told Chauncey Depew afterward that Conkling "neither omitted nor interpolated a word from the beginning to the end." Depew, *My Memories of Eighty Years,* p. 48.

12. Conkling, *Life and Letters,* p. 120.

V

1. Conkling, *Life and Letters,* p. 199.

2. Yet there was coolness between the men before long, and though they never fought openly, they were respectively identified with warring factions. Depew believed that this was Conkling's fault. They were companions in a campaign tour of the state in 1868; and Roscoe Conkling was the star performer, Depew being decidedly a secondary figure. Conkling had made it known that he had a cold and would not consider giving any address out of doors. At Lockport it was learned that the local committee had announced arrangements for an open-air meeting on the fair grounds: twenty thousand persons were promised. Conkling, furious, refused to speak there; and another meeting was hastily arranged for his benefit in the Lockport Opera House, while Depew was told off to speak at the fair grounds. Later, while Conkling was spluttering to Depew about the poor audience in the Opera House, some committeemen indiscreetly rushed up to congratulate Depew upon the wonderful crowd at the fair grounds, which had applauded the younger man's talk to the last echo. "The cordial relations which had existed up to that time were somehow severed," wrote Depew in *My Memories of Eighty Years,* "and he became very hostile."

3. ". . . when life was made up so largely of doing disagreeable things, it was surely policy to use a man who did them with masterly ease and a connoisseur's perfection." Bradford, *Union Portraits,* p. 181.

4. Nicolay and Hay, *Abraham Lincoln,* IX, 250. *See also* Barnes, *Memoir of Thurlow Weed.*

5. Alexander, *Political History of the State of New York,* III, 104.

6. Item 130, Lot No. 99, Lincoln letters at the New York Public Library.

7. Conkling, *Life and Letters,* pp. 239–243.

8. Conkling, *Life and Letters,* p. 245.

VI

1. Hugh McCulloch, Secretary of the Treasury, for the four years of Johnson's Presidency had occasion to see him almost daily, "frequently at night," but never once found him under the influence. *Men and Measures,* pp. 373–374. And Colonel Crook, his bodyguard, says the President seldom drank anything at all. *Through Five Administrations,* pp. 82–83.

2. *New York Herald,* September 8, 1865. Stevens' ideas on reconstruction are best summed up in this speech at Lancaster, Pa., on September 7, and in his famous address from the floor of the House, December 18, 1865. *See Congressional Globe* (39th Cong., 1st Sess.), Pt. I, pp. 72–75.

3. Reid, *After the War: A Southern Tour,* p. 576.

4. Charles Sumner and William Lloyd Garrison, for example. But for the most part, even ex-Abolitionists of the North had no thought of giving the Negro the franchise. Vermont and Maine are the only states admitted to the Union before 1865 which did not at one time or other impose some legal restriction upon Negro voting; and there were practically no members of the race in those states anyway. Of the thirty-six states in 1865, only six permitted Negroes to vote. Five of these were New England states, Connecticut being the exception. The sixth was New York, which imposed special property qualifications upon Negroes. Constitutional amendments which would have established Negro suffrage were rejected in Connecticut, Wisconsin, and Minnesota in 1865; in Kansas, Ohio, and Minnesota in 1867; in Michigan and Missouri, 1868; and in New York a proposal to remove the special property qualification was voted down in 1869. Iowa and Minnesota were the only states to grant the Negro suffrage between the close of the Civil War and the final ratification of the Fifteenth Amendment. Smith, *Negro Suffrage in the South;* Mathews, *Legislative and Judicial History of the Fifteenth Amendment.* During the war, Lincoln's own state, Illinois, voted down a Negro suffrage proposal, 6–1.

5. *House Reports* (39th Cong., 1st Sess.), No. 30.

VII

1. Ghost writing was almost an unknown practice then, but Andrew Johnson's first message to Congress was so very well written that from the beginning nobody in Washington supposed he had done it himself. There were only two members of the cabinet, it was generally thought, who were capable of writing such a message. These were Stanton and Seward. Blaine thought Seward had done it, and so probably did most of the other guessers. See *The Nation,* December 14, 1865. It was many years later that Professor Dunning, almost by accident, learned that the real author was George Bancroft. Genteelly gloating because the much-discussed masterpiece had proved to be the work not of an unschooled Tennessean but of one "whose early life had been passed amid the best cultural influences of his native Massachusetts," Professor Dunning announced his find at a meeting of the Massachusetts Historical Society in November, 1905. The talk later was incorporated into a paper for the *American Historical Review* and was published in April, 1906.

2. *Congressional Globe* (39th Cong., 1st Sess.), p. 1079.

3. Williams, *Rutherford B. Hayes,* I, 278 n.

4. Hamilton, *Southern Legislation in Respect to Freedmen, 1865–1866.*

5. Of 144 witnesses heard, 10 were Northerners who had traveled through the South since the war, 39 were Northern army officers stationed in the South, 10 were Northern officeholders in the South, 15 were officials of the Freedmen's Bureau, 3 were Northerners who recently had moved south, 21 were Southern white "loyalists," 8 were Negroes. Beale, *The Critical Year*, pp. 94–96; Kendrick, *Journal of the Committee of Fifteen*, pp. 264–291.

6. *Congressional Globe* (39th Cong., 1st Sess.), Pt. I, pp. 351–359.

7. *Congressional Globe* (39th Cong., 1st Sess.), Pt. I, pp. 376–377.

VIII

1. Stanwood, *American Tariff Controversies in the Nineteenth Century*, II, 144. *See also* Smith, *The United States Federal Internal Tax History from 1861 to 1871.*

2. Taussig, *The Tariff History of the United States*, p. 164; also Smith, *Federal Internal Tax History*, and Seligman, *The Income Tax.*

3. This plan received much favorable attention when Conkling first proposed it, in 1861; but it was rejected as probably impractical, possibly unconstitutional, and certainly designed to prevent a huge enlargement of the patronage, then chiefly controlled by members of the lower house. *Globe* (37th Cong., 1st Sess.), p. 247.

4. All the testimony taken by the subcommittees of the Committee of Fifteen—none was taken by the committee itself—is contained in *House Reports* (39th Cong., 1st Sess.), No. 30. Part 1 of this volume contains the testimony concerning Tennessee. The figure above is to be found on page 91. One hundred and fifty thousand copies of this testimony were ordered printed, at the public expense, chiefly for use as campaign documents in the coming Congressional election. Kendrick, *Journal of the Committee of Fifteen*, pp. 265–291. Beale, *The Critical Year*, pp. 94–96.

5. It was modified in Grant's first administration, on motion of Roscoe Conkling, and in the first Cleveland administration it was repealed, before its constitutionality ever was tested. However, a recent Supreme Court decision—*Myers* v. *United States*, 272 U.S. 52 (1926)—has been taken as a complete vindication of Andrew Johnson's position on the tenure of office act.

6. Fish, *The Civil Service and the Patronage*, p. 200.

IX

1. According to the general's own version, *The Conkling and Blaine-Fry Controversy*, published in 1893, twenty-seven years after the event. The general's blood had cooled by then, and his book is admirably subdued in tone. There are many other accounts; the above, however, is based chiefly upon the *Congressional Globe* (39th Cong., 1st Sess.), Pt. I, pp. 2–151 for the original fight, p. 2293 for the reading of Fry's letter and for Conkling's response; Pt. V, same Sess., p. 3935, for the report of the investigating committee.

2. General Grant's name frequently was dragged back and forth in debates like this, for all the poor fellow's efforts to keep out of trouble. His prestige was infinitely greater than that of any other man in the nation at the time, and his endorsement was besought for all sorts of matters he didn't understand. In this particular instance, his opinion would have been

valuable. What it really was, we don't know. It should be mentioned that neither Conkling nor Blaine was specially friendly with Grant at this time.

X

1. *Congressional Globe* (39th Cong., 1st Sess.), p. 1147.

2. See Owen's article in the *Atlantic Monthly* for June, 1875, "The Political Results from the Varioloid." The reason for this curious title is the conversation Owen reports with Stevens after the rejection of the plan. The radical leader, Owen says, told him that the plan had been agreed upon and was to have been reported, but Fessenden was ill of the varioloid at the time, and it was thought courteous to hold back the report for a few days in order to give him, the chairman, a chance to present it in person. During those few days, according to Stevens as quoted by Owen, details of the plan became public and members of the committee were approached by congressmen who feared that any official mention of Negro enfranchisement would hurt their chances of reëlection: hence the whole plan was killed and removed, Fessenden's illness acting as the abortifacient. The story rests upon young Owen's unsupported word.

3. *House Reports* (39th Cong., 1st Sess.), Vol. I, pp. 16–21.

4. "The original Constitution was framed under very difficult and trying circumstances. The Fathers were very careful to word it so as to confer great power and yet to have it in such a form that the people might not fully realize the power that was being conferred. We are venturing little, we believe, in saying that this was apparently the problem that confronted the Radical leaders of the Thirty-ninth Congress, and that their main purpose in proposing the first section of the Amendment was to increase the power of the Federal Government very much, but to do it in such a way that the people would not understand the great changes intended to be wrought in the fundamental law of the land. Their failure to do this is due to the strained construction put upon their work by the Supreme Court." Flack, *The Adoption of the Fourteenth Amendment*, p. 69.

5. This section, as the committee originally reported it, would have disenfranchised all rebels until the year 1870. In the debate in the House, Roscoe Conkling fought a movement to have it eliminated, and won, 84–79; but later the Senate forced the modification.

6. *Journal of the Joint Committee of Fifteen*, p. 350.

XI

1. *New York World,* October 19, 1866; Stebbins, *Political History of the State of New York,* pp. 115–117.

2. *The Nation,* September 20, 1866.

3. Conkling, *Life and Letters,* p. 270.

4. Sumner, for instance: "Witness Memphis; witness New Orleans. Who can doubt that the President is the author of these tragedies? Charles IX of France was not more completely the author of the massacre of St. Bartholomew than Andrew Johnson is the author of those recent massacres which now cry for judgment." *New York Herald,* October 3, 1866.

5. This speech, delivered at Mechanics' Hall, Utica, September 13, was made into a pamphlet, *Congress and the President: the Political Problem of*

1866, from which the quotations above are taken. The city editor of the *Utica Herald* asked for an advance copy, and Conkling gave him the manuscript. It filled eleven columns in the *Herald* (the pamphlet is more than forty pages) but Congressman Conkling delivered it "almost word for word," and made it seem extemporaneous. Conkling, *Life and Letters,* p. 278.

XII

1. John Hay noted other things on his return to Washington. "It is startling to see how utterly without friends the President is. . . . The whipped-out, stunned way of talking that I have seen in all the Conservatives, is very remarkable. No bitterness, no energetic denunciation, no threats; but a bewildered sort of incapacity to comprehend the earnest deviltry of the other side, characterizes them all—but Seward, who is the same placid, philosophic optimist that he always was, the truest and most single-hearted Republican alive." Thayer, *Life and Letters of John Hay,* I, 255. Seward, however, a few months earlier had attended a Democratic state convention, helping to nominate a Democratic candidate.

2. *New York Herald,* Friday, November 9, 1877. The *Herald* was, most of the time, the only New York City newspaper friendly to Roscoe Conkling. The *Times* usually was cool, though seldom antagonistic. The *Post, Sun,* and *World* rarely had anything but harsh words for him; and the powerful *Tribune,* under Greeley and later under Whitelaw Reid, fought him ceaselessly.

3. In a letter to Horace Greeley, from Utica, April 25, 1864, he specifically denied that he was planning to run for governor, as an "indiscreet friend" had written to Frederick Conkling, who relayed the information to Greeley. "I entirely agree with you about the Convention. . . . General Wadsworth should be the only candidate." The letter is among the Greeley Papers, in the Ford Collection at the New York Public Library.

4. Rhodes, *History of the United States,* VI, 45; Kendrick, *Journal of the Committee of Fifteen,* p. 379.

5. White, *Autobiography,* I, 134. The same story has been told of at least one other Senator, so it may be untrue. However, it is noteworthy that it was told of Harris at all. Nobody could conceive of Roscoe Conkling hiding under a bed, for whatever purpose.

6. Conkling, *Life and Letters,* pp. 286–287. The custom of deliberately buying elections to the United States Senate, a custom which led eventually to the adoption of the Seventeenth Amendment, was just beginning at this time. Alexander, *Political History of the State of New York,* Vol. III, chap. 16.

7. Cary, *George William Curtis,* p. 193.

8. M. E. W. (Mrs. John) Sherwood, in the *Utica Daily Press,* October 26, 1893. It should be noted that Sumner was not given to flattery. On the contrary, though he was adored by all women, from duchesses to slaveys (with the single exception of his own wife, who left him after less than a year of marriage), he never was distracted by mere beauty or the easy tricks which pass for graciousness and social charm; he was experienced, difficult to please, and outspoken.

9. In a letter to his friend Rhodes, October 12, 1862. Smith, *James Abram Garfield,* I, 242.

XIII

1. Welles, *Diary*, III, 157.

2. *See* Colonel Moore's notes, published in the *American Historical Review*, October, 1913.

3. From Utica, September 14, 1867. The original is among the Greeley Papers in the Ford Collection at the New York Public Library.

4. *Congressional Globe* (40th Cong.), p. 1316. A summary and explanation of the entire debate is contained in Professor Mathews' *Legislative and Judicial History of the Fifteenth Amendment*. For other information on Conkling's attitude toward Negro Suffrage, *see Globe* (39th Cong.), Pt. I, p. 358, and *Globe* (40th Cong.), Pt. II, p. 2666.

5. The others were Ferry, Morgan, and Patterson of New Hampshire. Rhodes, *History of the United States*, VI, 222–224.

6. The suggestion shocked a not very tiger-like young correspondent for the Paris *Temps*, one Georges Clemenceau, who wrote indignantly to his paper about it. For France in those days believed in the sanctity of governmental obligations. Clemenceau, *American Reconstruction, 1865–1870*, trans. by Margaret MacVeagh.

7. Oberholtzer, *Life of Jay Cooke*, II, 134. Later, it seemed possible that passage of such a bill, and its strict enforcement, would have averted Black Friday, the worst day Wall Street ever had known.

8. Welles, *Diary*, III, 285; Chadsey, *The Struggle Between President Johnson and Congress*, chap. VI. *See also* the biographies of Johnson by Stryker and Winston, and DeWitt's history of the impeachment proceedings.

9. *New York Tribune*, October 15, 1867.

10. Crook, *Through Five Administrations*, pp. 92–94. Colonel Crook, whose job it was to turn undesirable visitors from the door of the executive office, and who performed this duty for no less than five presidents, declared that none of them was so pestered by cranks of all sorts as was Andrew Johnson.

11. Both Webster and Clay had believed that the Senate had a constitutional right to advise and consent to removals from office, but such earlier authorities as Hamilton, Madison, and Marshall considered the removal power *ex officio*, not inherent in the appointment power. Fish, *The Civil Service and the Patronage*, pp. 141–142. McCulloch, who as a member of the Johnson cabinet was in a position to know, later averred that Stanton himself did not believe the tenure of office act constitutional, but clung to his portfolio as a matter of party loyalty. McCulloch, *Men and Measures*, pp. 401–402.

12. Wade was a radical of radicals. Garfield, writing to Rhodes, May 1, 1868, asserted that many Republicans thought him "a man of violent passions, extreme opinions, and narrow views; a man who has never studied or thought thoroughly or carefully on any subject except slavery, a grossly profane coarse nature who is surrounded by the worst and most violent elements in the Republican party; Chandler, the drunken extremist, being his bosom friend in the Senate, and Ben Eggleston, a low, coarse, pothouse politician being his next friend and champion in the House: . . . already the worst class of political cormorants from Ohio and elsewhere are thronging the lobbies and filling the hotels in high hopes of plunder when Wade is sworn in." Smith, *James Abram Garfield*, I, 425.

XIV

1. Badeau, *Grant in Peace,* p. 174.

2. Tilden denied it, then and later. Bigelow, *Life of Samuel J. Tilden,* I, 211–212.

3. He was remembering this ten years later, when he pleaded against repeal of the recently passed Federal election laws. "I say thousands of men voted upon fraudulent naturalization papers. But all this was tame and paltry compared with other enormities. The city of New York was so redistricted as to bisect blocks, and denizens of the same building could vote in different election precincts. In some cases the Democrat majority was larger than the whole number of men, women, children, horses, cats, and dogs in the district. . . . Repeating, ballot-box stuffing, ruffianism, and false counting decided everything." *The Extra Session of 1879: What it Teaches and What it Means,* political pamphlet comprising a Conkling speech before the Senate, April 24, 1879. Some authors have called this Federal election law a radical reconstruction measure, aimed at bulldozing the Southern states and maintaining carpetbag rule. But Roscoe Conkling's interest in it was a strictly local one: it would help keep Tammany from cheating too much. This, from a campaign speech in '70, epitomizes his feeling toward Tammany: "I believe it was the Queen of Sheba who could not appreciate the glory of Solomon until she went into a certain part of his temple. If any one wants to see the glory of Democracy, let him go to the city of New York, where, in a term of fifteen years, the taxes have been increased from three million dollars to twenty-three million dollars." Conkling, *Life and Letters,* p. 408.

4. Alexander, *Political History,* III, 219–222.

5. Moody, *The Railroad Builders,* p. 12.

6. Scott bought the paper from Manton Marble in '76 and sold it to Jay Gould in '79. Gould sold it to Joseph Pulitzer in '83. Seitz, *Joseph Pulitzer,* pp. 125–133.

7. Conkling, *Life and Letters,* pp. 319–322.

XV

1. In fact, his name wasn't Ulysses Simpson Grant at all, but Hiram Ulysses Grant. They got it wrong at West Point, when he entered, and he never took the trouble to correct the mistake. Simpson was his mother's family name, and the congressman who sent the youth's entrance certificate to West Point evidently guessed.

2. Stewart, *Reminiscences,* pp. 255–257.

3. Stewart, *Reminiscences,* p. 257; *The Nation,* July 14, 1870; Alexander, *Political History of the State of New York,* III, 232–235.

4. "No one not down in the ring himself can understand the manoeuvering of New York politicians; but the general battle seems to be simple in its outlines. Fenton wished to show the Administration and the Senate that he 'runs the machine' in this State, and that though Conkling may have the President's ear, it is he who lays down the law in the rural districts. . . . Mr. Conkling's simple game was to tell every Fenton man who was at all weak in the knees that to go for Fenton was to go against the Administration; or, to put it roughly, if he assisted Fenton's plans, Conkling would see that his office, if he had one, should be taken away from him, while, if he did

what Conkling wanted, an office, if he had none, should be given him." *The Nation,* September 15, 1870.

5. *New York Tribune,* May 19, 20, 25, 1871. But it mustn't be supposed that even Greeley was a greater master of vituperation than Roscoe Conkling. Beman Brockway, who knew both of them intimately, thought that Greeley "was a great wit, though he probably never undertook to say a smart thing in his life. He said cute things because he could not help it. They escaped his lips before he was aware of it. No man excelled him at repartee or in the command of language. . . . I was going to remark, no man ever excelled him in the use of adjectives except Roscoe Conkling. I am not sure but Roscoe would beat him in expressive words, terms, and phrases. He [Conkling] was terrific against an object of his dislike. If words would crush a man he would annihilate him." *Fifty Years in Journalism,* p. 99.

6. *Syracuse Daily Standard,* September 28, 1871.

7. Details of this famous disagreement were printed in the *New York Herald* of November 9, 1877, and the *New York Tribune* of the following day.

XVI

1. Foulke, *Life of Oliver P. Morton,* II, 178 n.

2. Roscoe Conkling, with a few others, supported Senator Fessenden's motion to postpone consideration of the Alaska purchase treaty, but this was defeated. On the final division Conkling voted for ratification. Oberholtzer, *History of the United States,* I, 545.

3. "I never saw father so grimly angry as at this time." Jesse Grant, *In the Days of My Father: General Grant,* p. 136. *See also* Holt, *Treaties Defeated by the Senate,* pp. 123–129, and the Bancroft-Dunning sketch of Carl Schurz's political career contained in Schurz's *Reminiscences,* Vol. III.

4. Nearly two months before the final vote on the Santo Domingo matter Grant told Badeau, a departing dinner guest, that he intended to remove Motley. He thought the historian (whom Badeau himself liked) was not only insubordinate but also unrepresentative. *Grant in Peace,* p. 206.

5. "As a matter of fact, his [Corbin's] attempts were very feeble and misdirected and of no consequence whatever." Boutwell, in *McClure's Magazine,* November, 1899. This probably was true; though Boutwell, as Secretary of the Treasury at the time, and a member of the court party, naturally would say something of the kind. *See also* Fuller's *Jubilee Jim: the Life of Colonel James Fisk, Jr.,* and Warshow's *Jay Gould.*

6. Hoar, *Autobiography,* I, 212.

7. "In any assemblage of that time, Charles Sumner was as conspicuous as an Indian in blanket and feathers." The boy Jesse Grant didn't like Sumner of Massachusetts, who patted his head in a patronizing manner—very much as he patted the heads of mature men. But he did like his father's friend Roscoe Conkling, who took him seriously, or pretended to. *In the Days of My Father: General Grant,* pp. 105–106, 113.

8. Welles, *Diary,* II, 393. England did pay us $15,500,000 in payment of claims. Rhodes says that President Grant was in favor of the United States arranging to purchase Canada and more than once broached this at cabinet meetings, but he gives no authority for this statement. *History of the United States,* VI, 354.

9. Conkling, in the campaign of '66, had compared Andrew Johnson with

Louis Napoleon, which comparison was at that time his conception of the worst possible insult to the Emperor. *See* p. 102. Serenaded in Saratoga, during the state convention of '70, he responded with a speech in which he mentioned "the sick man who dominates the land of Lafayette . . . the Emperor who plotted and schemed against us in the day of our trial," and praised Prussia and the Prussians. Conkling, *Life and Letters,* p. 327. When he went to Europe in 1876 he traveled both ways on a German ship, and his welcome-home speech included a period of praise of the conquering Prussians. *See* New York City papers of Saturday, August 12, 1876.

10. Schurz, *Reminiscences,* III, 335.

11. *Congressional Globe* (42d Cong., 2d Sess.), appendix. The record of the debate covers many pages. Quotations above are from pp. 60–87, 101–126, and 522–530. Conkling's speech of February 19 was made into a campaign pamphlet, *America, Germany, France: the Administration Vindicated.*

XVII

1. Conkling himself, toward the end of Grant's second administration, presented to the Senate a petition demanding passage of a Sixteenth Amendment prohibiting any state from denying suffrage to any citizen because of sex; it was signed by six hundred and ten New York residents, most of them women. Conkling, *Life and Letters,* p. 528. But this was a mere gesture, the same thing many a Senator and Representative of the time was doing, and it was harmless. Roscoe Conkling was characteristic in his attitude toward woman's suffrage, as toward prohibition. That is, he politely avoided all discussion. These might trouble another generation of statesmen: they were not for him.

2. Adams, *Charles Francis Adams,* p. 392.

3. The *New York Times* throughout the campaign carried in its editorial masthead the lines "For President Ulysses S. Grant, for Vice-President Henry L. Wheeler," and, underneath this, two acknowledged quotations from Greeley, both boosting Grant as a Presidential candidate.

4. *New York Times,* July 24, 1872. The story covers twelve small type columns, more than nine of which are occupied by the text of the Conkling speech. The speech, a matter of some nineteen thousand words, later was made into a campaign pamphlet, *The Issues of the Day,* which was widely circulated and hailed as a masterpiece.

5. August 26, 1871, from Utica. Conkling, *Life and Letters,* p. 336.

6. William Allen White in *McClure's Magazine,* December, 1901.

7. Conkling, *Life and Letters,* pp. 446–447.

XVIII

1. Colman, *White House Gossip,* pp. 77–81.

2. *White House Gossip,* p. 60.

3. The following dividends were declared, all payable in 1868—that is, at the time when the congressmen and senators were holding stock: December 12, 1867, 60% first mortgage bonds of the Union Pacific; same day, 60% Union Pacific stock; December 28, 40% stock; January 3, 1868, 20% first mortgage Union Pacific bonds; June 15, 40% stock; June 17, 60% cash; July 3, 75% income bonds (originally payable in first mortgage bonds);

July 8, 75% stock; December 28, 200% stock. Hazard, *The Crédit Mobilier of America.* Hazard, himself a Crédit Mobilier stockholder, was apologizing for the company when he gave these figures in his paper read before the Rhode Island Historical Society, Thursday evening, February 22, 1881. For another apology, *see* Crawford's *The Crédit Mobilier of America: Its Origin and History.*

4. *House Report* 77 (42d Cong., 3d Sess.).

5. *New York World,* February 19, 1873.

6. From 1789, when the national Government in its present form began, to 1861, when the Civil War was started, the South supplied 9 of the 15 Presidents, their terms aggregating 50 of the 72 years; 6 of the 14 Vice-Presidents, 29 of the 37 Supreme Court justices, 73 of the 153 cabinet members, 12 of the 23 speakers, and 47 of the 82 ambassadors to Great Britain, Spain, France, Austria, and Russia. But from 1861 to 1913 the South supplied no President or Vice-President, only 2 of the 11 speakers, 14 of the 125 cabinet members, 5 of the 20 Supreme Court justices, and 10 of the 112 ambassadors to Great Britain, France, Austria-Hungary, Russia, Germany, Italy, and Spain. Garner, *Southern Politics Since the Civil War. See also* Taylor, "The Solid South, a National Calamity," in *North American Review,* January, 1909, and unsigned editorial, "The Political Attitude of the South," in the June, 1880, *Atlantic Monthly.*

7. Kendrick, *Journal of the Committee of Fifteen,* p. 370.

8. *Harper's Illustrated Weekly,* March 11, 25, 1876. These editorials presumably were written by George William Curtis.

9. Conkling, *Life and Letters,* p. 463. Even Rhodes thought that Conkling should have accepted, that though he had only appeared once before the Supreme Court he would have made an excellent chief justice. *History,* VII, 25–26. So, unexpectedly, did the current *Nation.* After Conkling's refusal, Grant nominated Attorney-General George H. Williams, an incompetent; but this nomination was withdrawn when it became evident that the Senate would refuse to ratify it; and Caleb Cushing was named. Cushing was seventy-four years old and accused of party irregularity, so the Senate showed its teeth again, and Grant withdrew this nomination also, substituting that of Morrison R. Waite, which was found acceptable. Fuess, *Life of Caleb Cushing,* II, 364–376; Oberholtzer, *History,* III, 127. Foulke says that the chief justiceship was first offered, unofficially, to Morton, who refused because he feared that his Senate seat would be filled by a Democrat. *Life of Oliver P. Morton,* II, 337–340. And Coolidge, *Ulysses S. Grant,* pp. 493–495.

10. Conkling, *Life and Letters,* p. 333.

XIX

1. Erie is the classic example. In four years, from '68 to '72, it had been deliberately watered from $17,000,000 to $78,000,000. Ten years after the panic the lesson remained unlearned: at that time it was estimated that the total railroad indebtedness was $7,500,000,000, of which about $2,000,000,000 was water. Faulkner, *American Economic History,* p. 594.

2. To S. B. Chittenden, New York City, from Utica, August 24, 1863. In the Ford Collection at the New York Public Library.

3. Barry, *Forty Years in Washington,* pp. 71–74.

4. Conkling, *Life and Letters,* p. 409.

5. Poore, *Reminiscences,* pp. 374–375. The *World* interview appeared April 17, 1878. Senator Conkling later cried that he had been misquoted—though not about the Senator Gordon incident. Gordon and his friends indignantly denied that they carried pistols.

6. Rhodes, *History,* VII, 55–64; Lightner, *History of Business Depressions,* p. 165.

7. Barrett, *The Greenbacks and Resumption of Specie Payments,* pp. 25–56; *also* Mitchell, *A History of the Greenbacks,* pp. 403–420, and Bolles, *Financial History of the United States,* pp. 74–86.

8. "Had the demonetization of the silver dollar not been accomplished in 1873 and 1874, we should have found ourselves in 1876 with a single silver standard, and the resumption of specie payments on January 1, 1879, would have been in silver, not in gold; and 15 per cent of all our contracts and existing obligations would have been repudiated." Laughlin, *History of Bimetallism* (4th ed.), p. 93. *See also* Griffen, *The Case Against Bimetallism* (3d ed.), chap. VIII.

9. Badeau, *Grant in Peace,* p. 191; Boutwell, *Reminiscences,* II, 233. Alfred Conkling had this story from "a member of the cabinet." *Life and Letters,* p. 470. *See also* Rhodes, *History,* VII, 55–64; Edward Atkinson's "Veto of the Inflation Bill of 1874," in the *Journal of Political Economy,* December, 1892, and articles by John A. Kasson and Draper in the *Century Magazine,* respectively, April and July, 1897.

XX

1. Poore, *Reminiscences,* p. 299.
2. *Letters,* pp. 291–292.
3. Conkling, *Life and Letters,* p. 499.
4. *New York World,* April 18, 1878.
5. Hudson, *Recollections,* p. 86.
6. Hoar, *Autobiography,* I, 243.
7. Conkling, *Life and Letters,* p. 508.
8. Conkling, *Life and Letters,* pp. 508–512.

XXI

1. Not Abram S. Hewitt, the national Democratic chairman. This story is told in many forms, but the one given here is taken from Elmer Davis' *History of the New York Times,* pp. 130–142. Davis constructed it from the files, from office tradition, and from the stories of survivors; and there is every reason to believe that his version is accurate. John Bigelow, in his life of Samuel Tilden, later was to charge a conspiracy, and others took up the cry. It seems unlikely.

2. The literature on this election is enormous, but there has been only one full-length study, Professor Haworth's *Hayes-Tilden Election.* The Tilden papers at the New York Public Library, and the files of the *Nation, Harper's,* the *North American Review* and the *Atlantic Monthly* have been useful.

3. *House Miscellaneous Documents* (44th Cong., 2d Sess.), No. 13.

4. It might be that the writer intended these verses to be a campaign song but was late about getting around to sending them. The paper is endorsed (though not, to give him credit, in Tilden's own handwriting) "poetry." The

examples above were selected haphazardly from the Tilden collection. There were, of course, hundreds of others like them; and doubtless Hayes received many too.

5. From St. Louis, December 28, 1876. Tilden papers, item 310.

6. Marse Henry, though not able to deny that he had said this, later was to explain in his autobiography that he did not mean it literally. What he meant was only a "mass convention" exercising "the freeman's right of petition." But Pulitzer didn't understand it that way, and neither did the crowd, and neither did anybody else.

XXII

1. Childs, *Recollections*, pp. 77–80.

2. Conkling, *Life and Letters*, p. 528.

3. "After the whole contest was over, Senator Wallace of Pennsylvania told me that Edmunds and Conkling, who were Republican leaders in the Senate, had admitted to him that if the Democrats had insisted upon the joint rule, they would have yielded the point and allowed the question to be settled in accordance with the precedents of the three last Presidential elections. But they were far from admitting this openly." Wheeler, *Sixty Years,* p. 106.

4. Most of the letters sent to Tilden and to Hayes at this time were addressed either to "President" or "President-elect." The above, which is unnumbered in the Tilden collection, has been quoted but to the best of my knowledge has never before been printed in full.

5. Williams, *Rutherford B. Hayes,* I, 506–507, 514–516.

6. Williams, *Rutherford B. Hayes,* I, 521.

7. *New York World,* April 17, 1878.

8. Abram S. Hewitt admitted this shortly before his death. "How Hayes Became President," *McClure's Magazine,* May, 1904.

9. Poore, *Reminiscences,* p. 326.

10. From Garfield's diary. Smith, *James Abram Garfield,* I, 630.

11. *Our Presidents, and How We Make Them,* p. 269. The story had an amazing vitality, and of course the Senator never stooped to deny it. As late as June 30, 1900, in an article entitled "Democratic Conventions" in the *New York Evening Post,* it was stated that ". . . the anti-Hayes Republicans, left without a leader, fell back to their party lines and gave the vote of the state and Presidential certificate to Hayes. It is now known that Conkling was influenced by Mrs. Sprague, who thereby avenged the defeat of her father's nomination in 1868. A woman's ill-will lost Tilden the Presidency, to which he had been elected by a popular majority of over 250,000." It will be noticed that with the exception of one phrase this is identical with the McClure account, and possibly it was written for the *Post* by McClure. I have not been able to learn whether or not it was. The article is unsigned. Just a week later, on July 7, in the same paper, there was a sharp answer from W. George Hoadley, who resented publication of the silly story. Judge Hoadley was a former governor of Ohio, a prominent member of the independent movement in 1872, and an aspirant for the Democratic Presidential nomination in 1884. At the time of the events related he was in Washington —he was one of Tilden's counsel before the electoral commission—and he was a close personal friend of both the Senator and Mrs. Sprague, whom he helped to get a divorce.

XXIII

1. Not to be confused with that other friend of Blaine, General James B. Fry, whose proposed continuance as Provost Marshal General brought about that debate featured by the "turkey-gobbler" speech.
2. *New York Tribune,* July 28, 1877.
3. Hoar, *Autobiography,* I, 382–383.
4. "New York was the first state in which the offices were openly and continuously used for partisan purposes." Fish, *Civil Service and the Patronage,* p. 86.
5. All the New York City morning papers of August 12, 1877, carried long accounts of this home-coming, but that of the *World* seemed best, and the quotations given are from that paper.

XXIV

1. Brummer, *Political History of New York during the Civil War,* pp. 394–395.
2. The four principal reports, submitted May 24, July 4, July 21, and August 31, all 1877, are contained in *House Executive Documents* (45th Cong., 1st Sess.), No. 8.
3. Alexander, *Political History,* III, 358–377. Easily the best account of this convention.
4. Andrew White remembered this most quoted of all Conkling remarks as: "When Doctor-r-r Ja-a-awnson said that patr-r-riotism was the l-a-w-s-t r-r-refuge of a scoundr-r-rel, he ignor-r-red the enor-r-rmous possibilities of the word r-refa-awr-r-rm." *Autobiography,* I, 171. Others have agreed that the Senator out-Conklinged himself here. The greater his rage the slower he used to speak.
5. Curtis came from Richmond County.
6. To Charles Eliot Norton, from Ashfield, Mass., September 30, 1877. Cary, *George William Curtis,* p. 258.
7. Curtis' speech was either extemporaneous or hastily prepared as a result of the unexpected and shocking violence of Tom Platt's opening remarks. But Conkling's reply, though like all his great speeches it seemed extemporaneous and was generally accepted as such by those who heard it, in fact had been long and carefully prepared. Lawrence, the official Conkling listening-post, afterward told Chauncey Depew that he had heard the Curtis philippic many times before the convention. *My Memories of Eighty Years,* pp. 80–83.
8. October 18, 1877.
9. December 13, 1877.
10. Sherman's statement is contained in No. 8:83, *House Executive Documents* (45th Cong., 1st Sess.), Pt. I. Arthur's defense, probably written by the Senator himself, is No. 25, *House Executive Documents* (45th Cong., 2d Sess.).
11. *Recollections,* p. 682.
12. In a letter to John Jay, October 4, 1879. *Recollections,* p. 748.

XXV

1. The first of them, and by far the most important, was Allan Pinkerton, who had crossed the seas from Scotland in 1842, and had set up the first

American private detective agency in 1850, in Chicago. All of his original clients, and most of his clients at this time, were railroads. Richard Wilmer Rowan, *The Pinkertons: A Detective Dynasty*, pp. 25–26.

2. The Brotherhood itself took no official part in the strike. Commons and associates, *History of Labor in the United States*, pp. 177–191; Ware, *Labor Movement in the United States, 1860–1895*, pp. 45–49; Dacus, "The Great Strike," *Harper's Weekly*, August 11, 1877; Nevins, *Emergence of Modern America*, pp. 385–392; Adamic, *Dynamite*, pp. 28–36.

3. Thayer, *Life and Letters of John Hay*, II, 1–4. The father-in-law was Amasa Stone, a characteristic product of his time, one of the positive, growling, new Middle West millionaires. It was to him, as vice-president of the Lake Shore and Michigan Central Railroad, that young Rockefeller and his associates of the South Improvement Company first went with their rebate proposition. They got the rebate, too. It was the beginning of the notorious Rockefeller system—promptly imitated by every other industrialist able to do so—for choking competition. Amasa Stone was well remembered when, soon afterward, the Standard Oil Company was organized. He was one of the original directors. Tarbell, *History of the Standard Oil*, I, 47–48; Flynn, *God's Gold*, pp. 135–137. He lost a lot of money in the financial crash of '73, and ten years later killed himself. Dennett, *John Hay*, pp. 99–101.

4. This was one of the most famous of the Conkling speeches. Garfield, who took a keen professional interest in matters of oratory, and who was as watchful, as alertly critical, as any great singer attending the concert of a rival, managed to slip over from the other end of the building to listen. "It was a very strong and complete presentation of our views and entirely in accord with the position I took in my first speech," he recorded in his journal. "The senator's self-consciousness is always apparent and I think it marred the effectiveness of his speech. He spoke from notes without reading and when he completed the sheet of notes, tore it into small bits and threw them on the floor, taking some time to do it. He also held considerable *sotto voce* conferences with those around him. These little touches of self-consciousness detract from the effectiveness of his speaking. The more a man loses himself in his work, the better for the work. But notwithstanding these minor defects, his speech was very powerful and valuable. There were some extraordinarily strong passages." Smith, *James Abram Garfield*, II, 682.

5. Smith, *James Abram Garfield*, II, 670.

6. Conkling, *Life and Letters*, p. 649.

7. Hoar, *Autobiography*, II, 44.

8. For example, the tariff act of 1864 (when, however, Roscoe Conkling was not in Congress) was, according to Professor Taussig, "in many ways crude and ill-considered; it established protective duties more extreme than had been ventured on in any previous act in our country's history," raising the average level of duties to 47 per cent; yet the two houses devoted only five days "to this act, which was in its effects one of the most important financial measures ever passed in the United States." *Tariff History of the United States*, pp. 167–168. The act "remained for decades the basis of the American tariff system." Faulkner, *American Economic History*, p. 511.

9. Glasson's *Federal Military Pensions of the United States* is a monumental and much neglected work. Professor Glasson in 1900 published as one of the Columbia University Studies in Political Science his monograph

History of Military Pension Legislation in the United States. He lectured on the subject at Princeton, Johns Hopkins, and other universities, and in 1913, through the division of economics and history of the Carnegie Endowment for International Peace, he was enabled to complete the study, carrying it through the date of the entrance of the United States into the World War. Pension statistics given above, except where otherwise labeled, are from the larger work. *See also* articles by Charles Francis Adams in *The World's Work,* December, 1911, and January and February, 1912.

10. Williams, *Rutherford B. Hayes,* II, 339 n.

11. *See* Glasson. *See also* the chapters on pension legislation in the Nevins, Lynch, and McElroy biographies of Grover Cleveland. For it was Cleveland who reaped the whirlwind—or the beginning of it.

12. *Congressional Record* (45th Cong., 3d Sess.), Pt. I, pp. 484–494.

13. *Congressional Record* (45th Cong., 3d Sess.), Pt. III, p. 2050.

14. *House Executive Documents* (45th Cong., 2d Sess.), No. 23, pp. 10–16.

15. *International Review,* March, 1879.

XXVI

1. Senator Vest in the *Saturday Evening Post,* August 8, 1903.

2. *New York Herald,* November 9, 1877.

3. *Harper's,* February 8, 1879.

4. Cortissoz, *Whitelaw Reid,* I, 372.

5. April, 1880.

6. The pro and con arguments are well summarized by articles in the *North American Review* for March, 1880, Judge J. S. Black writing against the third term, E. W. Stoughton writing for it.

XXVII

1. Judge Hunt to the author. The incident serves to illustrate again the Conkling propensity for making enemies where he might have made friends. The following year, when the tyrant was toppling, Hunt was at Albany, actively engaged in the fight against Conkling's reëlection—the Senator's Waterloo. No doubt there were many other men like Isaac L. Hunt there too.

2. There are three other claimants, but Raleigh was almost certainly the author. The poem is popularly called "The Silent Lover," sometimes "To his Mistress" or "To his Queen," and occasionally is listed under its first line: "Our passions are most like to floods and streams." *See* Agnes Latham's definitive *Poems of Sir Walter Ralegh,* pp. 187–190. I have interviewed four men who were present at this convention, and each of them supposed the line to be Roscoe Conkling's own. He was fond of quoting, and it is probable that his admirers often credited him with originating lines written by the immortals.

3. May 16, 1880.

4. May 20, 1880.

5. Coolidge blamed the Senator for losing the nomination for his chief by "showing superb contempt for opposition, stirring resentment among friends of Blaine and other candidates, repelling by his domineering ways those whom another would have tried with tact to win, questioning their party loyalty, sneering at their political consistency, exulting in their hate."

Ulysses S. Grant, p. 544. For a friendlier account of Senator Conkling's behavior at this convention *see* Charles Emory Smith in the *Saturday Evening Post,* June 8, 1901.

6. Hoar, *Autobiography,* I, 390–392.

7. Smith, *James Abram Garfield,* II, 969.

8. "After the convention was over, however, it became apparent to every one not blinded by partisanship that the nomination of General Grant would have killed the party. A bolt would inevitably have occurred, and a second convention would have assembled within a month and put another Republican ticket in the field." Editorial in the *Atlantic Monthly,* August, 1880.

9. These lines of "Private Miles O'Reilly," one of the war poets, were suggested to the Senator only the previous night by Tom Murphy. The Senator, delighted, slapped them on top of his speech. Conkling, *Life and Letters,* p. 597. "Miles O'Reilly" was the pseudonym of Adjutant General Charles G. Halpine.

10. He was the postmaster of St. Louis, and a man whom George William Curtis, in scolding Hayes for his reappointment of Filley, had called the most conspicuous officeholder in the country for his active manipulation of politics. "He is a shining example of 'the thing to be reformed.'" *Harper's,* December 8, 1877.

11. Boutwell, however, makes no mention of this incident in his *Reminiscences.* Alexander had it from Morton in a letter dated September 14, 1908.

12. The popular belief at the time was that Conkling had forced the nomination of Arthur either to humiliate Garfield, and more emphatically Sherman, or else to have a close friend first in line for the throne. It is not likely that this is true. There are many conflicting reports about this dickering for the Vice-Presidential nomination, most of them founded upon nothing more substantial than rumor. Alfred Conkling, who was with his uncle in Chicago, says that the Senate refused to have anything to do with the nomination. *Life and Letters,* pp. 607–608. Alexander, in preparing this chapter of his *Political History,* interviewed Levi P. Morton, General Woodford, and Howard Carroll, all members of the New York delegation and close to the Senator. McElroy's account of this negotiation, in his biography of Morton, is taken chiefly from Alexander, whose narrative fits in too with probability.

13. May, 1880.

14. Bigelow, *Samuel J. Tilden,* II, 272.

15. *New York Tribune,* June 21, 1880.

XXVIII

1. Johnson Brigham, getting on a train at Corning, N. Y., to meet the candidate when Garfield was returning to Mentor from New York during the campaign, was disconcerted at finding him roaring with laughter at an exceptionally smutty tale, which Garfield insisted General Swayne retell for the benefit of the newcomer. Brigham confesses that it was "somewhat of a shock to me, for I had read much concerning the pure-mindedness of our Campbellite-preacher candidate." *Blaine, Conkling and Garfield,* p. 19.

2. *New York Tribune,* September 18, 1880.

3. "Had it been known that he [Garfield] desired the presidency, a combination would have been effected immediately, which would no doubt have

defeated him, regardless of his merits." Oliver P. Morton in the *Atlantic Monthly,* April, 1884.

4. There is some doubt about who proposed this visit, which certainly was unexpected. The version above is from Croley's *Marcus Alonzo Hanna,* pp. 116–117, and is taken from the account of a reporter present, James H. Kennedy in the *Cleveland Herald.* However, Mark Hanna had but recently bought the *Herald,* and Kennedy might have been patting the back of his new boss, who liked to get credit for "smart" things like this. Alfred Conkling says Si Cameron was responsible. *Life and Letters,* pp. 620–621.

5. "Whenever reconciliation seemed imminent, it vanished like a cloudshadow. I could never unite them. Blaine was ready, but Conkling would accept no advances." Senator Frye to Alexander. *Political History,* III, 471.

6. Platt, *Autobiography,* p. 135.

7. Conkling, *Life and Letters,* pp. 614–615. The Senator invariably refused to accept expense money while stumping.

XXIX

1. Morton, when it looked as though he wouldn't get the Treasury after all, pleaded by mail with the Senator to step into the contest. The Senator refused, coldly, firmly, January 10. McElroy, who publishes the letter in full, believes that the Senator really wished to see Tom Platt elected. *Levi P. Morton,* p. 123. Most authorities, however, believe that he was sincerely neutral.

2. *New York Tribune,* January 3, 1881.

3. Depew, *My Memories of Eighty Years,* p. 112; Depew to Alexander, *Political History,* III, 468; *New York Tribune,* January 9, 1882. Of course Platt doesn't mention the episode in his *Autobiography,* in which he asserts that his friends "insisted" he enter the contest, so that "I was forced to participate finally as an avowed candidate." The reference to a stepladder was intended only as a jibe at Conkling's length and general snootiness, but in view of what was to happen to Tom Platt a few months later it was remembered with many a grin.

4. *The Influence of Sea Power upon History,* 1660–1783, by Captain A. T. Mahan, D.C.L., LL.D. Little, Brown, and Company: Boston, 1890.

5. Connery, "Secret History of the Garfield-Conkling Tragedy," *Cosmopolitan Magazine,* June, 1897.

XXX

1. Poore, *Reminiscences,* p. 402.

2. *Brooklyn Daily Eagle,* March 8, 1885. The article, a colorful account of the Garfield-Conkling battle, is by-lined "Insider." Presumably this was Billy Hudson, then Washington correspondent for the *Eagle.* It reads like his copy. But nobody at the *Eagle* office now can say for certain that Hudson was the writer.

3. He was made resident minister in Belgium the following year, but not by Garfield. He was a son of Governor Hamilton Fish, who appointed Roscoe Conkling to his first political office and who later was Secretary of State under Grant, and father of that Sergeant Hamilton Fish, the Rough Rider, who was killed at Siboney. *National Cyclopaedia of American Biography,* XI, 27.

4. There was one protestation of amazement, however, which today would be called a baloney statement. "This is a complete surprise. To my knowledge no one has solicited for me any place under Garfield. It comes entirely unsought." Judge Robertson in an interview in the *New York Tribune,* March 22, 1881.

5. Cortissoz, *Whitelaw Reid,* II, 61. The President told a reporter, in the presence of Blaine: "I made the nominations deliberately and would do so again, and shall stand by them, especially Judge Robertson's. I made no promises, was reminded of none, and have broken none . . . I would not withdraw it if they carried me feet first out of this place." *Brooklyn Daily Eagle,* March 8, 1885.

6. Gorham, *Roscoe Conkling Vindicated.* True or false, it is an accurate expression of the attitude of the Democratic senators.

7. Dr. Gosnell says that Chauncey Depew told him, on September 25, 1922, that Platt first intended to support the Robertson nomination, opposing his chief. *Tom Platt and His New York Machine,* p. 27. It seems improbable. Platt was not of the stuff of which rebels, even momentary rebels, are made. If ever he revolted he kept it to himself. Depew makes no mention of this in his memoirs, published the year of the interview with Dr. Gosnell. Even Platt, in his own vainglorious autobiography, doesn't claim credit for such temerity.

8. Cortissoz, *Whitelaw Reid,* II, 63.

9. Smith, *James Abram Garfield,* II, 1119.

10. For example, Uncle Joe Cannon, who knew both men personally, liked Garfield and disliked Conkling, yet he thought "Garfield's indecision was as much to blame as Blaine's overweening ambition and desire for revenge and Conkling's vanity" for the fight which was "one of the most disastrous things that ever happened to the Republican party." Everybody knew, Uncle Joe says, that Garfield was making other senators all sorts of patronage promises in order to get their votes for confirmation of the Robertson appointment. Busby, *Uncle Joe Cannon,* pp. 153–158.

11. Dawes, "Garfield and Conkling," *Century Illustrated Monthly,* January, 1894.

XXXI

1. There was rain in Washington from 10.40 a.m. to 3.25 p.m.; from 3.40 p.m. to 5.15 p.m.; from 6.48 p.m. to 8.50 p.m.; from 9.30 p.m. to 10.20 p.m., and from 11.40 p.m. until 2.05 a.m. the next day—a total, at that, of only 0.21 inches. The maximum temperature was 59, the minimum 53. The sun set at 7.15 p.m. In New York City there was a total of 0.01 inches of rainfall, from 7.35 a.m. to 8.15 a.m., and from 5.15 p.m. to 6.35 p.m. The temperature ranged from 49 to 55. The sun set at 7.08. Figures supplied from the records by the climatological division of the weather bureau, United States Department of Agriculture at Washington.

2. "The followers of Conkling have undoubtedly a majority of the Republicans in the Legislature." Editorial in the *Tribune,* May 24, 1881. It was the same legislature, still in session, which had elected Tom Platt.

3. *New York Times,* May 17, 1881.

4. Platt, *Autobiography,* pp. 150–152.

5. Conkling, *Life and Letters,* p. 632.

6. "Many of his political acts were dictated by the lowest party considera-

tions; but his political and forensic speeches contain passages worthy of Cicero." Unsigned obituary in the *American Law Review,* July-August, 1888.

7. *New York Times,* May 23, 1881.

8. "Mr. Conkling was much misrepresented and of course he was much misunderstood. As a Senator from New York he claimed a right to be consulted in regard to the principal appointments in the State. His recommendations were few and they were made with great care. He confined himself to the chief appointments. It was quite difficult to secure his name or his favorable word in behalf of applicants for the subordinate places." Boutwell, *Sixty Years,* II, 274.

9. Robertson's "appointment was made on Boss principles and (so far as appears) on no others, and again, to all appearances by a Maine Boss instead of a New York Boss." *The Nation,* May 26, 1881.

10. Conkling, *Life and Letters,* pp. 642–643; Platt, *Autobiography,* pp. 159–160.

11. *New York Times,* May 25, 1881.

12. Thayer, *John Hay,* I, 452.

13. To J. D. Cox, May 22, 1881. Smith, *James Abram Garfield,* II, 1136.

14. *New York Times,* May 28, 1881.

15. Johnson Brigham to the author. Mr. Brigham, now Iowa State Librarian, was at that time a New York newspaperman.

16. Skinner, "A Memorable Senatorial Contest," *State Service Magazine,* January, 1920; Alexander, *Political History,* III, 480 n.

17. Hudson, *Random Recollections,* pp. 119–124.

18. Editorial, June 29, 1881. Conkling's friends contended that the matter would have been settled much earlier had it not been for a Half-Breed trick May 16, when Governor Cornell sent notice of the two resignations to the state senate. It was a Monday, and if the governor's communication was received that day the legislature could start balloting for United States senators the second Tuesday thereafter, that is, May 24. The assembly received the message, but when word of it was carried to the Senate Robertson and some others managed to put through an adjournment motion—even while the messenger was in the corridor outside. The message was sent again on Thursday, May 19, and then it was officially received. This meant a difference of a whole week in the time when balloting, by law, could be started. Which week, the Stalwarts contended, made all the difference. Gorham, *Roscoe Conkling Vindicated.* Possibly. It is true that time worked against the two resigned senators. But though Platt might have made up his mind to run again, by May 16, Conkling certainly hadn't.

19. Smith, *James Abram Garfield,* II, 1136.

20. *New York Tribune,* July 6, 1881.

21. *New York Tribune,* July 8, 1881.

XXXII

1. Bliss, *Story of President Garfield's Illness, Century Magazine-Scribner's Monthly,* December, 1881. Dr. D. W. Bliss was the physician in charge from the beginning.

2. Stoddard, *As I Knew Them,* p. 114.

3. An unnamed politician, who knew both men well, told Billy Hudson

that in his opinion this was the beginning of the rift between Conkling and Arthur. *Random Recollections,* pp. 125–127.

4. Eckenrode, *Rutherford B. Hayes,* p. 335.

5. *New York Sun,* January 21, 1890.

6. Strong, *Joseph H. Choate,* pp. 189–191.

7. Shipman, *Roscoe Conkling as a Lawyer,* Association of the Bar of the City of New York pamphlets, Vol. 48, No. 24.

8. "Mr. Conkling as a Lawyer," *National Law Review,* June, 1888 (unsigned).

9. Obituary in the *American Law Review,* July-August, 1888 (unsigned).

10. Conkling, *Life and Letters,* p. 671.

11. Alexander, *Political History,* III, 493–495.

12. *Letters,* p. 343.

XXXIII

1. As nothing so angered him as any accusation, however hazy, aimed at his integrity, so nothing delighted him as much as a tribute to his fond honesty. He fairly purred when Joseph H. Choate, in a court room when the two celebrated lawyers were on opposing sides of a famous case, unexpectedly offered this: "However we may differ one from another, or all of us from him, we owe the Senator one debt of gratitude for standing always steadfast and incorruptible in the halls of corruption. Shadrach, Meshach and Abednego won immortal glory for passing one day in the fiery furnace, but he has been twenty years there and has come out without even the smell of smoke upon his garments." Martin, *Joseph Hodges Choate,* I, 449.

2. Henry L. Stoddard tried to go along with this trio a few times, but he was unable to do so, and was afterward quietly warned by the ex-Senator that young newspapermen should not attempt to down as much wine as old politicians. He agreed. *As I Knew Them,* pp. 114–115.

3. *San Mateo County (Calif.)* v. *The Southern Pacific Railroad Company,* 116 U.S. 138.

4. 16 Wallace, 36, 76 (1873).

5. Frankfurter and Landis, *Business of the Supreme Court,* pp. 63–64.

6. This journal, surely one of the most interesting documents in our national history, was not even published until 1914, when it was brought out by Columbia University under the editorship of Benjamin B. Kendrick, who had with great difficulty located a copy. For its curious history, and for a review of Conkling's argument in the San Mateo case, *see* Dr. Kendrick's introduction to *The Journal of the Joint Committee of Fifteen on Reconstruction.* Where Conkling got his copy we don't know, but it was probably from Senator Morrill.

7. "The Fourteenth was a straight party measure, due to distrust of the states solely in respect of their possible treatment of the Negro." Hough, "Due Process of Law—Today," *Harvard Law Review,* January, 1919. For discussion *see also* Warren, "The New 'Liberty' under the Fourteenth Amendment," *Harvard Law Review,* February, 1926, the second chapter of Professor Corwin's recently published *Twilight of the Supreme Court,* and the preface of Dr. Flack's *Adoption of the Fourteenth Amendment.*

8. General Sherman continued to sniff at the thought of himself in the White House. "I am not a statesman," he told Boutwell. "My brother John is. If any Sherman is to be nominated, he is the man." *Sixty Years,* II, 263.

9. "With Mr. Conkling's aid in 1884, Mr. Arthur might have been nominated, and if nominated it is probable that he might have been elected with Mr. Conkling's aid." Boutwell, *Sixty Years,* II, 276.

10. Halstead, "Defeat of Blaine," *McClure's Magazine,* January, 1896.

11. Thomas, *Return of the Democratic Party,* pp. 161–162.

12. Davis, *History of the New York Times,* p. 120.

13. "There is something puzzling about Hay's fondness, even affection, for Blaine. . . . Blaine was the only political leader who ever bewitched Hay." Dennett, *John Hay,* p. 130.

14. Agar, *The People's Choice,* p. 224.

15. "It was only in praise of itself or in the arraignment of its opponents that either party was definite and positive." "Throughout the campaign there was a great deal of laudation by each party of itself for what it had done and a great deal of condemnation by its opponents for what it had not done, but there was a minimum of discussion as to what either party proposed to do. Neither had a definite program on any subject to present." Thomas, *Return of the Democratic Party,* pp. 143, 225.

16. To Stephen B. Elkins, July 27, 1884. Stanwood, *James Gillespie Blaine,* p. 285.

17. *Utica Daily Press,* September 8, 1884. This newspaper was started for this campaign, in opposition to Roberts' *Herald,* which was strongly pro-Blaine.

18. *Utica Daily Press,* October 26, 1884.

19. Bigelow, *Samuel J. Tilden,* II, 337.

20. There is very little published matter about this investigation of the "boodle aldermen," but the city newspapers carried many columns every day. *See also* Hendrick, *The Age of Big Business,* pp. 135–138; Josephson, *The Robber Barons,* pp. 385–386; and the collection of pamphlets, mostly anti-Conkling, at the New York Public Library.

21. Edmonds, *Ulysses S. Grant,* pp. 558–559.

22. Conkling, *Life and Letters,* pp. 564–567.

XXXIV

1. J. Phil Brannigan to the author.

2. It is, of course, possible that some of the oldsters have told us the truth about the Great Blizzard of Eighty-eight; and in any event, surely it ill behooves an author who was not among those present, who wasn't even alive then, to call them liars. Nevertheless, it is impossible not to suspect that Time, indubitably a worker of miracles, has heightened those snowbanks and quickened that dreadful wind. This account of the Blizzard was not taken from reports of eye witnesses, as given in later years, but from the New York City newspapers of the days in question, and notably the *Sun,* which got out several "Blizzard Editions." Mr. James H. Scarr, meteorologist in charge of the New York office of the Weather Bureau, has kindly supplied all the official data available there. An excellent scientific explanation of the Blizzard, by Everett Hayden, appeared in the very first issue of the *National Geographic Magazine,* in 1888.

3. Dr. D. H. Agnew was one of the physicians who had attended Garfield, both at Washington and later at Elberon.

4. The citizens of Utica survived the shock. No statue of the Senator has been erected in his home town, nor has any tablet been placed on the Rutger

Street house. No thoroughfare, hotel, playground, or public square has been named for him. A quarter of a century after his death the city was deeded considerable land for its park system, by Mr. and Mrs. Thomas Redfield Proctor, with the stipulation that the largest park should be called Roscoe Conkling Park. This was done. The statue in Madison Square, New York City (which it shares with statues of Seward, Chet Arthur and Admiral Farragut), was erected by a group of friends. John Quincy Adams Ward made it; it is eight feet tall, weighs 1,200 pounds, and cost $16,000. By request of the widow there was no ceremony of any kind at the unveiling. Indeed, through an oversight on the part of somebody on the committee, the Department of Parks was not even notified until three days afterward.

ADDENDA

XVI. 11 (*cont.*). There is a good account of the events leading up to this debate in the recently published Engelbrecht-Hanighen study of the munitions industry, *Merchants of Death,* pp. 48–51.

XXII. 10a. Cortissoz, *Whitelaw Reid,* I, 360.

XXIII. 6. The Senator used to drink a little wine, though so far as I can learn he never drank spirits. John Anthony ("Tony the Bartender") Weir, who, as a boy was a bellhop in the old Fifth Avenue Hotel—the Senator's headquarters—remembers Conkling as quiet, very dignified, never a member of any "sporting" circle. Tony, in his day, took many a bottle of whiskey up to the rooms of General Grant, Chester A. Arthur, Phil Sheridan, and other friends of Conkling; but he doesn't remember ever taking one to Conkling's room, or seeing Conkling in any poker game or drinking bout; indeed, he doesn't even remember seeing the Senator in the barroom at the old Fifth Avenue. Mr. Weir to the author.

Index

DATE DUE

GAYLORD			PRINTED IN U.S.A.